D1517836

A MILTON ENCYCLOPEDIA

A MILTON ENCYCLOPEDIA

VOLUME 2 C–Ec

Edited by

William B. Hunter, Jr., *General Editor*

John T. Shawcross *and* John M. Steadman, *Co-Editors*

Purvis E. Boyette *and* Leonard Nathanson,
Associate Editors

Lewisburg
Bucknell University Press
London: Associated University Presses

© 1978 by Associated University Presses, Inc.

Associated University Presses, Inc.
Cranbury, New Jersey 08512

Associated University Presses
Magdalen House
136–148 Tooley Street
London SE1 2TT, England

A Milton encyclopedia.
Includes bibliographical references.
1. Milton, John, 1608–1674—Dictionaries, indexes, etc.
I Hunter, William Bridges, 1915–
PR3580.M5   821'.4   75–21896
ISBN 0-8387-1835-3 (v. 2)

SYSTEM OF REFERENCES

Organization of the material in this Encyclopedia is alphabetical, with cross-referencing achieved in two ways. First, a subject may appear as an entry in the main alphabet, with citation of another entry under which that subject is treated. Second, subjects mentioned in an entry that are also discussed in other entries are marked with asterisks, with the exception of certain ones appearing too frequently for such treatment to be practical: the titles of all of Milton's works, each of which has a separate entry; the various named characters who appear in the works; and the names of Milton and his family, including his wife Mary Powell and her family, and his sister Anne Phillips and her family.

Titles of articles in serials have been removed, as have the places of publication of modern books. The titles of Milton's various works have been uniformly abbreviated in forms to be found in the front matter, as have references to the major modern editions and biographical works. All quotations of his writing are taken, unless otherwise indicated, from the complete edition published by the Columbia University Press (1931–1938).

SHORT FORMS USED
IN THIS ENCYCLOPEDIA

AdP	Ad Patrem
Animad	Animadversions upon the Remonstrant's Defense
Apol	An Apology
Arc	Arcades
Areop	Areopagitica
BrM	Bridgewater Manuscript
BN	Brief Notes upon a Late Sermon
Brit	The History of Britain
Bucer	The Judgement of Martin Bucer
CarEl	Carmina Elegiaca
Carrier 1, 2	On the University Carrier; Another on the Same
CB	Commonplace Book
CharLP	Character of the Long Parliament
Circum	Upon the Circumcision
CD	De Doctrina Christiana
CM	*The Works of John Milton* (New York : Columbia University Press, 1931–1938). 18 vols. The so-called Columbia Milton.
Colas	Colasterion
CivP	A Treatise of Civil Power
DDD	The Doctrine and Discipline of Divorce
1Def	Pro Populo Anglicano Defensio
2Def	Defensio Secunda
3Def	Pro Se Defensio
Educ	Of Education
Eff	In Effigiei ejus Sculptorem
Eikon	Eikonoklastes
El	Elegia
EpDam	Epitaphium Damonis
Epistol	Epistolarum Familiarium
EpWin	Epitaph on the Marchioness of Winchester
FInf	On the Death of a Fair Infant
French, *Life Records*	J. Milton French. *The Life Records of John Milton* (New Brunswick, N.J. : Rutgers University Press, 1949–1958). 5 vols.

Hire	Considerations Touching the Likeliest Means to Remove Hirelings from the Church
Hor	The Fifth Ode of Horace
Idea	De Idea Platonica
IlP	Il Penseroso
L'Al	L'Allegro
Literae	Literae Pseudo-Senatûs Anglicani Cromwellii
Lyc	Lycidas
Logic	Artis Logicae
Mask	A Mask (Comus)
Masson, *Life*	David Masson. *The Life of John Milton* (London, 1859–1880). 6 vols. plus Index.
May	Song : On May Morning
Mosc	A Brief History of Moscovia
Nat	On the Morning of Christ's Nativity
Naturam	Naturam non pati senium
NewF	On the New Forcers of Conscience
Parker, *Milton*	William Riley Parker. *Milton: A Biography* (Oxford : Clarendon Press, 1968). 2 vols.
Peace	Articles of Peace
PL	Paradise Lost
PR	Paradise Regained
PrelE	Of Prelatical Episcopacy
PresM	The Present Means
Prol	Prolusion
Ps	Psalm
QNov	In Quintum Novembris
RCG	Reason of Church Government
Ref	Of Reformation
Rous	Ad Ioannem Rousium
SA	Samson Agonistes
Shak	On Shakespeare
SolMus	At a Solemn Music
Sonn	Sonnet
StateP	State Papers
Tenure	The Tenure of Kings and Magistrates
Tetra	Tetrachordon
Time	Of Time
TM	Trinity Manuscript
TR	Of True Religion
Vac	At a Vacation Exercise
Variorum Commentary	*A Variorum Commentary on the Poems of John Milton.* 3 vols. to date (New York : Columbia University Press, 1970–).
Way	The Ready and Easy Way to Establish a Free Commonwealth
Yale *Prose*	*Complete Prose Works of John Milton.* 6 vols. to date. (New Haven, Conn. : Yale University Press, 1953–).

Wherever a reference is given by volume and page but without any other identification, *CM* (Columbia Milton) as given above is intended. Thus (11 : 21) refers to page 21 of volume 11 of that edition.

A MILTON ENCYCLOPEDIA

CABINET-COUNCIL, THE. According to Milton, he received the manuscript of the *Cabinet-Council* from a friend, who remains unidentified, and decided to offer it to the public after having found it some years later among his papers. Its full title indicates the sources of other titles assigned to it in later editions: *The Cabinet-Council: Containing the Chief Arts of Empire, and Mysteries of State; Discabineted in Political and Polemical Aphorisms, Grounded on Authority, and Experience; And Illustrated with the Choicest Examples and Historical Observations.* It was published by Thomas Newcomb for Thomas Johnson in 1658; it had been registered on May 4, 1658. The author is alleged to be Sir Walter Ralegh*, but Ernest A. Strathmann has shown that his initials were T. B. on the basis of other manuscript evidence. How Ralegh's name came to be associated with the manuscript is unknown, except as someone's educated guess because of the nature of the contents. The aphorisms are often accordant with Milton's own views, but not always. The book consists generally of maxims and observations paraphrased from such authors as Bodin*, Lipsius, Guicciardini and most sensationally, Machiavelli*. Milton published it with a two-page preface. It was reprinted in 1661 as *Aphorisms of State,* without Milton's name on the title page and without his preface because of Milton's low status during the early Restoration period. It appeared again in 1692 as *The Arts of Empire,* printed by G. Croom for Joseph Watts, with Milton's name on the title page and his preface restored. It was reissued in 1697 as *The Secrets of Govern-ment,* with no printer or bookseller being noted. This issue appears in two forms: one with sig. A, containing the title page with Milton's name, his preface, and a listing of the contents; and one without sig. A but with a single leaf of different paper stock substituted, giving only a title page with Milton's name. It was reprinted with Milton's name and preface in Thomas Birch's* 1751 edition of Ralegh's *Works* (1 : 39–170) and in the 1829 edition of the *Works* (8 : 35–150). [JTS]

CAEDMON: *see* JUNIUS, FRANCISCUS; ANGLO-SAXON.

CAESAR, JULIUS. While the name of Gaius Julius Caesar (100 B.C.–44 B.C.), general, statesman, ruler, was perpetuated as a synonym for imperial dignity, Milton's chief concern was with Caesar as historian, whose *Commentaries,* consisting of seven books about the civil strife that raised him to power, provided a basic source for Milton's own *Brit.* Although he was careful to supplement Caesar's report with more recent histories, Milton's regard may be measured by the fact that among the many writers, post-classical, ecclesiastical, medieval and modern, cited in *CB* the only reference to a classical historian is to Caesar. [PMZ]

CALAMY, EDMUND. One of the five divines who wrote under the name Smectymnuus*, Calamy (1600–1666) was baptized on February 24, 1600, at St. Thomas the Apostle, London; attended Pembroke Hall, Cambridge, from July 4, 1616, to 1619 (B.A.), received a B.D. degree in 1632, and was incorporated at

Oxford in 1639. His aversion to Arminianism* is said to have excluded him from receiving certain preferments. In certain ways he conformed to demands of the religious establishment of William Laud*, but not to all. Particularly he objected to Laud's demands concerning ceremonies, and this forced him to leave a lectureship at Bury St. Edmunds and to take up a lectureship at Rochford, Essex. In 1639 he became perpetual curate at St. Mary, Aldermanbury, London, where he enjoyed great popularity as a preacher. He was a moderate throughout his career, but he did speak out against those actions and beliefs which he found wrong. His first printed work was his part in *An Answer to a Booke Entituled, An Humble Remonstrance* (1641). His other major works are sermons. He was an original member of the Westminster Assembly*, but resigned with the rise of the Army dominance, and through the interregnum worked for the return of the monarchy. He became chaplain-in-ordinary to Charles II*, but then refused to subscribe to the Act of Uniformity. He was imprisoned briefly in 1663 (from January 6) for preaching while being ejected from the ministry; Charles aided in his release. He died in retirement on October 29, 1666. [JTS]

CALANDRINI, CAESAR (1595–1665), was directly acquainted with Milton, probably as early as the mid-1620s, when the poet's friendship with Charles Diodati* brought him into the circle of Italian exiles in Britain. It was to Caesar, not his brother Jean Louis of Geneva, that Milton turned for information from Leiden and Geneva about Salmasius* and More*. He was the son of Giovanni C. and Marie de Maistres of Antwerp who, like other members of prominent Lucchese families, such as the Florios, the Burlamacchis, or the Diodatis, abandoned Italy and as exiles had set up successive establishments in Switzerland, Germany, France, the United Provinces, and England. Shortly after marrying his second wife, Caterina de Petraviva, widow of Assuerius de

Reghemeester, Minister of the Dutch Reformed Church at Austin Friars*, Giovanni assumed management of the branch of the family banking firm in London, where Caesar joined him in 1611. Caesar studied divinity at Oxford and Leiden, and at the instigation of Marcantonio de Dominis, apostate Roman Catholic Archbishop of Spoleto, became minister of the Italian Church in London. In 1621 he married Elizabeth Harderet, of Walloon extraction, and shortly thereafter won the lasting affection of James Ussher* for his Reformed orthodoxy. During Archbishop Laud's* ascendancy, Caesar retired to his benefice of Stapleford Abbots, but in 1639 accepted the ministry of Austin Friars. For this, his continental background and command of languages were admirably suited, as his significance in the history of that church shows. [PPRS]

CALVIN, JOHN (1509–1564), French theologian of the Reformation, who studied for the priesthood but broke with the Roman Catholic Church in 1533 after a personal revelation convinced him that he was destined to return Christianity to its primitive purity. He achieved prominence in 1536 with the first (Latin) edition of the *Institutes of the Christian Religion* (enlarged 1539, translated into French 1541, in its final form 1559), which became the principal textbook of Reformation doctrine. He became a minister and reformer in Geneva in 1536, eventually establishing a theocratic rule there that lasted until his death.

Calvinism agrees with Lutheranism* upon Scripture as the sole rule of faith*, denial of free will* after the Fall* of Adam, and justification* by faith without works, but differs in insisting upon absolute predestination*, certainty of salvation, and the impossibility of falling from grace. In politics, whereas Luther subordinated the Church to the State, Calvin made the State subject to the Church.

Milton's theology accepts the views of Calvin rejecting confession, purgatory, intercession of saints, and papal authority, but emphatically parts company on the question of predestination. For Milton, God's absolute foreknowledge does not in any sense inhibit free will, and grace depends upon the will of man as well as of God. (The argument for Milton's Arminianism* by Maurice Kelley, *Publications of the Modern Language Association* 52 : 75–79, remains convincing.)

Milton's use of Calvin in disputation shows both independence and some dishonesty, for he cites the theologian wherever he offers a shadow of support and ignores him where he does not. In arguing for "a meet and happy conversation" as the chief purpose of marriage*, he accepts and loosely interprets Calvin's translation of Malachi 2 : 16 : *"He who hates let him divorce; that is, he who cannot love"* (*DDD* 3 : 403), finding this more convenient to his position than the contradictory King James version : "He [God] hateth putting away." He quotes Calvin against the Divine Right of Kings (*Tenure* 5 : 48), and he later, without evidence, declares that Calvin "asserted it lawful to depose a tyrant" (*1Def* 7 : 65, 347; cf. *2Def* 8 : 203). Yet, when Calvin has been quoted on the other side of a disputation, Milton declines to accept his authority unless his reasoning is given (*Animad* 3: 149). The single citation of Calvin in *CD* suggests that Calvin was unimportant as a direct authority for Milton's mature theology, though the Calvinist Beza* was.

Near the end of his life, arguing for toleration of error as distinct from heresy*, Milton casually excuses predestination as a Calvinist attempt, not to dishonor God, but to assert "his absolute power" (*TR* 6 : 169). It is the only time he mentions Calvin's name in all his writings upon free will. [EFD]

CALVISIUS, SETHUS (or Seth Kallwitz) (1556–1615), German astronomer, musician, poet, and chronologer, whose *Opus Chronologicum* (1605; expanded and revised, 1620, 1629) Milton relied upon for his chronology in *Brit,* using either the second or third edition. [WM]

CAMBRIDGE MANUSCRIPT: *see* TRINITY MANUSCRIPT.

CAMBRIDGE PLATONISTS, THE. The Platonist movement in seventeenth-century England was largely Christian and Puritan, its chief members clergymen of the Church of England. The Cambridge Platonists, whose name is almost synonymous with that of the whole movement, flourished at the University from about 1630 until the 1680s. The oldest member of the group, Benjamin Whichcote (1609–1683), was graduated from Emmanuel College in 1629 (M.A. 1633, B.D. 1640), and remained at Cambridge for all but the last twenty years of his life. While there he influenced a number of younger men to his way of thinking. For twenty years he preached every Sunday afternoon at Trinity Church, but none of his works were published until after his death (*Select Sermons*, 1698; *Several Discourses*, 1701–1707; *Moral and Religious Aphorisms*, 1703). John Smith (1618–1652) was tutored by Whichcote at Emmanuel, where he was graduated B.A. in 1640, M.A. in 1644. He remained at the University as a Fellow of Queen's for the rest of his short life. His *Select Discourses* was published in 1660. Henry More (1614–1687) entered Christ's College* the year before Milton left and remained there the rest of his life. There is some likelihood that he and Milton were acquainted. One of the most voluminous writers among the Platonists, and the only one who published much during his lifetime, More's best known prose works are those in which he opposed the mechanistic philosophy of Hobbes* (*An Antidote Against Atheism*, 1653; *The Immortality of the Soul*, 1659). His *Philosophical Poems* (1647) are generally extravagant developments of Neoplatonic themes. Ralph Cudworth (1617–1688), the greatest theorist of the group, entered Emmanuel in 1632, proceeded M.A., and became a Fellow in 1639, B.D. in 1645. Like More, he chose Hobbes as his principal target. His works include the monumental *True Intellectual System of the Universe* (1678), *A Treatise Concerning Immutable and Eternal Moralitie* (1731) and *A Treatise of Freewill* (ed. John Allen, London, 1838). His simplest and most beautiful work is the sermon on Christian love*, which he preached before the House of Commons in 1647 (in *The Cambridge Platonists*, ed. C. A. Patrides [1970], pp. 90–127).

The Cambridge Platonists sought, as Herschel Baker observes, "to reëstablish human reason as a valid epistemological instrument and to subordinate the doctrinal struggles of their age to a Christian morality of charity and toleration" (*The Wars of Truth* [1952], p. 125). In this effort they all held in common an appeal to the Platonic tradition. Their adherence to a rational philosophy caused them to speak in gentler voices than most of their contemporaries, including Milton, in expressing a dislike of Calvinism, especially the doctrine of predestination*, which they regarded as a form of determinism, and of Calvin's denigration of man. They favored toleration of divergent beliefs, however, except Catholicism, which was then regarded as a political menace rather than a faith to be freely chosen. Their attitude toward controversy is well expressed in one of Whichcote's aphorisms : "There is nothing more unnatural to religion than contentions about it" (in *The Cambridge Platonists*, ed G. R. Cragg [1968], p. 431).

More and Cudworth, especially, spoke out for liberty of conscience, but always with primary emphasis upon the guidance of reason and the presence of love. The Platonists were described by Simon Patrick in 1662 as advocating a "virtuous mediocrity" between "the meretricious gaudiness of the Church of Rome and the squalid sluttery of fanatic conventicles" (Cragg, p. 11). As philosophers, they gave rise to the idealist strain in British philosophy, which continued in the middle way the Platonists favored.

Although Coleridge's* remark that the seventeenth-century Platonists should rather be called Plotinists has frequently been quoted as a literal truth, the prevalence of Plotinus* and other Neoplatonists as sources in their works was never to the exclusion of Plato*, but represented to them rather extensions and further exposition of Plato's thought. Their

interpretations, it is true, were more metaphysical than what Plato wrote, and More especially, like Sir Thomas Browne, could not deny witches without denying spirit and ultimately God (Patrides, p. 32). In their context, chronology was not strained when they called Plato "that Atticke Moses," or when they made close identification between the Christian Trinity* and the Platonic. Cudworth was an especially good student of Plato. It is unfortunate that his philosophical works are so verbose that the quality of his thought is somewhat obscured. In battling the "atheism" of Hobbes he displayed a great arsenal of learning, and his concept of "plastic nature," worked out in this connection, had a strong influence on later idealism.

The chief link between Milton and the Cambridge Platonists was their common use of Augustine's* interpretation of major Christian doctrines in the terms of Platonism and Neoplatonism. Augustine's distinction and theirs between the two sources is not in substance but in emphasis. Such passages in Milton as the invocation to light (*PL* 3. 1–6) and the description of the scale of nature* (*PL* 5. 469–79) sound like Neoplatonism because they present concepts emphasized by the Neoplatonists. Both Milton and the Cambridge group, however, were well acquainted with the main doctrines of Plato, and the more strictly ethical parts of Plato assume a major importance in *PL* and even more in *PR* and *SA* (Irene Samuel, *Plato and Milton* [1947], p. 40). The denunciation of classical culture in *PR* (4. 285–364) was quite in accord with the belief of the Cambridge Platonists that supernatural truth, sought by man to the best of his capacity, was always superior to "other doctrine" (*PR* 4. 287).

Although no direct influence is detectable between Milton and the Platonists despite their proximity at Cambridge, they shared certain fundamental beliefs whose derivation from Plato is easily discernible : 1) against Calvin's insistence upon the utter depravity of man they opposed belief in his divine or "deiform" nature; 2) heaven* and hell*, for them, were not physical places to reward or punish man, but states of the soul, as Milton illustrates vividly in the character of Satan; 3) the law of nature was identical with God's will and was comprehended by man's reason; 4) reason*, right reason, had a moral definition, for the good man governed his life by it, as he could because of the law of nature written in his heart; 5) reason was equivalent to natural revelation, and faith* and reason were fundamentally alike. In Milton's prose works these beliefs were expressed most emphatically when he was opposing the validity of those man-made laws, ecclesiastical or civil, that restricted the exercise of right reason, or when he was seeking to establish the purity of Christian doctrine as he saw it. In his poetry they were exemplified dramatically in the actions of characters, or lyrically, as in the invocations in *PL*. Among the Platonists these ruling beliefs were expressed in a variety of ways.

"The deification of man is one of the most thoroughly Greek ideas espoused by the Cambridge Platonists," according to C. A. Patrides (p. 19). Benjamin Whichcote's favorite text with which to express the deiform nature of man was Proverbs 20 : 27, "The Spirit of a Man is the Candle of the Lord; Lighted by God, and Lighting us to God." His use of this text shows how easily Platonism and Christianity were brought together. In one of his sermons Whichcote explains "the great Benefits that accrue to us, by our Saviour's being in our Nature." The ruined nature of man is repaired, *"all Malignity, and naughty Habits"* expelled by contrary acts "in *Mental Transformation,* and DEIFICATION." For scriptural support he quotes 2 Peter 1 : 4 : *"Being made Partakers of the Divine Nature;* which is in effect our *Deification"* (Patrides, pp. 69, 70). The divine nature of man and his potential salvation through moral purification are among the strongest practical teachings of rational theology in the seventeenth century. It was a liberal belief

in a period of doctrinal contention, and Whichcote's preaching of it at Great St. Mary's church in Cambridge gave rise to a series of letters, a debate actually, between him and his former tutor, Antony Tuckney, a distinguished Puritan. Tuckney feared that Whichcote was placing the ancient philosophers above Scripture, and reason above faith, both "mistakes" being evidence of the pernicious influence of the Socinians* and Arminians (Robert A. Greene, "Introduction," Nathanael Culverwell, *Discourse of the Light of Nature*, ed. Greene and Hugh MacCallum [1971], pp. xxxv–xlviii).

John Smith gives in his *Discourses* the essential identification of religious knowledge with religious experience. In defining natural theology he steers a careful course between scholasticism on the one hand and popular "picture-thinking" on the other. Like Milton, he does not so much reject the popular mythology as substitute rational interpretations; but unlike Milton, who described Lucifer's fall as a physical event, Smith had it that the devils "fell from God not so much by a local descent as by a Mental apostasie and dissimilitude to God . . ." (*A Christian's Conflicts*, in Basil Willey, *The Seventeenth Century Background* [1934], p. 144).

The association of a pure life with the highest knowledge encountered throughout Milton's writings from *Mask* to *CD*, is the principal subject also of another of Smith's *Discourses*, "The True Way or Method of Attaining Divine Knowledge." Drawing heavily upon the *Enneads* of Plotinus, Smith defines the true method as attainable "not so much by notions as actions" (Cragg, p. 77). Smith's definition of "truths of natural inscription" as "those fundamental principles of truth which reason, by a naked intuition, may behold in God" (Cragg, p. 95) resembles Milton's concept of natural law as "in the hearts of all mankind" (*CD* 16 : 101).

In his controversy with Hobbes over materialism, More reveals some ideas in consonance with Milton's. His notion of reason as receptive to the supernatural, for example, was directly opposed to

Hobbes's materialism, nominalism, and self-centered philosophy. If the law of nature was identical with God's will, as the Platonists and Milton believed, then Hobbes's ethical relativism was unacceptable. In the *Antidote Against Atheism* and the *Immortality of the Soul,* More argued for the independent existence of spirit. The soul, he believed, did not require sense experience to apprehend spirit. The orderliness of nature, "being guided according to the most Exquisite Wisdom imaginable," could not be the effect of "the mere motion of Matter, but of some Immaterial Principle" (*Antidote,* in Samuel I. Mintz, *The Hunting of Leviathan* [1962], p. 85). Many similarities are found by Marjorie H. Nicolson between More's descriptions of the soul after the death of the body, in *The Immortality of the Soul,* and the angels*, good and bad, in *PL* (*Studies in Philology* 22 : 433–52). More's book was the standard "demonology" of the period, and although not the only source of ideas the two men held in common, it surely would have been read with great interest by Milton.

Perhaps it is the essential Protestantism of Milton and the Platonists that accounts for their similarities. Believing in reason as that which brought them closest to God and best able to do His will, each had confidence in his own ability to use his mind, even when it meant opposing arbitrary sectarian demands for which he could find no justification in his philosophy. In their writings they dealt less with things as they were than with things as they ought to be, but their actions showed a will to live their beliefs as well as to explain them. [GDM]

CAMDEN, WILLIAM (1551–1623), teacher, historian, archaeologist, chorographer, humanist, a towering figure in the intellectual life of late sixteenth- and early seventeenth-century England. Schooled at St. Paul's School* and Oxford, he later became master at Westminster School, where Ben Jonson* was one of his pupils, and ultimately Clarencieux King-of-Arms, occupations that allowed him much time to pursue his antiquarian studies. More than any other single scholar, he was responsible for the emergence of English historiography* from the chaos of the chronicles into an order, method, and critical objectivity distinctly modern. His great monument is the *Britannia* (Latin eds. 1586, 1587, 1590, 1594, 1600, 1607; English trans. by Philemon Holland, 1610, 1637), which begins with a judicious examination of evidence bearing on the earliest British inhabitants, the extent and impact of Roman occupation and subsequent invasions by Angles, Saxons, Danes, and Normans, with attendant effects on the language, customs, and institutions of England. The bulk of the work, however, consists of a county-by-county survey of England, Scotland, Ireland, and the English islands, with generous comment on their outstanding topographical features, their illustrious families, their place names, and the sites of famous historical events. To his deep knowledge of classical writings concerning Britain, he added Anglo-Saxon* and Welsh in order to avail himself of native sources. He traveled extensively for first-hand study of archaeological remains, coins, and local records. In his own words, he "neglected nothing that could give any considerable light towards the discovery of Truth in matters of Antiquity." For nearly two centuries the *Britannia* carried an authority that was matched by no other single work of antiquarian interest. Milton used it extensively in his own *Brit,* and many other historians depended on it. Camden himself had early plans for writing a complete history of England but found the project too vast. His chief example of purely historical writing is his *Annales* (1615–27) of Elizabeth's reign to her death, regarded in its own day and since as one of the best examples of the new "politic" history then developing. Camden edited (Frankfurt, 1603) little-known medieval chronicles, he published the left-overs from the *Britannia* as his *Remaines* (London, 1605; 7 eds. in the 17th century), he wrote a Greek grammar for schools widely popular for over a century, he was a dominant figure in the noted Society of Antiquaries, and he endowed the first chair of history at Oxford in 1622. His enormous intellectual energy, his genius for ordering complex materials, and his vast learning, combined with his great humanity and love of country, earned him the highest reputation both at home and abroad as a leader in establishing new standards for the study of the English past. [FF]

CAMÕES, LUIS DE ([English, Camoëns] 1524?–1580), Portuguese poet and playwright, most famous for his *Os Lusíadas* (1572), an epic in ten cantos of *ottava rima* recounting the voyage of Vasco da Gama around Africa to India and back. Though the epic covers an action of a little over two years (July 1497–September 1499), it includes a condensation of four centuries of Portuguese history narrated by Vasco and Paulo da Gama (Cantos III–IV and VII–VIII respectively) and a foreview of Portuguese colonial expansion in the sixteenth century prophesied by Jupiter (Canto II), Adamastor (Canto V), and a Siren and the goddess Tethys (Canto X). Its intense patriotism, vigor and clarity of style, and allegorical realism made it immensely popular; twelve Portuguese editions were published by 1631, some 20,000 copies having been sold by 1624. A four-volume commentary was published in Spanish in 1639, and earlier Spanish translations had begun appearing in 1580.

Sir Richard Fanshawe Englished the epic in 1655. Although *Os Lusíadas* and *PL* contain intriguing parallels, there is no conclusive evidence that Milton knew of Camões or his poetry. Similarities are mentioned or explored in William Julius Mickle, *The Lusiads of Luis de Camoens* (1776); Allan H. Gilbert, *A Geographical Dictionary of Milton* (1919); Luis Cardim, *Projecção de Camões nas Letras Inglesas* (1940); C. M. Bowra, *From Virgil to Milton* (1945); R. R. Cawley, *Milton and the Literature of Travel* (1951); E. M. W. Tillyard, *The English Epic and Its Background* (1954); Madonna Letzring, "The Influence of Camoens in English Literature" *Revista Camoniana* 1 (1964): 158–80; and James H. Sims, *University of Tulsa Department of English Series* 8 (1969): 36–46 (reprinted in *Revista Camoniana* 3 [1971]: 135–44); *Renaissance Papers* (1971), pp. 79–87; *CL* 24 (1972): 338–56; and *Ocidente: Revista Portuguesa de Cultino* (Nov. 1972), pp. 163–72; and Louis Martz, ibid., pp. 45–49. [JHS]

CAMPION, EDMUND (1540–1581), Irish Jesuit and author of a history of Ireland published, together with those of Meredith Hanmer and Edmund Spenser*, in 1633. In *CB* Milton cited two examples from Campion illustrating "Justice," but found no further use for the history. [WBH]

CANON. There are few questions concerning the canon of Milton's works. His poems were published in *Poems &c. Upon Several Occasions* (1673), in *Paradise Lost* (1674), in *Paradise Regain'd ... To Which is Added Samson Agonistes* (1671), and *Letters of State* (1694). The last volume, containing Edward Phillips's translation of Milton's official correspondence* and his biography of his uncle, gives garbled versions of four "political" sonnets (nos. 15, 16, 17, and 22), which are recorded in *TM*. Whether all the poetry that Milton wrote has come down to us can probably not be determined. At least it seems plausible that other early poems (such as *FInf*, which found its way into only the second edition of the minor poems) and particularly additional psalm translations existed. Perhaps such works were considered either inferior or too similar to others for inclusion in the collected volumes.

Almost all the prose works were published and acknowledged by Milton: see *Ref, PrelE, Animad, RCG, Apol, DDD, Educ, Bucer, Areop, Colas, Tetra, Tenure, Peace, Eikon, 1Def, 2Def, 3Def,* "Sir Walter Ralegh's" *The Cabinet-Council* (editor), *CPow, Hire, Way, BN,* the English Grammar, *Brit, Logic, TR, Epistol,* and *A Declaration, or Letters Patents.* Posthumous publications were *StateP, CharLP, Mosc, A Letter to a Friend, Con-*

cerning the Ruptures of the Common-wealth and *PresM* in *A Complete Collection of the Historical, Political, and Miscellaneous Works of John Milton, both English and Latin* (1698), which also gives a revised and augmented version of *Brit.* In addition *CD* and *CB* were published posthumously. There is no reason to question Milton's authorship of any of these poems or prose works, which the reader should refer to under separate entries. However, there are three or four poems, three or four prose items, and some state papers that retain some question. (*See also* ATTRIBUTIONS.)

The two poetic exercises entitled *Carmina Elegiaca*, beginning "Surge, age, surge, leves, iam convenit, excute somnos" and "Ignavus satrapam dedecet insyltum," have generally been accepted as Milton's. These holograph fragments were discovered in 1874 by Alfred J. Horwood* among Sir Frederick Graham's papers at Netherby Hall, Longtown, Cumberland, where the manuscript remains today. An autotype of the single foolscap leaf (formerly with Milton's name in the left margin) is in the Public Record Office (cat: Autotypes / Milton, &c. / Fac. 6 / Library / Shelf 156a) and a photograph of this autotype can be found in the British Museum (cat: Additional MS 410631, f. 85). The verses are written on the reverse of the leaf. They have been included in most editions of the poetry since Horwood first published them in 1876.

Two lines of poetry, ascribed to Milton and apparently in his hand, appear on the back of a letter from Henry Lawes* (written ca. April 1638) attached to *CB*, also discovered by Horwood in 1874. Horwood published the lines in 1876; they have not been included in poetic collections, however. The manuscript is now in the British Museum (cat: Additional MS 36354).

A third poem on Thomas Hobson, the carrier of Cambridge, was proposed as Milton's by W. R. Parker in 1938; its most frequent title is "Hobson's Epitaph"

and its first line is usually "Here *Hobson* lies amongst his many betters." Similarities to the two acknowledged verses on Hobson and the poem's frequent occurrence with one or the other of those verses suggest Milton's authorship. Parker reasoned that Milton may have omitted the poem from the 1645 collection, if indeed it is his, because two poems on the subject and in this vein may have been considered sufficient. The poem was printed in popular miscellanies, including *A Banquet of Jests* (1640, 1657), *Wit's Recreation* (1640), and *Wit Restor'd* (1658); it has been discovered in twenty-one manuscript miscellanies. Its first two lines begin another poem entitled "On Hobson the Carrier" in another manuscript. The poem is not generally admitted into the canon.

An early Latin prolusion, entitled "Mane citus lectum fuge," appears on the recto of the holograph leaf that records *CarEl.* Authorship is generally accepted; it was published by Horwood in 1876 and in *CM* and the Yale *Prose.*

"A Postscript" to Smectymnuus's *An Answer to a Booke Entituled, An Humble Remonstrance* (1641) has elicited a fair share of comment. Arguments for authorship include internal evidence, style, verbal parallels, historical sources and their use, Milton's relationship with Thomas Young*, and spelling. A comment in the Preface to *Bucer* seems to deny Milton's knowledge of Bucer's work prior to ca. May 1644, although "A Postscript" refers to Bucer's *De Regno Christi*, but this position has been challenged on the basis of interpretation of the comment and Milton's reading practices. The question of authorship can not thus be considered settled. "A Postscript" has been included in the Yale *Prose.*

"Proposalls of certaine expedients for the preventing of a civill war now feard, & the settling of a firme government" has been assigned to Milton because of its inclusion in the Columbia MS, pp. 19–21. Internal evidence of content and style likewise suggest authorship. It has been published in *CM* and the Yale *Prose.*

The various materials that Milton wrote or translated in his official capacity as Secretary for Foreign Tongues* are discussed under the heading *Papers, State.* A number of such documents from the Cromwellian government have been alleged, at times, to come from Milton's hand, but one should be cautious in making such assignment when the document has not appeared in *Literæ,* in Daniel Skinner's* transcription, or, generally, in the Columbia MS, the three major sources for these materials.

Two other canonical questions have frequently been raised : Milton's alleged contribution to Edward Phillips's *Theatrum Poetarum* (1675) and the existence of a Latin and a (separate) Greek thesaurus reportedly produced by Milton. The first problem has been solved through examination of Phillips's sources by Sanford B. Golding, who found such close paraphrases that Miltonic influence, let alone Miltonic authorship, is clearly refuted (see *Publications of the Modern Language Association* 76 : 48–53). The Latin thesaurus, however, remains a bibliographic mystery. Edward Phillips, Cyriac Skinner*, and John Aubrey* all remark in their lives of Milton that he had been amassing a Latin thesaurus, the last citing it as a "dictionary called 'Idioma Linguae Latinae.'" Probably such a compilation was begun in Milton's early years of tutoring (the inference that Phillips's remarks yield) and was not completed (as Phillips and Aubrey both state), although Skinner says it was begun and finished after the Restoration. Phillips adds that the thesaurus "was made use of for another dictionary," and according to Anthony Wood* in *Athenae Oxonienses* there were two such volumes published in 1684 : *Enchiridion Linguae Latinae* and *Speculum Linguae Latinae.* But no copy of either volume is known, nor is either registered or listed in the Term Catalogues. On the other hand *Linguae Romanae Dictionarium Luculentum Novum* (1693) was registered on November 1692 and advertised in the Term Catalogues (No. 48) for 1693 with the statement that the work was drawn from many authors including Adam Littleton and three manuscript volumes compiled by Milton. Further entries in the Stationers' Register under August 21, 1693 (seven entries for *Linguae Latinae Dictionarium* and six for *Linguae Romanae Dictionarium*) do not mention Milton. The allegation is repeated in eighteenth-century editions of Littleton's dictionary (1703 and 1719) and in Robert Ainsworth's *Thesaurus Linguae Latinae* (1763). D. T. Starnes has shown, however, that *Linguae Romanae Dictionarium* derives largely from Littleton's 1678 volume, *Linguae Latinae Liber Dictionarium.* Might Milton's work have been used by Littleton, and this was known to Phillips? or did Phillips perhaps add his comment that it "was made use of for another dictionary" as a result of the 1693 *Linguae Romanae Dictionarium* title page? In any case, a Latin thesaurus seems to have been compiled by Milton and to have disappeared in any "original" state. But these speculations do not solve the mystery of the volumes cited by Wood. Further, it should be noted that Cyriac Skinner, and only he, lists a Greek thesaurus, otherwise unknown. [JTS]

CANTACUZENUS, JOHN (ca. 1292–1383), generally known as John VI (or V) Cantacuzene, Emperor of the East. A Byzantine soldier, statesman, emperor, monk, and historian, Cantacuzenus served Andronicus III until the latter's death in 1341, then declared himself regent over the infant John V. Civil war resulted. Cantacuzenus claimed the empire and was crowned in 1347. He was opposed by the Patriarch of the Orthodox Church, among others, and his reign was beset by social and religious upheavals. Another civil war forced his abdication in favor of John V in 1354. Cantacuzenus retired to a monastery, where he wrote a history of his own time (*Historiarum Libri IV*) dealing with the events of 1320–1356. Milton refers to the *Historiarum* in *CB,* on Pope Innocent's condemnation of athletic games. He does not refer to the work again; he evidently had read the Latin translation by Jacobus Portanus (Ingolstadt, 1603). [WBH]

CARMINA ELEGIACA. These twenty lines of Latin elegiac verse were not printed by Milton during his lifetime. Together with a second set of verses (eight lines of lesser Asclepiad meter) and a Latin prose essay, they appear on a single leaf of foolscap belonging to the Graham family of Netherby Hall, Longtown, Cumberland. This leaf, along with Milton's *CB,* was discovered by Alfred J. Horwood* in 1874 and printed by him in his edition of *CB* (Camden Society, n.s., 16 [1876]; rev. ed., 1877). Little doubt exists that the handwriting is Milton's or that the works are his.

The authors whom Milton employs suggest that the three pieces were probably composed during his last years at St. Paul's School*, that is, around 1624 or 1625. The best attempt to relate them to their intellectual setting is that of Donald Lemen Clark in *John Milton at St. Paul's School* [1948], pp. 178–80; 230–37). They deserve to be studied together, for the evidence is strong that collectively they represent at least a part of a grammar school exercise. These exercises were among the many means by which students of Milton's day were drilled in the classics to a degree that it is now difficult to comprehend. The one in question was the ancient and widely approved "paraphrase." Authority for it as good pedagogical procedure could be found, among other authors, in Erasmus*, whose educational theories were so widely influential during the Renaissance. In his *De ratione studii* (1511), he recommended "the turning of poetry to prose and prose to poetry, and the turning of poetry from one meter to another . . ." (Clark, p. 180). Thus, the interrelationships are close among these works on the proverb *"In the Morning Rise up Early."*

The proverb itself, a common enough one, Milton could have found in the standard Latin grammar of William Lily.

His development in praise of it, however, suggests that he patterned his theme after an example in Aphthonius's *Progymnasmata,* a text on theme writing with models. The rhetorical patterning of the two themes—the praise of the proverb, the paraphrase of it, the reasons why it is so, and so on—is strikingly similar and bears witness to the conventional and imitative origins of Milton's work. Further, Milton's source dealt specifically with the idea that "a counsellor should not sleep all night," and Milton reproduced similar material in his own work, although he broadened it to include praise of the morning's beauty and dispraise of the ill health attendant upon sleeping late.

The first twelve lines of *CarEl* turn into verse those portions of the theme which treat the morning's beauty; the remaining eight lines, the ills of sleeping late. Not surprisingly, given Milton's training, the poem contains a number of classical allusions; the sun, for example, is referred to as "the flame-bearing Titan." Even the birds and flowers that adorn the poem testify to literary tradition rather than observation of nature.

To the other set of eight verses, which are obviously unfinished, Milton gave no title. The work versifies the idea that "ignoble sleep ill becomes a famous ruler who presides over a numerous people." Having stated this, Milton drew from Virgil's* *Aeneid* the example of Turnus, a military leader whose camp was successfully raided while he slept.

Despite their lack of originality, the theme and the two sets of verses are significant. A mark of the mature Milton is his continual ability to knit traditional images and patterns, often drawn from Latin and Greek literature, into strikingly original works. If at age fifteen or sixteen, he not surprisingly lacked that ability, he was nevertheless well on his way to a thorough grounding in the classics and in the images and patterns themselves. These works suggest then the great importance of Milton's early intellectual training as background to a fuller comprehension of his mature work. [ERG]

CAROLUS I., BRITANNIARUM REX:
see ANTAGONISTS.

CARPENTER, WILLIAM: *see* IN-
FLUENCE ON THE LITERATURE OF NINE-
TEENTH-CENTURY ENGLAND, MILTON'S.

CARYL, JOSEPH (1602–1673), Indepen-
dent divine, member of the Westminster
Assembly*, Lincoln's Inn preacher, and
a licenser in the 1640s. His voluminous
Exposition on Job began to appear in
1643, and was complete in 1666. His
printers* were the same as Milton's:
Matthew Simmons*, his wife, Mary, and
his nephew Samuel. Caryl became rector
of St. Magnus, London Bridge, in April
1645, succeeding Samuel Bourman. He
was the licenser of the anonymous *An
Answer to a Book, Intituled, The Doctrine
and Discipline of Divorce*, on November
14, 1644. To his imprimatur he added a
comment that showed him unalterably
opposed to divorce*. Milton takes him to
task in *Colas* and says that he has been
informed that Caryl so overstepped his
job as licenser as to have revised the
manuscript by omission, alteration, and
addition. Caryl also licensed *Eikon
Basilike** in 1649 for Matthew Simmons,
who as parliamentary printer had regis-
tered the work as a blocking action for the
Council of State*. [JTS]

CASA, GIOVANNI DELLA (1503–
1556), Archbishop of Benevento. Born at
Mugello near Florence, Della Casa studied
at Florence, Bologna (where he became a
friend of Beccadelli), and Padua (where
he became personally acquainted with
Bembo). At Rome he participated in
the literary revels of a convivial circle
of poets—Berni*, Firenzuola, Molza,
Capilupi—who called themselves the Ac-
cademia de' Vignaiuoli. His ecclesiastical
duties as Apostolic Clerk, Apostolic Com-
missary, Papal Nuncio at Venice, and
papal Secretary of State gave him a first-
hand knowledge of contemporary political
affairs, and several of his orations are
concerned with Italian politics or inter-

national diplomacy. Though his most
popular book was his *Galateo ovvero de'
costumi*, an urbanely written courtesy-
book, his lyric poems—chiefly sonnets
interspersed with *canzoni*—were widely
admired and sometimes imitated by other
sixteenth century poets. He exchanged
sonnets with Bembo, Marmitta, Capello,
Varchi, and Rota; and his versification
left its impact on Tasso* and Milton. He
also composed satirical or burlesque verses
(*capitoli*) in Berni's manner, political
orations, and eulogistic biographies of
Bembo and Cardinal Contarini, and made
translations from Demosthenes and Thu-
cydides.

In December 1629, Milton purchased
a copy of the 1563 edition of the *Rime
e Prose di Giovanni della Casa*. This
volume, now in the New York Public
Library, contains Milton's genuine auto-
graph and record of purchase. In Maurice
Kelley's opinion, Milton's hand "almost
certainly" appears in another entry in the
same volume, while the transcript of
another sonnet by Della Casa ("Dopo si
lungo error") on folio 28r is in "the script
of the Milton amanuesis who made . . .
the Berni and Boiardo notes on pp. 71, 77,
187, of Milton's Commonplace Book."
The amanuensis has now been identified
as Milton's nephew, John Phillips, by
John T. Shawcross. Though there is sub-
stantial external evidence that Milton
knew Della Casa's poetry, for the nature
and extent of its influence scholars have
had to rely largely on internal evidence.
In 1846 James Glassford noted structural
resemblances between the sonnets of the
two poets. More recently a stronger case
for Milton's indebtedness to Della Casa
has been argued by J. S. Smart* (1921)
and F. T. Prince (1949, 1954).

In Smart's opinion, Della Casa con-
sciously sought to break with the smooth
and regular versification of the Petrarchan
tradition and to achieve new effects "by
some sudden and striking departure from
the familiar flow of language and verse,"
avoiding the conventional pauses at the
end of a line of verse or at the conclusion
of a quatrain or tercet, ignoring metrical

divisions and allowing his sentences to pass "imperceptibly from line to line, . . . ending abruptly where an ear attuned to Petrarch's modulations might least have expected. . . ." Prince, in turn, emphasized Della Casa's contribution to the development of the form that Tasso termed the "heroic Sonnet" (a category that, in Prince's opinion, includes "almost all" of Milton's sonnets*). Placing Della Casa's innovations in the tradition of sixteenth-century humanistic attempts to "latinize Italian verse," Prince regards Tasso's *Heroic Sonnets* as a vulgarization of Della Casa's style. Even though Tasso's sonnets may have helped to shape Milton's conception of the sonnet-form as a vehicle for celebrating contemporary leaders and events, Milton was directly indebted to Della Casa's "rhythmic innovations" rather than to Tasso for the style and structure of his major sonnets. On the other hand, in Milton's epic style* Prince detects the direct influence of Tasso's theory and practice and the indirect influence of Della Casa. The techniques for achieving elevation and surprise (or "marvel")—distortions of natural word order, breaking up the verses through enjambment, "the placing of strong pauses within the lines, and the deliberate accumulations of elisions"—are common to all three authors. Della Casa (Prince concludes) was "the chief Italian model" for Tasso's "magnificent" style, which "in its turn" influenced Milton's heroic verse. [JMS]

CASTELVETRO, LODOVICO (1505?– 1571), gifted and outspokenly original Italian humanist, poet, and literary critic. He studied at Bologna, Ferrara, Padua, and Siena, where he received a doctoral degree in law and devoted himself to the study of letters, producing there a comedy, *Gli ingannati*, in 1531. Named to a Readership in Civil Law at the Academy of his native city in 1532, his censure of a panegyric composed by the influential Annibale Caro at the charge of Alessandro Farnese, nephew of Pope Paul III, precipitated a celebrated quarrel among Italian

literati in the mid-Cinquecento. In 1557, when proceedings were resumed by the Inquisition against Modena academics, who were accused of deviation in matters of faith, Castelvetro was implicated, partly through the malice of his enemies. Already suspected of translating heretical writers such as Melancthon, Castelvetro fled the threatened torments of the Holy Office, and accordingly he was condemned and excommunicated. Having obtained a promise of safe-conduct, he presented himself at Rome in 1560 to clear his name, but managed to escape from confinement just as the tribunal was sentencing him to death and sequestration as an "impenitent heretic." After appeals to the Council of Trent* proved fruitless, he left Italy, finding refuge at Geneva (1564–1566), Lyons (1567), Chiavenna (then harboring known radicals like Camillo Renatus and Laelius Socinus*, the uncle of Faustus) and Vienna, where he dedicated his translation of Aristotle's* *Poetics* to the Emperor Maximilian. Besides his famous exchanges with Caro and manuscripts lost during the vicissitudes of exile, Castelvetro wrote several important works on literary subjects, including commentaries on Petrarch*, Virgil*, Dante*, and the Roman comic poets. His most famous piece is a landmark of Cinquecento criticism. The first of the great translations and commentaries on the *Poetics* in any modern language, the *Poetica d'Aristotele Vulgarizzata Et Sposta* (1570) is responsible for formulating the doctrine of the three "unities" (time, place, and action) that pervades later neoclassical criticism.

Castelvetro is one of the very few Cinquecento critics whom Milton actually names, referring to him in *Educ* (4 : 286) as an authority on "that sublime Art" which teaches the "laws" of a "true" epic* and lyric poem, as well as the nature of "decorum," the "grand masterpiece to observe." In *SA* (as well as *Mask*) Milton does indeed observe the three unities, though his Preface speaks only of the "circumscription" of "time," and that in terms conforming better to Aristotle's

Greek than to Castelvetro's insistence on twelve hours. It has also been suggested that Milton accepted the license granted by Italian commentators, including Castelvetro, in allowing the epic poet to speak in his own person. Nevertheless, the theory of tragedy* suggested by statements in the Preface to *SA* and elsewhere differs from Castelvetro's in several crucial respects. The Italian critic locates the principles of tragedy frankly in the pleasure of the ignorant multitude, not in an elevated notion of moral utility regardless of the preferences of common taste. He views catharsis* as instrumental to pleasure, whereas for Milton it is the final end of tragedy, and the process is likewise conceived as one of expelling pity and fear, not tempering them. For Milton, history and poetry appear to be separate arts, but in Castelvetro they become essentially one. [PRS]

CASTIGLIONE, BALDASSARE (1478–1529), diplomat and writer. He served at the Court of Duke Ludovico Sforza and with the Duke of Urbino, Guidobaldo da Montefeltro, distinguishing himself as a diplomat, chiefly as an envoy from Urbino to Ferrara, to Mantua, to the Pope, and to the King of England, Henry VII. Later he was appointed by Pope Clement VII as Apostolic Nuncio to Emperor Charles V in Spain, and during his last years he was primarily a mediator between the Holy See and Charles V.

Castiglione's major contribution to literature, *The Book of the Courtier* (*Il Libro del Cortegiano*), displays his devotion to, and admiration for, the gracious Elizabetta Gonzaga, Duchess of Urbino and wife to Guidobaldo da Montefeltro. *The Courtier*, which is set at Urbino, reflects the leisurely but sophisticated conversations of the Duchess and other noble ladies with the courtiers and with distinguished visitors. Written in four books and in dialogue form, *The Courtier* is a Renaissance courtesy or conduct book that describes the traits of the ideal courtier, his service to his prince, and the Platonic love* relationship that he could

develop with a courtly lady. The ideal courtier is graceful and handsome, witty and entertaining in discourse, proficient at letter writing, expert in arms, athletic, valorous, and resolute; he should speak the truth to his prince and avoid flattery; and he could achieve spiritual exaltation by contemplating the beauty of a courtly lady. Composed between 1508 and 1516, *The Courtier* was not printed until 1528 in Venice, a year before Castiglione's death. In 1561 an English translation by Sir Thomas Hoby was published, and Castiglione's conception of the ideal courtier and gentleman was widely disseminated and often discussed by nobleman and literati throughout England.

Castiglione's influence on Milton is difficult to determine. Though Milton did not write a courtesy book, his treatise *Educ*, like *The Courtier*, aims to inculcate gentlemanly perfection by describing "a compleat and generous Education [as] that which fits a man to perform justly, skilfully and magnanimously all the offices both private and publick of Peace and War" (4 : 280). Furthermore, Castiglione in *The Courtier* and Milton in several writings borrow from Aristotle's description of the ideal ethical character and, in particular, from his conception of the virtue magnanimity, which is "greatness of soul" and "a crowning ornament of the virtues" (*Nicomachean Ethics*, 4. iii. 16). In the fourth book of *The Courtier*, for instance, Lord Octavian, when explaining the virtues of the ideal courtier, lays greatest stress on *magnanimità*. Similarly, in the exordium of the second book to *Ref*, Milton asserts that a ruler should be "a spirit of the greatest size, and divinest mettle" and should display "magnanimity" (3 : 37). In *CD* (17 : 240–41), moreover, Milton states that magnanimity is exemplified "when in the seeking or avoiding, the acceptance or refusal of riches, advantages, or honors, we are actuated by a regard to our own dignity, rightly understood," and in *PR* (2. 481–83) Christ, who manifests Aristotelian magnanimity, rejects Satan's offer of the Kingdoms of this world, because

. . . to give a Kingdom hath been thought
Greater and nobler done, and to lay down
Far more magnanimous, then to assume.
(2. 481–83)

Perhaps the most renowned passage of *The Courtier* is Pietro Bembo's impassioned discourse on Platonic love in the fourth book. This passage reflects Castiglione's knowledge of Italian treatises of love (*trattati d'amore*), and his selection of Bembo as the spokesman for this philosophy of love probably expresses some indebtedness to Bembo's recently published *Gli Asolani* (1505), which describes in dialogue form and in a courtly setting how a gentleman's contemplation of a beautiful lady can lead to a union of their souls, to a vision of divine beauty, and, ultimately, to contemplative union with the deity. The two Platonic dialogues that comment extensively on love are the *Symposium* and *Phaedrus*, and both dialogues generated numerous commentaries on, and poetic expressions of, the Platonic philosophy of love. Italian Platonists like Marsilio Ficino, Pico della Mirandola, Girolamo Benivieni, Guido Cavalcanti, Bembo, and Castiglione, and many others fostered interest in Plato's doctrine of love. Their influence extended into England, probably to Spenser*, for example, whose *Four Hymnes* appear to reflect it, and perhaps to Milton. Milton's ideas on Platonic or heavenly love are expressed in his poetry (including, for example, the Latin poetry, the Italian sonnets, *Mask, PL* and in his prose (including, for instance, *CD, DDD, Apol*), but he frequently derived his ideas directly from Plato, whom he acknowledges as a major influence on his thought. Though he surely knew the intellectual trend cultivated by the Italian Platonists, in which Plato's doctrine of love was studied and interpreted, Castiglione's influence on Milton cannot be ascertained.

Castiglione's *Alcon*, a Latin elegy written in 1506 to commemorate the death of Falcone, a boyhood friend, is sometimes compared with *Lyc* and with *EpDam*. Some structural parallels between Castiglione's poem and Milton's two pastoral* elegies may possibly be attributed to Milton's indebtedness to *Alcon*, but other similarities may, more probably, be ascribed to Castiglione's and Milton's use of the same classical models for the Renaissance pastoral elegy, namely Theocritus's* second idyl, Moschus's* *Lament for Bion*, Bion's* *Lament for Adonis*, and the fifth and tenth eclogues of Virgil's* *Bucolics*. [ACL]

CASTON FAMILY: *see* BIOGRAPHY.

CATHARSIS, a Greek work meaning "purification" or "purgation." The concept of catharsis has it roots in Pythagorean lore that was handed down by later Greek philosophers, especially Plato* and his disciples. In his famous definition of tragedy* (*Poetics* 1449 b 21–31), Aristotle* classifies tragedy as a kind of imitation that "through pity and fear" effects "the catharsis of such passions." Cartharsis was a problem to which Milton devoted much careful thought, and it is important in coming to understand his thinking about dramatic art. Indeed, he refers directly to the concept several times in his works. *RCG* for example speaks of "Dramatick constitutions" that are of "power" to "allay the perturbations of the mind, and set the affections in right tune" (3 : 237–38). The epigraph on the title page to *SA* quotes the Greek text of Aristotle's definition verbatim and translates the word "cartharsis" as a *lustratio* ("lustration," ceremonial "cleansing") of *talium* ("such") passions. The Preface to this work also gives a quite formal, and fully developed, explication of the concept, formulating Aristotle's meaning thus: "Tragedy [is] said by *Aristotle* to be of power by raising pity and fear, or terror, to purge the mind of those and such like passions, that is to temper and reduce them to a just measure with a kind of delight, stirr'd up by reading or seeing those passions well imitated." Catharsis seems even to be woven into the events of Milton's larger works, the chorus in *SA* leaving the stage with "calm of mind all passion spent" (line 1758), and Adam and Eve experience something akin to it at the end of *PL* (12. 558–60, 595–605, 645) —though the kind of experience Milton's characters seem to undergo appears to differ from the cathartic effect he envisioned tragedy as working on an audience. Milton's remarks reflect careful choice between conflicting schools of thought in the Renaissance, for the history of classical philology and criticism from antiquity to the present reflects constant uncertainty as to what precisely Aristotle meant. In the first place, Milton's wording distinguishes his views sharply from modern "aesthetic" interpretations of catharsis, in which catharsis is thought to ensue concomitantly from the formal qualities of a "beautiful" tragedy.

With rare exceptions (for example, Mazzoni*), the Renaissance thought of catharsis as something tragedy is specifically organized to achieve, rather than a concomitant effect. Milton's initial assertion to the effect that Aristotle assigned tragedy the "power" of catharsis because antiquity thought of it as the most serious and moral form of poetry, implies that in Milton's eyes catharsis is the final end of tragedy. Furthermore, his view is not that of many modern critics who, though they think of catharsis as the function of tragedy, interpret it as a process of evoking and refining emotions, or as productive of pleasure through emotional relief. Apart from exceptional critics such as Castelvetro* or, again, Mazzoni, the Renaissance insisted on justifying poetry on utilitarian grounds, and hence Cinquecento critics almost universally interpreted catharsis as the ethical or political benefit that tragedy conferred on an audience. Both the remarks just quoted as well as the celebrated passage in *RCG* (3 : 238) demonstrate clearly that Milton conformed to the standard Renaissance position on the matter. But as to what exactly catharsis was or how it worked, Renaissance commentators were anything but agreed, and hardly any conceivable possibility, however far-fetched, wanted an advocate. In the main, critics disagreed on 1) what

exactly the nature of the cathartive process was, and 2) what its agents and objects were. As to what catharsis is and does, critics were and are usually divided over whether it extirpates passions from the mind entirely in a stoic fashion, or whether it tempers or moderates them. Extirpative critics might think of the arousal of "good" passions such as pity and fear as the means of expelling undesirable emotions such as wrath or lust from the soul. Their opponents believed that virtue consists not in the complete absence of passions, as in Plato, but in a proper balance of the emotions, as in Aristotle's ethical theories, and they thought of catharsis as remedying the excess of passions and restoring them to their proper state. Milton's definition of the "power" of tragedy to "purge the mind" as a process of "temper[ing] and reduc[ing] them to just measure" (cf. *RCG* 3 : 238) shows clearly that he chose not an extirpative but a moderating theory of catharsis. His preference for *lustratio* as the proper Latin translation of the Greek confirms his adherence to this principle. Regarding the second issue—that is, the agents and objects of "purging"—critics divided over the peculiar special pronoun that Aristotle used in specifying the passions purged. Does a catharsis of passions mean simply "such passions"—implying that pity and fear purged other passions as well?—or should "such" be taken as equivalent to "these," a strict demonstrative limiting the meaning to just these two passions alone? Milton's choice, "these" and "such like passions," seems to equivocate. The passage in *RCG* where he speaks of tragedy "allay[ing] the perturbations of the mind and set[ting] the affections in right tune" can be read as referring not to just pity and fear but to the emotions generally, in which case it appears that Milton thinks of the objects of catharsis as pity, fear, and other passions that weaken us if not in proper balance. However, one can as well, if not better, hold that he read "such" as "these," meaning that pity and fear purged pity and fear alone, for in the phrase "the affections" in *RCG* the use of the article is ambiguous, leaving the question of which "affections" are set in "right tune" unanswered. Moreover, if Milton did not intend to read "such" as "these," why did his Preface not content itself with the simple word "such" instead of insisting on "such like," an embarrassingly clumsy construction? If one also considers that Milton's Latin epigraph reads "talium" ("of such quality") and not "similis" ("similar," "like"), which is common in many Renaissance translations of the *Poetics,* the proper conclusion is that Milton intended the purgation not of " 'such-like' passions" but "such 'like' passions." Hence, to Milton the objects of purgation probably are not pity, fear, and other passions as well, but only pity, fear, and pitylike or fearlike passions such as terror, horror, commiseration, rue, and so on. If this is so, then Milton's view links him with another great seventeenth-century dramatist, Jean Racine, who also thought of focusing his art on the catharsis of only these two passions, which he likewise refers to with the ambivalent expressions "ces sortes de" and "ces" passions back-to-back. The last problem relevant to Milton's catharsis is the "delight" that according to him comes "with" catharsis. Some commentators, seeking to link great poets like Milton and Racine with modern theories far in advance of their time, have held that Milton's "with" implies that catharsis is instrumental to pleasure. Milton's phrases derive directly from slippery Greek datives in Aristotle's Greek, however, and they are datives of accompaniment, not instrumentality. Milton, thus, explicitly states that the source of delight is the viewing of skillfully constructed imitations of human behavior, not the process of catharsis itself. Hence, delight springs not from the purgation of pity and fear, but from the imitative means that, through arousing the passions, effects catharsis. [PRS]

CATHOLICISM, MILTON'S ALLEGED ROMAN. After his death there is mention of Milton's having become a Roman Catholic during the last ten years of his life, and because of the fears of a Popish plot the rumor seems to have been fanned into belief. Frequently the allegation is conjoined with another that Milton's brother, Christopher, had also been a Papist. There seems to be no truth in either piece of gossip, and certainly anyone who had read *TR* (1673) would have ridiculed such a strange idea.

The first appearance of the rumor seems to be a deliberate aside on Titus Oates's part to vilify his opponents; he wrote, "The Popish Lord is not forgotten, or unknown, who brought a Petition to the late Regicides and Usurpers, signed by almost Five hundred principal Papists in *England*. . . . Who more disheartned the Loyalty and patience of your best Subjects, then their confident Scriblers, *White* and others? And *Milton* was a known frequenter of a Popish Club. Who more forward to set up *Cromwell,* and to put the Crown of our Kings upon his head, than they?" (*A True Narrative of the Horrid Plot and Conspiracy of the Popish Party* [1679], p. [v]; see also *Les Conspirations d'Angleterre, ou l'Histoire des Troubles Suscités dans ce Royaume, de puis l'an 1600. Jusques à l'an 1679, inclusivement* [Cologne, 1680], where Oates's work is translated as *Recit Veritable de l'Execrable Conspiration du Parti Papiste,* with the allusion on p. 428). The next year Edward Pelling cited Oates's remark in *The Good Old Way* (1680), p. 115, adding that it was "credible enough, that he was a *Jesuit in disguise.*" Sir Roger L'Estrange* picked up Oates's phraseology and speeded it on to become "fact" (see *A Further Discovery of the Plot: Dedicated to Dr. Titus Oates* [1680], pp. 26–27). L'Estrange's disbelief that Rome should be charged with aiding the Puritan rebellion was rebutted by a B. W. (in *An Additional Discovery of Mr. Roger L'Estrange His Further Discovery of the Popish Plot* [1680], p. 15), who saw the Jesuits as main culprits, and alleged that Milton had worked with Jesuits according to their own records. L'Estrange's answer accepted B. W.'s account (*L'Estrange's Narrative of the Plot* [1680], p. 7). A patently fictitious account of the rumor was provided by Edward Pettit in *The Vision of Purgatory* (1680), pp. 99–101, where Milton's advancement of the Puritan cause (the burden of Oates's comments) was in reality the advancement of the Jesuit cause. Milton is said to have been "very earnest with a Provincial of the Jesuits." Pettit has Milton beg for preferment from the Roman Catholics, only to be brushed aside as a useless anachronism.

Robert Hancock likewise traced an affinity between papists and antimonarchists, and hearing of the rumor of Milton's Roman tendencies, alluded twice to such a possible religious persuasion (*The Loyalty of Popish Principles Examin'd* [1682], pp. 35–50). A sermon by George Hickes iterates Milton's imbibing of popish principles of rebellion (*A Sermon Preached . . . on the 30th of January 1681/2* [1682], pp. 17–19, 23), and Thomas Wilson pointed out parallels between the Jesuits and Milton in *Tenure* and *Eikon* (*A Sermon on the Martyrdom of King Charles I* [1682], p. 32). *A Vindication of the Primitive Christians* (1683), pp. 192–96, offered proof of his papal leanings by recalling Milton's trip to Rome and by translating that part of *1Def* concerning the deposition of Childeric. Milton was, thus, a Jesuit in disguise according to the author Thomas Long, who asked the reader to "judge how diligent an Advocate *Milton* was for the Pope."

The ensuing years did not drop the rumor, which was repeated by L'Estrange in *The Observator*, No. 457, December 17, 1683; in *Matchiavel Junior* (1683), p. 23; by Long in *A Compendious History of All the Popish and Fanaticall Plots* (1684), pp. 92–93; by Pettit in *The Visions of Government* (1684), pp. 148–49; by Richard Forsters in *Prerogative and Privilege Represented in a Sermon . . . March 18. 1683/4* (1684), p. 32; by John Moore in *Of Patience and submission to Authority* (1684), p. 40; by Robert Brady in *An Introduction to the Old English History* (1684), p. 355; by Edward Cooke in *Certain Passages Which happened at Newport* (1690). pp. [6–7]; and in *Oliver Crom-*

well's Letters to Foreign Princes and States (1700), pp. 46–48.

The continuance of the allegation as the century closed and as the new one began may owe something to (justified) incredulity, although "proof" seemed to rest for some in noting that Christopher was a papist. John Evelyn* referred to Christopher as a papist in his diary, under date of June 9, 1686 (ed. E. S. de Beer [1915], 4 : 514), as did John Lord Campbell around the same time (British Museum, Additional MS 19142, f. 79v). The diary of Zachary Merrill, under date of November 7, 1698 (Bodleian, Rawlinson MS D.1120, f. 67v) specifically connected the two brothers' religious precepts: "He had a brother y^t was a Papist, and he ('was thot) dyed one." William Binckes, in *A Sermon Preach'd before the Honourable House of Commons . . . November 5. 1704* (1705), p. 16 and n., called Christopher "a professed Papist" and assigned to him public declaration to several gentlemen and justices that his brother was a Roman Catholic. John Ward repeated the charge against John (*Diary*, ed. Charles Severn [1839], p. 141) and G. R. Clarke, in *The History and Description of the Town and Borough of Ipswich* (Ipswich, 1830), p. 226, referred to Christopher's "Catholic chapel." John Oldmixon was also to repeat the allegation in *The History of England, During the Reigns of the Royal House of Stuart* (1730), p. 708. But Thomas Hearne twice recorded that William Joyner, himself a Catholic and "an intimate friend" of Milton's, assured him that the story was not true. Nonetheless, Hearne adds that Christopher's position was "credibly reported" (see *Reliquiae Hearnianae: The Remains of Thomas Hearne, M.A.*, ed. Philip Bliss [2d ed., 1869], 1 : 2 [under July 4, 1705], and 1 : 115 [under September 16, 1706]). According to Christopher, John "had liv'd in y^t Communion for above ten years." *The State of Church Affairs* (1687), which draws upon *Brit* and "answers" Milton, presents a Roman Catholic point of view. Interestingly, but without foundation, it has been attributed to both John and Christopher in more recent years. [JTS]

CATS, JACOB (1577–1660), Dutch states-man and poet. Because he is a copious, moralizing poet and emblematist who used his art to urge domestic moral values centered in love, marriage, and religion, his popularity has practically disappeared. During the seventeenth, eighteenth, and even nineteenth century, however, he attained a place in Dutch households akin to that once enjoyed by Quarles, Bunyan, and Milton himself. Learned, but simple and unpretentiously genial, his virtues are evident in his earliest works (1618), *Maechden-plicht* and *Sinn' en Minne-Beelden,* a collection of emblemata famous for generations at home and abroad—in-deed, the work was translated into English by Thomas Heywood in 1637. *Selfstryt* (1620); *Houwelyck* (i.e., "Marriage," 1625); a second emblem collection, *Spiegel van den Ouden en Nieuwen Tijdt* (1632); *Klagende Maeghden* (1633); and his most extensive work, *Trou-Ringh* ("The Mar-riage Ring," 1637), soon followed. Public service silenced his muse until retirement, his *Wercken* appearing in 1655, his *Tach-tigjarige bedenckingen* and *Tachtig-jarig leven* in 1658. A rimed autobiography, *Twee-en-tachtig-jaerig leven,* the most important source of personal information, was not published until 1700.

Numerous parallels (as well as some differences) between the first part of *Trou-Ringh,* which treats the original of mar-riage in Eden, and Milton's handling of the relationship between Adam and Eve in Books 4 and 8 in *PL* have been noted. Though no responsible observers dare sug-gest that the similarity of ideas in the two poems proves that Milton used Cats, it is clear that both poems stem from a common Calvinist* culture, and that each poet is enriched by the study of the other. Nevertheless, for Milton access to Cats's work would have been simple. *Sinn'-en Minne-Beelden* could reach foreigners even if, unlike Milton, they knew no Dutch, for the work was in three tongues, Latin and French as well as Dutch, and its impact on Englishmen such as Sir Joshua Reynolds later has been doc-umented. As for *Trou-Ringh,* the subject was of longstanding interest to the author of the divorce tracts; it was Cats's chef d'oeuvre; and again, even had Milton known nothing of the tongue, a Latin version was published in 1643 and re-printed in 1653 with a dedication to the daughter of Elizabeth, the Queen of Bohemia. Furthermore, Milton certainly knew Cats by reputation, and probably in person. As the Commonwealth and the United Provinces drifted into war toward the end of 1651, the Dutch sent a special embassy to London to forestall hostilities, where the legation was ceremoniously received and richly entertained. As Secre-tary for Foreign Tongues* to the Council of State*, Milton was directly involved in the negotiations, translating the Dutch proposals from Latin into English and the Council's answers into Latin; when nego-tiations broke down in July 1652, he possibly oversaw the Latin translation of the Declaration of the Causes of War against the Dutch—indeed, the Sonnet to Henry Vane the Younger expresses his appreciation of the delicate statesmanship the affair had required—and members of the mission are known to have consulted and visited Milton. Since the leader of the Dutch embassy was none other than the just retired Grand Pensionary Cats, who, though reluctant, had been pressed to serve in the emergency, it is almost certain that Milton encountered the elderly poet-statesman face to face, though under circumstances that both regretted. It is perhaps emblematic that in an English translation of a poem by Cats in 1680, readers are urged not to reject the counsel of the book, though not sung by a Cowley* or a Milton. [PRS]

CATULLUS, GAIUS VALERIUS (84? B.C.–54), Latin lyric poet. Catullus had great impact on Renaissance lyric poetry in general, although his explicit and, to some, obscene poems were a sub-ject of controversy. His direct influence on Milton's poetry appears to be slight, although there are many suggestive echoes to be found along with a few specific references. Catullus would appear to be one of the "smooth elegiac poets" Milton admired in his youth and later repudiated as wanton, lacking in seriousness, and trivial.

Milton had apparently read Catullus well. In a prose note for his Latin ode to John Rous, Milton says that "there are two Phaleucian verses which admit a spondee in the third foot, a practice which Catullus freely followed in the second foot." The regular Phaleucian line consists of a spondee, a dactyl, and three trochees, and Milton cited Catullus to justify his metrical experimentation. Some readers have found Milton's appeal to Catullus misjudged or badly reasoned, but most modern editors think his point well taken.

Milton evidently knew Catullus better than most of his contemporaries, considering the fact that an English edition of Catullus's *Carmina* did not appear until 1684. Such a late appearance of Catullus in England may have been a consequence of the Licensing Act of June 14, 1643, which invasion of the rights of a free press Milton condemned in *Areop* by observing that not even Rome interdicted "the Satyricall sharpnesse, or naked plainnes of *Lucilius* or *Catullus* or *Flaccus*" (4 : 301).

Apart from the references in *Areop* and the ode to Rous, Milton cited Catullus five times in *Logic*. Of these citations, only one was cited by Ramus* in the original *De Dialectica*. This evidence shows that Milton was familiar with Catullus's poetry. But on balance, when one considers the imprecision of Catullian echoes that some readers have found in Milton, one must conclude that Milton generally found Catullus inharmonious as a poetic influence. [RCR]

CEDREN, GEORGES, eleventh-century Byzantine monk and historian (*Compendium Historiarum a mundo condito*). In *CB* Milton cites him as opposing clerical celibacy ("On Marriage") and twice quotes him as an authority on Eastern history in *PrelE*. [WBH]

CELSUS, AULUS CORNELIUS (1st century A.D.), ancient medical authority and member of the noble family of Cornelii of Rome. He wrote an encyclopedic treatise that consisted of six parts: Agriculture, Medicine, Military Arts, Rhetoric, Philosophy, and Jurisprudence, of which only Part II, *De re Medicina,* remains. Extracts from Celsus on pharmacy were published under the title of "Flowers of Celsus" in an *Enchiridion medicum* in 1619 in England, and fortynine editions of the complete Part II had appeared by 1841. This work is a landmark in the history of medicine.

Edward Phillips, Milton's nephew, includes Celsus's *De re Medicina* in the list of Latin works studied by the poet's pupils in the 1640s. In *Educ,* Milton states that he would have this treatise available to his students because of scientific usefulness (4 : 283), but he was also aware of the elegance of the Latin : see his quotation from Celsus in *Accedence Commenc't Grammar* (6 : 329). [MRM]

CENSURE OF THE ROTA, THE: *see* ANTAGONISTS; HARRINGTON, JAMES.

CHALFONT ST. GILES, BUCKS. Thomas Ellwood*, Milton's friend, found a "pretty box" for him on the outskirts of the village of Chalfont St. Giles as a country retreat during the time the plague raged in London. Milton, his wife Elizabeth, and family stayed there from June 1665 until February or March 1666. In this cottage Milton may have made final alterations on *PL*; Ellwood reports that Milton, while there, showed him the poem in manuscript. The cottage was purchased in 1887 and turned into a Milton museum; it is the only residence of the poet that still stands. [WM]

CHANCERY PROCEEDINGS. John Milton, Sr.'s occupation as scrivener brought him into numerous court actions. From the end of the sixteenth century scriveners functioned as brokers, real estate agents, and even legal advisers. Frequently suits were brought before Chancery Court in London for settlement; these were usually for larger sums, of longer duration, or the result of default. The standard discussion of the Miltons' activities in Chancery is J. Milton French's *Milton in Chancery* (New York, 1939). Milton, Jr., was at times directly involved, as was his brother Christopher, acting for their father. Their sister's two husbands, Edward Phillips and Thomas Agar, were also both Deputy Clerks of the Crown in the Court of Chancery.

The affairs of Milton's father with John Cotton began around 1590 with arrangements to lend Cotton's capital at regular interest rates of 8 to 10%. A number of such loans are on record (for example, that to John and Thomas Harvey on November 30, 1605), which may or may not have been repaid without incident. By 1620 Milton was investing money for Cotton and his partner John Downer (a "long acquaintance") in various enterprises. Frequently, when defaults of payments occurred or there were changes of ownership of loans or businesses, Milton deposed in Chancery suits for his clients. One instance is the court action that he brought in February 1623 against Edward Raymond and James Ayloffe. On February 9, 1622, he had made a loan to Raymond, an attorney, who transmitted the bond to John Lane, with Ayloffe standing surety. The loan was not repaid and Milton sued. In 1624 he and John Lane joined in suing Ayloffe, who submitted a bill on May 1 through his lawyer, Edward Breres. Milton and Lane answered this bill on May 10. Through this action Lane became a close associate of Milton. The suit was still not settled in April 1630, when Milton made a deposition about it in the County of Exeter.

An upshot of Milton's lending money for John Downer, a tallow-chandler, who died in 1624, was that Downer's widow, Rose, called in moneys in early June 1628. One such loan for Mrs. Downer had been to Sir Francis Leigh in November 1624.

Milton's partner, Thomas Bower, persuaded her to reinvest the money and add more to the outstanding capital as well. Fifty pounds of Mrs. Downer's money was lent to Matthew Ewens, with William Keyner standing surety. Later the loan was called in but not paid, and on April 26, 1631, Mrs. Downer sued Milton and Bower. On May 3 answers were filed, and on June 20, 1632, Milton returned her money out of his own pocket. He apparently tried to get half the sum from Bower, who was now an attorney, and all of it from Ewens. By this time, however, Ewens had died and his son and heir, Matthew, had sold much of the property he inherited in December 1629 to Dr. Arthur Duck (1580–1648). Matthew died sometime before February 14, 1633, but had given William Child, a scrivener, moneys to pay off his debts, but Child died on February 27, 1638. In 1633 Milton and Bower tried to obtain their money by bringing suit against Alexander Ewens, the brother and executor of Matthew's estate. Another bill was entered in Mrs. Downer's name in May 1635, but Milton and Bower had to bring suit again on February 16, 1637. This was answered by Duck and Child on March 16, 1637. On June 12, 1640, the Court absolved Duck and his deceased child of legal responsibility, ordered Milton and Bower to pay the court costs, and told them to seek satisfaction from Alexander Ewens. Whether the case was ever settled is unknown.

Another long litigation involved a loan of £150 to Sir John Cope on February 1, 1638. He died in October 1638, but interest was paid regularly until November 1641, when his heirs claimed they had no funds. Milton's suit to recoup his money had no success. John, Jr., brought suit on June 16, 1654, with the help of his brother Christopher. An answer came on October 21 and Milton immediately filed exceptions, but failure to respond brought a protest by Christopher on February 6, 1655. This the court upheld, yet it took until May 28 to issue a subpoena. Lady Elizabeth Cope filed an additional answer on June 18, and the litigation continued through at least June 1659. Lady Cope died in 1660, and the outcome of the suit is unknown.

A final example of the kind of chancery proceedings in which Milton the younger was involved is the suit brought against him by Sir Robert Pye, MP, on February 11, 1647. Milton's legal counsel was John Bradshaw*, who later was a regicide and President of the Council of State*. This suit came as a result of the involved financial dealings of Milton's late father-in-law Richard Powell. Powell had bequeathed his estate at Forest Hill* to his son Richard, but he had previously mortgaged it to Pye for thirty-one years in June 1640. An answer by Milton was ready on February 22, 1647, and on November 27 Pye entered a denial. Forest Hill was indentured to Pye's son John on December 3, and on June 16, 1649, the court dismissed the case with costs being awarded to Milton.

The importance of these legal matters for a study of Milton lies, of course, in their biographical information, such as dates, activities, residences, and acquaintances, and in the realization of the nature of Milton's income. [JTS]

CHANNING, WILLIAM ELLERY (1780–1842), New England Unitarian. In his review of Milton's *CD* for the liberal Boston periodical the *Christian Examiner* when it first appeared in America in Charles R. Sumner's edition of 1825, he saw Milton as a great precursor of the Unitarian movement. Minister of the Federal Street Church of Boston from 1803 until his death, Channing had been a leading spokesman for the Unitarians since 1815, when he responded to a *Panoplist* accusation that Boston clergymen were not Christians, but "Unitarians." By 1819, he had accepted the label *Unitarian;* and in his widely-read "Baltimore Sermon" (delivered at the ordination of Jared Sparks), Channing outlined the beliefs of those who argued for "God's unity" and "the unity of Jesus

Christ [who is] distinct from the one God." The "Moral Argument Against Calvinism" (1820), in which he denied the doctrine of natural human depravity, and "Unitarian Christianity Most Favorable to Piety" (1826) further enhanced his reputation as a champion of free thought in America.

When his "Remarks on the Character and Writings of John Milton" (1826) and his "Analysis of the Life and Character of Napoleon Bonaparte" (1828) appeared in England, Channing quickly gained the admiration of the London *Monthly Magazine* and the *Westminster Review;* only William Hazlitt* of the *Edinburgh Review* objected that Channing's evaluation of Milton was "full of commonplace eulogy," his essay on Napoleon of "commonplace invective." In 1839, thirteen years after its original publication in the *Christian Examiner* and nine years after its being reprinted in Channing's *Discourses, Reviews, and Miscellanies* (1830), the *Edinburgh Review* again attacked the "Remarks on . . . Milton." This time it was Henry Brougham who accused Channing of poor taste, of affected diction, and of obscure thought. More typical, however, of the English response to Channing's moral criticism was the *Westminster Review*'s evaluation of him "as an incarnation of the intellectual spirit of Christianity . . . the tenth Avatar of the principle of reformation"; only the criticism of Washington Irving and James Fenimore Cooper was admired more by English reviewers.

In the first part of the "Remarks on . . . Milton," Channing praises "the sublime intelligence of Milton" as it is expressed in his poetry and the remainder of his prose. Reflecting the most *avant-garde* literary theories of the early nineteenth century, Channing extols the moral grandeur, the energy, and the seriousness of Milton's vision and style. One may hear echoes of the theories of Wordsworth*, whom Channing met in 1822 and whose works he had introduced to Boston literary circles, in Channing's praise of Milton's poetic genius: "With a few strong or delicate touches, he impresses, as it were, his own mind on the scenes he would describe, and kindles the imagination of the gifted reader to clothe them with the same radiant hues under which they appeared to his own." And one is reminded of Carlyle's later theory of the literary man as hero when one reads that Milton is "an illustration of what all, who are true to their nature, will become in the progress of their being."

Although he is disappointed to find few passages in the *CD* "in which Milton's mind is laid open to us," and although he is surprised by Milton's views on polygamy* and divorce*, Channing is pleased to find in the *CD* a "calm earnestness, and that profound veneration for Scripture which certain denominations of Christians, who have little congeniality with Milton, seem to claim as a monopoly"; a defense of "human freedom, in opposition to the Calvinistic doctrine of predestination"; and a declaration of "Anti-trinitarianism." Channing celebrates Milton, Locke, and Newton, "the three noblest minds of modern times, and, we may add, of the Christian era, [all] witnesses to the great truth . . . of God's proper unity." In the "Baltimore Sermon" Channing had asserted that the Unitarians "feel it our bounden duty to exercise our reason upon [the Bible] perpetually . . . to seek the nature of the subject, and the aim of the writer, his true meaning"; Milton, in spite of his disturbing notion of the "twofold Scripture," seems to believe "that the Holy Spirit works with and by our own understandings, and instead of superseding reason, invigorates and extends it." And so Milton's close examination of Scripture makes him, for Channing, a pattern for all Christians who desire to join "the pursuit of high and ever-growing attainments in intellect and virtue." Other Unitarians have since then frequently claimed Milton as their very own. [EHH]

CHAOS: *see* METAPHYSICS; COSMOLOGY.

CHAPPELL, WILLIAM (1582–1649), Milton's first tutor* at Christ's College*, Cambridge. A quarrel between them resulted in Milton's rustication* in spring 1626; upon his return he was placed under Nathaniel Tovey*. The reason for their quarrel is unknown; it is possible that Milton was whipped, as Aubrey* states, but more likely the cause was the two men's unbending natures, probably brought to a head by either Milton's course of study or some doctrinal point. Chappell was known as a staunch supporter of episcopacy; later, he was accused of being an Arminian* and even charged with having papistic views and leanings. Milton, in his first elegy to Diodati*, refers to his dislike for Chappell, and some critics suggest that Old Damaetas, in *Lyc*, is Chappell, although no positive identification is possible. [WM]

CHARACTER OF THE LONG PARLIAMENT. A posthumous volume listed in the Term Catalogues for the Easter Term (April), 1681, *CharLP* was originally a digression included in the third book of *Brit*. It would seem to have been written during 1648 when the Long Parliament was in power and the Civil War was either in abeyance or seemingly at an end. Perhaps the first four months of 1648 are most likely. Milton saw a parallel between the Long Parliament and the Westminster Assembly* on the one hand and the state of Britain after the Roman conquest on the other; the work is an indictment of selfish, corrupt, and tyrannic leaders. It was excised from *Brit* in 1670, but why and by whom is not clear. Henry Brome, the publisher*, says that it was deleted for some unseasonable harshness, but what would not have been harsh in 1681 that was considered so in 1670 is difficult to understand. Brome's remarks do not disagree with the thought that Milton himself struck out the passage, perhaps because he did not wish to obtrude such an obviously opinionated passage into an otherwise straightforward historical work. How Brome obtained the manuscript is unknown.

A variant text is extant in manuscript in the Harvard University Library (Eng. MS 14496.34). Entitled "The Digression to com in Lib. 3 pages 110 after these words [from one misery to another]," its twelve pages, in scribal hand, are somewhat longer than the printed version, with frequent variations in orthography. It has been considered closer to Milton's original, although it is keyed to the 1670 edition of *Brit* in a hand contemporary with that of the text. Its place of insertion into *Brit* is different from that in *CharLP*.

CharLP was briefly summarized and discussed in Thomas Flatman's *Heraclitus Ridens*, No. 10, April 4, 1681. It was omitted from Phillips's list of his uncle's works and from the prose collections of 1697 and 1698. It was first reinserted into *Brit* by Thomas Birch* in 1738, and was reprinted in the *Harleian Miscellany* in 1745, and later. [JTS]

CHARITOPULUS, MANUEL, patriarch of Constantinople in the first half of the thirteenth century. Renowned for his learning, he wrote *Solutiones Quarundum Quaestionum (Answers to Certain Questions), Decretum de Jure Patronatus (Decree Concerning the Law of Patronage),* and *Decretum de Translatione Episcoporum (Decree Concerning the Transfer of Bishops).* These works were the result of the many legal questions put to him by his bishops in Cappadocia, to one of which, on whether, if men left their wives for five years or more and it was uncertain where they were, their wives might marry again, Bishop Manuel replied affirmatively. All three of Charitopulus's works were reprinted in Frankfurt in 1596 by Johann Löwenklau (1533–1593), or Leunclavius*, as he Latinized his name, in his compilation of Graeco-Roman law *Iuris Graeco-Romani . . . Tomi Duo,* which, he says, was "dug out of various libraries of Europe and Asia and rendered into Latin." It was Bishop Manuel's affirmative reply that Milton entered in the *CB* under "Of Divorce." [RM]

CHARITY, or love, is the third and greatest of the theological virtues*. In *CD* Milton distinguishes between love in the wider sense of the term as identified with holiness (the subject of Book 1) and love in a more particular sense with reference to its object (the subject of Book 2). The latter is defined as "a general virtue, infused into believers by God the Father* in Christ through the Spirit, and comprehending the whole duty of love which each individual owes to himself and his neighbor" (17 : 197). Nowhere is it more fully described than in 1 Corinthians 13 : 13 : "And now abideth faith*, hope*, charity, these three; but the greatest of these is charity." The opposite vice is uncharitableness, which "renders all our other qualities and actions, however excellent in appearance, of no account." Milton treats together love (*caritas*) and righteousness (*iustitia*) on the grounds that they are the two general virtues concerned with one's duty toward men. The distinction between them seems to be based on the distinction between an infused and an acquired virtue. Love is infused directly by God, whereas righteousness, defined as the virtue by which "we render to each his due" (17 : 199), corresponds to the cardinal virtue of justice. In a much-debated passage of *Mask* Milton substitutes Charity for Chastity, probably because of the occasion. Michael's final admonition to Adam in *PL* is to add deeds and virtues to his newly acquired knowledge*, above all, to "add Love, / By name to come call'd Charitie, the soul / Of all the rest" (*PL* 12. 583–85). Then Adam will no longer be loath to leave this Paradise* but shall possess within himself a paradise "happier far." [RF]

CHARLES I (1600–1649) King of Great Britain from 1625 to 1649. The second son of James I*, he became heir apparent on the death of Prince Henry in 1612 and king on the death of his father on March 27, 1625. His marriage to Princess Henrietta Maria of France was unpopular because of the renewal of Roman Catholic influences. Charles's early reign was dominated by the influence of his disliked prime minister George Villiers, Duke of Buckingham*, who was assassinated in 1628. Charles's first three parliaments were dissolved over the members' opposition to his financial bills and eleven leaders were imprisoned at various times. The third parliament introduced the people's Petition of Right. From 1628 to 1639 he ruled without a parliament through his advisers Archbishop William Laud*· and Sir Thomas Wentworth (Earl of Strafford). Bills concerned with poundage and tonnage, loans, and the like, were put into effect by his Star Chamber and High Commission. Through Laud he attempted to impose episcopacy, to which the Scots reacted with the Solemn League and Covenant on February 28, 1638, and the restoration of Presbyterianism*. The "Short Parliament" was called in 1639 but Charles's demands for money to fight the Scots were turned down and peace demanded. On November 3, 1640, the "Long Parliament" was convened because Charles's intervening attack on Scotland, which brought retaliation and the Scot's occupation of Newcastle and Durham, had drained his financial resources. This parliament was not legally disbanded until 1660, for a bill was passed that it could not be dissolved without its own consent.

The "Long Parliament," led by John Pym, impeached and imprisoned Laud and Strafford, who were finally executed under a forced warrant from Charles. Conditions worsened and Civil War broke out in 1642, with victories on both sides during the next few years. The defeat of the Royalists by the Parliamentarian forces at Marston Moor (July 2, 1644) and Naseby (June 14, 1645) and their aftermath caused Charles to give himself over to the Scottish army at Newark on May 5, 1646. Turned over to the English, he escaped from Holmby House to Carisbrooke Castle on the Isle of Wight, but was there again imprisoned. Negotiations had been in progress between the king and Parliament until "No More Addresses" was passed on January 3, 1648. The Scots, who had also been in negotiation with

Charles primarily to enable the establishment of Presbyterianism in Scotland and England, invaded England under the Duke of Hamilton. This second Civil War ended with Cromwell's* defeat of the Scots at Preston, August 17–20, 1648. Charles had been removed from Wight to Hurst Castle and then to Windsor on December 23, 1648. The purge of Presbyterian members of Parliament by Colonel Pride on December 6 had left a Rump Parliament that represented the Army, and the Rump appointed a court to try the king. The trial began on January 6, 1649; Charles was taken to Westminster Hall on January 20, but he declared the trial illegal and refused to plead before the court. The trial ended on January 25; the king was condemned on January 26–27 by 67 of the original 70 judges; the sentence of execution was signed on January 29; and he was beheaded at Whitehall on January 30.

While the political actions of Charles and parliamentary leaders had influence indirectly upon Milton's life and may perhaps be read into some of the early poems, it was not until the controversy over episcopacy erupted in 1641 that Milton entered into such public concerns. Directly, Charles's actions and person were important to *Tenure, Peace, Eikon,* and *1Def.* Charles was the alleged author of *Eikon Basilike*, "The King's Book," and the sympathy that it elicited for him as a martyr had to be countered by the new government under Cromwell. To achieve this Milton was ordered by the Council of State* to write *Eikon.* [JTS]

CHARLES II (1630–1685) King of England. Milton mentions Charles II numerous times in *Eikon, 1Def, 2Def,* and *3Def.* Overall, Charles is depicted as no better than his father, ill-instructed and not to be trusted. Milton worked hard to prevent Charles's Restoration, and the poet's courage in publishing *Way* so close to the return of Charles must be admired (perhaps Milton felt that he had nothing to lose). Thomas Tomkyns, the censor who granted the licence for *PL* in 1665, was reported by Toland* to have objected to some supposed references to Charles II and his Court, at 1. 594–99, and 7. 32–34. There is an anecdote of a meeting between Charles and Milton where the two discussed some of the poet's prose endeavors; this piece of apocrypha dates from the late eighteenth century. However, Milton's widow did state "that her husband was applied to by message from the King, and invited to write for the Court," which, true to his principles, Milton declined. Perhaps Charles, who was at various times considering a divorce from his childless wife, Catherine of Braganza, had a specific assignment in mind for Milton. [WM]

CHARTISM: see INFLUENCE ON THE LITERATURE OF NINETEENTH-CENTURY ENGLAND, MILTON'S.

CHASTITY. In *CD* Milton defines chastity as "temperance as regards the unlawful lusts of the flesh"; opposed to chastity are all kinds of impurity such as effeminacy, sodomy, and bestiality (17: 217). A more personal note is struck in *Apol* where Milton, in defending himself against the charge of dissolute living, reveals his high regard for chastity and his idealistic attitude toward women (3 : 301–7). *Mask* is a dramatic embodiment of these attitudes. Milton goes so far as to substitute chastity for charity* in the Lady's allusion to the theological virtues (3 : 213–15). This substitution has evoked criticism, but the association between *castitas* and *caritas* was a Renaissance commonplace; *castitas* was regarded as a step toward, a symbol of, and, in its truest sense, a virtue identical with *caritas*. In *Apol* Milton cites Plato* and Xenophon* as authorities in identifying "true love" (love of virtue) with chastity.

Milton everywhere treats unchastity with severity, but for him lust is not the primal sin*. On several occasions in his major poetical works he depicts the contention of St. Augustine* that the rebellion of the flesh against the spirit (lust) is a symbol and a consequence of the rebellion of the spirit against God (pride). A mythic embodiment of this notion occurs

in the episode of Satan and Sin in *PL*. At the moment Satan begins his rebellion, the personified Sin springs full-grown from his brow; he becomes enamored of this daughter, and the two soon join in an incestuous union to beget the monster Death (2. 747–67). With Adam and Eve, acts of lust immediately follow the eating of the forbidden fruit (9. 1011–45). A similar progression occurs in *SA*. Samson falls into the snare of "fair fallacious looks, venereal trains" but only after becoming "swoll'n with pride" and walking about "like a petty God" (529–40). [RF]

CHATEAUBRIAND, FRANÇOIS-RENÉ DE (1768–1848), was born to a noble Breton family at Saint-Malo on September 4, 1768. He became an outstanding man of letters, and, of all French writers other than academic scholars, was the most thoroughly appreciative of English literature, particularly of the poetry of Milton. He attended several lycées for short periods, but very early entered military service in the Garde de Marine. At about the same time, his interest in religion led him to become a knight of the Order of Malta. Though his marriage was financially advantageous, it was not happy, and throughout his life he engaged in liaisons with women of social or cultural distinction. The most notable of these was his long and tender devotion to the celebrated Madame Récamier. His flair for romanticism was responsible for his voyage to the United States in 1791. He was received by George Washington, traveled inland to Niagara Falls and the shores of the Great Lakes, lived with Indians, and left for home deeply impressed by wild landscapes and primitivism. His experiences are reflected in *Atala* (1801), *Les Natchez* (1801), and *René* (1805). He held high offices of state for brief terms, but the clash of his ideals with political loyalty caused him always to resign or be dismissed. His deep religiosity found expression chiefly in his *Génie du Christianisme* (1801), a long and passionate apologia for the Roman

Catholic Church, particularly its essential doctrines and its forms of worship. In this massive work he discusses *inter alia* the function of poetry in the interpretation of Christian traditions and concepts. *PL* receives perceptive treatment in chapters on Milton's presentation of Hell*, Adam and Eve, the angels*, and Satan. His *Essai sur la littérature anglaise* (1836), however, offers full and richly appreciative consideration of *PL* as a whole. Chateaubriand's thorough analysis and sensitive interpretation of the epic are the climax of an extended account of Milton's life and art. Though he presents no new facts of biographical* interest, he is copious and accurate in his use of the information available in his day. For all the poetry, he gives judgments that are both perceptive and objective. But his most notable contribution to Milton studies was his translation of *PL* (1836) into French prose. Though he gently boasted that his understanding of poetry would have enabled him to make an "elegant" translation, he affirmed his intention to produce a literal version, "line by line and word for word," but retaining every poetic subtlety and excellence of the original. That he succeeded in his purpose, despite occasional lapses, two crucial passages attest : 1. 1–16 : "La première désobéissance de l'homme et le fruit de cet arbre défendu, dont le mortel goût apporta la mort dans le monde, et tous nos malheurs, avec la perte d'Eden, jusqu'à ce qu'un homme plus grand que nous rétablit et reconquit le séjour bienheureux, chante, Muse celeste ! Sur le sommet secret d'Oreb et de Sinai [Milton wrote *or*, not *and*] tu inspiras le berger qui le premier apprit à la race choisie comment, dans le commencement, le ciel et la terre sortirent du chaos. Où si le colline de Sion, le ruisseau de Siloe qui coulait rapidement [Milton wrote *fast by*, not *rapidly*] près de l'Oracle de Dieu, te plaisant d'avantage, j'invoque ton aide pour mon chant adventureux : ce n'est pas d'un vol tempéré qu'il veut prendre l'essor au dessus des monts d'Aonie, tandis qu'il poursuit des choses qui n'ont encore été tentées ni

en prose ni en vers," and 3. 1–12 : "Salut, lumière sacré, fille du ciel née la première où de l'Eternel rayon coéternel! Ne puis-je nommer ainsi sans être blamé? Puisque Dieu est la lumière, et que de toute éternité il habita jamais que dans une lumière, inaccessible, il habita en toi, brillante éffusion d'un brillante essence incrée. Où préfères-tu t'entendre appeler ruisseau de pur éther? Qui dira ta source? Avant le soleil, avant les cieux, tu étais, et à la voix de Dieu tu couvris, comme d'un manteau, le monde s'élevant des eaux ténébreuses et profondes, conquête faite sur l'infini vide et sans forme." Chateaubriand is respected for *Génie du Christianisme,* but he is best known for *Atala, René, and Mémoires d'outre tombe* (1848–1850). Though he was preceded as a translator of *PL* by others, he remains with Voltaire* the most important French man of letters interested in Milton as a poet. [DAR]

CHAUCER, GEOFFREY. Seventeenth-century readers knew Chaucer's writings in the editions of Thomas Speght, 1598, 1602, 1687, which superseded William Thynne's (1532, 1542) and John Stow's (1561). Page references in Milton's *CB* prove that Milton read Speght's second edition (1602), which had profited from Francis (son of William) Thynne's *Animadversions* (1599) upon the first. It is pleasant to conjecture that the young Milton was introduced to Chaucer's (and Spenser's*?) poetry in 1616 when his father's friend John Lane first prepared for the press a fair copy of his continuation of Chaucer's *Squire's Tale* that added, in undistinguished couplets, ten new sections to Chaucer's two, to which Lane affixed an account of Spenser's prior effort at continuation of the tale in canto three of the fourth book of the *Faerie Queene.* Lane prepared another, revised, copy of his continuation (like the first, not published in his lifetime) in 1630, within a year of the composition of *IlP,* in lines 109–15 of which, alluding to the incomplete *Squire's Tale,* Milton penned his most eloquent and haunting echo of Chaucer's verse.

Echoes of Chaucer have been fairly

confidently identified in three of Milton's Latin university poems, despite the uncertainty inherent in the fact that both poets drew upon many of the same classical sources. Lines 139–54 of *QNov* recall the description of the temple of Mars in the *Knight's Tale,* lines 1109–82; the description of the tower of Fama, lines 170–93, as MacKellar insists, is indebted to the *Hous of Fame,* lines 711–24, as well as to Ovid*. Likewise the young poet's imagined empyreal flight, lines 45–64 of *In Obitum Praesulis Eliensis,* owes much to the airy journey in Book 2 of the *Hous of Fame.* Lines 63–65 of *Nat* echo an idea common to Ovid, Horace*, Boethius*, and Chaucer; but the only parallel of one phrase "sub aquis gemmas" is in Chaucer's *The Former Age*: "in the riveres . . . gemmes." In writing *IlP* shortly before leaving the university, Milton recalled a line from Chaucer's *Wife of Bath's Tale,* line 868, "As thikke as motes in the sonne-beem"; in *IlP,* lines 7–8, "As thick and numberless / As the gay motes that people the Sun Beam." One reference to Chaucer appropriates Spenser's appellation for the poet, Tityrus, who, as he now, had once in Naples, Manso*, he glancingly compares himself to another young English poet, Tityrus, who, as he knew, had once long before traveled to Italian shores (*Mansus,* lines 30–34). All of these are instances of poet responding to poet.

The best gloss on the Chaucerian allusions in *Ref* are the references to Chaucer added in the second edition (1570 and subsequently) of John Foxe's* *Actes and Monumentes.* As evidence of prelatical corruption, Foxe instances "sects of Fryers," citing Chaucer (1 : 341); Milton, taking up the hint, adduces "the merry Frier in Chaucer" and quotes lines 221–23 from the sketch of the friar in the *General Prologue.* In 2 : 965, Foxe characterizes Chaucer as one "Who (no doubt) saw in Religion as much almost, as euen we do now, . . . and semeth to be a right Wiclevian"; he has been informed of many who by "readying of Chaucers workes . . . were brought to the true knowledge of Religion," instancing and

discussing "the talke of the ploughman"; that is, the stanzaic allegory of the griffin and the pelican, which is included in both Thynne's and Speght's editions as Chaucer's *Plowman's Tale.* Again Milton follows suit in the course of several citations (*Ref* 3 : 28, 44–45, 54), commenting upon and quoting two appropriate stanzas from Speght, 1602 : "Thus hee [Chaucer] brings in the Plow-man speaking, 2. Part. Stanz. 28. . . . And in the next *stanza* which begins the third part. . . ."

The passing reference to "our learned Chaucer" in *Animad* (3 : 110–11) commends him along with the "elegantest Authors" as not being servile to a "capricious *Paedantrie*" in the spelling of proper names—citing, as spelled in Speght's edition, "K. Sejes for K. Ceyz" in the *Book of the Duchess* and others from the *Parlement of Foules* and *Troilus.* Finally, Chaucerian references in Milton's *CB,* all dated 1640–1642, reflect interests and activities of those years. First, there is ". . . the discommodities of mariage. See Chaucer merchants tale, and wife of Baths prologue" (18 : 151). Under a rubric on the education of children, lines 65–69 of the *Physician's Tale* are paraphrased on the dangers of "feestes, revels and . . . daunces" as making young people "To soon ripe and bold" (18 : 154). The sermon on gentilesse in the *Wife of Bath's Tale* is cited twice, under *"Paupertas"* ("no poverty but sin") and, along with a passage in the *Romaunt of the Rose* (included by Speght as Chaucer's), under *"Nobilitas."*

There are no allusions to Chaucer in Milton's prose or poetry after 1642. Thus, between 1626 and 1642, the young poet, controversialist, and moralist ranged widely and profitably over the canon of Chaucer's poetry as he found it presented in Speght's black-letter folio volume, recommended by Spenser and John Lane, and expounded especially by Foxe and perhaps other late sixteenth- and early seventeenth-century Reformers. His appropriation of Chaucer, while uniquely his own, was consonant with that of his time. [EHD]

CHEKE, SIR JOHN (1514–1557), Professor of Greek, early Protestant, tutor and privy councilor to Edward VI. He was elected first Regius Professor of Greek at St. John's, Cambridge, in 1540. With his colleague Sir Thomas Smith (d. 1577) he changed the pronunciation of Greek from the prevailing Modern to the Ancient as demonstrated by Erasmus*. Cheke defended his practice against the Chancellor, Bishop Gardiner, but conservative authority forbade the innovation. He published his exchange of letters with Gardiner in *De Pronunciatione Graecae* (1555). Cheke's fortune rose in a succession of offices: tutor to Edward, Prince of Wales, provost of King's College, member of Parliament, secretary of state, and privy councilor. Upon the accession of Mary (1553), misfortunes beset him and he took refuge in Strasbourg. In 1556, traveling near Brussels, he was seized by Spanish authorities, taken to London, and terrified into public recantation of his Protestantism. He died soon after.

Milton probably noticed Ascham's valedictory praise of Cheke, "our moste helpe and furtheraunce to learnynge," newly made tutor to Edward (*Toxophilus* [1545], 1.33r; cf. *CB* 18:214). Citing from the *Scripta Anglicana* of Martin Bucer* (1577), which came into his hands in April or May 1644, Milton includes among the testimonials for Bucer one sentence translated from Cheke's *De Obitu . . . Martini Buceri* (1551), "*pag.* 864" *Bucer* (4:2). He learned from John Foxe's* preface to *Reformatio Legum Ecclesiasticarum* (1571; 1640) that Cheke was a member of the committee of thirty-two appointed by Edward to search into the old ecclesiastical law books of England and to frame therefrom English laws to replace canon laws: "of whom *Cranmer* the Archbishop, *Peter Martyr,* and *Walter Haddon* (not without the assistance of Sir *John Cheeke* the Kings Tutor, a man at that time counted the learnedest of Englishmen, & for piety not inferior) were the chief . . ." (4:231). This passage in *Tetra* reflects Milton's happy discovery that among the laws framed by Edward's

committee, in Latin polished by Cheke, was the legalization of divorce* and second marriage *"not only for adultery or desertions, but for any capital enmity or plot against the others life,"* or for *"lesser contentions, if they be perpetual"*—which, says Milton, is "all one really with the position by me held in the former treatise publisht on this argument" (4:231–32).

In the final sestet of *Sonn* 12, Milton invokes Cheke in a quip: "Thy age, like ours, O soul of Sir *John Cheek,* / Hated not Learning wors then Toad or Asp; / When thou taught'st Cambridge, and King *Edward* Greek." Does Milton say that Cheke's age also hated learning, or that his own age contrasts with Cheke's receptive times? Masson (*Life,* 2:283) claims the latter, Smart (*Sonnets,* pp. 73–74) the former solution, arguing from *De Pronunciatione Graecae* that "many men in that age" hated learning. Schultz (*Modern Language Notes* 69:497) agrees with Smart that Milton scorns both ages for neglect of learning, citing Gerard Langbaine's* description of bigotry at Cambridge in the preface to the 1641 reprint of Cheke's *The Hurt of Sedition* (1549), which Milton possibly knew and recalled. French disagrees (*MLN* 70:404–5), contending that Milton in *Tetra* and elsewhere refers to the age of Cheke as "those times which are on record for the purest and sincerest that ever shon yet on the reformation of this Iland, the time of *Edward* the 6th" (4:231). All that is certain is that Milton knew of Cheke as a famous Greek scholar, a friend of Bucer, a royal commissioner on church law reform, and a learned influence upon the most Protestant of English kings. [TLH]

CHERON, LOUIS: *see* ILLUSTRATIONS.

CHERON, DE BOISMORAND, C. J. *see* TRANSLATIONS OF MILTON'S WORKS.

CHERUBINI, ALESSANDRO. A precocious intellectual from Rome whom Milton met during his first visit there in 1638, Cherubini is mentioned in *Epistol* 9 to Holstenius*, the librarian of the Vatican. Milton supposes that Cherubini may have spoken of him to Holstenius prior to his visit to the library. Cherubini died at age twenty-eight. [JTS]

CHILDREN, MILTON'S. Milton fathered five children: four by his first wife, Mary Powell, one by his second wife, Katherine Woodcock, and none by his third wife, Elizabeth Minshull. Anne was born on July 29, 1646; Mary, on October 25, 1648; John, on March 16, 1651; Deborah, on May 2, 1652; and Katherine, on October 19, 1657.

Anne had some kind of physical handicap; it has been suggested that she was a spastic or retarded. She had difficulty in speaking, and is described as being lame and almost helpless. She was deformed but had a handsome face. Although she was illiterate, she did acquire the trade of making gold and silver lace. She seems to have left Milton's home around 1669. A special arrangement for her was given in Milton's will; £100 was to be invested for her by her uncles Christopher Milton and Richard Powell. Soon after Milton's death she married, ca. 1675, a master builder. An Anne Milton married a Michael Smith at St. Giles, Cripplegate, on November 2, 1676, but whether this was Milton's daughter is uncertain. She probably died in 1677 in childbed with her first child, who also died.

Mary was baptized at St. Giles in the Fields on November 7, 1648. She is reported to have looked more like her mother than her father. Like her sisters she learned a trade and left her father's home around 1669. She seems to have read to Milton, including material in foreign languages, though without real comprehension. Mary seems never to have married and apparently died between 1681 and 1694. Through Milton's nuncupative will* she received £100 and signed a release to her step-mother on February 22, 1675, and she was named in her grandmother Anne Powell's will dated October 24, 1678. Milton's reputed reference to his unkind children and their

being undutiful to him has led to various speculations about his relationship with the three surviving daughters. Perhaps Milton referred only to their lack of attention to him from around 1669 until his death in 1674, for there is no real evidence of strained relationships before, nor of their presence in his last years. Mary is reported to have shown dislike of her father shortly before his third marriage; but such rumors cited during the deposition on Milton's will may not deserve the unfavorable light that has often been cast upon them. They are vague and not always reliable in detail, particularly in chronology. Difficulties may have ensued as a result of his third marriage to Elizabeth Minshull on February 24, 1663. Elizabeth was only twenty-four, and Anne was seventeen, Mary fifteen, and Deborah eleven.

Milton's only son, John, died around June 16, 1652. The entry in Milton's Bible reads, "And my son about 6. weeks after his mother." The death and burial probably occurred elsewhere than in Westminster, because the mother's confinement with Deborah shortly before in May was probably at Mary's mother's home, the location of which is unknown.

It appears that Deborah was Milton's favorite daughter. She had been taught to read and write; she read to Milton in various languages; and like her sisters she learned a trade (probably embroidery). Specifically, she cited reading Isaiah in Hebrew, Homer* in Greek, and Ovid's* *Metamorphoses* in Latin. Many years later she could still recall at least one long passage from something she had often read to her father. Probably, however, she did not really understand what she read. Aubrey* remarked that she was his amanuensis*; the truth is more likely that at most she wrote down little things for him, not any part of a major work, as the remark has been interpreted in the past. Deborah looked like her father, and is reported to have said that he was "delightful company, the life of the conversation" and a man of "unaffected cheerfulness and civility." She left Milton's household around 1669 and soon became a companion to a lady named Merian, with whom she went to Ireland around 1672 to live. On June 1, 1674, in Dublin, she married Abraham Clarke, a weaver. Whether Milton knew of the marriage is unknown; her sisters were not aware of it. The Clarkes had ten children, seven sons and three daughters. The names of only three of the children are known: Elizabeth, born in Ireland in November 1688; Caleb; and Urban.

Deborah and Abraham Clarke's release of inheritance in her father's will was signed on March 27, 1675, a month after her sisters' releases. Apparently Deborah demanded and got, in addition to the £100, some personal articles or furniture. One item seems to have been a small silver seal, drawn from the coat of arms. It passed from Deborah to her daughter Elizabeth, to her husband, Thomas Foster, from him to John Payne, a bookseller, and then to Thomas Hollis. Its present whereabouts are not known. Deborah returned to England sometime after November 1688, when Elizabeth was born, and, according to John Toland*, was living in London in 1698. Her husband must have died after 1687, possibly in 1688, which was thus the reason for Deborah's return to England. More probably he died around 1702 when his children Caleb and Elizabeth left Ireland. (There is no evidence that the Abraham Clarke admitted to the Company of Weavers on May 9, 1709, was related, though he may have been one of the unnamed sons.) Around 1704–1708, Milton's daughter was "in a very low and destitute condition." She petitioned Robert Harley, Secretary of State, for financial aid, though she hoped to be able to maintain herself in her own work. He wrote a note that says he relieved her often. Later she lived in a little street near Moorfields where she kept a school for young children. Since the age of eighteen, however, Deborah had had poor eyesight and worn glasses, and when her eyesight failed further, she gave up conducting school and went to live with her daughter and son-in-law in

Pelham Street, Spitalfields. In 1719 she was befriended by Joseph Addison* shortly before he died, and on April 29, 1727, a public appeal was made for her support. Many contributed, including Queen Caroline. Deborah died at her daughter's home in Lower Holloway on August 24, 1727.

In the last years of her life she was visited by at least two people interested in her father. George Vertue saw her on August 10, 1721, to check on portraits*. The pastel by William Faithorne* was shown her and she exclaimed immediately upon its likeness to her father; her exact words are reported in two slightly differing versions. Another portrait (uncertain which) did not appear to be of her father; and she said she knew of only two which her step-mother would have owned (probably that by Janssen and that owned by Onslow). She was interviewed by John Ward* around August 1727; his notes often seem confused and unreliable, but they were communicated to Thomas Birch* and used in Birch's "Life" in his edition of Milton prose (1738).

Deborah's daughter Elizabeth curiously remained in Ireland until about 1702; she married Thomas Foster, a weaver, and survived her children (see FOSTER, ELIZABETH). Her brother Urban, also a weaver, came to live with the Fosters and died at their home in Lower Holloway. Nothing further is known of him. Deborah's other son, Caleb, migrated to India by 1702, when he is listed at Fort St. George in Madras. He and his wife, Mary, had at least three children: Abraham, baptized at St. George's on June 2, 1703; Mary, on March 17, 1707; and Isaac, on February 13, 1711. Mary was buried in Madras on December 15, 1716; nothing further is known about Isaac. Abraham came to England in 1719, reputedly with the late Governor Harrison (?); undoubtedly he would have seen his grandmother and his aunt Elizabeth Foster. He returned to India after news of his father's death reached him. Caleb had been clerk of St. George's parish since 1717 and died in October 1719. His wife was perhaps the

Mary Clarke buried in Madras on October 4, 1729. Abraham married Anna Clark on September 22, 1725, and had a daughter baptized on April 5, 1727. This child may, of course, have been the Mary Clarke buried on October 4. An Abraham Clarke, perhaps Milton's grandson, was buried in Madras on September 5, 1743. Further descendents are not known, although there is the possibility that new evidence will uncover a few additional relatives.

Milton's last-born child, Katherine, died on March 17, 1658, at the age of five months. This was about five weeks after her mother, Milton's second wife, had died, having fallen ill "of a consumption" after having given birth. The daughter was buried on March 20 from St. Margaret, Westminster. [JTS]

CHIMENTELLI, VALERIO, a priest and a member of the Florentine academy of the Apatisti, whose meetings Milton probably attended both times that he was in Florence. Chimentelli later became a professor at Pisa. He is apparently "Clementillo the young," to whom Milton sent greetings by way of Carlo Dati* in *Epistol* 10. Milton mentions him in *2Def* along with other Florentine friends. Milton is supposed to have written six Italian sonnets to him, but these have never been found and probably never existed. He died around 1670. [JTS]

CHORUS. The possibility of using a full dramatic chorus appealed to Milton's imagination at least twice before he produced the extraordinary "Chorus of Danites" for *SA*. In the late 1630s Milton sketched a number of poetic projects that incorporate a functioning chorus. In fractured form, the general possibility had presented itself many times before. At Cambridge, Milton had delivered *Vac,* a humorous college enactment in which the "Ten Sons of Ens" personifying the Aristotelian predicaments were called across the platform to speak appropriate words and group themselves around their "Father." Milton's lyric poetry had frequently invoked the motif of a singing choir (as in *El* 3, *Nat,* and *Lyc*). In more dramatic vein, he had produced *Mask* with its choric group of Comus's followers. Stage directions for their song, dance, and motion display the force of Comus's presence, if not a separable interest in the conflict. Reflecting the "double chorus" highly precedented in both classical drama and masque, Comus's group is balanced by the "country-dancers" and shepherds of Ludlow Town who attend their President's seat. Milton had also read the classical dramatists with an eye to staging (see his marginal note on Euripides' chorus, 18 : 309). He knew the Italian critics who had shaped theoretical considerations for a proper chorus after Aristotle* (Bernard Weinberg, *A History of Literary Criticism of the Italian Renaissance,* 2 vols. [1961], "chorus," *passim*). He was familiar with the neo-Senecan and pastoral drama of Tasso*, Guarini, Trissino, and Andreini*, which had attempted in various ways to revive the chorus of ancient times. By Milton's day Italian dramatists had abandoned the attempt in literary drama (J. S. Kennard, *The Italian Theater,* 2 vols. [1932], *passim*), but in Florence and Rome, Milton could have seen contemporary developments of Italian "melo" drama (or proto-opera), which employed the chorus singing in recitative (J. H. Hanford and J. G. Taffe, *A Milton Handbook,* 5th ed. [1970], pp. 334–38; French, *Life Records,* 1 : 378–92 and 5 : 386–87). Each of these experiences suggests a possible stimulus to Milton's grasp of the nature, function, and appropriate speech for a dramatic chorus.

After he returned from the Continent, Milton put some of these ideas into tentative form. Preserved on pp. 35–41 of *TM,* his notes record groups of characters, possible plot outlines, and lists of biblical and British topics that might furnish a major tragedy*. Most of the longer entries stipulate a chorus.

Milton shows concern for "the probability of persons" in requiring a "Chorus of Angels" for a play on the loss of paradise*. A projected tragedy on the destruction of Sodom calls for a chorus of "Lots Shepherds" as well as a "Chorus of Angels." Some "Elders of Israel" bear witness in a sketch labeled "Abias Thersaeus." A double chorus composed of Abraham's followers as well as Melchizedec's shepherds appears in "Abram from Morea, or Isack redeemed." For a New Testament subject, "Christus patiens," Jesus' betrayal and arrest "may receav noble expressions" both "by message & chorus," presumably consisting of those apostles and followers who remain at Gethsemene. A play on Dinah specifies both "Nuncius" and "Chorus."

It also appears that Milton required more than mechanical service from his chorus. Successive drafts show some development for the chorus, from being an obligatory adjunct or expository convenience to serving more intrinsic purposes. The action of Milton's first *PL* sketch is curious in being mainly invisible to its audience of mortal sinners. Moses, as prologue, author of Genesis, and sole human authority for the Adam and Eve story, explains why this must be so. To develop the first three acts of his invisible and highly lyric drama, Milton uses his chorus of angels and many allegoric persons, but they do not seem to interact in dialogue. The chorus discharge an expository function in singing a "hymne of the creation"; at the end of Act 2, they "describe Paradise" and "sing the marriage song" of Adam and Eve. As the play proceeds, the chorus becomes slightly more interactive and less reportorial. It "feares for Adam" in Act 3, and relates "Lucifers rebellion and fall." Responding to the situation in Acts 4 and 5, the chorus "bewails" Adam's fall and "tells the good Adam hath lost." Finally, after Faith*, Hope*, and Charity* instruct Adam in Act 5, the Chorus "breifly concludes." In addition to a major burden of exposition and a small amount of reactive or interactive speech, Milton's chorus serves a structural function in the sketch. The materials of the play are divided into five segments; a balancing choral part concludes each act; after Moses, the chorus serves both as "presenter" and final interpreter of the events; their voice occupies nearly half of the proposed whole.

A revised draft called "Adam unparadized" develops a more dramatic, less lyric role for the chorus. They still "sing a hymn of the creation*" and bewail Adams' fall* as before, thus providing information and establishing tones and images that Milton could not otherwise motivate. Gabriel opens, however, with a description of Paradise, and then the chorus, as though trailing him, explains the reason for Gabriel's watch from their knowledge of God's command. They express a desire "to see, & know more concerning this excellent new creature man." When Gabriel passes by "the station of the chorus," they ask him to say what he knows of Adam and Eve's creation "with their love, & marriage." The chorus become seekers of information rather than deliverers. It appears that the "apostrophe to wedded love" in *PL* 4 had its origins in choric song or in Gabriel's reply. When Lucifer appears, the chorus "prepare resistance," suggesting that Milton's imagination, having played with lyric and allegoric aspects of tragedy, begins to grasp more obvious elements of dramatic confrontation. "After discourse of enmity on either side" Satan departs. The chorus displaces its hostility at this point by singing "the battell, & victorie in heavn against him, & his accomplices." Perhaps with mimed counterpoint that breaks into speech when the departing chorus end their song, "heer again may appear Lucifer relating, & insulting in what he had don to the destruction of man." The chorus does not witness Satan's gloating, nor Adam and Eve's entrance "confusedly cover'd with leaves." They reenter the stage and are told "by some angel" the manner of Adam's fall. Once again, the chorus "bewailes" the event, and then converses directly with Adam, warning him to heed Lucifer's example of "impenitance."

Both of these plays and the Sodom

play suggest that a different kind of chorus was also present in Milton's imagination, groups of anti-masquers like Comus's crew. Before Adam's banishment, "a mask of all the evills of this life & world" "passe before his eyes in Shapes." In "Cupids funeral pile. Sodom Burning" "the Gallantry of the town passe by in Procession with musick and song to the temple of Venus Urania or Peor." As well as supplying spectacle, this chorus functions in a character role in that they "send 2 of thire choycest youth with the preist" to invite Lot's two angelic visitors to join the orgy. When Lot's outrage is communicated to the Sodomites, they return in force to "taxe him of praesumption, singularity, breach of citty customs, in fine offer violence."

In addition to using a choric group for spectacle and character functions, the Sodom play suggests a double, or perhaps a triple chorus, which would emphasize the force and scope of interests engaged in the dramatic conflict. The chorus of Lot's shepherds "praepare resistance in thire maisters defense" when attacked by the mob. Classic propriety is observed and a stage battle averted when the angelic guests reveal themselves. But at the end of the play, a full "Chorus of Angels" narrate the concluding events of Lot's journey and the fate of his wife. The expository function still seems to dominate Milton, however. He reminds himself in afterthought that just as an angelic chorus might conclude this play, so his chorus of shepherds could just as well begin it by relating "the course of the citty each evening every one with mistresse, or Ganymed, gittering along the streets, or solacing on the banks of Jordan." It would have been a fine piece of descriptive verse. And since there is no reason to think that Milton was not intending these plays for production, he might have imagined the shepherds' words echoed in pantomime by the chorus of city dwellers.

A few years after these preliminary and private plans for a major work, Milton publicly declared his poetic intentions in *RCG* (1642), suggesting now a wider range of genres than he had considered earlier. For a second time, Milton envisions the chorus as a necessary element of drama. But he cites scriptural and exegetical authority rather than suggesting classical or Italian practice. Since the London theaters would be closed 2 Sept. 1642, perhaps Milton sought more telling precedent for the writing and production of "Dramatick constitutions." Solomon's "divine pastoral Drama" (as Milton apprehends the Book of Canticles) models "two persons and a double Chorus, as Origen rightly judges." Given Milton's musical* interest and the existence of pastoral*, musical drama in Italy, it is reasonable to suppose that Milton's thoughts embrace a stage blending of "voice and verse" (cf. G. L. Finney, *Studies in Philology* 37 : 482–500). Two years later Milton was to praise Henry Lawes* for teaching "English Music how to span / Words with just note and accent" (*Sonn* 13). Moving from pastoral to more serious drama in his *RCG* discussion, Milton next cites Revelation and its chorus. "The Apocalyps of Saint John is the majestick image of a high and stately Tragedy, shutting up and intermingling her solemn Scenes and Acts with a sevenfold Chorus of halleluja's and harping symphonies : and this my opinion the grave autority of Pareus* commenting that booke is sufficient to confirm." The use of a chorus not only to enhance a theme, but to modulate the flow of narrative matter, as suggested in the early *PL* sketches, is still viable in 1642 although on different authority.

Which of these possibilities became actual in Milton's later poetry? The chorus as an imaged presence, a passive group of observant, echoing attendants, is signified in both *PL* and *PR*. Neither poem provides for a dramatically functional chorus, each being told by a first-person narrator. The action of *PR*, the opening paragraphs declare, was originally played out before the observing angels. Their witness of the forty days and comprehension of its meaning are indicated at the end by their providing the banquet and singing the penultimate verse paragraph. In *PL,* a chorus of angels attend the Father with constant song and praise. Full participants in the heavenly debate, they stand mute in response to the Father's awesome question, but shout and sing their understanding of the Son's* voluntary offer for man's redemption. With their song the bard imperceptibly blends his voice (*PL* 3. 410).

But the fruit of Milton's speculations about a dramatic chorus appears in *SA.* Because the play was not stage-intended and Milton rejects music as a proper adjunct, there is no determining the question whether Milton imagined the odes and speeches to be chanted in unison or spoken by one or several leaders on behalf of the rest. There are no cues for patterned or dancelike motion, it being more *coro stabile* than *mobile.* Nor is there division of personality until the dialectic implied by one semi-choral exchange following the Messenger's report. The Chorus attend Samson's progress as if a single person, even though their poetic speech rhythms are distinct from all other verse in the play. In company with the other characters, however, the Chorus also provokes the hero's progress. Being "friends" of the fallen hero and elders of his tribe of Dan, their unanimous but ambivalent interest ultimately reflects the situation, capability, and spiritual potential of men who, "by thir vices brought to servitude" under the Philistine, love "Bondage with ease" more than "strenuous liberty." Critics have speculated upon the moral posture and metrical language of this Chorus, as well as the models Milton might have turned to when contriving a dramatic element unique in English literature.

Popular English drama provides no satisfactory prototypes for the conception. Apart from minor flurries of academic revivalism, the English stage chorus is confined to such examples as the one-character "chorus" in Shakespeare's* *Henry V* or "Time" in *The Winter's Tale.* Jonson* and Webster justify the omission of "a proper and sententious Chorus" in their prefaces to *Sejanus* and *The White Devil.* Jonson writes that the chorus's "Habite, and Moodes are such, and so difficult, as not any, whome I have seene since the Auntients, (no, not they who have most presently affected Lawes) have yet" succeeded. "Nor is it needful, or almost possible, in these our Times," Jonson continues, "and to such Auditors . . . to observe the ould state, and splendour of Dramatick Poemes, with preservation of any popular delight." Milton proudly exempts his tragedy from these popular and economic restrictions, for it comes forth "after the antient manner, much different from what among us passes for best."

Looking for the literary origins of Milton's chorus, W. R. Parker (*Milton's Debt to Greek Tragedy in SA* [1937], pp. 139–50) turned to the classical tragedians, finding Milton's chorus "Sophoclean," but with considerable difference. In their delivering the final word, in the division of "semi-chorus" at the end, and in their continuous stage presence, Milton's Chorus is not untypical. Even Dalila's "damsel train," introduced as mute visual pageantry, finds classical precedent. But the great number of short speeches in dialogue, the frequency and length of sustained choral odes, and the total proportion of space (the Chorus occupying about a fourth of the total length of *SA*) set Milton's Chorus apart from all classical models. According to Parker, its essence is Sophoclean in two respects. They bear sympathetic but not omniscient witness to the protagonist's experience. Their thoughts spring from and bear constant reference to issues raised by the central action, rather than to their own fates or to extra-dramatic philosophical concerns.

Gretchen Finney (*Publications of the Modern Language Association* 58: 649–64) proposed a link between ancient practice and Milton's play through seventeenth-century Italian musical drama and its derivative, the oratorio. Her plausible account of the Chorus's literary history substantiates Milton's otherwise cryptic claim in the preface to *SA,* that the "Chorus is here introduc'd after the Greek manner, not antient only but modern, and still in use among the Italians. In the modelling therefore of this Poem, with good reason, the Antients and Italians are rather follow'd, as of much more authority and fame." Her thesis answers Dr. Johnson's* scornful judgment: "It could only be by long prejudice, and the bigotry of learning, that Milton could prefer the ancient tragedies, with their encumbrance of a chorus" to the plays currently produced in England and France. Finney concludes that Milton was neither a learned bigot nor a self-evolved accident in creating his Chorus. When Milton asserted that music was not essential to drama, he echoed Aristotle and repudiated excesses of sung Italian drama; he acknowledged the true rhythmic origins of Hellenic tragedy; and he returned from Italian models to the purer ideals enunciated by the sixteenth-century Italian Aristotelians.

An analytic description of the Chorus's verse form begins with Milton's own prefatory statement to *SA* : "The measure of Verse us'd . . . is of all sorts, call'd by the Greeks Monostrophic, or rather Apolelymenon [i.e., single stanzas without recurrent metrical pattern], without regard had to Strophe, Antistrophe or Epod [i.e., balanced stanzaic patterning], which were a kind of Stanza's fram'd only for the Music, then us'd with the Chorus that sung; not essential to the Poem, and therefore not material; or being divided into Stanza's or Pauses, they may be call'd Allaeostropha [i.e., stanzas of varied form]." F. T. Prince (*The Italian Element in Milton's Verse* [1954], pp. 145–68) traces the irregular combination of long and short lines (at most 12 syllables, at least 5 syllables in length), each with terminal emphasis, to a unique extension of English blank verse in the light of poetic rhythms developed in Greek lyric poetry and particularly in the Italian canzone form. Robert Beum (*Texas Studies in Language and Literature* 4: 177–82) notices the appearance of over a

hundred rhymed lines (rhyming words within four lines of each other), most of which mark the symbolic, interpretive, incantatory, and evocative voice of the Chorus as distinct from the voice and language in which they converse with Samson directly. The discussion of Milton's prosody and its Italian* source is summarized by M. Y. Hughes (*Complete Poems and Major Prose* [1957], pp. 537–39) and extended by E. Weismiller (*The Lyric and Dramatic Milton,* ed. J. Summers [1965], pp. 115–52). (*See* VERSIFICATION.)

A great variety of published opinion concerning the Chorus's moral posture—its motives, its static or evolving perception of Samson's case, its own constant or developing personality, as well as the meaning, authority, and bearing of its final statement—invites each reader to a personal assessment of the Chorus's role in the play. Some commentators have seen the Chorus as interpreting Samson's experience with the omniscience of God, others, with the prejudice of Milton. Still others have suggested that the Chorus, although it rises to partial understanding of Samson's enfranchisement, begins its conversation with hypocritical self-satisfaction, and remains throughout more blind and bound than the man sent to be Israel's deliverer. In that respect the chorus reflects the condition of those who vaguely ask what shall we do to be saved, but cannot wholly perceive the enacted answer.

The influence of Milton's Chorus on later English drama is minimal, but can be traced through Dryden* (who wistfully embraced the classical ideal, but found the English stage and audience still inhospitable in "A Parallel of Poetry and Painting"), more strongly through masque, opera, and oratorio, very slightly in literary drama through the eighteenth and nineteenth centuries (R. D. Havens, *The Influence of Milton on English Poetry* [1922], pp. 346, 556–60), up to Eliot's *Murder in the Cathedral,* that classical tragedy with a religious theme, on an English subject, for a theater audience

—all of which Milton long considered, but never wrote. [JFH]

CHRIST: *see* SON, THE.

CHRISTIAN DOCTRINE, OF: *see* DE DOCTRINA CHRISTIANA.

CHRISTINA, QUEEN OF SWEDEN (1626–1689), was a celebrity from her birth to her death, and it is not surprising that Milton took note of her. The only surviving child of the Swedish hero Gustavus Adolphus, she succeeded to the crown at the age of six, when her father died in the Battle of Lutzen. She ruled through a regency, astutely contrived by Gustavus, until her eighteenth birthday when she assumed full powers as monarch. She enjoyed the trust, even the affection, of the Rad and the Riksdag, the two houses of the Swedish parliament, and, though erratic in temperament and apparently distraught by inner conflicts, she applied herself assiduously to the duties of her office. Her deep concern for the reconciliation of Protestant Europe led her to take a large part in effecting the Treaty of Westphalia in 1648. In order to establish an improved system of schools in Sweden she sought the advice of John Amos Comenius*, the eminent Bohemian educational theorist. She introduced measures to encourage agricultural productivity and international trade. And, above all, she strove to raise the cultural level of her nation by gathering in Stockholm a notable library of rare books and manuscripts and a massive collection of excellent works of art. Her own skill in languages and her good taste were abetted by bibliophiles and connoisseurs throughout Europe. Her zeal for the enrichment of the national culture was further expressed in her lavish entertainment of eminent scholars at her court. Among those who visited Stockholm, besides Comenius, were : René Descartes, for whom the Swedish climate was fatal; Hugo Grotius*, who died in Christina's service as Ambassador to France and whom Milton met in Paris with fruitful

result; Claudius Salmasius*, early antagonist of Milton whose friendship with the Queen seems first to have brought her to the poet's notice; Isaac Vossius*, collector of manuscripts and classical scholar; and Samuel Pufendorf, author of important studies in law, and historiographer of Sweden.

It may be assumed that through either hearsay or his acquaintance with Bulstrode Whitelock*, British Ambassador to Sweden and admirer of the Queen, Milton had some awareness of positive aspects of Christina's character and career. It is impossible to believe, however, that, when he freely praised her, he knew of her gross extravagance, which tended to beggar her impecunious nation; her fanciful and reckless international policies, which endangered the peace and security of Sweden; her steadfast aversion to marriage, which threatened the stability of the dynasty; her lesbian affection for her lady-in-waiting, Ella Sparre; her perverse insistence on abdication; and her conversion to the Roman Catholic Church, which she flamboyantly paraded across Europe. It is ironic that her formal reception by the papacy at Innsbruck was presided over, as papal legate, by Lucas Holstenius*, Milton's friend and erstwhile mentor in Rome.

After her conversion Christina, renamed Alexandra, took up residence in Rome, where she was warmly received. For her residence and library she was given a rambling palace on the Janiculum. She lived there in state until her death on April 19, 1689, but her last years were clouded by emotional upsets and painful physical illness. As a mark of special honor her body was interred in the crypt of St. Peter's, but, contrary to her wishes, her funeral arrangements were elaborate. Her own text for the inscription on her tomb, which was disregarded, indicated that at life's end she had reached a state of humility that she had never before known.

Milton's tribute to Christina in *2Def* and in *3Def* is ardent but deficient in facts. He lauds her as a new Queen of

Sheba, "Queen of the North"—beautiful, wise, truly regal, beneficent in word and deed. On the basis of the evidence his judgment was uncritical and seriously misleading. Even under the greatest temptation Milton did not lie, but on occasion he accepted inadequate data. In praising Christina he used the classic form of argument known as panegyric; he sought to associate himself with a renowned and, as he believed, noble figure in contemporary life and thus to mitigate the fury of his opponent's unscrupulous attacks on his private and public life. He honored the Queen as a sensitive and learned woman who had preferred his writings to those of Salmasius and had therefore dismissed the latter from her presence. And he exalted her as a prime Protestant monarch who ruled her realm with justice and wisdom, the very antithesis of a tyrant. On the first point he was only partly right; on the second he was almost entirely wrong. Since he obviously did not base his opinions on substantive evidence, he fell into a logical fallacy. It seems clear that he was grasping at straws in argument; that, on the basis of widely disseminated rumors, he found grounds for believing that he had totally destroyed Salmasius; and that he honestly thought Christina offered striking confirmation of his cherished dichotomy of true king and tyrant. Though his knowledge of Sweden was surprisingly accurate, he was essentially ignorant of the Queen's appearance, character, and behavior. His judgment, though not false in intent, was superficial and justifiably open to attack. [DAR]

CHRISTOLOGY: *see* RELIGION, MILTON'S; THE SON.

CHRIST'S COLLEGE, Cambridge University, Milton's undergraduate and graduate school. The third largest college of sixteen (behind Trinity and St. John's), Christ's was a community of about 265 persons. Then as now, its buildings were close on a main street of Cambridge, not far from other colleges of the university

church, Great St. Mary's. Its spacious quadrangle was surrounded by the chapel, the hall, and living quarters, and beyond to the rear of the structures were fields. The college was crowded and students were lodged two to four to a room. There were studies attached to each room. Milton apparently was first lodged in Rats' Hall, a small, temporary, wooden building in the Second Court. It was built in 1613 and destroyed in 1731. In 1740 Dr. William Stukely (1687–1765) was told that Milton had roomed there. Later Milton may have been assigned a choice room in the main building on the First Court, as tradition has it. The curriculum that Milton followed is not detailed, but its rough outlines were traditional. (See Harris F. Fletcher, *The Intellectual Development of John Milton* [1961], vol. 2, and William T. Costello, S. J., *The Scholastic Curriculum at Early Seventeenth-Century Cambridge* [1958], for full discussions.) Milton, as a student preparing for the ministry, pursued rhetoric*, logic*, metaphysics*, languages* (Hebrew and Greek), mathematics, and the like. In his graduate studies he was more independent of specific subjects and books. For example, while the undergraduate regularly studied Aristotle* and through him came to know about Plato*, the graduate student often progressed to Plato directly, as Milton did in 1629 and after. The three years that Milton took for his graduate education was standard. Generally, after having received a graduate degree, a student preparing for the ministry would stay at his college for three or so more years acquiring a divinity degree and/or take a year or so off to travel on the Continent. An undergraduate student was assigned to a tutor*, who examined him on his studies from time to time and who was supposed to give advice on reading. Milton was expected to attend both college lectures and university lectures, and there were many important scholars attached to the colleges in Milton's day. In demonstration of his own proficiency and learning, a student had to present public orations on assigned topics. (*See* PROLUSIONS.) Extant are three exercises delivered in the public schools (local college audiences), three exercises delivered in the college (larger university audience), and a declamation delivered in the college.

Milton was admitted to Christ's from St. Paul's School* on February 12, 1625, and matriculated on April 9 as a lesser pensioner. That is, his status, which depended on his financial circumstances, was average, neither requiring chores and the like to meet payment nor allowing him better living conditions and privileges. The master of Christ's was Thomas Bainbridge and there were thirteen Fellows (listed by Parker in *Milton,* p. 727), among whom were William Chappell*, Joseph Mead*, Nathaniel Tovey*, Andrew Sandelands*, and Robert Gell. As pastor of St. Mary's, Aldermary, Gell may have officiated at Milton's wedding many years later to Elizabeth Minshull, on February 24, 1663. Milton was placed under Chappell, but a disagreement with him in the Lent Term of 1626 caused Milton's rustication*. Upon his return to Christ's at the beginning of the Easter Term Milton was placed under Tovey, and this arrangement was apparently satisfactory. Tovey became Christopher Milton's tutor also when he entered Christ's on February 15, 1631.

Milton was graduated B.A. on March 26, 1629, and was listed fourth on the University honors list (*ordo senioritatis*), which numbered twenty-four. There were three others from Christ's. During most of 1630 Milton was not in Cambridge due to the plague. The University closed down on April 17, and though it was reopened in October, relatively few students seem to have returned before Hillary Term in January 1631. Presumably Milton was in London at his father's home in Bread Street during this time. On July 3, 1632, Milton received the M.A. degree cum laude, subscribing to the three articles of religion enjoined in the thirty-sixth of the ecclesiastical canons of 1603–1604. These articles acknowledged the liturgy and doctrines of the Church of England and royal supremacy in all matters. Whether such subscription was perfunctory or whether it can be concluded that Milton was still intending a ministerial career within the standard procedures is debatable. Much has been made of Milton's not receiving a fellowship (and of Edward King's* becoming a Fellow in 1630), but aside from possible uncertainty as to a career, Milton's responsibilities to his parents in 1632 may have deflected him from continued study at the college or travel. He, of course, pursued such study on his own until 1638 when he did set out to travel for about a year and a half.

From various remarks made in his letters, prolusions, and poems it is clear that Milton was not happy with the kind of education he was experiencing at Christ's, nor with his fellow students*. Milton seems to have been serious about his studies, to have had high morals, and to have been generally disassociated with many undergraduate social activities. These personality traits plus his fair complexion and good looks seem to have acquired for him the epithet "The Lady of Christ's." He discusses the matter in *Prol* 6 (1628), by which time he seems to have come to an understanding with his fellow students and was able to treat the matter as a joke. His unhappiness with his unserious colleagues and with the unchanging and stultifying system of educational chores can be seen in this same oration, and contempt for those students and that system can be read into his letter to Alexander Gill, Jr.*, dated July 2, 1628. He apparently felt no moral compunction in ghostwriting an oration of some nature for one of the Fellows, who was obviously too far advanced for that kind of exercise. It seems that eventually Milton was held in high esteem, particularly by the Fellows, probably because of his scholastic achievement and his amused acceptance of collegiate ways.

The library of Christ's College has an extensive collection of early editions of Milton's works. It owns the receipt for £5 given to Samuel Simmons* on April 26, 1669, in payment of royalty for *PL,* as well as Elizabeth Milton's receipt for £8 and her release of rights, dated December 21, 1680. Also owned by the college is the clay bust said to have been executed from life around 1651 (more probably after 1660) by a sculptor named either Edward Pierce or, less likely, Abraham Simon. It has frequently been reproduced and was acquired by George Vertue prior to his engraving from it for Birch's* 1753 edition of the prose works. [JTS]

CHRONOLOGY OF MILTON'S WORKS, THE. While most of Milton's prose works are dated by the occasion that provoked them, dating of the poems largely depends upon dates that he himself attached to them, their order in the collected editions of the minor poems, some external evidence, and at times subject matter or internal evidence. Dates attached to the poems are sometimes demonstrably in error and often in Latin as well as reckoned according to Latin practice (that is, "aet. 17" means during that year when Milton was seventeen— December 9, 1625, through December 8, 1626). The order of the poems in his collected editions seems to apply within categories (religious poems, secular poems, sonnets*, others—such as pastorals*, elegiac verse*, verse in other meters), except that the *Nat* is placed out of order to achieve a memorable first poem in the collection, *Mask* is placed after *Lyc* because of length, and the typesetting of Greek poems may have necessitated some rearrangement. Further, the 1673 edition does not always maintain such chronological ordering; for example, Psalms 1–8 are placed before Psalms 80–88 because of their numbering, but this is in reverse of their composition. Although specific dates are sometimes disputed, for most of the works a general chronology can be given. The works can be divided into periods: those written before Milton's graduation from Cambridge with a masters degree; those written during the studious retirement* or associated with the European trip; those written during public life and

governmental service; and those written in later life.

Period I (1624–1632). The prose state papers. The majority of *CB* entries includes the seven prolusions and some personal letters, but the specific dates are disputed. Perhaps the prolusions can be assigned to 1628–1629 and 1631; the dates attached to the letters have been challenged.

Poems include many of the Latin works, some of which are schoolboy exercises or are dated by their academic occasion; most problematic are the short Gunpowder Plot poems, *El 7, Naturam,* and *Idea.* The Italian poems and some English poems, including notably the *Nat, L'Al,* and *IlP,* also fall into this period. Milton's earliest surviving works are two English paraphrases of Psalms 114 and 136 (dated 1624). Some scholars would date Milton's translation of Horace's Fifth Ode in this period; others would place it in Period III.

Period II (1632–1640). Little prose was written during this period; a few letters survive, including the uncertainly dated letter to an unknown friend*, and *CB* was begun.

Poetic production was limited in quantity during this period, yet such great poems as *Mask, Time,* and *Lyc* were written prior to Milton's trip to the Continent. With only two exceptions, the remainder of Milton's foreign-language poems (including *EpDam*) were written at this time, five of them when he was abroad. The most debated dates are those for the English odes (1631–1637?) and *AdP* (1631–1638?).

Period III (1641–1660). Most of the prose (English and Latin) was produced at this time: the five antiprelatical tracts, the four divorce tracts, *Educ* and *Areop,* the antimonarchial pamphlets, the three *Defenses,* some personal letters, *CivP, Hire* (1659?), *Way,* and the state papers. The majority of *CB* entries date in the earliest part of this period, also. Uncertainly dated prose works are those published after the Restoration though written during this period: *Accedence Commenc't*

Grammar (early 1640s?), *Logic* (middle 1640s?), *Mosc* (ante 1648?), *CharLP* (1648?), *Brit* (1648–1650?), *CD* (1658–1660?).

Poems written during this period include all the remaining minor poems (*Sonn* 8–23, *NewF*, the psalm translations, *In Effigiei Ejus Sculptorem*, and *Rous*). Uncertain is the date of *Hor*. *PL* was begun during this period, with first attempts as early as 1640 and apparently more concerted attention from around 1655 onward. It has also been argued that *SA* and *PR* were begun, or even largely written, during the later 1640s and middle 1650s.

Period IV (1660–1674). Prose works are few : *TR* and *Declaration*, plus a few personal letters. Possibly there was further work on *CD*.

Poetic work was the completion of *PL* (1660–1665) and the writing or revision of *PR* (1665–1670?) and *SA* (around 1670?). [JTS]

CHRYSOSTOM, JOHN (ca. 347–407), an important Doctor of the Church. His powers of oratory, which earned him the name "golden-mouthed," were directed to the instruction and moral reformation of the nominally Christian church at Antioch, and his series of "Homilies" on the Scriptures reveal him as the foremost of Christian expositors. He opposed the allegorical* interpretation of the Scriptures, which he insisted should be interpreted literally. As Bishop of Constantinople, he set about reforming the corrupt court, clergy, and people. His combination of honesty and asceticism was a source of inspiration to all, but his tactlessness in dealing with the court eventually brought about his exile.

Milton greatly admired Chrysostom and used him often for support in his tracts on civil government, church government, and freedom of the press. In *Tenure*, Milton asserts that Chrysostom was appalled by those evil magistrates who used their power for evil means rather than for the punishment of offenders and encouragement of good; the churchman, says Milton, taught that such tyrants do not have their abused powers "ordain'd of God, and by consequence no obligation [is] laid upon us to obey them and not to resist them." In *1Def* Milton reminds his readers of Chrysostom's famous contention that all princes are not necessarily appointed by God and that all sorts of magisterial powers are not of God, but only lawful ones, those ordained or ordered by God. Chrysostom says that even Paul "speaks not of the person of the prince, but of the thing. He does not say, there is no prince but of God; he says there is no power but of God." Later in *1Def*, Milton alludes to another of Chrysostom's teachings, namely, that all subjects are to be obedient to their leaders, but that Christ introduced this principle of obedience* "with no intent to overthrow the civil government, but rather to establish it upon truer foundations." This doctrine does not mean that slaves are to be subject to tyrants; on the contrary, the Apostles did such things as made them suspected of all tyrants. Christ, Chrysostom says, in intending "to dissuade from unnecessary and fruitless wars, never intended that tyrants be beyond all laws and penalties, that they be cruel despots over all mankind," and never condemned "a war taken up against a tyrant, a bosom enemy of his own country." Milton concludes his reference to Chrysostom in this tract by extolling the churchman for his integrity, since the great insurrection in Constantinople against the emperor Arcadius was the reason for Chrysostom's exile. In his teaching on church reform in *Eikon*, Milton tells the reader to bear in mind what Chrysostom said about ministers becoming involved with material possessions and wealth : "Religion brought forth riches in the Church, and the Daughter devour'd the Mother." In *CB* Milton commends Chrysostom's argument in *Gen: orat 8*, which urges us not to wish "our alms to be known unto men, because men are apt to envy where they ought to praise. There is no reason why we should hope much from human commendation." Two further citations appear elsewhere in *CB*. In *Areop*, on the suppression of books, Milton maintains that Chrysostom not only studied nightly the works of Aristophanes, the loosest writer of all the old comedians, but "had the art to cleanse a scurrilous vehemence into the stile of a rousing Sermon." [PAF]

CHURCH, BENJAMIN: *see* INFLUENCE IN AMERICA, MILTON'S.

CHURCH OF ENGLAND: *see* ECCLESIOLOGY.

CHURCHES. In seventeenth-century England the parish church dominated family and social life; the members of a specific church would normally have lived in the specific area served by the church and would, earlier in the period, generally have known most of the other parishioners. Marriages, birth, and deaths would be recorded in the parish register, which is therefore a major source of knowledge of biography as well as of a person's community of relatives and friends. Some parish registers have disappeared or been destroyed over the years; in some areas lying outside London registers were not begun until well after a church community had been formed. Obviously omissions from a parish register of known marriages, births, or deaths suggest that an inhabitant of that parish at that time may have lived temporarily elsewhere or the event occurred elsewhere. For example, the death of Mary Powell Milton and the birth of her daughter Deborah in 1652 are not recorded in the register of St. Margaret, Westminster, as would be expected from Milton's residence then in Petty France. The explanation may be that Mary was with her mother during her confinement, and Mrs. Powell's residence in May 1652 is unknown.

The record of Milton's residences* gives a fairly clear picture of which churches Milton and his family attended. Although other churches bear upon Milton's biography, or may do so, by supplying evidence concerned with relatives and friends or possible relatives, the following are the churches of London having direct and important connection with Milton. The family of John Milton, Sr., lived in the parish of All Hallows, Bread Street, when Milton was born. The pertinent entry in the register is as follows, "The xxth daye of Decēber 1608. was also baptized John the sonne of John Mylton scrivenor." Various other entries —such as the death of one of his father's servants*, Oliver Lowe, or the baptism of his sister Sara—are also found in the register. Undoubtedly the Miltons also attended important services and functions at St. Paul's Cathedral, which was only a few blocks from their home, and near which was St. Paul's School* where Milton was in attendance from around 1620 through 1624. During the years when Milton lived on Bread Street, the Dean of St. Paul's was John Donne, well known for his sermons. During this period also St. Stephen, Walbrook, was the scene of Milton's sister Anne's marriage to Edward Phillips on November 22, 1623, perhaps because the rector was a friend, Thomas Myriell*. The Phillipses moved to the parish of St. Martin in the Fields, where entries of births and deaths appear from 1625 through August 1631 when Edward was buried. The births of Edward and John Phillips, Milton's nephews, in August 1630 and October 1631 are not recorded, suggesting that Anne was elsewhere at both times, perhaps Hammersmith*, to which Milton's father moved around 1631. Possibly Milton's father also had a home in the parish of St. Martin in the Fields (he owned property there), and Milton, as well as his sister, may have been a communicant of the church. The widowed Anne, with two young children, married Thomas Agar, a widower with a young daughter, on January 5, 1632, in St. Dunstan in the East; the location is unexplained. Agar's daughter Anne, by his first wife, Mary Rugeley, seems to have been buried from St. Martin in the Fields on November 13, 1633. However, whether Anne and Thomas Agar lived steadily in her former parish in 1632–1633 is uncertain. Two other parish churches may be mentioned here for indirect but important connection with Milton. His second wife, Katherine Woodcock, was baptized at St. Dunstan in the West on April 2, 1628, and Charles Diodati* was buried from St. Anne, Blackfriars, on August 27, 1638.

Upon his return from the Continent Milton lived in the parish of St. Bride's (1639–1640), then moved to St. Botolph without Aldersgate (1640–1645). His move to the Barbican placed him in the parish of St. Giles, Cripplegate (1645–1647), where his father was buried in March 1647. His residence in Holborn (1647–1649) made him a parishioner of St. Giles in the Fields, where the baptism of his daughter Mary is registered on November 7, 1648. While he was Secretary to the Council of State* he lived in Westminster and was a communicant of St. Margaret. During the late 1640s and the 1650s Milton's brother Christopher was residing in the parish of St. Clement Danes. Milton's removal to Red Lion Fields, Holborn, in 1660–1661, returned him to St. Giles in the Fields, and his two subsequent moves to Jewin Street and to Artillery Walk placed him again in St. Giles, Cripplegate. The register records his burial in the chancel on November 12, 1674. [JTS]

CICERO. In his brief treatise *Educ* Milton recommends Marcus Tullius Cicero (106–43 B.C.) in three capacities : (1) as an authority on rhetoric*; (2) as a model of rhetorical achievement in his "Political Orations"; and (3) as a source of ethical* instruction (4 : 284–86), a recommendation that serves bare notice of the profound and extensive influence the most famous of Roman orators had on the Renaissance and on Milton.

Drawing upon his thorough acquaintance with Greek rhetorical theory and practice, Cicero formulated a philosophy of rhetoric in three related treatises (frequently printed together in Renaissance editions), *De Oratore, Brutus,* and *Orator.* The first of these extensively discusses the elements of making an effective speech, the second critically evaluates Greek and especially Roman orators, and the third sets forth Cicero's conception of the ideal orator. This ideal speaker is no less than an intelligent man, perfected in knowledge and virtue, who contributes actively and constructively to the political life of a free republic by means of his oratorical skills in the Senate and Forum of the people. Milton conceives of his polemical and indeed his poetical career in just this way. The good poet, like the orator-statesman, must be a well-educated, good man (*El* 6, especially lines 55–78, *AdP* and *Apol,* 3, pt. 1, 302–5). Milton twice explains his career as pamphleteer, interrupting further poetic efforts, in terms of Cicero's ideal of the orator-statesman whose duty it is to exercise his talents for the common good (*RCG* 3, pt. 1, 235–42, and *2Def* 8 : 69–71 and 119–39). He characterizes his polemical efforts as defenses of "ecclesiastical, domestic or private, and civil" liberties (p. 131).

Cicero also influenced Milton's more technical ideas about the interrelated natures of rhetoric and logic*. Following the sixteenth-century French scholar Ramus*, Milton considered the invention or finding and disposition of arguments (two of five traditional elements of rhetoric) to be the art of logic, but the art of his treatise *Logic* (11) is much more the rhetorical logic of persuasion and debate than the demonstrative, scientific reasoning of Aristotle's* *Analytics.* Appropriately, *Logic* cites Cicero some seventy-five times and leans heavily upon the theoretical support of his *De Inventione, De Oratore II,* and *Topica.*

Milton, of course, was denied the opportunity of speaking before Parliament, but like some ancient orators and with the modern assistance of the printing press he wrote his speeches, sometimes to Parliament and its leaders, sometimes to the English public, and sometimes to the larger forum of Europe. This last group of polemics, written in Latin, justifies the execution of Charles I* in 1649 and the establishment of an English commonwealth in the European community of

nations. Here, too, Milton found service-
able the memorable pronouncements of
Cicero against the dictatorial pretensions
of Catiline, Crassus, Caesar, Antony, and
others (see *1Def* 7 : 97, 183, 219, 305, 327,
387, 425, 477, and *2Def* 8 : 197).

Milton's frequent reliance on personal
attacks against his opponents and theirs
against him to aid the refutation of
arguments is characteristic of an age
taught out of the book of Cicero. Over
fifty of Cicero's orations in part or whole
were transmitted to Renaissance Europe.
They were the acknowledged models of
rhetorical skill and a staple of rhetorical
education and imitative practice. Milton
himself refers to Cicero in *Prol* 6 as
the "most renowned of all the orators"
(12 : 243) and in his prose works takes
material explicitly from half of them.

Cicero was a master of invective,
ranging from the most subtle irony and
humor (at his opponent's expense) to
caustic sarcasm and the most vicious and
coarsest kind of abuse. His attacks on
Verres (a corrupt governor of Sicily),
Catiline (a revolutionary thwarted by
Cicero), and Mark Antony (who finally
had Cicero proscribed and put to death)
are some of the most colorful displays of
his talents. His opposition to Lucius Cal-
purnius Piso (Julius Caesar's father-in-law)
reveals a pattern of attack and counter-
attack growing more and more personal.
Piso was instrumental in Cicero's being
banished (58–57 B.C.). Returned and
reinstated in the Senate, Cicero attacked
Piso's genuinely corrupt government of
Macedonia in an extant speech, *De
Provinciis Consularibus*. Piso was recalled
but vigorously defended his administration
to the Senate against Cicero. Thereupon
Cicero delivered a brutal (extant) per-
sonal attack, *In Pisonem*. Milton's in-
volvement in the episcopal controversy
follows a similar course. Balanced and
mainly reasonable pamphlets are suc-
ceeded by the severely ridiculing invec-
tives, *Animad* and *Apol* (both in 3, pt. 1).
A similar descent to personalities alone
characterizes Milton's *3Def* (9), which
stands in poor comparison with his

earlier and more balanced defenses of the
regicides, in which his arguments are well
seasoned with the biting sauce of invective
but are not stifled by it.

Giving a personal estimation of one's
opponent and oneself in public con-
troversy is warranted, of course, only by
the orator's being virtuous in private and
public life and hence his being as credible
a source of opinion as possible. This
important consideration, and the fact that
the orator as statesman or as pleader
before the courts must obviously have a
thorough acquaintance with the norms
and eccentricities of human behavior,
explains Cicero's great interest in ethics
and his lack of interest in metaphysical
speculation. The Ciceronian contribution
to ethical thought was not particularly
original. It was, however, immensely
authoritative. St. Jerome*, as Milton
recalls (*Areop* 4 : 307), knew Cicero well.
Indeed he, more than any other figure in
pagan antiquity, influenced Christian
ethics and the Christian understanding of
classical ethics.

De Finibus presents in dialogue form
a carefully detailed and generally objec-
tive statement of the ethical teachings of
each of the major Hellenistic-Roman
schools, followed by a refutation of each
from the point of view of another. The
Epicurean position is introduced and then
rebutted by a Stoic spokesman. Stoic
views are propounded only to be rejected
by the New Academy (revived and much
transformed Platonism). The Peripatetic
approach (school of Aristotle beginning
with Theophrastus) follows. It is refuted
by the Stoics. Cicero generally lumps the
ethical teachings of Plato*, Aristotle, and
their followers together under the guiding
spirit of Socrates, who, Cicero says,
brought philosophy down to earth, to
ethics (*Tusculan Disputations* 5. 4). Three
categories of Greek ethics emerge : the
schools of the Stoics, the Epicureans, and
the Academy-Peripatetics. The wisdom
with which Satan tempts Christ in *PR*
has three sources: Old Testament writings,
Athenian eloquence in poetry and or-

atory, and Greek philosophy (*PR* 4. 221–84). Satan's description of philosophy is ethically, not metaphysically, oriented and is precisely Cicero's :

To sage Philosophy next lend thine ear,
From Heaven descended to the low-rooft house
Of *Socrates,* see there his Tenement,
Whom well inspir'd the Oracle pronounc'd
Wisest of men; from whose mouth issu'd forth
Mellifluous streams that water'd all the schools
Of Academics old and new, with those
Sirnam'd *Peripatetics,* and the Sect
Epicurean, and the *Stoic* severe.
(4. 272–80)

Cicero's own ethical views are expressed in *De Officiis* and the *Tusculan Disputations.* Both syncretically draw on all the Hellenistic schools except the Epicurean, a recurrent whipping boy. The Fathers of the Church appropriated the four cardinal virtues* (wisdom, courage, justice, and temperance) from *De Officiis,* and both it and *Tusc. Disp.* were continuing sources of inspiration to educated Christians. According to Cicero the happy man is the virtuous one. Virtue is a state of right reasoning* whereby the mind is proof against all external circumstances and is so conditioned as to avoid every sort of mental and emotional disturbance (fear, grief, anger, and so on). Virtue is free and invincible (*Tusc. Disp.* 5. 18). Temperance* is the heart of all the virtues and intemperance the source of all evil (*Tusc. Disp.* 4. 9 *et passim*).

For Milton censorship becomes a facet of Epicureanism. It is that "fugitive and cloister'd virtue" which he condemns (*Areop* 4:311) while recommending temperance (4 : 309–11), because, as Cicero observes, the Epicurean tries to avoid all painful external circumstances in his pursuit of pleasures as happiness, instead of so fortifying his mind with right reason that he will be able to withstand the mental and emotional disturbances incited by all kinds of pain (and pleasure). Like the Epicurean, the proponent of censorship tries to avoid the conflict of truth and error by suppression. Cicero's virtue is active (see esp. *Tusc. Disp.* 5. 25) but

tolerant (*Tusc. Disp.* 4. 4), allowing everyone his own opinion. The stated impulse for presenting an objective view of the various Greek ethical schools in *De Finibus* is to let the Romans make an educated decision for themselves. Milton recalls and approves the tradition that Cicero edited Lucretius :

And therefore *Lucretius* without impeachment versifies his Epicurism to *Memmius,* and had the honour to be set forth the second time by *Cicero* so great a father of the Commonwealth; although himselfe disputes against that opinion in his own writings. (4: 301).

Milton's poetry also reflects Ciceronian ethics. The conflict between the Lady and Comus is strongly influenced by the Ciceronian polarity of the temperate as opposed to the intemperate life. The Lady's chastity*, as in Book 3 of Spenser's *Faerie Queene,* is the female version of temperance. Comus, the male tempter, is a spokesman for effeminate intemperance, Epicureanism. He is branded as a sophist by the Lady (*Mask,* lines 756–59 and 790–91) as Epicurus is branded by Cicero (*Tusc. Disp.* 5. 26). The Lady's virtue, like Cicero's, is free and invincible (lines 663, 780–82, and 1019). Her right reason triumphs, as the Attendant Spirit attests, *"O're sensual Folly, and Intemperance"* (line 975). The fallen angel Belial in *PL* and *PR* is another sophistic Epicurean, and, of course, all of Milton's heroes are defined to a large extent by the better or worse condition of their right reason.

Ciceronian ethics and rhetoric exercised a pervasive influence on Christian Europe. Like Erasmus*, Gabriel Harvey, and others, Milton rejected the kind of slavish imitation of Ciceronian style* and diction so popular in the Renaissance. Milton gently chides St. Jerome for addiction to Ciceronian modes of expression (*Areop* 4 : 307). However, Milton was more thoroughly imbued than most men of his age with Ciceronian attitudes, the essence not the form of Ciceronianism. In many respects the two are kindred spirits. Their kinship was rendered more compelling to Milton, no doubt, as his own developing life revealed curious echoes of Cicero's life and thought. Both men rose to prominence from modest, middle-class families. Both fathers expended every effort to provide the best possible educations for talented children, supporting the leisure of study well beyond formal schooling and into adulthood. Both men defended republican government, and both suffered political persecution for it. Cicero was banished and later proscribed and executed. Milton narrowly and mysteriously escaped the same fate on the return of monarchy and a new monarch, Charles II*, to England in 1660. Both men experienced domestic problems. Cicero was divorced twice, the second second time from a woman much younger than he. All of Milton's three wives were considerably younger than he was. Cicero's ideal man (described in *Tusc. Disp.* 5. 24–25) should be extraordinarily intelligent and learned. He must be dedicated to discovering the truth and presenting it to the world (a purpose Milton enunciates in the exordium to *PL*, esp. lines 24–26). This ideal man, fortified by a highly developed right reason, can be truly happy, even if, as Cicero argues at length (*Tusc. Disp.* 5. 38–39), he is blind. But the heart of Milton's affinity with Cicero is this : both were perfectly assured that they were very close to being such ideal men. Neither was given a false humility or lacked confidence in his own virtue, wisdom, and intelligence. [PBR]

CLARENDON, EDWARD HYDE, EARL OF, was almost exactly Milton's contemporary : he was born on February 18, 1609, two months later, and died on December 9, 1674, one month later. Differences in background, temperament, and training led them to take different sides in the civil wars. It is almost certain they never encountered each other or read each other's major work : *PL* appeared just as Hyde, created first Earl of Clarendon at the coronation of Charles II* in 1661, was dismissed as Lord Chancellor and banished from England;

his *History of the Rebellion and Civil Wars in England* appeared posthumously, in 1702–1704. The *History* is silent concerning Milton, though Hyde knew his divorce tracts, *Eikon,* and *1Def*. He also knew what Milton did not : who wrote the *Eikon Basilike**. In *Eikon* Milton suggested the possibility of a "secret *Coadjutor,*" but took Charles I* as its author (5 : 72). Hyde's most important reference to Milton occurs in a letter of March 13, 1661 (not 1661/62, as French suggests [*Life Records* (4 : 370]) to this "secret *Coadjutor,*" John Gauden*. Gauden, who became Bishop of Exeter at the Restoration, found the revenues of his diocese an unsatisfactory reward for working up papers of Charles I into the *Eikon* and addressed to the Chancellor a number of decorous but increasingly explicit threats to reveal what he had done. Hyde, when he at last responded with promises of something better, acknowledged Gauden's role and added, "truly, when it ceases to be secrett, I know nobody will be glad of it but Mr. Milton."

In 1640 Hyde was elected to both the Short and the Long Parliament. He was not yet a royalist; rather, he was notably active in opposing the king and, in particular, in calling him to account for his administration of justice during the eleven years he had refused to summon Parliament. But Hyde's position—to limit the king's power by restoring Parliament to its own—was essentially conservative. Milton's was radical : to complete what he regarded as the yet imperfect reformation of God's true religion in England, he looked to the future, not to the past.

As Parliament limited the king's power, however, it enlarged its own and claimed more than what men like Hyde and Falkland considered its lawful rights and duties. When their attempts to moderate between king and Parliament failed, first Falkland and then Hyde undertook to serve the king; Hyde joined the king at York in June 1642, as both sides readied their troops. He had already served the king, and continued to do so, by writing his answers to Parliament's declarations, all of which were published. In them he persuasively argued, in the king's name, that the king claimed no more than his lawful rights and duties, which Parliament denied him and claimed for itself; by presenting Charles I as the true upholder of the known constitution of England, he won him the support that enabled him to raise his armies. Hyde was an effective propagandist, more effective than Milton, even when left to defend as lawful those actions he advised the king against and privately deplored. He loyally followed the king to Oxford, where he remained until March 1645; he was knighted in February 1643, when he joined the Privy Council, and in March became Chancellor of the Exchequer. Then, after a succession of royalist defeats, the king sent him with Prince Charles to the army in the west. In February 1646, when it was defeated, they escaped, first to Scilly and then to Jersey; from there the prince, against Hyde's advice, left for Paris.

When Hyde rejoined the prince, soon to be Charles II, he put aside for what would be twenty years his history, which he had begun during his exile in Scilly and Jersey. It had nevertheless informed him what was to be done, and he urged the exiled king to heed what it taught, that his father forfeited the loyalty of his subjects when he tried to rule without Parliament, and that Parliament in turn, ruling without him, became far more oppressive and tyrannical. Therefore his son was to wait upon events in England rather than looking to Scotland, Ireland, or Europe. Charles II, reluctant to adopt Hyde's policy, eventually did so only for want of a better. In the interim, while Milton defended the execution of Charles I, served as Secretary for Foreign Tongues* to the Council of State*, and retired from public life, Hyde loyally followed Charles II and his impoverished court from Paris to Cologne to Bruges, burdened by the royal correspondence and often paying its postage out of his own ill-furnished pocket; in January 1658 the king appointed him Lord Chancellor of

an England ruled by Cromwell*. Not until 1660 were the lessons of his history vindicated in history: then, after negotiations in which Hyde played an active part, Charles II was restored as the lawful king of England.

Hyde returned to England as the king's first minister and for seven years experienced the rewards of power and its dangers. Royalists discontented with the Restoration settlement blamed him for it; the Act of Indemnity and Oblivion, which spared Milton among others, they jestingly described as bringing indemnity to the king's enemies and oblivion to his friends. Parliament regarded him as highhanded; Charles II regarded him as too sturdy a defender of its power. Then in August 1667 the king sacrificed him to Parliament by dismissing him from office; in October, when the king promised Parliament never again to employ him, he was accused of treason, and in November, acceding to the king's wish that he not defend himself, he fled to France.

There he turned again to reading and writing. What he wrote, from July 1668 to August 1670, was an account of his own life from birth to the Restoration, drawn entirely from memory; the sources he had collected to complete the history begun in 1646–1648 remained in England until June 1671, when his younger son was permitted to visit him. Then, working rapidly, he conflated the 1646–1648 history with the 1668–1670 life and added to them. The *History,* which he completed within the year, is a composite work: for events through 1644 its text is the history supplemented by the life, and for the rest, the life supplemented by the 1671–1672 additions. The life, written as a surrogate for history, and in the third rather than the first person, he converted to history simply by replacing some of its *he*'s; at times he named himself, usually as the Chancellor of the Exchequer; at times he disguised himself as an unnamed royalist adviser. As a result he appears on stage in the *History* as a less-critical royalist than in point of fact he was. But the off-stage historian remained critical: writing the 1668–1670 life, he repeated and extended the analysis of events in England that he worked out when writing the 1646–1648 history. This analysis, grounded in an acute and far-reaching perception that the English assented to the rule of what they knew as the constitution of England because they were loyal to their own institutions and their own past, informs the *History* and gives it unity and coherence.

Clarendon was the first English historian to meet the challenge of Livy* and Tacitus*. Milton, though he wrote *Brit* in accord with the same precepts of Renaissance historiography*, stood closer to Holinshed* and Stow*; it was drawn from the same sources as their chronicles because he lacked the knowledge necessary to interpret other records of pre-Conquest England. His account of a thousand years is thin, the analysis he imposed upon it schematic; "the immediate finger and wrath of God" are plainly visible and its lessons straightforward. Clarendon also held a providential view of history, but he was a more diligent observer of "natural causes and means" : when he designated the Restoration miraculous he did so because it seemed impossible during the years Cromwell ruled England, not because he was unable to explain it after it happened. And the lessons of the *History* emerge from his observation and analysis; while he commemorated those who discerned the public consequences of their actions and did what ought to be done, he was also attentive to those who did not and equally concerned to understand the permutations and combinations of reason and will that led them to do what they did. If Livy and Tacitus were congenial to him by temperament and experience, Virgil* was to Milton, who in a letter of December 20, 1659, wrote to Henry Oldenburg* : "Of any such work as compiling the history of our political troubles, which you seem to advise, I have no thought whatever : they are worthier of silence than of commemoration" (12: 108–11).

Clarendon bequeathed the history and other manuscripts to his sons, with directions to publish or suppress them in consultation with the Archbishop of Canterbury and the Bishop of Winchester, then Gilbert Sheldon and George Morley, both friends from Great Tew. The history was published at Oxford some thirty years after his death, in 1702–1704, under the supervision of his younger son, Laurence, the Earl of Rochester. [JEH]

CLARKE, DEBORAH MILTON: *see* CHILDREN, MILTON'S.

CLEMENT OF ALEXANDRIA (ca. 150–ca. 215), Church Father. Nothing is known of the birth and early life of Titus Flavius Clemens, or Clement of Alexandria, but it would appear that he was born into a wealthy Athenian family. A cultured pagan or a "Greek of the Greeks," he was steeped in both pagan mysteries and Hellenistic thought, although he may have come into contact with Christianity in his youth. In Alexandria he became a disciple of Pantaenus, who was in charge of the Catechetical School, and whom he succeeded. In 203 he fled the persecution of Severus and did not return to Egypt.

Milton was familiar with all three of Clements's major works : *Protrepticus* (The Exhortation to the Greeks), *Paedagogus* (Christ the Educator of Little Ones), and *Stromateis* (Miscellanies). He repudiated many of the doctrines of the Gnostics, yet Milton's statement that he "would be term'd a Gnostick" (*PrelE* 3: 86) properly describes Clement's attitude toward *gnosis* in his exposition of Christian Gnosticism, which he defines as "striving . . . to attain to the summit of knowledge (gnosis)" (*Strom.* 7.11), and which includes both the "milk" and the "meat" of St. Paul.

To most of the Gnostics, mankind was divided into three groups : the spiritual, the natural, and the material. Only the first group was foreordained to eternal life. Clement held that knowledge of the truth was available to all seekers, and that the Gnostic depreciation of the material—and therefore the body—led to heresy and sin. The practice of the Gnostics to allegorize the Scriptures led ultimately to the doctrine that the Word had not really come in the flesh, but that "there had been only a temporary association of the Divine with the human, nothing more." Gnosticism held great appeal for the intellectuals in Alexandria's Christian community, even though its adherents subscribed to a wide variety of opinions, many of which, protested Clement, were in conflict with one another. Clement's insistence on adding knowledge to faith, testing every doctrine by the Word, kept him from the often ridiculous positions to which the Gnostics were ultimately driven. However, Gnostic allegorizing of the Scriptures, particularly of Moses and the prophets, no doubt justified Milton's inclusion of Clement in his list of ancient fathers when he wrote, "Who is ignorant of the foul errors, the ridiculous wresting of Scripture, the Heresies, the vanities thick sown through the colums of *Justin Martyr**, *Clemens*, *Origen**, *Tertullian** and others of the eldest time?" (*Ref* 3 : 21). For example, in *Paedagogus* 10 Clement "wrests" the Scriptures when he interprets Moses' prohibition, "Do not eat the hare nor the hyena" (Deut. 14 : 7), as a commandment not to lust after adultery.

With reference to the Anglican insistence on the primacy of bishops, Milton distinguishes the frequently confused Clement of Alexandria and Clement of Rome (fl. 90) and rightly states that "authority of *Clemens Alexandrinus* is not to be found in all his workes, and wherever it be extant, it is in controversie, whether it be Clements or no; or if it were it sayes onely that Saint *John* in some places constituted Bishops : questionlesse he did, but where does *Clement* say he set them above *Presbyters*?" (*PrelE* 3 : 98). Actually, the discussion of bishops appears in the *First Epistle to the Corinthians* (chap. 44), a work frequently attributed to Clement of Rome, with which Milton was obviously familiar. Other references to Clement of Rome

appear in *PrelE* 3 : 96 and 97; *RCG* 3 : 211 and 221.

Milton usually includes Clement among the orthodox. In the reply to Salmasius* (*1Def* 7 : 91) he upbraids his adversary for defending the principle of the divine right of kings "in opposition to all the expositors [including Clement of Alexandria], especially the orthodox. . . ." Again, Milton counters Alexander More's* argument against intermixing "on divers occasions, words more indelicate indeed, and subjects abundantly gross, with matters of greater seriousness" (*3Def* 9 : 111) by citing "Clemens Alexandrinus, Arnobius, Lactantius*, Eusebius*, when they uncover and cast derision upon the obscene mysteries of the old religions!" in support of his own position. He is referring to *Protrepticus*, Clement's exposure of the evil practices of paganism in an attempt to convert men to Christianity. Similarly in *Areop* (4 : 312) when he catalogues the books that must be prohibited if all discussion of heresy is to be avoided, he writes, "The ancientest Fathers must be next remov'd, as *Clement* of *Alexandria*, and that *Eusebian* book of Evangelick preparation, transmitting our ears through a hoard of heathenish obscenities to receive the Gospel."

CB contains three further references to Clement, alluding to his chapter on marriage; to his discussion of the good man's practice of speaking the truth "unless at any time, medicinally, as a physician for the safety of the sick, he may deceive or tell an untruth"; and to his description of proper dress for women: "For neither is it seemly for the clothes to be above the knee . . . nor is it becoming for any part of a woman to be exposed. . . . It has also been enjoined that the head should be veiled and thē face covered; for it is a wicked thing for beauty to be a snare to men." [MRM]

CODINUS, GEORGIUS, late fifteenth-century (?) historian and author in part of *Byzantinae Historiae Scriptores* (Paris, 1648). He is cited in *CB* under "Kings" as to rules governing Greek emperors, but does not otherwise appear in Milton's work. [WBH]

COKE, SIR EDWARD (1552–1634). With an unrivaled knowledge of common law from medieval times, Coke, Lord Chief Justice of England, joined the issue of *lex* vs. *rex,* often infuriating King James* with his rulings against the Crown. Even as Chief Justice of the King's Bench, Coke maintained audaciously that common law is supreme over all except Parliament. Dismissed in 1616, Coke maneuvered himself into the privy council the next year. In Parliament in 1628, he presented a bill of liberties that were incorporated into the Petition of Right, based upon "good laws and statutes of this realm" from the time of Edward III and the "Great Charter of the Liberties of England." Coke's contribution to legal history is the *Institutes of the Laws of England* (First Part, 1628–1629; Second, 1642; Third, 1644; Fourth, 1644). In *1Def* Milton attacks Salmasius* for quoting Coke's *Institutes* out of context (7 : 478–79), though Milton himself twists Coke's meaning (Yale *Prose* 4, pt. 1, 505). In *Hire,* Milton cites the *Second Part of the Institutes* to show that before a decretal from the Third Lateran Council (1179) and another decretal of Innocent III interfered, an Englishman was free to give *"his tithes to what spiritual person he would"* (6 : 74). It is surprising that Milton does not cite from the *Institutes* in his *CB* during the early 1640s. He must have known of Coke by fame and through his pupil, Cyriack Skinner*, Coke's grandson. He refers to Coke in *Sonn* 21, addressed to Skinner. [TLH]

COLASTERION. Milton's fourth and last tract on divorce*, *Colasterion: a Reply to a nameless answer against The Doctrine and Discipline of Divorce,* published with "J.M" on its title page and without license or registration, or any indication of the printer* (possibly Matthew Simmons*), on or before March 4, 1645 (the date on Thomason's* copy), is an attack on an anonymous tract that had appeared in London in November 1644, *An Answer to a Book, Intituled, The Doctrine and Discipline of Divorce, or, A Plea for Ladies and Gentlewomen, and all other Maried Women against Divorce.* The "nameless answer," which was licensed with special praise on November 14 by Joseph Caryl* and published by William Lee, was a methodical refutation of Milton's own first edition of *DDD* (1643). *Colas,* consisting of twenty-seven pages without a preface, probably appeared simultaneously with *Tetra* (to which it refers but does not name, and to which it serves as a kind of comic relief) and was probably set by the same printer(s). The tract was not reissued in Milton's lifetime.

Intended primarily as an attack on the writer of the *Answer* (who Milton says he has learned was a servingman turned solicitor but who may have been a minor clergyman), Caryl, and William Prynne* (who had condemned Milton's idea of "divorce at pleasure" in *Twelve Considerable Serious Questions Touching Church Government,* 1644), *Colas* ("punishment," "a place or an instrument of torture") broadens into a general assault upon the various detractors of Milton's earlier divorce tracts, none of whom has proved to be an opponent worthy of his attention. In a mixture of anger, scorn, and ridicule, Milton turns in order from one to another of his adversaries, employing a full range of humor, invective, and scurrilous abuse.

Milton's initial target is Prynne, from whom he might have expected worthier opposition. Prynne's "jolly [bold] slander" is more of a disappointment than a serious threat, far from the reasonable view of truth that should be expected of a man "who hath suffer'd much and long" —fines, the pillory, imprisonment, and loss of ears—in its defense.

Caryl also comes in for Milton's tongue-lashing for his audacity in not merely licensing the *Answer* but in praising it as a necessary antidote against the "sad breaches" and "dangerous abuses" created in "unstaied mindes." Such an assertedly estimable man, one noted for discretion, religiousness, and honesty, has shown no regard for justice or civility in writing this "brute Libel" against "a name and person deserving of the Church and State equally to [himself] and one who hath don more to the present advancement" of the English clergy than Caryl himself.

Milton's major effort, however, is directed against the "illiterat, and arrogant presumer," the "mechanic," the "gross . . . sluggish . . . contentious and overweening pretender," the "puny Clark," the "hucster," the "opinionastrous" fellow, the "doult," the "Pork," the "frivolous . . . disputer," the "Idiot," the "Country Hinde," the "mongrel," the "rank Pettifogger," the "presumptuous lozel," the "brazen Asse," the "Serving-man . . . turn'd . . . paltry Solliciter" who, with "peasantly rudenes," displayed "his own contemptible ignorance" in attacking the excellent ideas set forth in *DDD*. Milton is particularly irritated by the anonymity of the tract, conveniently forgetting that the first edition of *DDD* was also published anonymously, as was his *Colas* itself. He is also displeased that the *Answer* is directed against the early version of *DDD* rather than the fully developed version of 1644.

The object of this attack hardly merits such ferocity. The *Answer's* forty-four pages are clearly organized, opening with three major points to be discussed: the proper doctrine and discipline of divorce, the reasons that incompatibility is an insufficient ground for divorce, and the problems inherent in *DDD*. Most attention is devoted to the third point. That the writer read Milton's tract carefully and imaginatively is suggested by a comment that must have especially displeased Milton: "The Reader is to take notice of one thing, namely, that all his Arguments, to prove a man may put away his wife for disagreement of minde or disposition, except it be his Argument from *Deu.* 24. 1. they prove as effectually, that the Wife may sue a Divorce from her Husband upon the same grounds" (p. 13).

Although the *Answer* is weak in its understanding of the basic premises of Milton's tract, especially his views of the true purposes of marriage, it does recognize various practical difficulties in realizing Milton's goals. In the light of seventeenth-century polemical writings, it is distinctly polite and reserved; and its point-by-point discussion and refutation of the highlights of Milton's tract suggest a well-trained, analytical mind. Milton must have recognized some of the methodical care that had gone into the *Answer*, for in a very similar step-by-step progression he in turn refutes each of its major points. Perhaps the imitation is more in mockery, however, than in admiration. And perhaps his entire tone is deliberately exaggerated more as a display of wit and bravado than sincere anger. Clearly Milton does not see the writer of the *Answer* as worthy of serious opposition, but as an apt victim for his "talent of sport." His lightness of mood is perhaps best seen in his threat to write a satiric poem (a genre in which he is as witty as he is caustic) if provocation continues: "Nay perhaps, as the provocation may bee, I may bee driv'n to curle up this gliding prose into a rough *Sotadic* [scurrilous satire], that shall rime him into such a condition, as instead of judging good Books to bee burnt by the executioner, hee shall be readier to be his own hangman" (4:272). Unfortunately, no further provocation ensued, so we have lost what might have been a stunning poem delivering one final drubbing of choice epithets upon his unfortunate opponent. [AA]

COLERIDGE, SAMUEL TAYLOR. Humphrey House's statement that "the shadow of *Paradise Lost* hung over all Coleridge's life" (*Coleridge* [1962], p. 66) should be modified to include the name of Milton himself, who provided, both as man and poet, a bracing but occasionally stultifying shade for Coleridge's poetic aspirations: "My poetic vanity," Coleridge wrote in 1796, "and my political *furor* have been exhaled; and I would rather be a self-maintaining gardener than a Milton, if I could not unite both" (J. A. Wittreich, Jr., *The Romantics on Milton* [1970], p. 156). The absolute reverence in which he held Milton is best seen in what is actually a superfluous note to "The Nightingale" (1798). In the course of caricaturing the poet who imposes his own melancholic feelings on Nature, he quoted *IlP*, line 62, and acknowledged apologetically that he had removed the line from its dramatic context in Milton's poem and that he was not treating the verse with levity : if such a charge were made, he continued, "none could be more painful to him, except perhaps of having ridiculed his Bible" (Wittreich, p. 160).

As if to give them greater weight, Coleridge borrowed frequently from Milton to ornament his slighter poems, but the borrowings rest uncomfortably in their new settings. He twice used the dismissals at the outset of *L'Al* and *IlP* to begin "Music" (1791) and "To Disappointment" (1792). He quoted line 62 of *IlP* in "To the Nightingale" (1795), line 17; cited line 14 of *Lyc* (slightly altered) in "To a Friend" (1796), line 19; and echoed the opening lines of *SA* in "The Wanderings of Cain" (1798). He also borrowed line 594 from *SA* in his "Dejection : An Ode" (1802), line 39, very effectively equating his loss of imaginative light with Samson's dispiriting blindness; the form of the third stanza of "Dejection," in which the quotation appears, is rime royal and similar to the proem to Milton's *Nat*.

One of Coleridge's earliest poems, "The Monody on the Death of Chatterton" (1790), imitates not only the title and subject of *Lyc* but its varying line lengths and rhyme scheme as well. "Inside the Coach" (1791) is an imitation of *L'Al* and *IlP*, and "Song of Pixies" (1793) borrows from *Nat;* Coleridge's "Ode to Georgiana, Duchess of Devonshire" (1799) quotes from and emulates the verse effects of Milton's "On the late Massacre in Piemont." His most ambitious imitative attempts were "Religious Musings" (1794) and "The Destiny of Nations. A Vision" (1796). "Musings" is infused with considerable indignation against social injustice, but its force is dissipated in the turgid blank verse and heavy-handed attempts at capturing the apocalyptic tone of *Nat*.

With the assistance of words such as "operant" (line 256), "immitigable" (line 79), "Omnific" (line 106), and "connatural" (line 173), the poem is quilted from sections of *PL;* the most successful passage is constructed from *PL* 4. 641–58 and begins: "Fair the vernal mead, / Fair the high grove, the sea, the sun, the stars" (lines 14–15). "The Destiny of Nations" is only slightly longer than "Musings," but is an even greater attempt to embrace in poetic form the subjects Milton synthesized in *PL* : the result is less the "Vision" Coleridge subtitled the poem than "a "romantico-politico-religious patchwork" (Carl R. Woodring, *Politics in the Poetry of Coleridge* [1961], p. 169). The poetry is obscured by contorted syntax and involved epical similes (notably lines 64–75), and it is filled with turbulent divinities :

> From his obscure haunt
> Shrieked Fear, of Cruelty the ghastly Dame,
> Feverous yet freezing, eager-paced yet slow,
> As she that creeps from forth her swampy reeds,
> Ague, the biform Hag!
>
> (lines 315–19)

Although Coleridge often became enraptured by an apocalyptic argot and lapsed into bombastic imitativeness, it is clear that he sensed his inability to write in Milton's own idiom and he virtually parodied his efforts in "Devonshire Roads" (1791) and "Monody on a Tea-kettle" (1790). Coleridge was also ambitious of devoting not "less than 20 years to an Epic—Ten to collecting materials and warm my mind with universal science. . . . the next five to the composition of the poem—and the five last to the correction of it" (Wittreich, p. 159); fortunately, Coleridge early recognized that the strength he could draw from Milton lay not in Milton's epic style and scope, but elsewhere.

Like many of his contemporaries, Coleridge fell out of sympathy with the revolutionists in France and, from a radical utopian in his student days at Jesus College, moved gradually to a more conservative position (cf. David P. Calleo, *Coleridge and the Idea of the Modern*

State [1966]). In both positions, he found support in Milton. During the period of December 1794, and January 1795, Coleridge contributed a series of "Sonnets on Eminent Characters" to the *Morning Chronicle*. Each of the sonnets shows not only the influence of Milton's political sonnets* (especially those on Cromwell, Fairfax, and Vane), but also the diction and images of the other sonnets as well (cf. Coleridge's "Burke" [1794] and Milton's "Me thought I saw my late espoused Saint"). Coleridge's revolutionary, reformist zeal, much like Milton's own, became rapidly modified: just as Coleridge argued in his Bristol addresses (1795) that he had never been truly affiliated with "republicanism," he was also able to assert from his new vantage point that Milton was "an advocate for . . . religious and moral aristocracy . . . the direct antipode of modern jacobinism" (Wittreich, p. 215). He agreed with Milton's stand on religious freedom and on the execution of Charles (Wittreich, pp. 178, 192, 181); and in his later political and philosophical essays, although without specific reference to Milton, Coleridge strongly advocated the individual's necessary moral and civic allegiance to the autonomous institutions of Church and State. He detected, however, Milton's opposition to democracy; in a conversation with Henry Crabbe Robinson, Coleridge said Milton was "a determined aristocrat, an enemy of popular elections. . . . He would have thought our popular freedom excessive . . . he thought the people fools" (Wittreich, p. 192). He took Milton's defense of Cromwell's dissolution of Parliament to be an inexcusable error (Wittreich, pp. 279–80). Coleridge's political views are intricate, and in spite of his criticism of Milton and his own support of democratic causes such as Catholic Emancipation and universal education, his position and Milton's are not at such variance—especially when the inherent irony of his following observation is taken into account:

> It was the error of Milton, Sidney, and others of that age, to think it possible to construct a purely aristocratic government, defecated of all passion, and ignorance, and sordid motive. The truth is, such a government would be weak from its utter want of sympathy with the people to be governed by it. (Wittreich, p. 273)

While he generally praised Milton's political works, Coleridge felt them to be too sectarian—in short, "of a party"—while Milton's poetry, he was convinced, "belongs to the whole world!" (Wittreich, p. 181). It was by means of intensive reading and study of Milton's poetry that Coleridge was able to organize his critical doctrines and to write his greatest poetry.

It is impossible to say with much certainty whether Coleridge deduced critical principles from his reading of Milton, or —and this is perhaps more likely— whether he affirmed his own ideas in Milton's poems. On several occasions, Coleridge quoted passages from *PL* in the *Biographia Literaria* (1815–16) to clarify an issue. For example, he cites *PL* 4. 139–42 and 11. 637 when he considers the metaphoric use of "scene" (Wittreich, pp. 224–25), and when he argues the propriety of the imagination over the fancy he quotes *PL* 9. 1101–1110. Two most important sections in the *Biographia,* chapter 10 and chapter 13, "On the imagination, or esemplastic power," are concerned with the discrimination of the "primary" and "secondary" imagination: both chapters take their departure from Raphael's discussion with Adam concerning the difference between the human and the angelic mind (*PL* 5. 469–90).

Milton, as well as Shakespeare, was the subject of the five-lecture series given by Coleridge between 1808–1819. Although the lectures were never recorded completely, the notes taken by those in attendance, the extant syllabuses, and Coleridge's own notebooks indicate the range of his considerations to have been extensive and to have included discussions of the quality of Milton's blank verse*, the minor poems, and the characters of Satan and Milton as they emerge in *PL*. It was an awareness of Milton's presence in *PL* that permitted Coleridge to make his famous distinction between Shakespeare and Milton in the *Biographia* : both poets are compeers, but Shakespeare merges into his creations, while Milton "attracts all forms and things to himself, into the unity of his own IDEAL" (Wittreich, p. 222; cf. p. 194).

Coleridge often indicated his preference for those passages in *PL* which are "the revelations of Milton's own mind, producing itself and evolving its own greatness . . . ," and wherein Milton "developes his own feelings" (Wittreich, pp. 245, 159). In all of Milton's poems, Coleridge said, "it is Milton himself whom you see; his Satan, his Adam, his Raphael, almost his Eve—are all John Milton . . . this intense egotism . . . gives me the greatest pleasure in reading Milton's work. The egotism of such a man is a revelation of spirit" (Wittreich, p. 277). What Samuel Johnson* condemned as egocentricity in Milton, Coleridge identified and praised as Milton's most significant creative quality. In the finest recorded passage in one of the last lectures (given March 4, 1819), Coleridge, perhaps inadvertently, revealed a personal reason for his interest in Milton's character :

No one can rise from the perusal of this immortal poem [*PL*] without a deep sense of the grandeur and the purity of Milton's soul, or without feeling how susceptible of domestic enjoyments he really was, notwithstanding the discomforts which actually resulted from an apparently unhappy choice in marriage. He was, as every truly great poet has ever been, a good man, but finding it impossible to realize his own aspirations, either in religion or politics, or socially, he gave up his heart to the living spirit and light within him, and avenged himself on the world by enriching it with his record of his own transcendental ideal. (Wittreich, p. 245)

In Sarah Fricker, Coleridge had also made an "unhappy choice in marriage," and he no doubt found excellent comfort in Milton's success in the face of similar adversity. It is also of interest to note, in this connection, that two of the earliest "conversation poems," "The Eolian Harp" and "Reflections on having left a Place of Retirement," which were both written during the idyllic first year (1795) of his marriage to Sarah, are filled with the rusticity and conviviality of Eden before the Temptation. Even though Coleridge refers to these poems as *sermone propriora* after Horace (*The Poems of Samuel Taylor Coleridge* [1912], pp. 106, 258,) it is probable that the remarkably graceful and casual cadence of the blank verse is indebted to the style of the conversations between Adam and Eve (especially *PL* 4. 634–88). It is almost irresistible to complete the pattern by suggesting that the serpent in the Garden was Sara Hutchinson, Wordsworth's future sister-in-law and the woman Coleridge came to love in 1799, but that would be unfair to that charming woman. Instead it would be more appropriate to identify the serpent as Coleridge's abstruse, imagination-deadening metaphysical preoccupations: "my idol, Milton," Coleridge remarked, "has represented Metaphysics as the subjects which the bad Spirits in Hell delight in discussing" (Wittreich, p. 189; elsewhere, having *PL* 4. 195, in mind, Coleridge wrote : "I sate myself, like a cormorant, once / Hard by the tree of knowledge" [Wittreich, p. 161]).

Coleridge's intense philosophical investigations, at least in part, were motivated by the desire to acquire sufficient erudition to attempt an epic* poem : "I would thoroughly know mechanics, Hydrostatics, Optics, and Astronomy, Botany, Metallurgy, Fossilism, Chemistry, Geology, Anatomy, Medicine —then the *mind of man*—then the *minds of men*—in all Travels, Voyages and Histories" (Wittreich, p. 159). Even if the advances in all these disciplines since Milton's time are not taken into account, Coleridge's resolve could not be supported by his ill health or his temperament. It is apparent, however, especially from the studies of J. L. Lowes (*The Road to Xanadu* [1927]), Maud Bodkin (*Archetypal Patterns in Poetry* [1934]), and J. B. Beer (*Coleridge the Visionary* [1959]) that both "The Rime of the Ancient Mariner" (1797) and "Kubla

Khan" (1799 or 1800?)—and "Christabel" (1797) should be unhesitatingly added— no matter to what else they owe their inspiration, are saturated with Milton and the results of Coleridge's attempts to "swell his intellect" as Milton did (Wittreich, p. 159). Rather than reiterate the numerous Miltonic echoes, direct and oblique, that the critics have discerned, it would be more useful to consider in more general terms the Miltonic elements that recur in the three poems.

Milton was a "platonizing Spirit," Coleridge observed, "who wrote nothing without an interior meaning" (Wittreich, p. 166); it is precisely this same "Spirit" that haunts these three poems with emblems and persistent hints that beg for symbolic interpretation. One way Coleridge achieved this mysterious atmosphere is by borrowing a device he commended in Milton by instancing his description of Death (*PL* 2. 666–73; Wittreich, pp. 200– 201): the use of shadowy images and forms rather than distinct images. "The substitution of a sublime feeling of the unimaginable for a mere image," argued Coleridge, is not only the highest order of imaginative writing, but also provokes an imaginative response from the reader. Coleridge unequivocally succeeds in his impalpable depictions of the topology of Xanadu, in the Mariner's pathological isolation, and in the physiognomy and character of Geraldine.

Another way Coleridge increased the preternaturalism of these poems was by adopting Milton's frequent use of intense opposites((for example, light/dark, cold/ heat). As Coleridge made clear in chapter 14 of the *Biographia*, the poet, "described in ideal perfection," reveals his imaginative genius "in the balance or reconciliation of opposite or discordant qualities" (*Biographia Literaria*, ed. Shaw- cross, 2 : 12); as he put it more tersely in his notebooks, "EXTREMES MEET," and he cited as an example *PL* 2. 594–95 (Wittreich, p. 169). The principal set of opposites in *PL*, as Coleridge understood, is good and evil* (Wittreich, p. 241). It is possible in Coleridge's three great poems

to set aside the rudimentary opposites, such as the desert ocean of the Ancient Mariner, the "sunny pleasure-dome with caves of ice" ("Kubla Khan," line 36), and the deceptive beauty and white silken robes of Geraldine ("Christabel," line 59), and apprehend Coleridge's unifying fac- ulty of the imagination striving to bring to a Miltonic resolution the "combat of Evil and Good" (Wittreich, p. 241) and failing: the mariner must relive his struggle through all eternity; Kubla Khan's success is fitful and fugitive; and *Christabel* breaks off with Evil in firm command. In the winter of 1800, imme- diately succeeding this concentrated period of poetic activity, Coleridge made the following enigmatic entry: "To have a continued Dream, representing visually and audibly all Milton's Paradise Lost" (Wittreich, p. 162); in a way, Coleridge's three greatest poems were that dream. [APA].

COLMAN, GEORGE, the elder (1732– 1794), dramatist and author. Born in Florence, Colman during his later twenties became a member of the theatrical group of which David Garrick was a major force. With others, Colman purchased the Covent Garden Theatre, which became his base of operations. Important plays include *The Jealous Wife* (1761), pro- duced anonymously, *Philaster* (1763), an adaptation of the Beaumont and Fletcher play, and *The Clandestine Marriage* (1766), written with Garrick. Colman revised the version of *Mask* that John Dalton* had made so successful. From 1772 it was this second adaptation* that held the boards into the nineteenth cen- tury. Editions came out in 1772, 1774, 1776, 1777 (3), 1779, 1780, 1784, 1791 (2), 1792, 1797, 1799 (2), 1809, 1815, as well as two undated printings. Colman's ver- sion is in two acts, Dalton's Act 2 becom- ing Scene 3 of Act 1 and Dalton's Act 3 becoming Act 2. The long speeches are drastically cut, and songs are rearranged and some lines (like "Come and trip it," taken out of Dalton's third act and put into Scene 1 of the first act) are made into songs. The section from *L'Al* now in Act 2 is greatly revised.

Colman also frequently alluded to Milton or quoted from his works, and was influenced by *Educ* in his own discussion of that subject. Allusions or quotations will be found in an article in *The Adventurer*, no. 90 (September 15, 1753), in the Prologue to *Philaster* ("Upon Mr. Powell's First Appearance at Drury Lane, October 8, 1763"), in his translation of *Q. Horatii Flacci Epistola ad Pisones, De Arte Poetica* (1783), in "Prologue to the French Piece of Pygmalion, Performed by Monsieur Tessier, Spoken by Lord Malden" (see *New Foundling Hospital For Wit* [1784], 6 : 34), in *The Genius*, in the Appendix to the Comedies of Terence," and in "Ode to Obscurity." Colman's "Orthopaedia : or, Thoughts on Publick Education," first published in his *Prose on Several Occasions; Accompanied with Some Pieces in Verse* (1787), quotes and discusses *Educ* (2 : 236–37, 248–51). [JTS]

COLTELLINI, AGOSTINO (1613–1693). A Florentine friend greeted by Milton in his letter to Carlo Dati (*Epistol* 10) and cited in *2Def*, Coltellini was a lawyer and the young founder of the Academy of the Apatisti, whose meetings Milton probably attended. The Apatisti were known by anagrams, Coltellini being "Ostilio Contalgeni." He frequently used the name in later years. He was a member of the Accademia della Crusca as well, and was four times president or consul of Florence (during 1659–1693). His *Endecasillabi*, published in two parts in Florence in 1641 and 1652, frequently alludes to other members of the Apatisti. [JTS]

COLUMBIA MANUSCRIPT. Once owned by Sir Thomas Phillipps and now the property of Columbia University Library (purchased in 1921), the manuscript (X823 M64 / S52) is in the hand of two scribes, Phillipps, and Bernard Gardiner, a former owner. There are seventy-eight leaves, one scribe beginning on p. 3 and working toward the center, the other starting on p. 154 and working backwards toward the center. Many of the items are not associated with Milton; those that are include : *Proposals of Certain Expedients*, pp. 19–21; *A Letter to a Friend*, pp. 21–23; and transcriptions of 156 letters of state, pp. 23–79, all by the first-mentioned scribe. The letters of state omit three given in *StateP*, give ten not found in *StateP* but included in the Skinner MS*, and include ten more not found in *StateP* that can be attributed to Milton only with uncertainty. (One letter, *CM* 71, appears twice as Nos. 59 and 85, the latter being crossed out.)

The scribe working forward from the back of the manuscript records under seven rubrics notes concerned with legal matters; there is a table to this Legal Index, or commonplace book. Whether these notes should be assigned to Milton is most debatable, the inclusion of the items above in the same manuscript being the only reason for such attribution. [JTS]

COMENIUS (KOMENSKY), JOHN AMOS (1592–1670), a Moravian churchman and an advocate of educational reform. He visited England in 1641 at the urging of Samuel Hartlib*, who had translated his *Janua Linguarum Reserata* [*The Door to Languages Unlocked*] (1631) and a summary of *The Great Didactic* (1639). The fundamental tenets of Comenius's program were compulsory free education for rich and poor children of both sexes in schools conducted by the state, a more rapid and practical method of teaching languages, a strong emphasis on vocational as opposed to liberal subjects, and the use of encyclopedic compilations of knowledge with the ultimate aim of achieving "Pansophia," the understanding of a universal harmony. Despite the support of Hartlib, John Dury* and others, Comenius's advocacy of universal education and his proposal for a new college in England for scholars dedicated to the pursuit of Pansophia were not acted upon by Parliament.

Milton wrote his tractate *Educ* at the entreaty of Hartlib, stimulated by the latter's translation of Comenius's *A*

Reformation of Schooles (1642). In his own work Milton declares his independence of Comenius: "To search what many modern *Janua's* and *Didactics*, more than ever I shall read, have projected, my inclination leads me not" (*Educ* 4 : 276). Despite agreement on such general ideas as the importance of religious and moral instruction, the principle of proceeding in education from sense experience to the abstract, and the need of reform in curriculum and methods, Milton's tractate clearly diverges from the most characteristic positions of Comenius. [JAD]

COMES, NATALIS (1520–1582), or Natale Conti, historian, poet, and translator, best known for his *Mythologiae sive explicationum fabularum (Mythology or accounts of ancient stories)*. First published in 1561 and reprinted in numerous editions thereafter, it was popular throughout Europe in the sixteenth and seventeenth centuries. Comes summarizes the mythological narratives, gives their Greek source when appropriate together with a Latin translation, and provides interpretations of each story and a good index. The preface announces that his purpose is not only to retell the classical myths* but to uncover the hidden sense attached to them by the ancients, for the stories of the gods were invented to provide us with a key to the understanding of nature as well as a guide to human conduct. Comes thus carries on the medieval and Renaissance tradition of interpreting pagan mythology in terms of Christian belief and morality.

The *Mythologiae* proved most useful to such English writers as Spenser*, Chapman, and Bacon*. Even Milton, for all his classical learning, relied like his contemporaries on such useful compilations. Copies of Comes were certainly to be found at St. Paul's School* and at Christ's College*, Cambridge. Milton's use of the work is treated in detail by D. T. Starnes and E. W. Talbert in *Classical Myth and Legend in Renaissance Dictionaries*. The authors are cautious in ascribing a given allusion to Comes alone, since Milton also

consulted other compendia, especially those of Robert and of Charles Stephanus, as well as his own prodigious memory of the original sources. But whatever the origin of his mythological facts, Milton always subordinated them to poetic and to Christian truth. [JAD]

COMINES, PHILIPPE DE (ca. 1447–1511), French statesman and historian. Milton's *CB* contains five entries from the *Mémoires* of Comines. Considering that Milton thought him "a weighty authority," "a keen eyed witness," and "a great statesman and courtier," it is surprising that he found use for only two of the entries in other works.

The most fruitful quotation proved to be that entered under the topic "On Consultation," for it was echoed in *Colas, Educ,* and *2Def.* According to Milton, Comines "shows how far credence and consent should be given to the advice of experts . . ." who "often make mistakes under the influence of their emotions. . . ." The observation that "princes ought to be learned especially in histories" appeared in *Educ.* Other citations from the *Mémoires* were recorded under the headings of "Concubinage," "Tyrants," "Property," and "Taxes."

In his *Eikon,* Milton drew a parallel between the publication of King Charles's letter and the exposure of Marie of Burgundy's correspondence with Louis XI by her ambassadors, taking the latter incident from Comines's *Mémoires.*

Comines, an ambitious courtier, diplomat, and historian, served first Charles the Bold of Burgundy, then deserted to the side of the French monarch Louis XI. His fortunes at court varied; though he fell from favor after Louis's death, he served Charles VIII as ambassador to Venice after the French invasion of Italy, finally retiring to expand and revise his *Mémoires.* Milton apparently used the Gaillot du Pré edition (1552), although Ruth Mohl notes a number of descrepancies in paging. [RMa]

COMMELIN, JEROME (d. 1598), printer. A French Protestant, Commelin took refuge in Geneva, where he became a printer. Later, he was appointed curator of the electoral library in the County Palatine. Milton used his editions of the British historians compiled in *Rerum Britannicarum . . . Scriptores,* which contained seven histories including Gildas*, Bede*, and Geoffrey of Monmouth*. His annotated copy is owned by the Harvard University Library. [RMa]

COMMONPLACE BOOK. Milton's *Commonplace Book* is the notebook he kept on his general reading from his school days to about 1665 or 1667, according to the methods taught in St. Paul's Latin grammar school* in London. Deriving its name from its ancient Greek and Roman origins, it is important for its many examples of Milton's handwriting and for its evidence of the wide range of his reading, but especially for the insight it gives into his mind and the use he made of his notes in both his prose and poetry. To him a good book was "the pretious life-blood of a master spirit," and in his youth he began collecting books for his own library that were to serve him for the rest of his life. They included the works of historians, ancient, medieval, and contemporary; the Greek and Latin fathers of the church; theologians like Peter Martyr* and André Rivet*; jurists and political theorists like Justinian*, Sir Thomas Smith*, John Selden*, and Machiavelli*; military men; educators; philosophers; travelers; reformers; a professor of medicine; as well as ten poets, Prudentius*, Chaucer*, Dante*, Gower*, Boiardo*, Berni*, Ariosto*, Tasso*, Sidney*, and Spenser*. That this is not a literary notebook, however, is evident from the fact that the few quotations from the poets are from their prose or from such verse as contains some bit of practical wisdom. Neither does it reflect all of Milton's reading. Many sources he often referred to in his other works, such as the Bible and the classics, are not included. His purpose in his reading was to acquire the breadth of knowledge and philosophical objectivity necessary to a Renaissance scholar and humanist concerning the principles and problems affecting life in all ages.

From his reading Milton noted both facts and ideas, some that were purely informational, some that corroborated his own beliefs, and others that plainly differed from them. His entries were made from ninety-two authors, in Greek, Latin, French, Italian, or English, depending on the text being used. He arranged his notes in three groups suggested by Aristotle's* *Rhetoric*: the Index Ethicus, the Index Economicus (i.e. Domestic), and the Index Politicus. In several places Milton refers to his Theological Index*, which has not been discovered. In *CM* 18 : 221–26, 509–10, a Legal Index is also ascribed to Milton, but its true identity has yet to be established. Of the three Indexes in the *CB,* the Political Index is longer than the other two combined and is largely the work of the mature Milton.

CB was discovered in 1874 by Alfred J. Horwood*, who, as a representative of the Royal Commission on Historical Manuscripts, went to Netherby Hall, Longtown, Cumberland, to examine the manuscripts of Sir Frederick Graham. The document was stained with dampness and bound in rough brown sheepskin. It consisted of pages numbered from 1 to 250, but some had been cut away, and there were 136 blank pages. An Index of headings on an unnumbered page at the end shows that none of the material referred to in it is missing. Milton's notes, most of them in his own handwriting, appear on 71 pages. After 1650, when his sight was beginning to fail, Milton employed several scribes, and after 1652, when his blindness* was complete, he was forced to depend on some five or six scribes, besides those who made the entries from Machiavelli. The elder brother of an ancestor of Sir Frederick Graham, Lord Preston (1648–1695), who seems to have acquired the manuscript from Daniel Skinner*, Milton's last scribe, made some notes of his own on 15 pages otherwise blank, as well as on parts of pages already used by Milton or his scribes. The handwriting, form, and ideas of Lord Preston's entries are quite different from all the rest and have, of course, been omitted in the later editions of *CB*. The manuscript was later repaired and rebound, and in 1900, according to the British Museum catalogue, was acquired by the Museum (M.S. Add. 36354).

In 1876 Horwood, realizing the importance of his discovery, asked permission to edit the manuscript for printing, and, with Sir Frederick Graham's approval, the Camden Society published it, including three facsimile pages. Later in 1876 the Royal Society of Literature had one hundred facsimile copies of the whole manuscript printed. A revised edition of Horwood's text appeared in 1877. A third printing appeared in 1938 in *CM* 18, in which for the first time the foreign-language entries were accompanied by English translations, and the true importance of *CB* began to appear. Earlier, the editor of this edition, James Holly Hanford*, had pointed out the significance of the notebook as "affording an insight into the real and abiding intellectual temper of Milton and as a revelation of the preparatory intellectual processes which culminated in his greatest work," but also as a clue to the chronology* of Milton's entries and to the identity of the authors cited. Horwood had begun the work of identification, but Hanford completed it, often with the exact edition used by Milton as indicated by Milton's page numbers. The fourth and last printing to date appeared in 1953 in the Yale *Prose* 1, in which the text, in English translation only, is accompanied by notes on the sources from which the entries were made and quotations from them.

The keeping of a commonplace book was an important part of the curriculum of the sixteenth- and seventeenth-century Latin grammar school in England. The program of study at St. Paul's in London, where Milton was a student from about 1620 to 1624, was planned by Erasmus*

at the request of John Colet, founder of the school, and became the program on which all the other English grammar schools were founded. In his *De Ratione Studii* Erasmus outlined his course of study of grammar* and rhetoric*, with just enough logic* to make the rhetoric understandable. This modified trivium was based on the reading of the best authors and the careful taking of notes from them. In his *De Copia* Erasmus specified authors to be read and explained how the notes were to be taken. They were to consist of propositions or "places" of proof, arranged under topics or headings of significance and called "commonplaces." Hence the commonplace book. The plan was derived from Aristotle, whose analysis of the *topos koinos* (the *locus communis* of Latin and the *commonplace* of English) led to his discovery of deductive reasoning and the syllogism. It was modified by Cicero* in his *Topica* and by Quintilian* later in his *Institutio Oratoria*. The schools of ancient Greece and Rome, as well as those of the Middle Ages, followed such a plan, and many commonplace books still survive in the schools and libraries of Europe. The notes taken were used in themes, essays, speeches, orations, and other forms of expression. The schoolmaster would assign a topic sentence, such as a proverb, a figure of speech, a historical statement, or some well-expressed thought, and from his notebook the student would develop it, using the notes on his reading under that topic. Milton's "Theme on Early Rising" is an example of how he, as a schoolboy, developed a proverb (12 : 288–91). Other schoolboys similarly trained were Francis Bacon*, Thomas Traherne, Thomas Ellwood*, John Locke, and Thomas Jefferson. The training was recommended by Bacon, Roger Ascham*, Sir Thomas Wilson, Sir Thomas Elyot, and Hugh Blair, renowned eighteenth-century professor of rhetoric at Edinburgh University. Some dissatisfaction arose in the later seventeenth century over too narrow a range of "topics" and too slavish following of the commonplaces. Milton's own remarks in his *Apol* (3 : 334) and *Areop* (4 : 335) illustrate this dissatisfaction.

The range of topics in Milton's *CB* is by no means narrow. Though he began his note-taking as a student, he continued it into maturity. Most of his notes were made from 1640 to 1644, in the middle period of his life, and hence show best his growth as a thinker, scholar, teacher, and reformer, but chiefly as a pamphleteer and poet. From twenty-four headings on goodness and evil* in the Ethical Index, he proceeded to twelve on domestic matters in the Economic Index, and to eight on the State, the King, the Tyrant, Subjects, Laws, Property and Taxes, Military Discipline, and War*, among twenty-one others, in his Political Index. There are thirteen entries under Laws, some compounded from several authors; forty-six under King, ten compounded; seventeen under Tyrant; sixteen under Subjects; fifteen under Property and Taxes, plus eight under Official Extortion; seventeen under Military Discipline; and thirteen under War and Civil War. Almost all the notes are meticulously referred to an author, work read, book, chapter, and page number, often abbreviated since the notebook was for Milton's use only. Sometimes Milton paraphrased what he read; sometimes he quoted exactly, omitting, however, the quotation marks. Frequently he added a comment of his own that suggests uses to which he put his entry in his other works.

The uses he made of this mine of ideas are many. The most obvious are those in which he gives the exact words of his source. For example, in *Areop* on censorship he has two quotations from Bacon's *Wise and Moderate Discourse, Concerning Church-Affaires* (18 : 180, and 4 : 326, 332–33); and in *Tenure* he quotes Sir Thomas Smith's definition of a king (18 : 176, and 5 : 10–11). Similarly in *Apol* he quotes Johannes Sleidan* on Luther's* use of harsh speech in reforming the church (18 : 145, and 3 : 314–15). In *Ref* and in *Hire* he cites and quotes Sulpicius Severus's* *Sacred History* to contrast the poverty of three fourth-century British bishops with the rich dioceses of his own day (18 : 160–61, and 3 : 98, 6 : 87). Sometimes the title of a prized authority like John Selden's *Of the Law of Nature and of Nations* is fashioned into a line of poetry, as in line 890 of *SA* (18 : 152, and 1 : 368). Even when sources are not quoted, authors are named, as when in *Ref* he cites Dante's* views on the avarice of the clergy (18 : 131, and 3 : 26–27) and on the necessity of discovery of individual differences in education in his own *Educ* (18 : 153 and 4 : 290). From his *CB* he also drew significant examples for his *Brit,* such as that of Alfred's method of coping with theft and highway robbery (18 : 143, and 10 : 221); the dramatic incident of Anlaf's faithful soldier (18 : 143, and 10 : 233–34); and the familiar story of King Canute's lesson to his courtiers, beside the sea, on "the small power of Kings in respect of God" (18 : 144, and 10 : 280–81). Perhaps his most significant use of his notebook in his other works, however, is in his treatment of such general topics as good and evil, based on his notes from Tertullian*, Lactantius*, and Chrysostom* (18 : 128–29). So pervasive are these ideas in Milton's prose and especially in *PL, PR,* and *SA* that they become wholly Milton's, and the reader is likely to forget their source. These are only a few examples of how he put his notebook to work.

Milton was a scholar, and the wide range of his reading contributed in large measure to his greatness. His purpose in his reading and note-taking was a search for truth, moral, economic, and political, with which he might serve England, mankind, and God. His ultimate goal, however, was to write something that men in aftertimes would not willingly let die. In the achievement of that goal, with a poet's imagination and emotion, he was able to transform scholarship into great art in both prose and poetry and to become "a contemporary of time itself" (12 : 267). [RM]

**COMPLETE COLLECTION OF THE
. . . WORKS, A:** *see* EDITIONS, PROSE.

**COMPOSITION, MILTON'S HABITS
OF.** Surviving stories of Milton's methods
of composing verse relate to the writing
of *PL.* He rose early, had his secretary
read to him (usually in Hebrew from the
Scriptures), sat in contemplation, and then
was read to and dictated until dinner
time. He composed and kept verses in
his head until his secretary could take
them down; when the amanuensis* was
late, the Anonymous Biographer reports,
"he would complain, saying he 'wanted to
be milked.' " A typical group of lines
would number forty and these would then
be reduced to about half. The composition,
however, seems to have been in syntactical
units rather than in lines; and this is
understandable for *PL* in view of the way
in which "the sense [is] variously drawn
out from one Verse into another." Phillips
talks of correcting a parcel of ten, twenty,
or thirty verses at a time when he visited
his uncle, because such verses had been
written down by "whatever hand came
next." According to Jonathan Richard-
son*, when he dictated, Milton leaned
back obliquely in an easy chair, with his
leg flung over the elbow of it, or he
frequently composed lying in bed in the
morning. The composition in bed occurred
in the winter, he adds, and Phillips and
Aubrey* tell us that Milton's poetic vein
usually flowed from the autumnal through
the vernal equinoxes (*see* INSPIRATION,
SEASONAL).

From manuscript material, biography*,
and a study of *PL*, however, we can dis-
cern other habits of composition. As Mil-
ton himself remarks in *RCG*, he prepared
himself long for his task of writing a work
that man would not willingly let die. He
was writing prose in the early 1640s out
of his own season when he had not yet
completed to his own mind the full circle
of his private studies. Surveying the biog-
raphy and being influenced by this state-
ment, Parker comments that Milton rarely
mixed original composition in poetry with
prose writing. Suggested, therefore, is a

habit of extensive preliminary work, out
of which would come a rather fully
developed piece of writing, not a work
basically evolved as writing took place.
The prose outlines for dramas that are
extant in *TM,* including the development
of what came to be *PL,* attest to the second
stage in Milton's writing (*see also* DRA-
MATIC PLANS). The prose summaries for
each book of *PL* and for *SA* likewise
illustrate a further stage in this planning.
But these summaries show too that further
attention was paid to the finished poem,
for they do not agree in all details with
the completed work. As Milton added in
RCG, he hoped for time enough to permit
him to apply "all the curious touches of
art" to the great poems he contemplated.
Thus his general procedure would seem
to be 1) contemplation of a work and
mental planning, 2) for a longer work, a
prose outline perhaps to be developed
further at a later stage, 3) the actual
writing out of the work, or, for a longer
work, of sizable sections of verse, 4) re-
vision of the work or the section, and
5) the application of "all the curious
touches of art." In the manuscript of *Lyc*
we see stage 3 as a first rendering of lines
1–14, followed by a full development of
the poem, and then stages 4 and 5. The
fifth stage continued after its first publica-
tion in 1638. This stage of compositional
procedure can be seen in such alterations
as "opening" for "glimmering" in line 26;
"westring" for "burnisht" in line 31; "Or
with" for "Hid in" in line 69; and "wheel-
ing" for 'humming" in line 157. In the
manuscript of *SolMus* we see a fully
worked out poem set down, with indica-
tions of variant readings that Milton was
considering. As stages 4 and 5 evolved,
the original writing was so revised that
what remains in the completed poem in-
cludes only six lines of the first draft,
among them the first two lines of the
poem. But between writing the final ver-
sion in *TM* and publishing the poem in
1645, Milton altered the last line to a
more logical wording; that is, from "To
live and sing with him [God]" to "To live
with him, and sing."

Study of the manuscript development of *Mask* impresses two further habits of composition upon us. That is, Milton frequently reused sections of longer poems in different places from their "original" positions, adapting as needed for the new contexts, and he expanded a few lines into more or picked up dramatic or character hints and developed them into full-scale episodes. Realization of these habits of composition are central to Allan H. Gilbert's contention as to the development of Milton's major work (see *On the Composition of Paradise Lost* [1947]), which he views as being worked up out of a series of briefer tragedies, compounded and shifted next into a chronological version of the narrative, and then finally reorganized into an epic form. [JTS]

COMUS: *see* MASK, A.

COMUS, A MASQUE: *see* MASK, A; ARNE, THOMAS; COLMAN, GEORGE; DALTON, JOHN.

CONCORDANCES. The first attempts at concordances to Milton's works were incomplete indexes to certain key ideas or words. *1Def* has such an index attached to the quarto reprint, perhaps from Gouda (Madan No. 3); the index is six pages [105–10]. Although Madan No. 4a (with date of 1650) and 4b (with date of 1651) advertise themselves on the title page as "Cum Indice," there is none. This is a duodecimo reprint by Theodorus ab Ackersdijck in Utrecht. The index appears again in Madan no. 6 (duodecimo, by Daniel Elzevir*, Amsterdam, pp. [261–72]), in Madan no. 10 (duodecimo, pp. [390–410]), and in Madan no. 13 (duodecimo, by Theodorus ab Ackersdijk and Gisbertus à Zijel, Utrecht, pp. [277–88]). All other editions omit the index except that No. 3 was reissued in Paris by Mathurini du Pius in 1651 with Salmasius's* *Defensio Regii.* It is reprinted in *CM* 18.

Brit likewise contains an index, pp. [309–61] of the first edition in 1670, reissued in 1671. The index appears in the second edition, pp. [359–416], in 1677,

reissued in 1678; in the third edition, pp. [359–416], in 1695, reissued in 1695. It is included in *A Complete Collection,* 1698; Francis Maseres's edition, 1818; Robert Fletcher's *The Prose Works,* but not until published by William Bell in 1838; and, separated from the text, in *CM* 18.

"A Table to the Poem" appears in many of the copies of the 1695 edition of *PL,* but not all. It has been assigned to Patrick Hume*, who wrote "Explanatory Notes Upon Each Book," included also in many of the copies of this edition. The table lists descriptions, similes, and speeches. "An Index of the Principal Matters in *Paradise Lost*" appears in Thomas Tickell's edition of *The Poetical Works,* printed for Jacob Tonson* in 1720, 1 : [591–603]. It was reprinted very often in the eighteenth century. Jonathan Richardson* added a brief index to *Explanatory Notes and Remarks on Paradise Lost* (1734), and James Paterson provided a kind of dictionary as *A Complete Commentary, with Etymological, Explanatory, Critical and Classical Notes on Milton's Paradise Lost* (1744). "A Verbal Index to *Paradise Lost*" by Thomas Coxeter came much closer to a full concordance; it appeared in an edition by Innys and Browne in 1741. With Bishop Newton's* variorum edition of the poem in 1749, the two indexes by Tickell and by Coxeter in vol. 2 became standard for most of the numerous editions in the second half of the century. Henry John Todd* supplied a new and superior verbal index in his 1809 edition of *The Poetical Works.*

The first actual concordance to the poetical works was a two-volume text by G. L. Prendergast, published in Madras in 1857–1859; much of the inadequate and erroneous citation can be excused by foreign publication, but it is far from complete. Charles D. Cleveland's poetical concordance in 1867 is not complete and not much better than its predecessor. The standard concordance to the English poetical works had been John Bradshaw's (1894; rptd. 1965), but it must be used with caution. *A Lexicon to the English Poetical Works* (1907; rptd. 1966) by Laura E. Lockwood* provides a verbal index while defining vocabulary in terms of usage. Lane Cooper's *A Concordance of the Latin, Greek, and Italian Poems of John Milton* (1923) is a competent and reliable work. A computer-based concordance of *Paradise Lost,* compiled by Gladys W. Hudson, using the 1674 edition, has been published recently (Detroit, 1970). The computerized concordance, but to all the poetical works (early editions) and poetic manuscript material, from Oxford University Press, edited by Kathleen M. Swaim and William H. Ingram is now the standard volume. The first of a series of computerized concordances to the prose is to appear from Southern Illinois University Press, edited by Laurence Sterne and others; the text concorded is that in the Yale *Prose.* [JTS]

CONSCIENCE: *see* REASON.

CONSIDERATIONS TOUCHING THE LIKELIEST MEANS TO REMOVE HIRELINGS OUT OF THE CHURCH. State-enforced tithing was an active source of disagreement among various religious groups during the entire period of the Civil Wars, the Commonwealth, and the Protectorate, causing the dissolution of more sittings of Parliament than any other reason. The immediacy of the subject resulted from strong economic and religious feelings; in the former, the state-enforced support of a ministry toward which the taxed individual might well be hostile; in the latter, the reciprocal support of Church and State, with its implied Erastianism*.

A previous generation had seen the state tax that underwrote the established Church questioned by John Selden* who, in his *History of Tithes* (1618), had tested the legality of the practice, employing his immense erudition to show that the collection of tithes had not been made by the primitive Christian Church, and that it had only dubious authority in English history. The clergy, threatened with disestablishment. appealed at once to King James*, who directed that Selden was to write no more on the subject, despite the attacks to which he was being subjected.

The subject became an active public issue in May 1646, when a great crowd unsuccessfully petitioned Commons that tithes be abolished. As Selden's argument had elicited printed rebuttals, so did this public display; probably the most scholarly was the collection of pamphlets, *Tithes Too Hot to be Touched* (1646), mostly written by the late antiquary Henry Spelman*, a recognized authority on British ecclesiastical history.

Again in 1652 the issue was raised by the Parliamentary Committee for the Propagation of the Gospel, asking for state support of an Independent ministry. This time the most important publication in support of tithing was probably William Prynne's* *A Gospel Plea* (1653), a more emotional and less scholarly work than Spelman's, though it too was based on biblical authority and historical practices. One should notice that the Episcopalian Spelman, the Presbyterian Prynne, and the Independent Committee all supported the practice of enforced tithing, the issue between them being not state support of a church but state support of *which* church.

A proposal to abolish tithes broke up the Nominated Parliament in 1654, and the issue was again raised before the Restored Rump in the summer of 1659. Perhaps in response to a letter from Moses Wall* written to him in May, Milton contributed *Hire* to the public discussion. It had no effect; Parliament was again dissolved over the issue. In retrospect, one realizes only too clearly the difficulties of separating Church and State.

When Milton became a firm disestablishmentarian is impossible to say. *Lyc* shows his dissatisfaction with ministers who serve "for their bellies' sake." *Sonn* 16, responding to the Committee for the Propagation of the Gospel, pleads that Cromwell "save free Conscience from the paw / Of hireling wolves," and the missing Index Theologicus* almost certainly had a lengthy series of entries under "Church Property" or "Tithing." But

Hire is Milton's major statement, an argument that to withhold pay from the ministry will drive the hirelings out and leave only the truly dedicated. Its opening sentence shows that it should be matched with the anti-Erastian *CivP* in an attempt to limit civil and religious power each to its own separate function. (*See also* ECCLESIOLOGY.)

The main attack is directed against Prynne's *Gospel Plea,* published six years earlier, and the Spelman collection twelve years earlier rather than against any work more recent, though *Hire* does seem to refer to Prynne's *Ten Considerable Queries,* dated by Thomason* June 27, 1659, only two months before Milton's appeared. But his major argument centers on the two earlier works, suggesting that he had compiled much of the material used in *Hire* some years earlier and perhaps had even written much of the pamphlet in 1653, a date reinforced by his mention of the recalcitrance of "the presbyters of late in *Scotland*" (6 : 99), where the General Assembly had to be forcibly dissolved in July 21, 1653, ancient history by the summer of 1659. The style of *Hire* also is quite different from that of *CivP,* published the same year.

Aside from its disestablishmentarian position, Milton's pamphlet is interesting for the careful scholarship on which it is argued. He drew heavily for support of his position from Selden's *History* and from his own profound knowledge of English history, more fully evidenced in his *Brit.* Thus he unhesitatingly engages the historian Spelman, citing from Spelman's *Concilia* (1639) in support of his position and attacking his *Tithes Too Hot to be Touched.*

Particularly interesting arguments are derived from Waldensian* practices, with which Milton shows close familiarity (but without any mention of their "massacre" in 1655, further evidence for an earlier date of composition). He cites the standard authorities, Pierre Gilles*, Jean Paul Perrin, and John Dubrau. The Waldensians are significant for him because they represent the practices of the primitive church. In a somewhat similar vein, much of his argument derives from the non-tithing practices of the pre-Levitical Jews, interpreted by Prynne in Abraham's gifts to Melchizedek (Gen. 14 : 18ff.) as authorizing tithes but sharply reinterpreted by Milton as authorizing only optional rather than required presents to the church.

Finally, a good deal of critical attention has recently been accorded the pamphlet because it disavows the need for a highly educated ministry, a requirement that had been supported by both Spelman and Prynne to justify reimbursement by way of state payments to the minister for the outlays he had made for his education and his books. The *Resolution of a Doubt* (included in the aforementioned collection of 1646) argues that such an education costs £600. Milton answers that rather than £600, it can be had for £60 (6 : 95), and that a classical education is not really necessary anyhow. This brings the polemical position in the pamphlet very close to that of Jesus in the depreciation of classical learning in *PR* and aligns Milton with various sects led by laymen today [WBH]

CONSTANTINE THE GREAT (d. 337), proclaimed Augustus of Gaul in 306, invaded Italy in 312. He told his biographer, Eusebius* of Caesarea, that the vision of a cross in the sky was decisive in his conversion to Christianity and in the victories that made him senior Augustus over all the western provinces of the Roman Empire. Together with Licinius, sole ruler of the eastern provinces, he proclaimed full religious toleration in 313. By defeating Licinius in 324, Constantine became Emperor. Presiding at the Council of Nicaea in 325, he proposed the crucial formula, "of one substance with the Father," which made possible the official unifying of disparate Christian elements.

Milton represents Constantine as baptizing the Roman Empire (*DDD* 3 : 377), but rejects certain legends (*Brit* 10 : 92–93, 118, 122–23). He laments Constantine's heresies, particularly his favoring of Arius (*Ref* 3 : 23). He praises Constantine's suggestion of silence with respect to difficult interpretations for the prevention of schism (*CB* 18 : 138), his attitude toward divorce (*Tetra* 4 : 215), and his rejection of lordly titles (*CB* 18 : 170). The struggle between eastern and western divisions of the Empire reminds Milton of that between Charles I* and Parliament (*1Def* 7 : 251, 253, 375), and Constantine's attempt to control the clergy reminds him of Charles's similar attempt (*Eikon* 5 : 261).

Milton is not unaware of the shortcomings and strengths of the pre-Constantine church (*Ref* 3 : 21, 23, 25; *1Def* 7 : 251, 257; *CB* 18 : 161; *Hire* 6 : 81). He notes the growing emphasis under Constantine of superstition, wealth, clericalism, and ceremonialism (*CB* 18 : 163; *Ref* 3 : 24–25, 42; *Animad* 3 : 169; *Hire* 6 : 48, contrast 6 : 64). Though aware that the donation of Constantine is spurious (*Ref* 3 : 43–44), Milton says that it poisoned the church (*Eikon* 5 : 230), changed "woodden Chalices and golden *Preists*" into "golden Chalices and woodden *Preists*" (*Ref* 3 : 25–28), and was deplored by a voice from heaven (*Apol* 3 : 259–60; *Eikon* 5 : 187; *2Def* 8 : 183; *Hire* 6 : 49).

Constantine, weighed in Milton's balances, brought not good but evil to the church (*CB* 18 : 168–69; *Ref* 3 : 21, 26, 28), to his spiritual successors (*CB* 18 : 173; *Ref* 3 : 21, 23, 28, 44; *Animad* 3 : 138; *Eikon* 5 : 187), and to his descendants (*Ref* 3 : 25). The "spotless *Truth*" is not dependent on the "dim Taper" of Constantine's time (*Ref* 3 : 10, 24). [MCP]

CONSTITUTIONS AND CANONS: see LAW, ECCLESIASTICAL.

CONTEMPTUS MUNDI. By *contemptus mundi* is meant a total rejection of the things of this world and a turning toward those of the spirit. The phrase gained currency through the popularity of two medieval Latin works bearing the title *De Contemptu Mundi*, one by Bernard of Cluny (or Morlaix) and the other by the future Pope Innocent III, both of which date from the late twelfth century. The

rejection of the offers of Satan by the Christ of *PR* can be seen as a part of this tradition. Merritt Y. Hughes contends that "*contemptus mundi* was never carried further by medieval pope or doctor of the Church than it was by Milton in this poem" (*Studies in Philology* 35 : 257). Arnold Stein offers a rejoinder; quoting the words of Hughes, he adds the following comment : "Milton does not declare the business of the world bankrupt. Satan has gotten control of some of the world's enterprises, but his power is usurped, and it is not complete; nor is the world incorrigibly rotten : Christ rejects the false allurements of Satan. Old heroes and old possibilities are respected" (*Heroic Knowledge* [1957], pp. 130–31). John M. Steadman accepts the distinction made by Stein but finds that it actually strengthens the *contemptus mundi* theme. A method common among seventeenth-century theologians was to compare and contrast the "true and eternal values of Heaven with the false and transitory goods of the world." Milton's Christ employs this same process of distinction, which "provides Christian ethics with an additional argument for despising the goods of this world as inferior to those of Heaven" (*Milton's Epic Characters: Image and Idol* [1968], pp. 131–32). [RF]

CONTROVERSIES. During his lifetime Milton was involved in the antiprelatical controversy in 1641ff.; the dispute over divorce, 1643ff.; the argument over regicide and the King's Book, 1649ff.; the antimonarchial debate, 1649ff.; and the settlement of the Restoration, 1660. For the first see *Animad, Apol, PrelE,* Joseph Hall, *A Postscript, RCG, Ref,* and Smectymnuus. For the second see *Bucer, Colas, DDD, Divorce, Marriage and divorce, Tetra.* For the third see Charles I, *Eikon Basilike, Eikon,* and Kingship. The question of authorship of *Eikon Basilike* continued long after Milton's death with the attendant wrangle over Pamela's prayer. For the fourth see *1Def, 2Def, 3Def,* Peter Du Moulin, Alexander More, *Responsio ad Apologia*

Anonymi, Salmasius, and *Tenure.* For the last see Antagonists, *Brief Notes, CivP, Hire,* Kingship, Sir Roger L'Estrange, and *Way.*

Since his death the major controversies have been those over blank verse*, Milton's alleged plagiarism (*see* William Lauder), Satan (*also see PL*), Arianism, and the dating of the works (*see* CHRONOLOGY). [JTS]

COOK, ALBERT S(TANBURROUGH) (1853–1927), scholar. After completing his undergraduate work at Rutgers University, Cook represented the considerable number of Americans who in the late-nineteenth and early-twentieth centuries went to Germany to complete their education. He studied there at the Universities of Göttingen and Leipzig and finally received his doctorate at Jena. Meanwhile he had organized on German lines the English Department at the new Johns Hopkins University. Until 1889 he was at the University of California at Berkeley; then he moved to Yale, where he remained until his retirement in the early 20s, its first professor of English language and literature and leader of its graduate program. In 1898 he served as president of the Modern Language Association, of which he had been a leader during its formative years.

Most of Cook's scholarship was done in Old and Middle English, but he produced several articles on Milton at the time when modern Milton scholarship was just being established. The most important is his extensive and still-valuable annotation of *Nat* (*Transactions of the Connecticut Academy of Arts and Sciences* 15 : 307–68), but he also suggested various sources for individual lines or images of other poems and analyzed Pareus's* view of the Apocalypse* as tragedy, to which Milton refers at the beginning of *SA* (*Archiv* 129 : 74–80). [WBH]

COPE FAMILY: *see* CHANCERY PRO-CEEDINGS.

COPERNICUS, NICOLAUS (1473–1543), Polish scientist, whose revolutionary doctrines helped awaken the world from the intellectual slumber of the Middle Ages. For 1400 years men had followed Ptolemy's theory that the earth was, in a sense, stationary and that the movements of heavenly bodies were real movements. Copernicus argued that the sun is the center of the universe, that the earth rotates on its own axis once every 24 hours, that the stars are vast objects, that some are planets, and that they are located at various distances from the earth. He reduced to order the "wandering" globes in the sky, in *De Revolutionibus Orbium Coelestium* (1543). Instead of the enclosed and finite universe of Ptolemy*, the new theory provided one of infinite space.

This revolutionary conception of space whetted Milton's imagination; throughout his life he was more interested in astronomy than in any other science* except geography*. Thus in *Educ* (4 : 283) Milton would require a thorough grounding in astronomy so that a student may pass an examination on general principles of this science before he moves on to the more theoretical subjects. He considers the study of heavenly bodies neither unlawful nor unprofitable in *CD* (17 : 151) and notes that astronomy flourished in England as early as the Saxons under Theodore of Canterbury (*Brit* 10 : 169). In *Logic* (11 : 317) he explains the importance of special precepts of astronomy, and in *1Def* (7 : 67) he laments ignorance of astronomy.

The heliocentric theory argued by Copernicus caused a complete revolution in man's conception of his relation to the universe. Problems associated with it are expressed in Raphael's description to Adam of the new cosmology in *PL* 8. 122ff. Raphael, however, warns Adam about inquiring too closely into "matters hid" when God is the only source of such occult knowledge; man's business is but to serve and fear God. Though relying upon the firm scientific conclusions of Copernicus, Milton seems to be skeptical of all more speculative, less scientific thinkers.

Though Copernicus's book had been dedicated (ironic as this fact is now) to Pope Paul III, it was not accepted but, after being merely tolerated for a brief period, was even openly renounced. Eventually in 1616 the Catholic Church made anti-Copernicanism an official church doctrine, and Protestants, reverting to pristine Christianity, discouraged its acceptance because the Bible might thus be dethroned. It was the church primarily that retarded recognition of Copernicus's discoveries, but Milton, inspired by truth, incorporates these recent discoveries into his epic as the highest angelic knowledge revealed to Adam. [ILD]

CORRESPONDENCE, PRINCIPLE OF.

A commonplace of the early Renaissance was a belief that the universe was harmoniously linked by a system of correspondences, whereby the natural order conformed to the divine. In the *Timaeus*, Plato* had asserted that in the world of ideas, each idea (or archetype) was the one eternal perfect form of all examples of any one kind. Along with the world of ideas was the world of space (or place), described as the nurse and receptacle of all generation; and under the agency of the Demiurgos, our world of appearances and the infinitely varied was created. This dualistic division opposed an ideal "real" world to a world of shadows and appearances, as described in Plato's myth of the cave (*Republic* 7. 514–18). It generated a subsequent assumption that the things seen in this world of change and appearances were *like* the things unseen in the other, that there was an image-likeness relationship between the phenomenal and nonphenomenal worlds.

Working on this assumption, Origen* said, citing St. Paul as his authority, that "the invisible things of God are understood by means of things that are visible, and that the things that are not seen are beheld through their relationship and likeness to things [seen]" (*Commentary on the Song of Songs*). Milton expressed a similar belief: "Our understanding cannot in this body found it selfe but on sensible things, nor arrive so clearly to the knowledge of God and things invisible as by the orderly conning over the visible and inferior creature . . ." (*Educ* 4 : 277; cf. *PL* 5. 568–76).

Based on these typical assumptions about correspondences, the principle allowed for analogies that ranged through every possible conception of human, divine, social, and cosmic relationship, and it was fundamental to the intricate correspondences between microcosm (man), geocosm (natural world), and macrocosm (universe), as most fully amplified by the quasi-occult writings of Paracelsus and Agrippa von Nettesheim. Astrology, alchemy, and hermeticism* are in great part based on application of these ideas, as the work of Marjorie Nicolson, Frances Yates, D. P. Walker, J. Mazzeo, and others has shown.

Following Cicero* (*De legibus* 3; *De re publica* 3) and Aquinas* (*Sum. Theo.* 1. 1. 90–97), Renaissance writers, including Milton, found a correspondence between the laws of nature*, man, and God, whereby the laws of man (society) were based on the laws of nature, and the laws of nature on the laws of God. A well-governed state was like a rational man in control of his desires and passions, and both were like a well-tended garden. Men ruled their wives as kings governed states, both displaying the rule of reason* over the "lower" passions. Such tidy beliefs were severely shaken by the emergence of empirical science* during the earlier seventeenth century, but Milton, like many of his contemporaries, persevered in the poetic use of these "conceits" and "similitudes"—images and figures he believed to be useful for conveying the symbolic truths of human nature. But perhaps even more important, Milton often qualified and reconsidered these commonplaces in ways that gave his poetry (more so than his prose) some of its distinctive brilliance. *See also* ACCOMMODATION, THEORY OF. [PEB]

CORRESPONDENTS. Milton wrote letters to his former tutors Alexander Gill*, Jr. (3), and Thomas Young* (2), to his friends Benedetto Bonmattei*, Carlo Dati*, Charles Diodati* (2), Lukas Holste*, and Henry Oldenburg* (4), to diplomatic friends Liewe van Aizema*, John Bradshaw*, Jean de Labadie*, Herman Mylius* (7), Leonard Philaras* (2), Ezekiel Spanheim*, and Bulstrode Whitelock*, to his former students* Richard Heath* and Richard Jones, Viscount Ranelagh* (4), and to acquaintances Emeric Bigot*, Henry de Brass* (2), and Peter Heimbach* (3). Manuscript letters to an unknown friend* and purportedly to his brother Christopher are also extant. These total forty-one letters and twenty-one recipients. These letters are reprinted in *CM* 12 and 18.

Extant letters to Milton come from Aizema, Dati (2), Diodati (2), Heimbach, Henry Lawes*, Andrew Marvell*, Mylius (16), Oldenburg (5) Andrew Sandelands* (2), Moses Wall*, and Sir Henry Wotton*. These total thirty-three letters and five additional correspondents, about whom separate entries are given. These letters are reprinted in *CM* 1, 12, 18, and in French's *Life Records* under dates of October 25, 1651; ca. June 1656; December 28, 1656; July 7, 1657; October 4, 1657; and December 12, 1659. Letter XLVII in the Columbia Milton (12 : 338–45) is from Mylius to George Weckerlin*, not to Milton. [JTS]

COSMOGRAPHY. "The study of Geography* is both profitable and delightfull," Milton wrote in his Preface to *Mosc* (10: 327). And in his essay *Educ* (4 : 283) he advises the pupil "to learn in any modern Author, the use of the Globes, and all the Maps; first with the old names, and then with the new." Even after he went blind we find him commissioning a friend traveling on the Continent to find out for him which is the best and most up-to-date atlas (12 : 83–85): "In the matter of the Atlas you have abundantly performed all I requested of you. . . . Be good enough, pray, to take so much farther trouble for me as to be able to inform me, when you return, how many volumes there are in the complete work, and which of the two issues, that of Blaeu or that of Jansen, is the larger and more correct." These passages are sufficient evidence to prove Milton's deep interest in cosmography, geography, and cartography. We know by his own admission in *Mosc* that he made extensive use of those two great authorities, Hakluyt's *Principal Navigations* (1598–1600) and Samuel Purchas* *His Pilgrimes* (1625). He was early aware of the seminal work in Abraham Ortelius's* *Theatrum Orbis Terrarum* and in Hexham's revision of Mercator, the former definitely more than the latter.

Three stages may be discerned in Milton's cosmographic knowledge. The first—and this stage is mainly reflected in the minor poems—is the one in which he is under the sway of classical and biblical traditions. There is then a stage when, it may be said, he is developing a geographic conscience. Here it would be hard to overestimate the influence of *Mosc* on his writing, for he clearly learned there the importance of making exact references to recent geographic discoveries. The third stage is one that is primarily operative in the late poems, *PL* and *PR*. The two most cosmographic passages in all of Milton occur in *PL* 11. 370ff. and *PR* 3. 267–321. In the first, the angel Michael surveys the whole known world as a lesson for Adam. In the latter, Satan, for his own evil ends, reveals to Christ the various kingdoms in all their glory and power. In both passages the determining influence is Peter Heylyn*. After blindness came on, it is noticeable that Milton resorted more and more to digests; that is to be expected. The amanuenses'* work would be made easier. Two matters should be observed in connection with Heylyn: his *Cosmographie* appeared in 1652 just prior to the time Milton again took up his work on *PL*; and it is in the nature of a compendium or digest. In an age of loose orthography it is characteristic of Milton that he should have been most accurate in his spelling of even complicated geographic terms. It is further remarkable how often his spelling squares with Heylyn's. Other travel books, such as Thomas Fuller's *A Pisgah-Sight of Palestine* (1650), together with George Sandys's popular *Relation of a Journey begun An. Dom. 1610* (1621), supplied Milton with updated material found in classical authors and in the Bible.

Generally speaking, Milton used the new cosmography to bring alive what had been traditional. While seeking analogies to the postlapsarian causeway built for Sin and Death across chaos to the created world (*PL* 10. 306–11), Milton could think of nothing better than Xerxes's bridge across the Hellespont. Herodotus* here dominates, but the passage gains freshness from Sandys's retelling (*Relation*, p. 25). Such is often Milton's procedure: a recent allusion is employed to move forward a passage into three-dimensional clarity. [RRC]

COSMOLOGY. At the end of *PL*, when Adam and Eve leave Eden, "The World [is] all before them where to choose / Thir place of rest" (12. 646–47), but the "world" of *PL* is larger than this, for it extends upward through the realms of the sun, the moon, the seven planets, the crystalline sphere, and the *primum mobile* to Chaos, a "void and formless infinite" (*PL* 3. 12). Above and beyond Chaos Milton places Heaven*, in which God is "high Thron'd above all highth" (*PL* 3. 58); below Chaos is Hell*, a "bottomless pit" (*PL* 6. 866). Since God's residence is of immeasurable height and Satan's of infinite depth, the exact shape of Milton's cosmos is difficult to define. The problem is compounded by Milton's assertions that Chaos is an "Illimitable Ocean without bound" (*PL* 2. 892), a "dark unbottom'd infinite Abyss" (*PL* 2. 405), "the nethermost Abyss" (*PL* 2. 956). Perhaps he means to imply that Chaos extends even below Hell; more likely, words like "unbottom'd" and "Illimitable" are qualitative, not quantitative terms. Certainly the vast distance between Heaven and Hell images their moral differences; the distance is so great that it took nine days

for Satan and his fellow angels to fall through Chaos to Hell (*PL* 6. 871–73); the fallen angels* are now "As far remov'd from God and light of Heav'n / As from the Center thrice to th'utmost Pole" (*PL* 1. 73–74). (Isabel G. MacCaffrey, *Paradise Lost as "Myth"* [1959], pp. 64–73; Jackson I. Cope, *ELH, A Journal of English Literary History* 26 [1959] : 497–513; and H. F. Robins, *Journal of English and Germanic Philology* 60 : 699–711, treat in some detail the moral meanings of place and direction in *PL*.)

In *Milton's Ontology, Cosmology, and Physics*, Walter Clyde Curry presents a workable diagram of a spherical cosmos with Hell at its base and a mountain of light at the top ([1966], p. 156, rptd. in Hughes's edition of the poetry and prose, p. 180). But the details of that diagram are debatable because, for example, nowhere in *PL* does Milton attribute shape to the whole cosmos. Curry portrays Heaven as round, and indeed Beelzebub remembers God's swearing "an Oath / That shook Heav'n's whole circumference" (*PL* 2. 352–53). Biblical precedent, on the other hand, would suggest that heaven is square (Rev. 21). Indeed, Sin, believing that Satan has succeeded in winning control of the Mundane World, contrasts God's "Quadrature" with Satan's "Orbicular World" (*PL* 10. 381); and Satan, viewing Heaven from a great physical and moral distance, sees it as "extended wide / In circuit, undetermined square or round" (*PL* 2. 1047–48). Nowhere in *PL*, however, does an altogether reliable witness define Heaven's shape.

In chapter 7, "Of the Creation," in *CD*, Milton distinguishes between the visible creation, which "comprises the material universe and all that is contained therein" (15 : 37), and the invisible creation, "the highest heaven, which is the throne and habitation of God, and the heavenly powers, or angels" (15 : 92). He hesitates to say when Heaven was created; it seems "improbable" that God should have formed it "only at so recent a period as at the beginning of the world," yet it "does not follow that heaven should be eternal" (15 : 29, 31). He does insist "that others have been too bold in affirming that the invisible and highest heaven was made on the first day, contemporaneously with that heaven which is within our sights. For it was of the latter heaven alone, and of the visible world, that Moses undertook to write" (15 : 31).

Neither is the chronology of Hell clear. But Milton contends that it was formed at some time distinctly before the six days in which the Mundane World was made. In *PL* Chaos complains that God seized part of his dominion when he created "first Hell / [Satan's] dungeon stretching far and wide beneath; / Now lately Heaven and Earth" (*PL* 2. 1002–4). Like Dante's* Hell, Milton's is a "hollow Deep" (*PL* 1. 314). In *CD* Milton quotes Luke 8 : 31 and Revelation 20 : 3 to prove that the "proper place" of the fallen angels is "the bottomless pit, from which they cannot escape without permission" (15 : 109). Milton departs from tradition in placing that pit below the rest of the cosmos, but in the argument to Book 1 of *PL,* he anticipates the surprise that his seventeenth-century readers must have felt at not finding it in the center of the earth. Hell, Milton explains, is "described here, *not in the Center* (for Heaven and Earth may be suppos'd as yet not made, certainly not yet accurst) *but in a place of utter darkness, fitliest called Chaos.*" In *CD* he argues that the writers of Luke, Matthew, and Revelation place Hell "beyond the limits of the universe . . . ; it does not seem probable that hell should have been prepared within the limits of this world, in the bowels of the earth, on which the curse had not as yet passed." Moreover, if Hell were at the center of the Mundane World, it would be destroyed by fire at the end of time, and that fate is "a consummation more to be desired than expected by the souls in perdition." Chrysostom*, Luther*, and "some other later divines," he maintains, hold similar views (16 : 373–75).

Although Heaven, Hell, and the Mundane World are protected from the inroads of Chaos—Heaven and Hell by walls and the Mundane World by its "firm opacous Globe" (*PL* 3.419), they are connected with one another by a system of gates and passageways. First, and most important in a poem dedicated to proving God's ultimate power over man's destiny, is the fact that "This pendant world" (i.e., the earth) hangs from Heaven by a "golden Chain" (*PL* 2. 1052, 51). Similarly, a stairway rather like the ladder on which Jacob saw angels ascending and descending (Gen. 28—cf. also the ladder connecting heaven and earth in Thomas Fuller's *A Pisgah-sight of Palestine* [1650] and the ladder that Dante sees in the Orb of Saturn [*Par.* 21]), is sometimes let down from the wall of Heaven to the shell of the World; beneath it is "A passage down to th'Earth" (*PL* 3. 528) upon which angels travel back and forth between Paradise and Heaven. A golden gate opens to permit Raphael to descend to Eden to converse with Adam and Eve; earlier, "Heav'n op'n'd wide / Her ever during Gates . . . / . . . to let forth the King of Glorie in his powerful Word / And Spirit coming to create new Worlds" (*PL* 7. 205–9).

Quite unlike the golden entryway to Heaven are the "thrice threefold" gates jealously guarded by Sin and Death at the "horrid Roof" of Hell : "three folds were Brass, / Three Iron, three of Adamantine Rock / Impenetrable, impal'd with circling fire / Yet unconsum'd" (*PL* 2. 645–48). Satan easily persuades Sin, who says she is forbidden by God to permit anyone to leave Hell, to use her key to unfasten those sturdy gates, and they "on a sudden op'n flie / With impetuous recoile and jarring sound"—not to be closed again (*PL* 2. 850–84). Following the precedent of Isaiah 14 and of medieval and Renaissance artists, Milton describes the "Yawning" Hell mouth as it admitted the fallen angels (*PL* 6. 636–37); at the end of time, he says, the Son of God will "obstruct the mouth of Hell / For ever, and seal up his ravenous Jawes" (*PL* 10. 636–37). But until that time, the gate of Hell welcomes sinful souls. After Satan enters Paradise*, Sin and Death build a "stupendious Bridge" (*PL* 10. 351), a "ridge of pendant Rock" (*PL* 10. 313), connecting the "Roots of Hell" (*PL* 10. 299) and the left-hand side of the shell of the Mundane World (*PL* 10. 322). (See Curry, pp. 153–54 for the view that this bridge is in fact a tunnel.) Satan proclaims that his bringing Sin into Paradise has "made one Realm / Hell and this World, one Realm, our Continent / Of easie thorough-fare" (*PL* 10. 391–93).

The terms with which Milton presents Sin and Death building the bridge joining Hell and this earth parody God's creation* of the World as it is described in the first verses of Genesis and in Book 7 of *PL* (E. M. W. Tillyard, *SP* 38 [1941] : 269). Sin and Death fly "divers, and with Power (thir Power was great) / Hovering upon the Waters," they crowd together whatever they find, "Solid or slimie" to build an "aggregated Soyle" (*PL* 10. 284–93). This episode brings into focus one of the principal problems in a description of Milton's cosmos: the relationships between God and Creator, the Mundane World He formed with His golden compass, and that wild abyss out of which the visible world is created. Clearly, "this pendant world" is the antithesis of Chaos, "The Womb of nature and perhaps her Grave" (*PL* 2. 911). Whereas the world within the *primum mobile* is carefully measured by God, Chaos is "without bound, / Without dimension, where length, breadth, & highth, / And time and place are lost" (*PL* 2. 892–94). Whereas God's will maintains the ceaseless motions of the spheres, in Chaos, "eldest Night / And *Chaos* . . . / Hold Eternal *Anarchie*"; "*Chance* governs all" (*PL* 2. 894–96, 910). In the sublunary world, the four elements, earth, air, fire, and water, "in quaternion run / Perpetual Circle, multiform; and mix / And nourish all things" (*PL* 5. 181–83), but in Chaos "hot, cold, moist, and dry," the qualities of the elements, "Strive . . . for Maistrie" (*PL* 2. 898, 899). Variously "light-arm'd or heavy, sharp, smooth, swift, or slow" (*PL* 2. 903), they constantly shift their allegiances to "warring Winds" (*PL* 2. 905).

The darkness of Chaos is a "palpable obscure" (*PL* 2. 406)—witness Satan's difficulty when "Ore bog or steep, through strait, rough, dense, or rare / . . . / [He] swims or sinks, or wades, or creeps, or flyes" (*PL* 2. 948–50). And yet, since these qualities are not atoms, but "embryon," that is, potential, atoms, they are incorporeal, and Chaos can be described as empty, as "the void immense" (*PL* 2. 829—see Lawrence Babb, *The Moral Cosmos of PL* [1970], pp. 106–9).

Precedents for the imagery defining the various attributes of Chaos are to be found in such widely different sources as Hesiod*, Plato*, the Greco-Roman atomists (including Aristotle*, Cicero*, Lucretius*, Ovid*, Epicurus, and Democritus), early commentators on hexameral* literature (among them Aquinas*, Ambrose*, Chrysostom*, and Basil*), and Renaissance cosmologists (including William Caxton, Robert Fludd*, and Thomas Vaughan). It is, however, to Milton's *CD* that one must look for a fairly complete understanding of the relationships between Milton's Chaos, which is a place, incorporeal matter within that place, and a personified character who threatens Satan but who obeys God's Word; the Mundane World; and God, "the primary, and absolute, and sole cause of all things" (15 : 21).

In *CD*, Milton "under the guidance of Scripture" proves "that God did not produce everything out of nothing, but of himself . . . all things are not only from God, but of God" (15 : 27). Milton uses Aristotelian terms to describe that creation : since God is "the sole cause of all things," He must be efficient, formal, final, *and* material cause of matter*. Matter, therefore, is "*substantially* [not accidentally] inherent in God"; unless one is willing to admit the existence of another, prior cause of matter, Milton argues, one must conclude that matter exists *in potentia* within a complete, perfect, infinite God (15 : 21–23). Matter is an "efflux of the Deity" (15 : 23); as Raphael tells Adam, "All things proceed" from God (*PL* 5. 470). To the objection that "body cannot emanate from spirit" Milton replies, "much less then can body emanate from nothing" (15 : 25). Matter has not always existed, he argues; it must have been created at some point in time, because it is "only a passive principle, dependent on the Deity, and subservient to him"; any other view is "inconceivable" (15 : 19–21). Original matter Milton describes as "not an evil* or trivial thing, but as intrinsically good. . . . It was a substance, and derivable from no other source than from the fountain of every substance, though at first confused and formless, being afterwards adorned and digested into order by the hand of God" (15 : 23—for an essentially Aristotelian understanding of the nature of matter and form, see William B. Hunter, Jr., *Journal of English and Germanic Philology* 45: 68–76 and *Journal of the History of Ideas* 13 : 551–62).

Milton's view of creation is somewhat like that of the Neoplatonists* Plotinus* and Proclus*, who also argue that matter emanates from God. Milton and the Neoplatonists differ, however, in that Plotinus and Proclus suppose that the creative act is eternal and necessary; Milton believes that matter was created at a point in time (15 : 19) by an act of God's will (see Curry, pp. 33–38). Certainly Milton's account of matter as an "efflux of Deity" and his asserting that original matter is "derivable . . . from the fountain of every substance" ("*ex fonte omnis substantiae derivanda*") (15 : 23, 22) has a Neoplatonic base. Similarly, the "embryon Atoms" (*PL* 2. 900) and "pregnant causes" (*PL* 2. 913) within Chaos are like Augustinian* "seminal reasons"; as A. B. Chambers says, Chaos "results from the implantation of active forms within a totally passive and formless matter." This formless matter is "perhaps identifiable with Night" (*Journal of the History of Ideas* 24 : 55–84). In *PL* 2, Milton portrays "eldest Night / And [her consort] Chaos, Ancestors of Nature" (2. 894–95), thus perhaps suggesting that mysterious Night, who is an entirely passive character in this epic, is indeed the "totally passive and formless matter"

out of which Chaos sprang. And yet one must pause to note that for Milton—as for Aristotle—matter and form are distinct only as logical categories; as Milton writes in the title to *Prol* 4, "In the destruction of any thing a resolution to primary matter does not occur" (see Hunter, *Journal of the History of Ideas* 13 : 553. Hunter also notes Christian commentators' appeals to Plato's notion of the Demiurgos who added form to matter; thus they explained how the first creation [Gen. 1 : 2] could be "without form.") Night, then, is a logical abstraction, nothing more; she is appropriately passive in *PL*.

The variously "hot, cold, moist, and dry" qualities warring within Chaos are potential earth, air, fire, and water, but they will not become material, corporeal elements "Unless th'Almighty Maker them ordain / His dark materials to create more Worlds (*PL* 2. 915–16). In the meantime, the undifferentiated space of Milton's Chaos is unlike Plato's in that Plato (in his *Timaeus*) assumes a prior, independent matter in his "receptacle" (see A. S. P. Woodhouse, *Philological Quarterly* 28: 220–21). Even so, Plato's "nurse of becoming" *is* like Milton's "Womb of nature," for "in both versions chaos is material, is possessed of qualities, and is elemental." And in both, chance, rather than necessity or Providence, rules (see Chambers, pp. 56–64). Alternately, Milton's chaotic space may be related to Aristotle's view of space as "that within which the presence of a concrete something is possible. . . . Matter cannot exist without space, and there is no space without matter" (see Babb, pp. 117–18); certainly Milton and Aristotle are alike in their monism.

And if there is no space without matter, neither can there be space without God; Milton's God tells His Son, "I am who fill / Infinitude, nor vacuous the space" (*PL* 7. 168–69). Denis Saurat's controversial "retraction theory," which supposes that God created this universe by withdrawing Himself from the realm of matter (see *Milton: Man and Thinker* [1925], esp. pp. 123–25), has been disputed by numerous recent scholars, among them

Woodhouse and Chambers, who argue that creation results "from the putting forth of God's active goodness into a passive and material principle eternally resident within himself" (Chambers, p. 70), and Curry, who suggests that "the finite worlds of creation are emanations 'within' the infinity of God, the incorporeal Being" (p. 42).

Milton's theory that original matter was "at first confused and formless, being afterwards adorned and digested into order by the hand of God" (*CD* 15 : 23) may suggest that he follows those Christians who—since Augustine—had distinguished two steps in God's creative process: the creation of the void and formless "deep" out of nothing, and the ordering of that chaotic deep into the perfect world. Yet Uriel, described by Curry as "a pious but not too perceptive physicist with inclinations towards atomistic philosophy" and Raphael, "the divine historian extraordinary . . . metaphysician, and indifferent physicist with Stoic or atomistic inclinations" (Curry, pp. 93, 102) both describe the process by which God transforms chaotic matter into the ordered, corporeal Mundane World as having a number of distinct steps. Whether or not they are the same steps as the four Aristotle suggests as logical distinctions (prime matter, four qualities, four elements, and corporeal matter—see Chambers, p. 81), those steps certainly indicate the intricacy of the distinction between incorporeal, material Chaos and the delicately ordered matter of the Mundane World. And so it is that Satan, having come from Hell through Chaos to the "opacous" shell of this world is astonished to discover what he sees; he "Looks down with wonder at the sudden view / Of all this World at once" (*PL* 3. 542–43).

Just before Satan, perched on the outer reaches of "the firm opacous Globe / Of this round World" (*PL* 3. 418–19), begins his descent to earth, Milton gives the reader a mirror image of his downward journey through the Mundane World in the account of the dying men who, ascending from earth, ". . . pass the

Planets seven, and pass the fixt, / And that Crystalline Sphear whose ballance weighs / The Trepidation talkt, and that first mov'd" (*PL* 3. 481–83). Although less explicitly, Satan encounters a similar universe as he pursues his devious route to his "journies end and our beginning woe" (*PL* 3. 633). Having passed through Chaos and now standing at a point on the outer edge of the prelapsarian cosmos where he may survey the Zodiac from eastern to western end, Satan plunges into the "pure marble Air" of the "Worlds first Region," winds his oblique way through the *primum mobile* and crystalline sphere to the "innumerable Starrs" of the eighth sphere, descends into the lower region of the planets, pauses at the "lucent Orbe" of the sun, and finally alights on earth's Mount Niphates to the north of Eden (*PL* 3. 555–742).

Although Satan's route through the Mundane World is no doubt intentionally vague—Milton describes it in Argument III merely as "his passage thence to the Orb of the Sun"—the earlier account of a ten-sphered world indicates clearly that the universe in *PL* is geocentric in static outline and based on the ancient Greek astronomical ideas summarized and modified in Claudius Ptolemy's* *Syntaxis* (or, as it was more popularly known, *Almagest*) of the second century A.D. To Ptolemy's basic system of a stationary earth surrounded by a nest of eight hollow revolving spheres containing the five planets, the sun and moon, and the fixed stars, later Arabian astronomers annexed two further spheres—the crystalline and the *primum mobile*. The Ptolemaic system, then, as represented in such handbooks available to Milton as seventeenth-century versions of Sacrobosco's [i.e., John Holywood's] *De Sphaera* (cf. A. H. Gilbert, *Publications of the Modern Language Association* 38: 297–307), consisted of ten spheres revolving about the immobile earth; outermost was the *primum mobile* (Milton's "first mov'd"), followed by the crystalline sphere, the sphere of fixed stars, and the seven spheres of the plants (Saturn, Jupiter, Mars, Sun, Venus, Mercury,

Moon). In traditional Ptolemaic cosmology, the region between the innermost or lunar sphere and earth was occupied by bands of fire and air, although Milton makes no mention in *PL* of this fiery division between sublunary and celestial areas. In the center of this great nest of concentric orbs lies earth, in Ptolemaic conception both "sedentarie" (*PL* 8. 32) or immobile and a mere "spot, a graine" (*PL* 8. 17) in comparison to the vast firmament.

While Milton uses the basic outlines of traditional Ptolemaic cosmology in *PL*, he introduces certain minor changes and emphasizes certain ideas to suit the demands of his epic. Hell, for instance, is not located within the confines of earth, as it is for Dante[*]; certain features from scriptural cosmology and some apparently from Milton's own invention augment the standard Ptolemaic constructions, aligning the Mundane World of *PL* with biblical text and creating for it a credible relationship with the supramundane universe. Furthermore, Milton does not activate his Ptolemaic universe into its complicated patterns of motion, although he does describe in simplified and metaphorical manner the visual image and audible results of these celestial motions.

The *primum mobile*, that "high first-moving Spheare" (*FInf* 39), was added by medieval Arabian astronomers to the Ptolemaic cosmos to account for the diurnal rotation of all heavenly bodies. Itself devoid of stars or planets, the *primum mobile*, set into perpetual motion by God, imparts this motion to all the spheres and orbs it encloses, except, of course, to earth. Moving with great speed, the *primum mobile* accomplishes one east-to-west revolution every twenty-four hours. As Adam notes, the heavens—presumably motivated by the Prime Mover—move at an "incorporeal speed . . . to describe whose swiftness Number failes" (*PL* 8. 37–38); even the "prime Orb," the sun, moves "incredible how swift" in its daily rotation (*PL* 4. 592–93). To explain the mechanics of this concept of celestial motion, some theorists held that the *primum mobile* simply swept the inner spheres along with it; others that the countermotion from west to east (or "proper" motion) of the sphere of fixed stars lessened the speed of the planetary spheres as they moved with the *primum mobile;* still others that all the planetary spheres enclosed within the *primum mobile* accomplished a contrary or proper motion and that the progressively slower sidereal revolutions of the outer spheres was caused by the neutralizing effect of the *primum mobile*. Hence, the sphere of the moon, furthest inward from the *primum mobile*, completed its rotation in the relatively shortest time ($27\frac{1}{3}$ days), while the sphere of Saturn, closest to the *primum mobile*, required the longest time (30 years). (See K. Svendsen, *Milton and Science* [1956], p. 54.)

For some readers, the *primum mobile* of *PL* serves another and different purpose of acting as the solid shell, "the firm opacous Globe" (*PL* 3. 418), around the created universe, which 1) protects it against the "ever-threatning storms / Of *Chaos* blustring round" (*PL* 3. 425–26); 2) supports the Golden Ladder let down from Heaven; 3) provides a foundation for the causeway from Hell; and 4) serves as a location for the Paradise of Fools. Although Milton says nothing explicit about the composition of the *primum mobile*—traditionally it was incorporeal and transparent, hence unsuitable for the purposes of protecting the universe and providing foundation—its supralunary position implies that it is an etherous body, and ether in *PL* may take a solid form, as it does in the planets. This fact, coupled with the scarcity of cosmological precedent for an outer shell separate from and external to the *primum mobile*, has led to the assumption that the outer shell and the *primum mobile* are in fact the same (see H. F. Robins *Studies in Honor of T. W. Baldwin*, ed. D. C. Allen [1958], pp. 211–19). However, since this encasing orb seems to be motionless, its opening remaining stationary beneath the Gate of Heaven and "just o're the blissful seat of

Paradise" (*PL* 3. 527), and since Milton's translation of *primum mobile* as "first mov'd" (as opposed to "First Mover") implies that the tenth sphere is in motion, other readers have concluded that the two are not the same and that the world of *PL* consists of the earth encircled by ten revolving spheres, all of which are enclosed by a solid, motionless, opaque shell, which Milton adds to his Mundane World because it requires protection from the turmoils of Chaos (see Babb, p. 62).

The crystalline or ninth sphere was added by the Arabians to the Ptolemaic eight-sphered world to account for "Trepidation," a theory of extensive and dubious speculation, as Milton's adjective "talkt" (*PL* 3. 483) implies. To explain the observable minute annual westward shift of the sun in relationship to the stars, Ptolemy proposed the idea of the precession of the equinoxes, or that the point of intersection between the ecliptic of the sun and the plane of the earth's equator advances slowly over a period of years. Arabian astronomers, noting incorrectly that precession did not advance uniformly in one direction but seemed to oscillate backwards and forwards, refined Ptolemy's theory into one of variable precession, or trepidation, the false notion that the point of intersection advances and recedes for an equal amount of time but for unequal distances (see J. L. E. Dreyer, *A History of Astronomy* [1953], pp. 202–5). The slow eastward motion of the crystalline sphere would account for the progression of the equinoxes through the heavens, while the supposition that the poles of the eighth sphere of fixed stars slowly described small circles on the inner surface of the crystalline sphere accounted for the presumed oscillation or variation in precession (see F. R. Johnson, *Astronomical Thought* [1937], pp. 54–55). Either Milton is uninterested in or unconvinced by trepidation—Tycho Brahe was the first to challenge the theory—for he mentions it and the crystalline sphere only once and briefly in *PL*.

Some controversy has resulted over the composition and function of Milton's crystalline sphere, which in traditional Ptolemaic cosmology is invisible or transparent and has the sole purpose of accounting for trepidation. Earlier commentators have maintained that the "waters above the firmament" of Genesis 1 : 7, which God divides from the "waters below," are synonymous with the "circumfluous Waters" of the "wide Crystalline Ocean" (*PL* 7. 270–71) or the "cleer *Hyaline*, the Glassie Sea" (*PL* 7. 619), and with the ninth or crystalline sphere. The "firmament," in other words, refers to the eighth sphere of fixed stars, as indeed it sometimes did in Renaissance and seventeenth-century cosmology (see Svendsen, p. 56), and the "waters above" occupy the crystalline sphere. But it has been convincingly argued that Milton mentions the crystalline sphere only once in *PL* (3. 482); reserves for it the sole function of accounting for trepidation; conceives of its composition in traditional Ptolemaic terms; and locates the biblical supercelestial waters referred to in *PL* 7. 270–71 and 619, beyond the outermost sphere of the universe, the "uttermost convex / Of this great Round" (*PL* 7. 266–67) or the intangible arc described by the Creator's golden compass (H. F. Robins, *Publications of the Modern Language Association* 69: 903–14). The "waters above" thus enclose the created universe and it is these same waters flowing about the stairs descending from the Gate of Heaven that Satan observes on the outer shell of the universe (Argument III). The outer shell protects the universe from the warring elements of Chaos; the supercelestial waters, however, provide an insulation for the Mundane World against the wide extremes of temperature in Chaos, "least fierce extreames / Contiguous . . . distemper the whole frame" (*PL* 7. 272–73). Just as the earth itself is "with her nether Ocean circumfus'd" (*PL* 7. 624), so the Mundane World is encompassed by its "Crystallin Ocean."

The eighth sphere, that of the innumerable "fixt Starrs, fixt in thir Orb that flies" (*PL* 5. 176), was already thought to contain well over a thousand stars in early catalogues. Its most famous member was the pole star, around which the others seemed to revolve and which coincided with the imaginary axis of the universe (cf. *AdP* 34 and *Vac* 34). As a group, the stars of this sphere, which derive most of their luminous quality from the sun (*PL* 7. 359–69), are incorruptible, unchanging and, as part of God's plan, serve benevolently with the planets to "divide the Day from Night," to be "Signes, for Seasons, and for Dayes, and circling Years," and "to illuminate the Earth" (*PL* 7. 340–50; cf. also *PL* 4. 660–73, and 9. 104ff.). After the Fall*, however, the stars are no longer incorruptible, unchanging, or necessarily benevolent. They may now possess an astrological "influence malignant" (*PL* 10. 662) and the phenomena of *novae* (or new stars) suggests that man's corruption has had a similar effect on the previously immutable heavens.

Of the seven planets that occupy the spheres between that of the fixed stars and earth, Milton pays most attention in *PL* to the sun and moon, as did the majority of his contemporaries. The sun, according to scriptural cosmology the receptacle of light created first among the celestial bodies (*PL* 7. 354–55), is "of this great World both Eye and Soule" (*PL* 5. 171) and holds the central or midway position among the seven planets. It gives light and life to the earth (*PL* 3. 581 and 609ff.; 5. 423ff.) and is the object of wonderment by the entire created universe, Satan included (*PL* 3. 591ff.). Originally following a prescribed course along the celestial equator, the sun passed directly over Eden daily so that "Spring / Perpetual smil'd on Earth with vernant Flours, / Equal in Days and Nights" (*PL* 10. 678–80). After the Fall, however, "Som say the Sun / Was bid turn Reines from th'Equinoctial Rode" (*PL* 10. 671–72). This dislocation of the center of the sun's orbit caused its path over the earth to be lower in winter than in summer, and thus to "affect the Earth with cold and heat / Scarce tollerable" (*PL* 10. 653–54).

Created next after the sun and less bright than it, the moon was set in the heavens to mirror the superior planet "with full face borrowing her Light / From him" (*PL* 7. 377–78). But in the postlapsarian cosmos, the "blanc Moon" too may have its bad effects prescribed by God (*PL* 10. 656ff.), just as it may be lured by the charms of Night-Hags and Lapland Witches into "labouring" eclipses (*PL* 2. 660–66). Like the moon, the other five planets are taught "thir planetarie motions and aspects / In *Sextile, Square,* and *Trine,* and *Opposite,* / Of noxious efficacie, and when to joyne / In Synod unbenigne" (*PL* 10. 658–61). To Milton, however, not all planetary influence is hostile, for while "Saturn's star has oft rested heavy on shepherds" (*EpDam* 79), while "the cross dire-looking Planet smites" (*Arc* 52), Jupiter and Phoebus and the grandson of Atlas must have "with kindly eyes surveyed" Manso* at birth (*Mansus* 85–86), just as the stars are "bending one way their pretious influence" (*Nat* 71). Planetary influence in the postlapsarian world simply carries out the order and plan of God; it consents "oftest with reason but never contrary" (*Tetra* 4 : 190).

At the center of the created universe lies the earth, which to Adam and to Ptolemaic cosmologists generally seems a mere atom, a "punctual spot" (*PL* 8. 23) in comparison with the vast size of the firmament. Traditionally, the sublunar world was thought to be ringed by concentric spheres of the terrestrial elements distributed according to their weight. Closest to earth, of course, is a region of water, then a middle region of several bands of air, and finally, just beneath the moon, a sphere of fire. To form these several sublunar zones, the four elements at the time of Creation sought out their proper levels—"Swift to thir several Quarters hasted then / The cumbrous Elements, Earth, Flood, Aire, Fire, / And this Ethereal quintessence of Heav'n / Flew upward" (*PL* 3. 714–17). Although Milton nowhere directly mentions the existence of the sphere of fire in the world of *PL*, his imagery of shooting stars, comets, meteors and the like (cf. *PL* 4.

556–60 and 12. 633–36) perhaps implies its existence, for these phenomena were thought to be evaporations or "exhalations" that rise from the earth and are ignited by heat from the sphere of fire or the sun. The middle region of air is itself divided into three spheres or zones. The upper zone, because of its proximity to the sphere of fire, is hot and dry; the middle zone is cold, often causing the condensation of rising aqueous vapors into snow, hail and rain (cf. *PL* 1. 515–17 and 4. 940); the lower zone, warmed by the reflection of the sun's rays from earth, contains the air mortals breathe.

Milton's conception that the "Earth self ballanc't on her Center hung" (*PL* 7. 242) might have derived from authorities as diverse as Ovid* and Galileo*, but more likely is based on Job 26 : 7 : "He hangeth the earth upon nothing" (Hughes, p. 352). With Eve's sin, "Earth felt the wound" (*PL* 9. 782), and with Adam's complicity, "Earth trembl'd from her entrails, as again / In pangs" (*PL* 9. 1000–1001). According to Ptolemaic theory, earth's "wound," the effect of man's corruption, caused an imbalance in the globe, a tilting of its axes : "Some say he [God] bid his Angels turne ascance / The Poles of Earth twice ten degrees and more / From the Suns Axle; they with labor push'd / Oblique the Centric Globe" (*PL* 10. 668–71). With the equator now $23\frac{1}{2}$ degrees south of Eden, the earth no longer enjoyed perpetual spring and was subjected to piercing extremes of cold and heat, to storms and winds, to "sideral blast, / Vapour, and Mist, and Exhalation hot, / Corrupt and Pestilent" (*PL* 10. 693–95).

Aside from minor additions and deletions, Milton's model for his created universe in *PL* is essentially Ptolemaic. But the complicated processes and patterns by which the Ptolemaic universe moves are only vaguely suggested in the epic. Brief allusion to the three primary motions of the planetary bodies in Ptolemaic theory—epicycles, eccentrics, and equants—occurs in Raphael's comparison of the dance of the angels* to that of the planets : "Mystical dance, which yonder starrie Spheare / Of Planets and of fixt in all her Wheeles / Resembles nearest, mazes intricate, / Eccentric, intervolv'd, yet regular / Then most, when most irregular they seem" (*PL* 5. 620–24). But Milton's cosmos in *PL* runs by no such complicated mechanism; indeed, Raphael mocks the "quaint Opinions wide" of those Ptolemaic astronomers who provoke God's laughter when they "come to model Heav'n / And calculate the Starrs, how they will weild / The mightie frame, how build, unbuild, contrive / To save appeerances, how gird the Sphear / With Centric and Eccentric scribl'd o're, / Cycle and Epicycle, Orb in Orb" (*PL* 8. 79–84).

Milton's universe in *PL* does move, even if in less complicated patterns, for he conceives of earth as a "Terrestrial Heav'n, danc't round by other Heav'ns" (*PL* 9. 103). The stars dance their "Starry dance" (*PL* 3. 580) and the planets "move in mystic Dance not without Song" (*PL* 5. 177–78). Audible proof of this heavenly dance is the music of the spheres, the beautifully harmonious sound produced by the motions of the heavenly bodies and their enclosing spheres. Milton frequently makes reference to this ancient Pythagorean conception of the universe as a huge, perfectly-tuned musical instrument (cf. *Nat* 125–32, *Arc* 62ff.), and he expresses the divinely ordered nature of the cosmos in *PL* through the "harmonie Divine" of the moving spheres (see S. Spaeth, *Milton's Knowledge of Music* [1913], pp. 100–123). This "ninefold harmony," delightful to God, was audible to unfallen man, but those now of "human mould with gross unpurged ear" (*Arc* 72) can no longer hear the sphere-music.

Although Milton uses the Ptolemaic model and makes passing reference to its mechanics in *PL,* there is ample evidence in the poem that he is familiar with other cosmological systems and models of his age. As Grant McColley has shown (*Studies in Philology* 34 : 209–47), Milton might have chosen a cosmological pattern from as many as four other competing schools of thought in the seventeenth century. Besides the Ptolemaists, there were the Copernicans*, who reproposed the ancient idea of a heliocentric universe with a planetary order of Mercury, Venus, Earth (which performed a double or triple motion) and Moon, Mars, Jupiter and, outermost from the sun, Saturn; the Tychonic school, which developed one of the oldest astronomical theories of a geoheliocentric universe in which the sun and moon revolve around the stationary earth, while the five lesser planets revolve in differing fashion around the sun; the "pluralists," who revived the concept condemned by the Church Fathers of an infinite number of world-universes, usually heliocentric, in which the other planets, particularly the moon, were inhabitable earths capable of supporting life; and those who believed in the diurnal rotation of the earth, a theory sometimes combined with one or more of the above cosmological systems (see McColley, *Isis* 26 : 392–402).

Of these five systems or theories, Milton mentions all but the geoheliocentric or Tychonic in *PL,* even though they have little relevance to the Ptolemaic universe set forth in Book 3. The heliocentric or Copernican system receives brief notice in the astronomical debate of *PL* 8, but it is clearly acknowledged in Raphael's question, "What if the Sun / Be Center to the World, and other Starrs, / By his attractive vertue and thir own / Incited, dance about him various rounds?" (*PL* 8. 122–25). More extensive discussion occurs about the theory of a plurality of worlds : Satan, as he passes through the eighth sphere, notes that the fixed stars "seemd other Worlds" (*PL* 3. 566); each new start of the Creation is "perhaps a World / Of destind habitation" (*PL* 7. 621–22); Raphaél suggests the possibility of "other Suns . . . with thir attendant Moons" (*PL* 8. 148–49). The possibility of the moon's being an inhabitable planet like earth also receives relatively major attention : the "*Tuscan* Artist" Galileo examines the moon with a telescope "to descry new Lands, / Rivers or Mountains in her spotty Globe" (*PL* 1. 288–91) and observes "Imagind Lands and Regions in the Moon" (*PL* 5. 262–63); Raphael inquires what "if Land be there, / Feilds and Inhabitants : Her spots thou seest / As Clouds, and Clouds may rain, and Rain produce / Fruits in her soft'nd Soile, for some to eate / Allotted there?" (*PL* 8. 144–48). Speculation concerning the diurnal rotation of the earth also occurs in the astronomical debate : Adam, for instance, questions why the "sedentarie Earth," less noble than the heavens, "attaines her end without least motion," while on the nobler heavens is imposed "restless revolution day by day" (*PL* 8. 25–38; cf. also 8. 129ff. and 160ff.).

The alternate cosmological systems mentioned in *PL,* however, are rejected. Concerning the plurality of worlds, Raphael tells Adam to "Dream not of other Worlds, what Creatures there / Live, in what state, condition or degree" (*PL* 8. 175–76). The other systems, including the celestial mechanics of the Ptolemaists, are likewise dismissed in Raphael's warning to Adam that God's ways are mysterious and that He "plac'd Heav'n from Earth so farr, that earthly sight, / If it presume, might erre in things too high, / And to no advantage gaine" (*PL* 8. 120–22). While Milton clearly recognizes and shows interest in other cosmologies than the Ptolemaic, he makes no value judgments about their relative worth. Why he chose the world model he did is problematic, but one must conclude that although Milton realized this system was somewhat outdated, as he hints throughout Book 8, it was nevertheless a cosmos entirely familiar to his audience, one that did not contradict or could accommodate scriptural details as divergent as Joshua's command that the earth be still and the sun move and the waters above, and one that allowed a poet ample opportuinty to set up a vast and ordered series of correspondences between the terrestrial and celestial, the mundane and supramundane. *See also* SCIENCE, MILTON AND. [SS and EHH]

COSTANZO, ANGELO DI (1507–1591), Neapolitan historian. Di Costanzo began collecting materials for a history of Naples about 1527 with the intention of correcting errors in Pandolfo Collenuccio's *Compendio delle storie del regno di Napoli.* Eight books appeared in 1572. For nine more years, he labored until twenty books were ready for publication in 1581. A second printing of the history appeared the next year. The work, which spans the years 1250–1486, is still a valuable source of Neapolitan history. In addition to the *Historia,* di Costanzo wrote poetry, but his *Rimes,* published posthumously, were apparently unknown to Milton.

Milton extracted two examples from di Costanzo's *Historia del Regno di Napoli* for *CB.* The first illustrated the topic the Good Man : "a noble Provençal knight" was not killed during the fury of the Sicilian Vespers (1282) "because of his great virtue and kindness." The second exemplified the right of a subject to rebel against a tyrant : Count Caserta, learning that King Manfred "was keeping the Countess of Caserta as his concubine," asked the Pope and King Charles whether or not he might be released from his allegiance to Manfred. They agreed that a vassal might withdraw his oath of loyalty in such circumstances. [RMa]

COTTON, JOHN: *see* CHANCERY PROCEEDINGS.

COUNCIL OF STATE, THE. With the execution of Charles I on January 30, 1649, England was left without an executive body, at least in the minds of those who denied the right of succession to the young Charles II*. Parliament moved swiftly to fill this constitutional gap and on February 17, 1649, the first Council of State of the Commonwealth met in Derby House. It shortly removed to its permanent seat in the Great Chamber of the old Whitehall Palace on the west side of King Street. The Council was a body of forty-one men elected by Parliament for the most part from their own ranks. Parliament, wary of the concentration of powers in the hands of any single person, directed that there would be no permanent president of the Council and that the membership would be determined by annual Parliamentary elections. The Council operated through several standing committees; among the most important were those for Admiralty, Ireland, Scotland, Army, Ordnance, and after December 1651, a Committee for Trade and Foreign Affairs. Business falling outside these areas was conducted by the appointment of a flood of *ad hoc* committees, and all of them reported their findings back to the Council for final decisions on major items.

Parliament established a quorum of nine, realistically as it developed, for attendance was erratic; during the first year, for example, there was an average of 13.4 members per meeting. The Council sat almost daily, except for Sunday, coordinating its hours with those of Parliament, for its members were called upon to attend sessions of both bodies, particularly in matters that required Parliamentary approval. The chief figures in the Council during its early years were John Bradshaw*, Oliver St. John, Sir Henry Vane*, the two Commissioners of the Great Seal, Bulstrode Whitelocke* and John Lisle, and, of course, Oliver Cromwell*. The "Lord Lieutenant," though immensely influential in establishing the body, had little direct influence on deliberations during its first years, since, except for a brief period in 1650, he was in the field campaigning until October 1651.

The Council was served by a secretariat headed by a General Secretary, Gualter Frost, Sr.; aided by his son, Gualter Frost, Jr.; Edward Dendy, Serjeant-at-arms; Sir Oliver Fleming, Master of Ceremonies; and after March 20, 1649, John Milton, Secretary for Foreign Tongues*. A number of others, including such figures as John Hall, Samuel Hartlib*, and Theodore Haak*, were engaged from time to time as the occasion arose. Milton was the only member of the permanent secretariat specifically designated as responsible for foreign affairs until March 1652, when Georg Weckherlin* was employed to assist him.

When Cromwell dismissed the Rump Parliament on April 20, 1653, he also dissolved the fifth Council of State, replacing it with an interim Council of Thirteen, the majority of whom were military figures. The Barebones Parliament, which convened on July 4, again elected members of the Council, now reduced to thirty-one in number, including all of the Council of Thirteen. This body was short-lived, however, for Cromwell again dismissed the Council when he dissolved Parliament in December 1653, making way for the establishment of the Protectorate.

Such was the Council of State for the Commonwealth. When Cromwell assumed the position of Protector on December 16, he established a Council very different in character and functions from its predecessors. It was designated the "Lord Protector's Council"; and after Cromwell had accepted the prerogatives of the king in all but name, it was called the "Privy Council." This body was far more stable in membership, since it was not subject to Parliamentary elections. It was composed of men selected by Cromwell, hence far more narrow in outlook, though it did reflect the political realities of England at the time, where the focus of power continued to be the New Model Army. It numbered fifteen members during most of its five-and-one-half years of existence and the majority of these, like the Council of Thirteen, were military figures. In 1654, for example, aside from Cromwell the membership included three major generals, five colonels, and one major. Changes in the body were very few, the most prominent additions being Nathaniel Fiennes (May 1654), Charles Fleetwood* (December 1655), John Thurloe* (June 1657), and Richard Cromwell* (December 1657); and the most important deletion that of John Lambert (June 1657), who refused to take the oath of loyalty to Cromwell. Henry Lawrence* presided as Lord President of the Council during its entire tenure.

The Council, in concert with the Lord Protector, continued to act as the executive body of the government, though inevitably, as Cromwell's powers waxed, his Council's waned. It met less frequently than its predecessors, until during the last months of Cromwell's life it was reduced to a carefully regulated nine meetings a month, alternating between Hampton House and Westminster. The authority of Council over domestic affairs continued to be all but absolute, but its influence in foreign affairs diminished as Cromwell and an inner circle of advisers, including Lawrence, Fiennes, and Thurloe, assumed the traditional prerogatives of the English monarch in that area.

The structure of the secretariat changed under the able direction of John Thurloe, who was engaged as General Secretary to the Council on the death of Gualter Frost, Sr., in March 1652. The two clerks, Henry Scobell and William Jessop, assumed the bulk of the routine duties for the Council, and Thurloe concentrated his efforts in the areas of intelligence and foreign affairs. John Milton's name almost disappears from the minutes of the Council of State, presumably because what duties he had were in the area of foreign affairs and in that capacity he was more often responsible directly to the Protector, through the office of Thurloe. Philip Meadows* was engaged as Latin Secretary in 1653; and after his appointment as Ambassador to Portugal and Denmark, Andrew Marvell* and Nathaniel Sterry were hired in that capacity (September 1657), with occasional assistance from Samuel Hartlib and John Dryden*.

The Lord Protector's Council continued to function under Richard Cromwell until May 1659, when the newly convened Long Parliament terminated the Protectorate and, asserting its authority, reestablished the old Council of State of thirty-one elected members. The month of May 1659 marks the last of Milton's *StateP* and presumably the last of his duties for the Council, though Masson concludes that he remained in office until February 1660. The Council continued to sit in one form or the other during the ensuing political chaos until it was dissolved upon the Restoration of Charles II in May 1660. [RTF]

COUNCIL OF TRENT: *see* COUNTER REFORMATION.

COUNTER REFORMATION, THE, a term applied to both internal reform of the Roman Catholic Church and the movement to regain those people and territories lost to Protestant groups. Internal reform had its origins within the early Church long before the beginning of the Protestant Reformation, and is thus called the "Catholic Reformation." The Oratory of Divine Love, begun at Genoa in 1497 and separate from the Protestant movement, is cited by Catholic authorities as one evidence of "Counter Reform" within the Church. Another is the creation of new Religious Orders, such as the Order of the Blessed Savior (Sweden, 1346), and the like. Outward reform begun under Pope Leo X (1513–1521) first sought to reestablish the strength of the Church by creation of new orders, such as the Theatines (1524), Capuchins (1525), and Barnabites (1530). Paul III (1534–1549) brought reformers like Giampietro Carafa, Gasparo Contarini, Jacopo Sadoleto, and Reginald Pole into the sacred college. The Society of Jesus was established in 1534 under the leadership of St. Ignatius of Loyola: and, in 1542, Paul III formed the papal Inquisition. Under Pope Paul IV (1555–1559) vigorous reforms were carried out, such as reduction of the size of the Curia and closer scrutiny of fiscal matters.

As a unified and organized force, the Counter Reformation may be said to have begun with the last session (1562–1563) of the Council of Trent (1545–1563). Pius IV (1559–1565) brought the Council of Trent to a conclusion and began to implement its recommendations. Pius V (1566–1572) continued the reforms, specifically com-

bating Protestant attacks on Thomistic philosophy by designating St. Thomas* a Doctor of the Church. Missionaries (usually Jesuits) went into those areas of Europe lost to the Protestants. In 1542 the Jesuits were established in Bavaria; they entered Poland in 1570, England in 1580, and Switzerland in 1586. There was also a strong effort by the Church to bring the arts back to religious purposes. Less measurable, but nevertheless significant, was a revitalization of the Catholic spirit in individuals. Some of these heroes were St. Charles Borromeo, St. Philip Neri, St. Francis of Sales, St. Teresa of Avila, St. John of the Cross, and St. Vincent de Paul. The Counter Reformation may be said to have come to an end by the latter half of the seventeenth century (although reforms within the Church have continued until modern times).

In *Areop* Milton declares that the practice of licensing of books "was never heard before, till that mysterious iniquity provokt and troubl'd at the first entrance of Reformation" (4 : 305), and that licensing was taken up "to no other purpose but to obstruct and hinder the first approach of Reformation" (4 : 306). Milton associates licensing with the Inquisition (4 : 299), speaks bitterly of the Council of Trent and the Spanish Inquisition for creating the indexes and catalogues of forbidden books, and calls these two institutions "the most Antichristian Councel, and the most tyrannous Inquisition that ever inquir'd" (4 : 305). Of particular significance is *TR*, which demonstrates an awareness of Catholic efforts to enlarge power in England. In this tract, Milton speaks of "the increase of Popery" and "the growth of this Romish weed" (6 : 165). Milton's purpose is to show "how to remove it [Popery] and hinder the growth thereof" (6 : 173); his underlying concern is the leaning of Charles II* (and the Duke of York) toward Roman Catholicism. [JWH]

COVENANT RELIGION. The term *covenant* calls to mind those agreements of the Old Testament between, for example, God and Moses concerning the role of the chosen people in the coming of Jesus, or the New Testament covenant between Jesus and those who believe in him. Protestantism gave the term new life. Calvin's* idea of covenant was strongly unilateral, with man accepting God's terms, but Calvinism subsequently modified toward a mutual covenant, closer to the orthodox dogma of Puritanism. Federalism, or federal covenant, the covenant of a group in a single place, conditional for its continuation upon group allegiance to God but not in itself meritorious toward salvation, was one extension of Calvinism, developed in particular by the writings of John Cocceius (d. 1669). Puritanism generally, especially the Separatists, for whom covenant theology was agreeable, emphasized mutual agreement in covenants. For Milton's contemporaries covenants were compacts made for mutual protection against external dangers, thus often used to provide organizational cohesiveness to otherwise loosely grouped sects of believers, and as such were agreements between men, rather than strictly between men and God, as part of the congregational impulse of Puritan church development.

Two notable covenants in Milton's day were the Solemn League and Covenant (1638) of the Scottish Presbyterians and the Presbyterian Covenant (1643) in support of the English presbyterian type of church against the prelates to which Milton presumably subscribed when it appeared but later (1649) scorned as a "ridling Covnant . . . seeming to sweare counter almost in the same breath Allegeance and no Allegeance" (*Tenure* 5:36). Milton's use of the idea of covenant extended beyond religion to, for example, marriage* : "Mariage is a cov'nant the very beeing whereof consists, not in a forc't cohabitation, and counterfet performance of duties, but in unfained love and peace" (*DDD* 3, pt. 2, 400). In other writings he pointed out the essential nature, as he saw it, of mutual consent between deliberate persons, for covenant can be "exercis'd on them only who have willingly joind themselves in that covnant of union" (*CivP* 6:10), thus excluding infants, even those baptized into faith. Furthermore, he stated, "Covnants are ever made according to the present state of persons and of things. If I make a voluntary Covnant as with a man, to doe him good, and he prove afterward a monster to me, I should conceave a disobligement" (*Tenure* 5:35). Milton's conception of covenant, while emphasizing the mutuality of the agreement, depended as well on the continued good faith and benefit of the parties. No "Law or Cov'nant how solemne or strait soever, either between God and man, or man and man, though of Gods joyning, should bind against a prime and principall scope of its own institution, and of both or either party cov'nanting" (*DDD* 3, pt. 2, 390). In *CD* he defined religious covenant in the following manner : "If our personal religion were not in some degree dependent on ourselves, and in our own power, God could not properly enter into a covenant with us" (15:215). Such a covenant was to Milton not Old Testament in nature, for there God imposed his will on people, but distinctly Christian, a new covenant of grace, a true covenant that allowed voluntary acceptance by man. Milton approved the idea of covenant with its sense of independence and freedom, though he was ready to criticize a forced covenant, for instance that of the Presbyterians*. [BEM]

COWLEY, ABRAHAM (1618–1667), poet whose first published book, *Poetical Blossoms*, appeared in 1633 when he was fifteen years old. Its earliest piece had been written five years earlier. Milton may allude to such precocity in *Sonn* 7 as the product of "some more timely-happy spirits," though he would have had to see the boy's work in manuscript. Cowley wrote steadily as he continued in school. With a B.A. (1639) and an M.A. (1642) from Cambridge, he turned to the Loyalist cause. A play, *The Guardian* (1642), was revised as *The Cutter of Coleman Street*, to achieve moderate success after the Restoration. *The Mistress* (1647), a collection of love poems, won him a large following and a high reputation that was enhanced by the appearance of his *Poems* in 1657, including his incomplete epic, the *Davideis*, written in college. After his death he rather quickly lost the immense popularity that had made him during his lifetime England's most popular poet.

Elizabeth Minshull reported that Cowley was one of Milton's favorite English poets, naming him together with Spenser* and Shakespeare*. If this statement can be believed, one must note that the Puritan shows no influence whatever of the ideas of the Loyalist. Weismiller has suggested (*Lyric and Dramatic Milton* [1965], pp. 139ff.) profound indebtedness of the choral structures of *SA* to Cowley's pseudo-Pindaric odes (of the *Poems,* 1657), though Cowley has far more rimed lines. But, he insists, "That the *Pindarique Odes* influenced Milton strongly . . . is hardly to be doubted" (p. 144), though one may question whether the evidence is overwhelming. [WBH]

COWLEY, WILLIAM (1731–1800), poet. Cowper's significance in Milton studies lies in the influence that Milton held over his poetry, in the important translations of the Italian and Latin poems and tributes, and in a series of notes for a projected edition of *PL*. Allusions to Milton also occur in numerous letters to various people over a number of years. Cowper's life was one of highs and lows through his frequent attacks of madness and suicidal attempts. His delusions involved religious rantings and terrors. His poetic work, translation, and commentary were often therefore interrupted and not all the projects he spent much time on were completed by the time of his death. *Poems by William Cowper, of the Inner Temple, Esq.* was first published in 1782. Successive editions added poems more recently composed. Around 1791, after his translation of Homer's *Iliad* and *Odyssey,* Cowper undertook to edit Milton's poems with Joseph Johnson, the publisher, who had produced Cowper's own first volume.

It was to be illustrated by Henry Fuseli* and to include Cowper's translations and commentary. Announcement was made in a subsequent eighteen-page pamphlet: *Milton. Proposals for Engraving and Publishing by Subscription Thirty Capital Plates, from Subjects in Milton; to be painted principally, if not entirely, by Henry Fuseli, R.A. And for copying them in a reduced size to accompany a correct and magnificent edition, embellished also with forty-five elegant vignettes, of his poetical works, with notes, illustrations, and translations of the Italian and Latin poems* ([London]: for J. Johnson and J. Edwards, [1791?]). It is dated September 1, 1791, and lists nineteen pictures from *PL* with texts quoted, and describes other possible pictures from other works with quotations from *PR* and *SA*.

Around 1792 Cowper met William Hayley*, who was working on a new life of Milton to be included in a new edition of the poetical works projected by John and Josiah Boydell and George Nicol, through Hayley's disclaimer to him that competition between the editions was not intended. (Hayley's three volumes appeared in 1794, 1795, and 1797, the "Life" appearing in Vol. 1.) They became fast friends and translated Andreini's* *Adamo* together. It was published in Hayley's four-volume edition of *Cowper's Milton* in 1810, which reprinted his translations and commentary on *PL* from the 1808 edition of *Latin and Italian Poems of Milton,* which included illustrations by John Flaxman. The translations, including those of the tributes from Milton's Italian friends, have often been reprinted, since they are about the best available in verse. "The Fragment of an Intended Commentary on *Paradise Lost*" (Books 1–3; dated around 1791–1792) stresses Milton's sublimity, language, and versification. Of Milton's narrative voice in the epic he writes (for 2. 496) "that there is more real worth and importance in a single reflection of his, than in all those of his heathen predecessors taken together. . . ." Hayley's life of Cowper appeared in 1803 (2 vols.), with a third volume the next year containing correspondence, and a fourth in

1806 including "Supplementary Pages," further correspondence, and "Yardley Oak." During the later 1790s Cowper's health failed and bouts of mental depression plagued him, though he managed to write a bit, including a revision of Homer in 1798 (published 1802). He died April 25, 1800.

The many editions of Cowper's letters register a deep reading of Milton and a debt to his poems. At least thirty-seven letters refer to Milton, ranging in date from October 31, 1779, to October 13, 1798, and including a Latin translation of a simile in *PL* (to William Unwin, dated June 8, 1780) and a Latin translation of Dryden's epigram (to William Unwin, dated July 11, 1780). Among Cowper's poems that show special influence are "Il Penseroso, an Evening's Contemplation in St. John's Churchyard" (1745?); "Verses Written in His 17th Year, On Finding the Heel of a Shoe" (1748), lines 4–9; "Table Talk" (1781), lines 556–67; "The Task" (1783–84), 4. 709–17, in which he says he first discovered Milton at age fourteen and, in a version of the common parody on Milton's epics, remarks that he "with regret suppos'd / Thy joy half lost because not sooner found"; "Stanzas on the Late Indecent Liberties Taken with the Remains of Milton" (August 1790), for which *see* NEVE, PHILIP, and whose first two stanzas derive from "Mansus," lines 91–93; and "Yardley Oak" (1791), lines 14–16, which refer to *PL* 9. 1084–1100. In his translation of Homer Cowper likewise reflects his study of Milton; see the Prefaces to both editions and *Iliad* 5. 641; 15. 168; 23. 195; and *Odyssey* 1. 178; 11. 19, 139; 24. 43. [JTS]

CREATION. Milton defines creation as "that act whereby God the Father* produced every thing that exists by his Word and Spirit, that is, by his will, for the manifestation of the glory of his power and goodness." God, of course, cannot himself be manifested since he is the absolute and one of his attributes is incomprehensibility. His power and his goodness are manifested, however, through the creation, which Milton defines as the addition of form to preexistent matter. God's sole act in the creation is to produce invisible matter by withdrawing his essence from a portion of infinity. "Matter, like the form and nature of the angels itself, proceeded incorruptible from God . . . " (15 : 23–25). This matter is free and uncontrolled. (*See* COSMOLOGY.)

Milton amplifies his definition of creation by explaining that "his Word" is the Son of God*, the creator of Heaven and earth. As the manifestation of his Wisdom* and as his agent in the creation, God wills that the Word come into being. The generation of the Word, which takes place within the freed area (*extra se*), is a great mystery called by Milton "the literal begetting" (14 : 181). It is from the substance of God that the Word creates the Holy Spirit, who "inasmuch as he is a minister of God, and therefore a creature, was created or produced of the substance of God, not by a natural necessity, but by the free will of the agent, probably before the foundations of the world were laid, but later than the Son, and far inferior to him" (14 : 403). The "Spirit" in Milton's definition of creation may be the spirit of God assisting the Son; it may be the spirit of the Son himself; it may be a minister of God, a separate entity, who, Milton points out, is "only represented as moving upon the face of the waters already created" (*CM* 15 : 15).

After the production of the Holy Spirit, the Word creates Heaven* and its inhabitants, the angels*; Hell* seems to have been created next, for it certainly exists prior to the three days' war in Heaven (*PL* 6. 183). This is, in Milton's term, "the invisible creation"; at least, he argues, it is "invisible to us" (15 : 29). Heaven, in *PL*, apparently had a lengthy history before the creation of the world; the angelic hosts present themselves before God bearing standards that

. . . in thir glittering Tissues bear imblaz'd
Holy Memorials, acts of Zeale and Love
Recorded eminent.
(5. 592–94)

In *PL* the invisible Word is made visible to the angels, acknowledged by God to be His only Son, anointed king, and designated head over the angels and ruler of Heaven; this ceremony dramatizes what in the *Christian Doctrine* Milton calls "the metaphorical begetting" (14 : 181). When Satan, thinking himself impaired, rebels through pride and malice and draws after him a third of the angels, God decrees the creation of things visible, the universe, so that in time mankind may replenish Heaven's loss of population. The creation of the visible universe is an instantaneous act; but, in order that man may better understand its nature, it is described as having taken place in six days. Like everything else, the universe is created from the freed substance of God by the Son, God's external agent.

The material that remains after the creation is completed is described in *PL* as Chaos, which extends beneath Heaven, surrounds the great globe of the world, and, far from the realms of light, engulfs Hell. In a crude parody of the creation, Sin and Death, unaware that they serve God, construct from the dregs of Chaos an immense bridge and tunnel reaching from Hell to the world,

> . . . a passage broad,
> Smooth, easie, inoffensive down to Hell.
> (10. 305)

A detailed poetic account of the creation occurs in *PL* 7. Essential also are the chapters on God, the Son, the Holy Spirit, and Creation in *CD* (14, 15). [HFR]

CREEDS, or church symbols as they are sometimes called, have been employed by Christians since their earliest times as summary statements of their faith. Somewhat as the Jew had affirmed with Moses, "Hear, O Israel, the Lord our God is one Lord," Christians affirmed a Trinity*. Supposedly the oldest creed had been uttered by the Apostles as assertion of the persons of the Trinity and the different kinds of activity in which each primarily participated. Church fathers assembled

in 325 at the Council of Nicaea found it necessary to draw up a far more detailed statement with which to combat the heresy of Arianism*, a statement that was revised by the Council of Constantinople in 381 to become the creed generally called the "Nicene" in modern times. Later, another statement of even greater length appeared, in an attempt to clarify the ramifications of Christian dogma. This is the so-called Athanasian Creed.

As Protestantism developed in the sixteenth and seventeenth centuries, many groups that emerged drew up formal statements of their faith. The Apostles' Creed met with general favor, both because of its supposed antiquity and because its contents were of such a general nature as to circumscribe only a few sects, most notably the Socinians*. It seems probable that Milton affirmed all of its clauses, none of which contradict any of his dogmatic conclusions. In this affirmation he is at one with both the Church of England and much of the Puritanism of the seventeenth century.

The second famous ancient creed, the Nicene, did not meet with so wide a favor, though it had found a central place in the communion service of the Church of England. As a youth Milton certainly affirmed its dogmatic contents many times and during his later life must have judged it to be to at least some extent a test of Christian orthodoxy. Close examination of the chapter on the Son of God* in *CD* shows that he is not in formal disagreement with it, a fact that he mentions at the end of the discussion (where he calls the Creed "that celebrated Confession of Faith"), adding that his views also do not violate the Apostles' Creed. Indeed, no one has ever successfully proved that Milton's dogmatic position contradicts either of these basic statements. His agreement with early creedal orthodoxy does not, however, extend to the Athanasian statement, which has possessed little or no authority for Protestantism.

As each Protestant sect appeared, it tended to produce its own dogmatic statement. For Milton the most important are the *Articles* of the Church of England and the Presbyterian* *Confession of Faith*. By his day the Articles had become the same thirty-nine that are affirmed in England today (though affirmation of them is not now and was not then a prerequisite for communion in the church). Milton certainly knew them as a student at Cambridge and certainly subscribed to all of them as a condition for the award of his university degrees. There is no reason to doubt the sincerity of his subscription, for he has not left a single piece of evidence from the early 1630s that he disagreed with any of them. The development of the dogmatic radicalism argued in *CD* came much later. Even though he testifies that he was "Church-outed by the Prelats" (*RCG*), and so was not ordained as he would have been in the normal course of events, all evidence discounts any disagreement on Milton's part as to the dogma of the Articles but emphasizes instead his distress with prelatry : with the episcopal system of government, which is not established by any Article. For this reason he left the Church of England, though the dogmatic position that he developed later in *CD* would have prevented his subscribing to the Articles then, especially the Second, on the Son of God.

When they achieved control of Parliament in 1643, the Presbyterians appointed a commission to draw up a formal statement of their faith. Meeting in Westminster Abbey, it produced the Confession, which is still the Presbyterian standard (though belief in all of its dogma is not required of communicants). Unlike his relationship with the Articles, there is no evidence that Milton ever affirmed the Confession. By the time it had appeared in 1647, he had evidently been totally disenchanted with Presbyterianism, especially with its system of government. He must have felt that the Confession had even singled him out for special attack as it affirmed the church's stand against divorce*, asserting that only "the corruption of man" leads one "to study arguments, unduly to put asunder those whom

God hath joined together in marriage" (24 : 6) as Milton himself had done quite recently. He resolutely ignored this Presbyterian creed for the rest of his life. Furthermore, his emerging position on such subjects as the Trinity, the Incarnation*, and Predestination* could not have been harmonized with it.

As he developed the dogmas of *CD* in his later years, Milton moved farther and farther from formal contemporary statements. In this respect he was aligning himself with sects like the Baptists (*see* ANABAPTISTS), a noncreedal church that expected each communicant to develop his own system of belief. The Quakers* likewise were an increasingly important noncreedal group. Thus *CD* is not a creed or a set of articles or a confession. It is Milton's attempt to present a system of theology for each reader to consider as he reflects and comes to his own conclusions. That it is in harmony with the creeds of the early church, the Apostles' and the Nicene, would be a relatively minor argument in its favor in the eyes of its author; its agreement or disagreement with contemporary statements would for him be quite insignificant, though there is no question that he had carefully pondered both the Articles and the Confession of Faith. The important fact for Milton was his use of the Bible alone to establish every detail of dogma. [WBH]

CROMWELL, OLIVER (1599–1658), general, regicide, Lord Protector, and subject of Milton's eulogies in *Sonn* 16 and *2Def,* came of a family that had risen to eminence in Huntingdonshire through his great-grandfather's service at Henry VIII's court, but was somewhat in decline by Charles I's time. He was subjected to strong Puritan influences at Huntingdon grammar school and Sydney Sussex College, Cambridge, though it was not until his late twenties that he underwent a personal and intense experience of conversion.

He first sat in Parliament in 1628–29, but two years later he sold what land he had and became a mere tenant farmer;

very possibly he contemplated emigrating to New England. If so, he changed his mind after inheriting his wife's uncle's estate in the Isle of Ely. When he was elected to the Short and Long Parliaments in 1640, he already had a local reputation as a militant Puritan and a champion of the poor commoners against the drainers of the local fens. In Parliament, he became more widely known by his fervor against the bishops and the court, his sometimes excessive vehemence of language, and his usefulness on committees. His national reputation really began, however, with the cavalry actions that he fought in 1643. Though he had had no previous military experience, his command rose within a year from a troop to a double regiment of horse, and in January 1644 he was made lieutenant-general of the army of the Eastern Association with command over all its cavalry. He led it to victory at Marston Moor on July 2, 1644, but in the ensuing months he quarreled with his own general, the Earl of Manchester, because the latter sought a negotiated peace rather than fighting the war to a finish. It was a crucial issue, and Cromwell brought it before Parliament. The outcomes were the Self-Denying Ordinance, which ousted Manchester and other peace-party commanders, and the New Model Ordinance, which forged a new national army, dedicated to total victory, out of the ruins of the old ones. Sir Thomas Fairfax* was appointed captain-general, Cromwell (after some delay) lieutenant-general. Cromwell's cavalry again clinched the crucial victories at Naseby and Langport in June–July 1645, and a year later the first Civil War was over.

In the divisions that by now split the Parliament, Cromwell was strongly identified with the Independents* against the Presbyterians*, on political as well as religious issues. He strove to avert the army's breach with the Parliament in 1647, but when the army defied the orders for disbandment and seized the king, he took its part. His aim then was to restore the king on the army's terms, but he was frustrated by Charles's slipperiness and by the growing opposition of the soldiers' elected spokesmen, the Agitators, who were strongly influenced by the Levellers. Charles himself broke the impasse by escaping from the army and signing an Engagement with the Scots, which precipitated the second Civil War in 1648. Cromwell annihilated the Scottish army at Preston in August, but he avoided involvement in the army's subsequent purging of the Parliament, which left the "Rump" holding supreme power. Thereafter, however, he threw all his weight behind the proceedings that led to the execution of the king (January 30, 1649).

His first task under the new Commonwealth was to suppress a Leveller mutiny in the army; he detested the Levellers' threat of social revolution. Thereafter he was almost continually absent on campaign, first in Ireland (1649–50) and then in Scotland (1650–51), until his conclusive victory at Worcester on September 3, 1651, finally released him from fighting. Milton's personal contacts with him in the Council of State* can have been very few. In 1650 Cromwell succeeded Fairfax as commander-in-chief, but his influence in state affairs was by no means paramount. His constant opposition to any forcing of conscience in religious matters prompted Milton to appeal to him in *Sonn* 16 in 1652, but how far he opposed the scheme for religious settlement that the Rump was then considering is uncertain.

Other issues, chief among them the Rump's long failure to provide satisfactorily for a successor to its own authority, finally induced Cromwell to expel the members on April 20, 1653, though only after he had long resisted the army's pressure for a dissolution. Dictatorship was in his grasp, but so little did he want it that he and the council of officers next handed over supreme political authority to a nominated assembly ("Barebone's Parliament") from which they almost totally excluded serving officers of the army. After five months, the moderate majority in it walked out rather than act any longer with the radical "saints," and

Cromwell on December 16, 1653, at last assumed the headship of the state as Lord Protector under a written constitution.

Milton's great panegyric in *2Def*, written shortly after, declares that Cromwell's virtues entitle him to supreme power, but it is followed by a lengthy exhortation which defines in broad terms how that power should be exercised. In this exhortation can be seen the main reasons why Milton's admiration turned slowly to disillusionment.

His most earnest plea was that the state should renounce all authority over the church and cease to maintain an established clergy by tithes or otherwise. Cromwell, by contrast, while protecting the dissident sects in their freedom of worship, believed it the duty of a Christian commonwealth to maintain a preaching ministry throughout the land. Milton also urged him to admit his old comrades to the first share in his counsels, hoping that he would be reconciled with Bradshaw*, Vane*, Overton*, and other republicans whom the poet had not ceased to admire, but the differences on both sides only widened. Again, Milton adjured Cromwell "to flee from the pomp of wealth and power"; but the Protector's long flirtation with Parliament's offer of the crown in 1657, the establishment that year of a new upper house of Parliament, the revival of a quasi-monarchial court at Whitehall, and the imposing estates acquired by the new "grandees," must have struck him as so many departures from the plain republican virtues that he had extolled. Nor can the author of *Areop* have relished the new restrictions on printing and news publishing introduced in 1655.

Yet Milton little appreciated what compromises Cromwell's political situation imposed. The Protectorate's enemies were many and diverse : royalists, Presbyterians, Levellers, republican politicians, army commonwealthsmen, and now the Fifth Monarchists and other proponents of a "rule of the saints." Cromwell was not a dictator by temperament or intent; he believed honestly in parliamentary liberties and constitutional restraints, and he strove to shift the basis of his power from the army to the political nation at large. But in his dealings both with his parliaments and with the gentry who ran the affairs of the counties, he experienced a constant conflict between the political attitudes of the traditional governing class and his own sense of obligation to what he called "the interest of the people of God." His notorious establishment of a regime of eleven major-generals in the fall of 1655 aimed partly at repressing royalist conspiracy, partly at bringing the county communities into closer cooperation with central government, and partly at promoting a "reformation of manners" by enforcing the laws against drunkenness, immorality, swearing, and sabbath-breaking. It is significant that he brought it to an end as soon as Parliament pronounced against it.

Cromwell gave England five years of domestic peace, certain genuine reforms, wide religious liberty, and a vast accession of power in Europe. Few irregular or revolutionary regimes have shed less blood, imposed less restraint on personal liberty, or striven more sincerely to observe the rule of law. But Cromwell's need and desire to win over the men of substance of the old political nation inevitably involved some conservative reaction, and every symptom of it alienated Milton. He never condemned Cromwell by name, but he almost certainly referred to the whole of the Protectorate as "a short but scandalous night of interruption" (in the Preface to *Hire*) and his repudiation of all its works is implicit in his tracts of 1659–60. In these, his first requirements of a free commonwealth are liberty of conscience and the rejection of government by a single person under any title or form. [AW]

CROMWELL, RICHARD (1626–1712), the third son of Oliver Cromwell* and the eldest to survive him. He was educated at Felsted School and Lincoln's Inn, and at 22 he married the heiress of Richard Major, the well-to-do squire of Hursley in

Hampshire. There he settled down to an easy round of country sports and pleasures, troubling his father periodically by his lack of serious purpose and his tendency to overspend his allowance. He took no part in public life except as a justice of the peace, and Oliver seems never to have thought of him as his political heir until the Humble Petition and Advice (May 1657) empowered him to name his own successor. In July 1657 Richard became Chancellor of Oxford University, but he was not appointed to the privy council until December. Next month he was given command of a cavalry regiment. These last two appointments probably mark Oliver's belated decision to prepare his son to succeed him. Earlier, the old Protector may have had someone else in mind—perhaps Charles Fleetwood*, as was alleged after the Restoration—but there is little doubt that he nominated Richard on his deathbed.

Richard's accession as Protector on September 3, 1658, was widely welcomed. His moderation, his affability, even his essential mediocrity, commended him to most of the country gentry, but the army resented coming under the ultimate authority of this young man whom it scarcely knew, and the "godly party" frowned upon his obvious lack of religious enthusiasm. Having little political experience or acumen, he depended heavily on advice, and he leaned too obviously on conservative, civilian counsellors whom the army and the sects distrusted. The Parliament that he summoned in January 1659 also displayed a conservative, anti-military temper, and soon the discontented army officers, republican politicians, and sectarian preachers were coalescing in opposition to what they considered to be a betrayal of the "Good Old Cause." Richard's downfall came when the chief officers, Fleetwood (his brother-in-law) and Desborough (his uncle by marriage), forced him to dissolve Parliament on April 22. Two weeks later the pressure of their own subordinates forced them to recall the Rump of the Long Parliament that the army had expelled six years

earlier. Richard tendered his submission in a dignified letter on May 25.

Milton wrote in *A Letter to a Friend* that he was overjoyed at the restoration of the Rump, which he addressed in enthusiastic terms in his preface to *Hire*. He had continued to draw his salary and to translate occasional letters of state during Richard's Protectorate, but shortly before its end he wrote to Moses Wall* complaining of "the non-progressency of the nation, and of its retrograde motion of late, in liberty and spiritual truths."

Richard lived for more than half a century after his brief tenure of power. After twenty years of lonely exile in France and Geneva, he ventured home in 1680 and lived out his days at Cheshunt as "Mr. Clarke." [AW]

CUDWORTH, RALPH: *see* CAMBRIDGE PLATONISTS, THE.

CULVERWWELL, NATHANAEL: *see* CAMBRIDGE PLATONISTS, THE.

CURIOSITY has been a particular concern of Christian moralists inasmuch as the Fall of Man consisted in the eating of forbidden fruit that promised knowledge of good and evil. Besides this special case, curiosity has been regarded as sinful when it is an indulgence of mere idle speculation without any worthy aim or objective, when it is motivated by pride or vanity, when it results in an injustice to another, and when illicit means such as witchcraft or sorcery are employed. Accusations of the sins of curiosity and of vain philosophy were especially prominent in the religious controversies of the seventeenth century. Howard Schultz opens his study of the subject by stating that "while Milton and modern England were growing up together within a period conveniently bound by the dates 1600 and 1660, it is safe to say that intellectual sin came in for a scolding somewhere in every influential kind of writing" (*Milton and Forbidden Knowledge* [1955], p. 1).

Milton gives due attention to such curiosity in his poetical works. In *PL*, after the dissolution of the infernal council, a group of the fallen angels gather to discuss such problems as providence*, foreknowledge, will, and fate*, but find "no end, in wandring mazes lost" (2. 546–69). Raphael warns Adam about the danger of an unrestricted appetite for knowledge (7. 110–30) but also commends him for his legitimate intellectual interests (8. 68ff.). Immediately after the Fall, Adam recognizes the similarity between curiosity and gluttony: both are characterized by an appetite that goes beyond the limits of reason (9. 1019–20). Near the end of *PL* he admits that his sin has been one of seeking "forbidd'n knowledge by forbidd'n means" (12. 279). In contrast to Adam, the Christ of *PR* refuses all offers of knowledge by forbidden means, asserting the sufficiency of God's revelation through Scriptures (4. 334–64). [RF]

CURRY, WALTER CLYDE (1887–1967), scholar from South Carolina who, following completion of his doctorate at Stanford University, spent his entire professional career at Vanderbilt University, where he helped raise the English graduate program to some distinction and was in his later years chairman. Earlier, in the 1920s, he had been a part of the Fugitive movement there, writing poetry under the nom de plume of Robin Goodfellow, but as this informal group broke up he moved to scholarship, producing three notable books: *Chaucer and the Medieval Sciences* (New York, 1926), *Shakespeare's Philosophical Patterns* (Baton Rouge, La., 1937), and *Milton's Ontology, Cosmogony, and Physics* (Lexington, Ky., 1957). The latter two draw especially upon Neoplatonism* to clarify their subjects. Of particular importance for Milton are the studies of creation* as it figures in his descriptions of chaos, the universe and the sun, and the scale of nature*. [WBH]

CUSPINIAN, JOHANNES (1473–1529), historian, Renaissance man of letters, diplomat, and teacher. He succeeded Conrad Celtes as curator of the imperial library at Vienna; his works, including the

histories, reveal his wide interests in law, medicine, philosophy, and literature.

Milton found no further use for the notes he gathered for *CB* from Cuspinian's *Historia Caesarum et Imperatorum Romanorum* (1601). The five entries, 1642–1644, include the following observations: on almsgiving: that a young nobleman had a reputation for giving alms, but as an adult, he was noted for his faithlessness; on kingship: that German emperors were elected from the time of Otto III; that Henry the Fowler out of humility refused to be anointed king; that Berengarius II of Italy was scorned by the Franks for his modest diet; that "severity in morals is of little use in trying to obtain authority or command"; and finally, that a city, having lost its liberty, cannot regain it. [RMa]

CYPRIAN. Caeilius Cyprianus, Saint Cyprian (ca. 200–258), was martyred at Carthage. Little is known about his life before 246. Then he became a priest and two years later Bishop of Carthage. At a time when persecutions caused many Christians to backslide, Cyprian gained fame for standing firm in faith and also forgiving apostates. His many theological writings had wide influence, extending to such early Fathers as St. Augustine*. Written in elegant style, they were sumptuously edited in 1471 and several times since. Milton uses citations from these works in *Ref,* especially in emphasizing the Bible as antidote to custom and tradition in religious matters (3 : 29). There are four citations in *CB*. [PMZ]

DALILA's name (as Milton preferred to spell it) appears in literature for the first time in Judges 16 : 4–20. Here she is simply described as a woman of Sorek whom Samson loves. In any case, the lords of the Philistines offer her 1,100 pieces of silver to entice Samson in order that they may "see wherein his great strength lieth." She makes three unsuccessful attempts, all at Samson's own suggestion. First she binds him with "seven fresh cords that were never dried," but he easily snaps these cords; second, she ties him with ropes "that never were occupied," and these too he easily breaks; third, she weaves his hair on a loom, but again he frees himself without difficulty. Finally, after she presses him daily and urges him "so that his soul was vexed unto death," Samson tells her that his strength lies in his uncut hair. Later, while he sleeps upon her knees she calls for a man to cut off "his seven locks"; and with Samson's strength now gone from him, Dalila wakes him and delivers him into the hands of the Philistines.

For the most part, the exegetes of the early Christian period say little to the characterization of Dalila. She was, however, frequently referred to in their literal homiletic treatments of the story, which were *exempla* designed to demonstrate the importance of chastity or the evils of intermarriage. Such treatment can be found in Clement of Rome's (1st century A.D.) *Two Letters Concerning Virginity* (2. 60; trans. B. L. Pratten, Ante-Nicene Christian Library, 14 : 389f.), and in Ambrose's* (4th century A.D.) *Epistola XIX* (*Pat. Lat.* 16 : 1026–36). Clement writes that Dalila was "a woman who brought a great man to ruin with her wretched body and her vile passion." (*See* F. Michael Krouse, *Milton's Samson and the Christian Tradition* [1949], pp. 31–45.)

But in the Patristic period, along with literal interpretations, allegorical explications of the Samson story began to develop as an attempt to resolve the many inconsistencies that arose out of strictly literal interpretations. Such important scholars as Origen* (ca. 185–253), Ambrose, and Augustine* (354–430) adopted the method of establishing parallels between the life of Christ and the life of Samson. Moreover, they began to place more emphasis on the culpability of Dalila. Hence, Isidore of Seville (7th century) suggests that the significance of Samson's submission to her and to the cutting of his hair is that if a man yields to the demands of the flesh he is "despoiled of the spirit" (Krouse, p. 43).

In the later Scholastic period of Christian hermeneutics, allegorical interpretation continued to flourish and in fact became the major method of exegesis, and it gave rise to extremely elaborate allegories. Rupert of St. Heribert (d. 1135) goes so far as to identify Dalila's betrayal of Samson with Judas's betrayal of Christ. But most important in this period, as Krouse points out, there was a significant shift of emphasis in the Samson story as more weight was given to the later part of Samson's life. Such a shift gave the story a more tragic shape and "for this reason Delilah came to occupy a position of greater importance in the Samson literature, and greater emphasis was placed upon her attempts to learn the secret of his strength" (Krouse, p. 55). Two twelfth-century examples of this new shift in focus are a sermon by Godefridius Admontenaius and a poem by Peter Abelard. Godefredius devoted a Palm Sunday sermon to Samson and Dalila in which he began with Samson's association with her and in which he concentrated on her insidious attempts to learn the secret of Samson's strength. Peter Abelard also called attention to her role in the story. In his eighty-seven-line poem *Planctus Israel super Samson,* he denounced her for her treason and blamed her for Samson's blindness (*ibid.*)

According to Krouse, Abelard's *Planctus,* which emphasized the tragic aspect of Samson's life, marked the beginning of secular poetic treatment of the Samson legend; and in the proliferation of non-ecclesiastic Samson literature which flourished throughout the Middle Ages and the Renaissance, women in general and Dalila in particular were almost always the object of denunciation and castigation. Boccaccio's* *De casibus virorum illustrium* (ca. 1350) includes a lengthy indictment of women, and he singles out Dalila for special criticism. Chaucer*, too, in "The Monk's Tale De Casibus Virorum Illustrium," chooses Dalila for special condemnation :

Unto his lemman Dalida he tolde
That in his heeris al his strengthe lay,
And falsly to his foomen she hym solde.
(2063–65)

. . . .
Beth war by this ensample oold and playn
That no men telle hir conseil til hir wyves
Of swich thyng as they wolde han secree fayn,
If that it touche hir lymes or her lyves.
(2091–94)

John Lydgate in *Fall of Princes* (ca. 1435) says that she was Samson's wife, but Lydgate then concludes that her treason was "one of the great domestic scandals of all time" (Watson Kirkconnell, *That Invincible Samson* [1964], p. 153).

In the many continental and English plays produced during the Renaissance, this concentration upon Dalila's treason continued. In an early play, *Samson Tragoedia nova* (Cologne, 1569) by Andreas Fabricus, the third act is almost entirely devoted to Dalila's temptations of Samson. In Marcus Andreas Wunstius's *Samson. Tragoedia Sacra* (Strasbourg, ca. 1600), the third act, in which her temptations undermine Samson's *hybris*, is one of the three dramatic climaxes of the play. Theodorus Rhodius's *Samson* (Heidelberg, 1600) calls for the action to take place in the street outside her home; and all five acts deal with the day of Samson's last temptation and blinding. And in Abraham de Konig's *Simsons Treur-spel* (Amsterdam, 1618) Dalila has a larger part than before. She sings three songs, the first when she confesses her love for Samson. At the outset she is sincere, but the Philistine lords tempt her with money and with appeals to her patriotism, to which she finally succumbs. Later she attempts to learn Samson's secret; finally, at the temple festival, Dalila is not only present but seated at a banquet with the Philistine lords. Vincenzo Giattini's oratorio, *Il Samsone,* was published in Palermo in 1638, the very year Milton arrived for a year's stay in Italy. In this oratorio there are only four characters: Dalila, a Philistine Captain, a Philistine Prince, and Samson. The action of this musical rendering of the story is limited to Samson's final day. It is worth mentioning here that Joost van den Vondel's* *Samson of Heilige Wraeck, Treurspel* (Amsterdam, 1660), which many critics believe to be

the closest play of all the forerunners to Milton's, has no part at all for Dalila (see Kirkconnell, pp. 152–81).

Hence, with but few exceptions, from the Middle Ages on through the Renaissance Dalila's role came to be considered crucial to the Samson story. She was not only regarded as the precipitator of his tragic fall, but she was also thought of as the prime example of all perfidious and iniquitous women. Indeed, in this long period she had only one defender—Cardinal Cajetan, who in the sixteenth century wrote that contrary to belief Dalila was not a Philistine, but a Hebrew, and that she had never bargained for the great cruelty that the Philistines ultimately inflicted upon Samson (Krouse p. 77). [CK]

DALTON, JOHN (1709–1763), poet and divine. The popularity of *Mask* during the eighteenth century is due largely to the theatrical revision that he created. During the period from around 1731 when he was tutor to Lord Beauchamp, the only son of the Earl of Hertford and the seventh duke of Somerset, Dalton adapted Milton's poem by revision, cuts, insertion of lines from *L'Al* partially cast as a song, and insertion of his own lines, many of which are cast as songs. *Comus,* as it was now called—the title by which Milton's poem is universally known—was first performed on March 4, 1738, at the Drury Lane Theatre. The music was by Thomas Arne* and was frequently published in 1738 (inspired by the centennial of its first publication) and later. The texts of the songs were also reproduced in *The Busy Bee, or, Vocal Repository* [1790], 1:33–42 (Songs 72–91). Four editions of the play appeared in 1738, and successive printings occurred in 1740, 1741 (?), 1750, 1759, 1760, 1762, 1766, 1777 (2), and 1811. A further revision by George Colman* was performed in 1772 and became the standard production thereafter, being frequently printed. The play's popularity helped lead to separate publications of Milton's original masque during the eighteenth century. In 1748 Dalton became canon of the fifth stall in Worcester Cathedral. He also aided in the benefit performance of the play for Milton's granddaughter, Elizabeth Foster, on April 5, 1750, at the Drury Lane Theatre. He died in Worcester, having also published other poetry and sermons.

Dalton's version of *Mask* is in three acts: Act 1 employs lines 1–330; Act 2, lines 331–658; and Act 3, lines 659–1023. It begins with a prologue by Dalton in heroic couplets. The attendant spirit's lines are divided among three spirits, and emphasis on Comus and his rout in their spirits, bacchanals, pastoral characters, and other vocal parts, dancers, &c." was added. Lines from *L'Al* are recited by Comus at the beginning of Act 3, followed by a song by Euphrosyne, which was written by Dalton. The temptation is particularly altered by insertions of non-Miltonic lines and song. A non-Miltonic epilogue, "to be spoken by Mrs. Clive in the Dress of Euphrosyne, with the Wand and Cup," ends the performance. The Euphrosyne (Mirth) along with "attendant songs and dances and the reduction of lines by the Spirit, the Lady, and the Brothers justify the change in title. [JTS]

DANIELLO, BERNARDINO (d. 1565),

author of a treatise on poetics (1536), a commentary on Petrarch (1541), and unrhymed translations into Italian of the Second Book of the *Aeneid* (1545) and Virgil's *Georgics* (1556). His commentary on Dante's *Commedia,* which was published posthumously at Venice in 1568 under the title *Dante con l'espositione di M. Bernardino Daniello da Lucca,* was known to Milton. In the "Index Oeconomicus" of *CB,* Milton cites Dante's* condemnation of usury (in Canto 11 of the *Inferno*) and Daniello's commentary on the passage (18 : 162): "Dante says that usury is a sin against nature and against art: against nature because it makes money beget money, which is an unnatural kind of birth; against art because it does not work. . . ." [JMS]

DANTE. Any discussion of the relations between Dante and Milton, both as thinkers and as poets, must be a cautious one. Perhaps no two poets were simultaneously more alike and more different; and few poets so widely separated geographically, culturally, and temperamentally have brought the language of poetry—each in a different vernacular— to such heights. The difficult question of their relationship has recently been the subject of a book-length study by Irene Samuel (*Dante and Milton* [1966]) which gathers all the known facts about Milton's knowledge of Dante and his work, contains appendixes listing Milton's references to Dante before *PL,* and a bibliography of books and articles that comment on the relation between Milton and Dante. Her book treats in some detail, and with considerable analysis, thematic and ideological relations between the *Commedia* and *PL.*

The relation between Dante and Milton is not so much a question of specific influences of one poet on the other as it is of similarity in scope. The relation, on the one hand, can be summarized in John Arthos's statement (*Dante, Michelangelo, and Milton* [1963]) that both poets believed "that works of art could be religiously inspired" and "rested in the conviction that poetry depended on truth" (p. xi). Both are metaphysical poets* in the most profound sense of the term: that is, poets whose major concern was the spiritual principle of being that informed men's lives; or, as William J. Grace says, both "attempted a comprehensive picture of the universe and of the relationship between Creator and created according to their respective cultural and theological traditions" (*Comparative Literature* 1 [1949]: 178).

The facts of Milton's knowledge of Dante are explicit, and all the more remarkable because, as Samuel tells us, Dante was very little read, or admired, even in Italy in the seventeenth century. That Milton was a reasonably accomplished Italianist is attested by the fact that he wrote six poems in Italian; that he was well read in Italian literature is evident from his own allusions in his prose, as well as by both explicit allusions and verbal and thematic echoes in his poetry (i.e., the passage denouncing bad pastors in *Lyc*, lines 108–31, has long been recognized as modeled on St. Peter's similar denunciation in *Paradise* 27. 19ff.). In *CB* Milton refers to the edition of the *Commedia* of Daniello* (1586). Although this is the only edition to which he refers, it is very probable that he was familiar with other editions and commentaries reprinted in the sixteenth century. From his own testimony, as well as from implicit allusion, it is clear that Milton knew Dante's *Commedia*, the *De Monarchia*, the *Convivio*. He owned a copy of the latter in the third edition (1529) which was bound up with the works of Giovanni della Casa* and the sonnets of Benedetto Varchi. He also refers to Boccaccio's* *Vita di Dante* from the edition that was published in the same volume as the *editio princeps* of *La Vita Nuova* (1576), so he undoubtedly knew the latter also. Samuel suggests that he probably also knew the *De Vulgari Eloquentia* and Dante's epistles.

It is, of course, the *Commedia* that chiefly interested Milton, and the evidence suggests that he not only knew it but also admired it, as a work of art if not for its "doctrine." He refers to *Inferno* 19. 115–17 and to *Paradise* 20. 55 in *Ref* (1641); in the sonnet to Lawes* (?1646) there is a reference to the Casella episode of *Purgatorio* 2. 76–119, and *CB* contains six citations to the *Commedia*, one of which has, in addition, the remarks of Bernardino Daniello da Lucca, making it clear that Milton at least knew his edition, with commentary. In each case, the references are admiring ones, as are his other references, in *CB*, to the *Monarchia* and to *Convivio IV*. Milton's references to Dante in *CB* are generally by way of giving examples of various moral characteristics and failings exemplified in the *Commedia* (i.e., the avarice of the clergy, suicide, sloth, usury, separation of church and state), or political-moral concerns, such as

the authority of the king and its basis, for which Milton goes to Dante's *De Monarchia* and Boccaccio's life of Dante. All of these uses in *CB*, to which might be added Milton's reference to Dante—in a letter to Benedetto Buonmattei, dated from Florence on September 10, 1638—as one of the Italian authors (the other who is explicitly mentioned is Petrarch*) to whom he is "glad to go for afeast," suggest not only a reading of Dante but an admiration for his work, enough so as to make him a model for study. This admiration is never more explicit than in the *Apol*, where Dante (together with Petrarch again) is read not simply as a great love poet, but as one of those men who inspired Milton to his lofty concept of poetry and of the poet as a "true poem," "a composition and pattern of the best and honorablest things"; for, as Milton saw them, Dante and Petrarch displayed nothing but "sublime and pure thoughts, without transgression." If, as Joseph Mazzeo maintains (*Renaissance and Revolution* [1965], p. 55), Dante, for the first time since antiquity, revived the tendency of the poet to think of himself as an inspired genius, a teacher of mankind, we can see a very general, but strong, relationship of continuity in Milton's concept of the function and mission of the poet. His remarks in *Apol* support this.

Assessing the nature and kind of influence Dante may have had on Milton is dependent upon alleged parallels. Literary echoes, allusions, and loose imitations of the *Commedia* abound; a few examples will give some sense of Milton's possible debt to it.

Samuel sees remarkable structural precedents for Milton's famous invocations in *PL* in the proems of the *Commedia* (pp. 51–59). The openings of each section of the *Commedia*—*Inferno, Purgatorio, Paradiso*—point consciously to the new kind of experience to be undergone in the succeeding cantos; they call attention to an elaborate structure. Milton uses proems in *PL* in a way that looks back to Dante, using them as Dante did early in the *Commedia,* to mark structural divisions in the poem. Thus the opening proem of Book 1 introduces the whole poem, and Books 1–6 in general, Books 1–2 in particular. The subsequent invocations and statements of theme and subject in *PL*—beginning Books 3, 7, 9— introduce large structural units in a manner comparable to the introductions to *Inferno-Purgatorio-Paradiso.* The multiple structural functions, according to Samuel, are even more elaborate in Milton's than those in Dante's poem because they mark shifts in theme as well as of place, and they measure the variations in tension in the poem as well as in narrative pattern.

There is little doubt that the description, in many general details, of Milton's Hell*, the shadowy and stark atmosphere of the place, owes something to Dante's Inferno, dependent on such specifics as the resemblances between Milton's concept of Hell as a place where "hope never comes / That comes to all" (1. 66–67) and Dante's famous "lasciate ogni speranza, voi ch'entrate"—"Abandon hope, all ye who enter here" (*Inferno,* 3. 9). This is a verbal resemblance that evokes a larger tonal and atmospheric resemblance. Or Milton's famous epic simile in which he compares the fallen angels in Hell to the autumnal leaves in Vallombrosa (1. 301ff.). while it may owe something to his own remembrances of that lovely spot outside of Florence, is unmistakably drawn from Dante's vision of the fallen souls in Hell as they are harassed by Charon at the Acheron (*Inferno* 3. 112): "Come d'autunno si levan le foglie / l'una appresso dell'altra, infin che il ramo / vede alla terra tutte le sue spoglie"—"As the leaves of autumn fall, one after the other, until the branch sees on the ground all its spoils." These can be multiplied; but it is not the collecting of parallels that is important, as Samuel says: it is what Milton did with them. Although Milton's Hell is different in specifics from Dante's, its atmosphere owes much to Dante, whose Hell is, like Milton's, a parody of Heaven.

It may be instructive to concentrate on one significant episode in each poem, and their similarities and differences. C. H. Herford some time ago recognized the possible relation between Virgil's last words to Dante in *Purgatorio* 27. 127ff. and Michael's final exhortation to Adam in *PL* 13. 575ff. (*Bulletin of the John Rylands Library* 8 [1924] : 191–235). These two scenes come at crucial moments in their respective poems; and it is significant that, structurally at least, Michael's speech parallels Virgil's. Dante, the pilgrim, has reached the point, with Virgil's guidance, where his will has been instructed and he has recovered from his dizzying descent; he is at the climax of the geographic configuration of Inferno just as he reaches the apex of his infernal experience. Virgil can now leave him on his own with assurance; for, as he says, "Libero, dritto e sano è tuo arbitrio, / e fallo fora non fare a suo senno"—"Free, upright, and whole is your will, / and it would be wrong not to follow its lead" (140–41). Dante is now prepared to *enter* the Garden of Eden. In Milton there is a reversal of this procedure, one that is informative both about the similarities and the differences between the two poets. Michael, too, has reached the end of his instructorship with his statement to Adam that "thou hast attain'd the sum / Of wisdom" and his exhortation to add deeds, virtue, patience, faith, temperance, and love to that wisdom. Like Dante the pilgrim, then, Adam—once he awakens Eve—is to be set off on his own. In *PL* this occurs at the very end of the poem, which is, in reality, the beginning of the course of life and history for humanity; in the *Commedia,* the comparable occurrence comes about two-thirds of the way through the poem and, significantly, before the central protagonist enters the Earthly Paradise preparatory to entering Paradise itself. Milton's hero is about to *leave* the Earthly Paradise* to enter the world of travail, solitariness, and suffering. Structurally, Milton's location of the final "briefing" comes at the moment in his poem that is comparable to Dante's preparation to enter the Earthly Paradise;

but the whole design of Milton's poem works to the moment when Adam and Eve leave the Garden. This is what the poem is *about* : our place in time, which is part of Adam and Eve's solitary way. Dante's poem, on the other hand, is a "comedy," its movement being upward; hence, his character who exists in time and history "now" (whether it be 13th century Florence or 20th century America), comes after the Fall*. He is the offspring of Adam and Eve and his movement is *back* and *up*. Dante's movement is to the "other world"; Milton's movement is to "this world." This is dictated by the different emphasis and direction of the two poems.

Echoes, allusions, and structural parallels, however, constitute only one kind of relationship. There are larger areas, which transcend the mere mechanics of echoes and parallels, no matter how conscious. The most obvious point of correspondence, of course, is between the two major poems of these two poets; but one could not, by any stretch of the imagination call *PL* an imitation of the *Commedia*; nor would it really do justice to Milton's achievement to refer to *PL* as a Protestant, or an English, *Commedia*. In these poems both poets reveal a pervasive concern with what we might call the "epic" of human salvation (a point that has nothing to do with the specific literary genre or genres of these two poems, a question that will be returned to below), described in poems that are epic* in scope and design. These poets are concerned with the design of the universe—design, not simply in the mechanical sense, but in the essential sense—with man's place in that universe, as part of its design, and his relation to it. Each incorporated that concern with and sense of the design of the universe in *the* poem of his age and culture, an epic in that it attempted to deal with man in the perspective of both the natural and the supernatural universes : a landscape more inclusive than that of a nation or a single race, which is the usual setting of traditional "epics." Both Milton and Dante, especially in these poems, reveal their similar-

ities most forcefully, as William Grace has shown, in making the demonstration of God's justice, of His transcendent and immanent aspect, essential to the scope and framework of their poems. They are equally concerned, in a manifest way in these poems, with the problem and meaning of evil, with free will, and with the salvation of man in the perspective of his place in the cosmic struggle (p. 178). More than this, both poets made these beliefs essential parts of the vast structures of their main poems. These beliefs and concerns, then, are not merely threads of intellectual biography, placed in a convenient category separate from aesthetic concerns; they infuse the aesthetics of these works and contribute integrally to their essential structure.

There is, in addition, a remarkable similarity in the way both Dante and Milton worked up to their great poems and developed this sense of the poet as "true poem," as a transmitter of "sublime and pure thoughts." *La Vita Nuova,* which precedes and looks toward the *Commedia,* is a book about love*, inseparable, in its way, from the troubadour tradition to which it owes so much; yet it is a book that places love in the larger perspective of *Divine Love* and initiates the process, through the narrator's memory, whereby Beatrice, the beloved, becomes a sanctified spirit (the *donna angelicata,* as the *stilnuovisti* would call her) that pulls him upward. This attraction is the force that results in the elevated sense Dante has of his poetic mission. It is, of course, to the love poetry that Milton seems to be referring in *Apol;* and while Milton has no Beatrice, as Dorothy Sayers wryly points out (*Further Papers on Dante* [1957], p. 151), he does develop, like Dante, from what might loosely be termed apparently "secular" concerns —which, as with Dante, are always in the perspective of some sense of Divine order—to the full emergence of the larger, transcendent one that had always been inherent and developing in his earlier thought. An example of this kind of thing—admittedly hypothetical—has recently been considered by A. Bartlett Giamatti in his annotations for the first volume of the *Variorum Commentary on the Poems* (1970). The poem under discussion is the third Italian sonnet ("Qual in colle aspro, al' imbrunir di sera"), and the problem is whether the phrase "e'l duro seno" at the end of line 13 is better read as it is, or "duro 'l seno," as one earlier editor preferred. Giamatti concurs with the accepted reading ("e'l duro seno") and in so doing sees the whole passage (the concluding couplet of the sonnet),

> Deh! foss' il mio cuor lento e'l duro seno
> A chi pianta dal ciel sì buon terreno.

> Oh, that my dull heart and hard breast might be
> As fertile soil for Him who plants from heaven.

as an echo of Beatrice's statement about Dante in *Purgatorio* 30:

> Ma tanto più maligno e più silvestro
> Si fa 'l terren col mal seme e non colto,
> Quant'elli ha più del buon vigor terrestro.
> (118–120)

> But as the ground becomes ranker and wilder with evil seed and not plowed, just so much more is its soil fertile.

Giamatti finds it interesting that—in addition to what he calls the "congruences in imagery" and the "similarity in language"—both poets tend to see themselves as arid earth that responds to cultivation in the person or inspiration of certain ladies (*Variorum*, pp. 379–80). Although the echo here, if one recognizes it as such, is from the *Commedia,* and it appears in one of Milton's earlier, lesser works, it suggests that same looking forward, the developing "higher strain," which Dante himself suggested throughout *La Vita Nuova* and, at the end of the work, stated explicitly as the ultimate direction of the experience rehearsed in his Book of Memory.

One thinks too of the political-social concerns of these two poets, never divorced from the larger sense of social order that should conform to the law of God, as each poet saw it. (See the allusion above to Milton's reference in *CB* to Dante's ideas of kingship in the *De Monarchia.*) Indeed, both poets seem to have suffered for their political and social beliefs and writings, Dante having to endure actual exile, Milton having to endure humiliation, retirement, and shame during the Restoration. It was during these periods of low fortune that both poets seem to have brought their major poems to completion (though they had been begun earlier), poems that relate man's path through life and ill fortune to his position in eternity. Both poets (and both poems) saw no divorce between the proper conduct of life in the world, between social and political action, and ethical standards. This is perhaps one of the most important areas of similarity. As Samuel puts it, both Milton and Dante saw politics* as related to ethics*, as the communal extension of the principles that guide individual, private life. If ethical principles are disdained or violated in public life, they are vitiated in private life. Samuel suggests that both the *Commedia* and *PL* are "political" poems, the former because it looks toward the "communion of saints" and therefore attempts to help toward that goal, and the latter because it relates the ethics of private morality to the larger concerns of human society in general (p. 218).

Thus far it has been suggested that Dante and Milton—perhaps it would be more accurate to say the intellectual and literary careers of Dante and Milton—are remarkably alike in general configuration. Their interest seems to have concentrated early on making their poetry some sort of divine force in man's salvation. For them, the true epic was the poem that would deal with essential truths about the human spirit. The scale would be cosmic and supernatural, but related to man's present time and place. The works they produced did not fall short of this goal. But something needs to be said about "genre" here. There can be no doubt that Milton—the poet who aimed to surpass Homer* and Virgil* in their own literary style and measure—felt that he was writing an epic in *PL;* it was the culmination and the marriage of his religious concerns, his classical training, and his unique style. But if he admired Dante's *Commedia,* as we have every right to assume, would he have considered it an epic, and could it then be said to be one of the poems that provided an epic pattern like the *Iliad* and the *Aeneid?* Or at least the basis for loose imitation, as Spenser* felt he was imitating Ariosto* and Tasso*, as well as Virgil and Homer, in *The Faerie Queene?*

The genre of the *Commedia* was something of an open question in the Renaissance (as, indeed, it may be today), and exactly how Milton may have regarded it is not absolutely determinable. Milton's probable position on this is itself an unresolved question; but John Steadman, for one, has attempted to confront it (*Huntington Library Quarterly* 23: 107–22). Italian critics and theoreticians of the sixteenth century were involved in a controversy about the genre of the *Commedia,* not unlike the controversies surrounding Ariosto's *Orlando Furioso* and Tasso's *Gerusalemme Liberata.* (These controversies are thoroughly treated by Bernard Weinberg in *A History of Literary Criticism in the Italian Renaissance,* 2 vols. [1961], 2 : 819ff.) In this controversy Mazzoni*, whom Milton had singled out for admiration in *Educ,* along with Castelvetro* and Tasso, as one of the best teachers of the laws of poetry and poetic genres, was a major voice; and, Steadman argues, it is legitimate to assume, in light of Milton's admiration for his critical theory, that Mazzoni's analysis of the genre of the *Commedia* was most influential on Milton. Steadman feels that from Mazzoni (who saw Dante's poem as a true "comedy," adhering to the "rules" of that genre) Milton would have recognized how different his own *PL* was from the *Commedia* in terms of genre. This would somewhat narrow the possible field of influence of the earlier poem on *PL.* Nevertheless, Steadman suggests, despite their essential difference in kind, style, and structure, both the *Commedia* and

PL are comparable as "extended poetic treatments of the cardinal doctrines of the Christian faith" (p. 121), and stand "on the bedrock of Christian tradition, not on the sandy foundation of the ancients" (p. 122).

Steadman does not represent a consensus, however; and Samuel may be taken as representative of the opposition. She agrees that Milton may not have taken the *Commedia* as an epic poem even though—she hastens to point out—both Mazzoni and Buonmattei found epic features in it. But, she hastens to point out, Tasso is also singled out, along with Mazzoni, for admiration by Milton, and Tasso considered the *Commedia* one of the four great models of epic poetry. Mazzoni himself regarded it as superior to the *Iliad, Odyssey,* and *Aeneid* not only as doctrine but as poetry. Given the fact that Milton often used in *PL* material that he did not consider epic (Genesis, Ovid's *Metamorphoses*), and the fact that Mazzoni and Buonmattei both regarded Dante as the greatest of poets for style, invention, fable, philosophic instruction, and organization, Samuel finds it highly probable that Milton also thought very highly of the *Commedia* in these terms :

> He nowhere names the *Commedia* as a model, but his promise in the *Reason of Church-Government* (1642) to undertake some great literary work has a marked similarity . . . to the promise at the end of the *Vita Nuova,* especially in conjunction with his praise of Dante in the *Apology for Smectymnuus* of the same year. He never regarded Dante as less than a great poet and an important thinker. (pp. 42–43)

Whatever Milton may have considered the genre of the *Commedia* to be may be ultimately unimportant; he quite obviously considered his own poem to be an epic, and only the most indiscriminate and injudicious would claim that *PL* is an imitation of or directly modeled on the *Commedia.* It is remarkable enough that two such culturally different poets saw their life work in writing, as Steadman aptly puts it, "extended poetic treatments of the cardinal doctrines of the Christian faith," and that, as Samuel puts it, Milton's promise "to undertake some great literary work has a marked similarity . . . to the promise at the end of the *Vita Nuova*. . . ." More than that, these promises were fulfilled in terms of an extended poetic treatment of the Christian faith. Certainly a poet of Milton's intelligence and sensibility, wide range of reading, and knowledge must have had some sense that his undertaking in *PL* was not unlike, even very like, Dante's in the *Commedia*, even if it was a different *kind* of poem with a different emphasis.

This is not to overlook, nor to underestimate, the differences between the two poems, differences that have been described by Grace and Sayers in the articles cited above. They might be summarized in Sayers's terms, that the characteristic differences between the two lies in the fact that Milton set out to justify the ways of God to man, while Dante did not think it necessary to justify God's ways; rather, his purpose was to show man the way to God. Milton starts from the problem of "Man's first disobedience," while Dante's problem is that "I went astray" (p. 166). One, then, is moving from the general or universal to the specific application; the other is dealing with the specific, the individual case as an example of and as a way of seeing the general and universal (a more Aristotelian-Thomistic approach, as one would expect of a Dante). But, by the same token, one might also describe the resemblances between Dante and Milton, in Samuel's terms, "in the reconcilement each effects between explicit theology and ethics and a primarily human action, mimetic of recognizable man in minutest detail and yet inclusive of the broadest generalities about the scheme of things" (p. 234). In the final analysis, this is perhaps the most pervasive and significant kind of influence one poet can have on another, the most recognizable parallel one great poem can have with another of similar grand design; and it far transcends the significance of mere verbal echoes,

parallels, and borrowings. It is the meaning, and not the name. [ARC]

DARBISHIRE, HELEN (1881–1961), editor, who after receiving her degree from Oxford remained there at Somerville College for most of her professional life and then transferred to Trinity College, Cambridge. Almost all of her work consisted in the careful editing of basic texts; she participated in the standard editions of the letters of the Wordsworths and of William's works. For Milton, she edited the manuscript of Book 1 of *PL* that survives in the Morgan Library (Oxford, 1931), work that has been superseded by Harris Fletcher's facsimile edition. Her edition of *The Early Lives of Milton* (London, 1932)—those by Aubrey*, "John Phillips" (the Anonymous Biographer, as she thought), Anthony Wood*, Edward Phillips, John Toland*, and Jonathan Richardson*—remains the accepted text. Later she edited the two-volume *Poetical Works* (Oxford, 1952–1955). Because this last is the standard Oxford edition, it has received considerable attention, but wide acceptance has not been accorded its editor's arguments for consistency in Milton's own spelling*, which was supposedly ignored by his amanuenses* and printers* and which she thought that she had recovered and employed to make this edition consistent with its author's purposes. [WBH]

DATI, CARLO (1619–1676), a member of the intellectual elite in Florence during Milton's two visits to that city in 1638–39. Though only eighteen years old when he befriended Milton, Dati had already established a reputation as a man of letters, an eloquent speaker, and a student of science. He actively participated in the academies of Florence; and when Milton first arrived in Florence, Dati was secretary of the Apatisti or the "Passionless," and a distinguished member of other academies, including, for example, the Svogliati* or the "Disgusted," and the Crusca, or the "Bran." Dati often welcomed visiting intellectuals to Florence and introduced them to the savants of the academies. No minutes of the meetings of the Apatisti survive, but Milton probably attended some of their sessions, which were devoted to classical and Tuscan literature, philology, and other related literary and historical studies. Milton's attendance at four meetings of the Svogliati is documented by surviving minutes, and during three of the sessions he read Latin poetry. In 2Def Milton mentions Carlo Dati, along with other members of the Apatisti and the Svogliati, while recalling his pleasant associations with the Italian academies (8 : 308–9). Among the Florentines Milton very rapidly established a reputation as an intellectual; and Dati, probably while Milton was in Florence, wrote and presented to him an encomium in Latin prose that celebrates Milton's erudition, his remarkable memory, his mastery of several languages, and his interest in history (1 : 164–67). This encomium and other testimonials (for example, a commendatory ode in Italian by Antonio Francini*, also a member of the Apatisti) are prefixed to the Latin poems in the 1645 edition of Milton's minor poems. In EpDam, lines 136–38, Milton may be alluding to these encomia when he mentions that Dati and Francini had sung praises of him. Furthermore, since Dati had studied with Galileo*, he possibly may have arranged Milton's meeting with the astronomer in Florence.

Almost eight years after having left Florence, Milton received his first letter from Dati. The letter is lost, but apparently Dati remarked that he had sent three earlier letters to Milton. In his reply, dated April 20, 1647, Milton states that he did not receive the earlier letters, which were evidently lost in transit (Epistol 10). Dati stated in his letter that he had received Milton's EpDam, which was printed separately about 1640. Milton comments in his reply that he had taken great care in sending Dati a copy of the poem, and no doubt he had mailed copies to other friends in Italy. He mentions the publication of his Poems (1645) and explains that because they are in English

he has not sent copies to friends in Italy. He promises, however, to mail the Latin poems of this edition, which perhaps were issued separately; and he explains, moreover, that he has been reluctant to mail them because of their adverse comments on the Pope (in the Gunpowder Plot poems). In this letter Milton also acknowledges reading Dati's description of the funeral rite of King Louis XIII, which was published in 1644, and he concludes by sending greetings to several of his friends in the Apatisti and the Svogliati.

In a letter dated November 1, 1647, Dati replied to Milton (12 : 296–313). He requests that Milton write some commendatory verses on Francesco Rovai, a Florentine poet who recently had died, and he mentions not having yet received Milton's Latin poems. Milton eventually did dispatch two copies of the Latin poems, for Dati acknowledges receiving them in a letter dated December 4, 1648 (12 : 312–15), but he apparently did not compose the memorial verses requested by Dati. In his letter of December 4, Dati mentions his appointment to the chair of classics in the renowned Florentine Academy, and he sends the greetings of several of Milton's Italian friends, including Galilei (probably Vincenzo Galilei, the natural son of the astronomer).

Other correspondence that may have been written between Milton and Dati does not survive, but news of Milton's literary reputation and his role as apologist for the Commonwealth continually reached Dati and the other Florentines through English travelers. [ACL]

DAVENANT, SIR WILLIAM (1606–1668), poet, playwright, theatrical manager, was born in Oxford, the son of a taverner. He came to London at sixteen and was initiated into courtly life by serving as a page in the houeholds first of the Duchess of Richmond and then of Lord Brooke. He rose rapidly in literary and fashionable circles. By 1638 he had written many plays for the public theater and masques for the court, had achieved the quasi-official title of poet laureate, and had become chief Court entertainer until the Civil Wars. He served in the King's army, was knighted at Gloucester in 1643, executed commissions for Queen Henrietta Maria*, and from 1645 to 1650 shared the exile of the Stuart court in France. In 1649 he wrote two books of a projected five-book heroic poem, *Gondibert*, published in 1651 with a prefatory epistle addressed to Thomas Hobbes*, in which he sets forth his literary creed. After a period of imprisonment in the Tower of London, Davenant began presenting entertainments (called *opera* in order to circumvent the Puritan ban on plays), and following the Restoration he was granted by royal warrant permission to operate one of the two authorized theatrical companies in London. He organized and directed the Duke's Company at Lincoln's Inn Fields until his death in 1668. "Through him more than any other the Restoration theatre was linked to its Elizabethan forerunner, and to the music, scenes, and machinery of the Caroline court masques" (Leslie Hotson, *The Commonwealth and Restoration Stage*, p. 223). The most important figure in the shaping of Restoration theatrical practice, Davenant introduced the use of movable scenery with a proscenium arch and curtain, innovations that became permanent features of the public playhouse.

Davenant's personal life may have intersected with Milton's at three points. In 1650, enroute to America with a commission from Charles II*, Davenant was captured by Parliamentary ships and imprisoned first on the Isle of Wight and later in the Tower. Milton may have been instrumental in helping obtain Davenant's release. The Anonymous biographer says that he "procured relief" for Davenant; and Davenant's son William told Jacob Tonson* that "when his father was in the tower he was very much assisted by Mr. Milton in gaining his liberty. . . ." Anthony Wood* had suggested that Milton had saved Davenant's life, a suggestion that scholars believe is a dramatic oversimplification of the facts. Parker reviews the evidence and concludes that we are probably justified in believing that Milton spoke up for Davenant but that reasons of state dictated the change of policy that actually saved his life (*Life*, p. 1017). Davenant may have interceded in turn on Milton's behalf in June 1660 when Milton was included on a "purge list" of a vengeful Commons. Parker comments that the story "is a good one and probably true," but points out that Milton had other influential friends (p. 572). The story seems to have been transmitted from the actor Thomas Betterton to Alexander Pope and then to Jonathan Richardson. Davenant's son William* studied Latin and Greek with Milton, but perhaps only after his father's death.

In dramatic theory and practice Davenant and Milton were poles apart. The contrast between Davenant's first court masque *The Temple of Love* and Milton's nearly contemporaneous *Mask* provides a good example : one celebrates the ideas then fashionable in the coterie of Queen Henrietta Maria; the other distinguishes the true doctrine of Platonic love* from the false one currently popular at court. Davenant wrote revenge tragedies, comedies of manners, masques flattering the Stuarts, operas and adaptations of Shakespeare. Both as a writer and as a producer he was concerned always with what succeeded on the stage, for the stage was his livelihood. Milton might prefer classical form and deplore "the Poet's error of intermixing Comic stuff with Tragic sadness and gravity" (Preface to *SA*), but records show the popularity of tragicomedy with the Restoration audience.

No documentary proof exists that Milton knew Davenant's *Preface to Gondibert*, though the likelihood is strong. Indeed, Tillyard writes that "Milton probably agreed with almost the whole of the critical matter given in Davenant's admirable preface . . ." (*The Miltonic Setting*, p. 203). Each poet believed that the audience for his heroic poem would be the "fit though few"; both emphasized the instructive value of poetry, its power to win people to virtue; both held allegiance to the doctrine of appropriate style. Davenant's *Preface* moves from a discussion of earlier heroic poetry, which he rejects as a model for imitation, to a detailed consideration of his own artistic intentions and finally to a generalized defense of poetry. Heroic poetry, he writes, should persuade men to admiration of the heroic virtue portrayed; it should provide a pattern of imitation for leaders of men who, adopting the morals of the poem, will then set a powerful example to the multitude. Poetry is above all useful: it can educate people's minds to virtue and thus aid the four chief instruments of government—religion, arms, politics, and law.

Davenant believed that English drama had found the most "pleasant and instructive" method for the "representment of great actions." Thus, though his poem is narrative, he has observed dramatic symmetry, "proportioning five Books to five *Acts,* & *Canto's* to *Scenes,*" and following dramatic practice of interweaving lesser plots ("underwalks") with the main design. Davenant's analogy between dramatic and epic structure was neither an innovation nor an affectation but had precedents both in critical theory and in practice. (Prose romances of heroic origin—Sidney's* canceled *Arcadia,* for example—often employed five-part structure.) *PL* in ten books (1667 edition) is seen by Arthur Barker as a firmly organized five-act epic, exemplifying the formal requirements set forth in Davenant's *Preface.* Emphasis comes down heavily on the fourth act —Davenant wrote that the fourth was usually the longest—Satan's successful achievement of man's Fall*. Milton's redivision of the poem into twelve books shifts the weight of emphasis, balancing the tragic implications of the Fall with the process of redemption and regeneration. But Barker believes the redivision neither repudiates the theory of the five-act epic nor obscures the five-act structure of the poem. Indeed, "the dramatic and epic structural patterns are thus brought into exact alignment" and *PL* becomes "the consummate example of five-act epic structure" (*Philological Quarterly* 28 : 28). [GFB]

DAVENANT, WILLIAM: *see* Tutoring by Milton.

DAVIES, SAMUEL: *see* Influence in America, Milton's.

DAVIS, MISS, unidentified friend. Edward Phillips, in speaking of the period when Mary Milton had left her husband (1642–1645), wrote that her return "put a stop or rather an end to a grand affair, which was more than probably thought to be then in agitation : It was indeed a design of marrying one of Dr. Davis's daughters, a very handsome and witty gentlewoman, but averse as it is said to this motion." Some slight corroboration comes from the Anonymous Biographer: Milton "thought upon a divorce that he might be free to marry another, concerning which he also was in treaty." Neither Dr. Davis nor his daughter has been identified, and nothing further is known about this possible second marriage. The suggestion that the lady of *Sonn* 9 was Miss Davis has no foundation. [JTS]

DE BRASS, HENRY. Not even life dates are known for this continental scholar whom Milton advised in two letters. In *Epistol* 23 to him (July 15, 1657) Milton stated his preference for Sallust* over any other Latin historian and gave his own ideas about the function of the historian and historiography*. In *Epistol* 26 (December 16, 1657) Milton discussed a passage from Aristotle* that De Brass thought referred to historians; Milton again presented his views on history. [WM]

DE DOCTRINA CHRISTIANA. The unique manuscript of Milton's *De Doctrina Christiana* (S.P. 9/61 in the Public Records Office, London) comprises 745 pages (misnumbered as 735). The greater part of the manuscript was written by Jeremie Picard*, Milton's amanuensis* from approximately 1658 to around 1660, but contains later insertions by diverse hands (amanuenses A, B, C, M, N, and O) as well as corrections by Daniel Skinner, Jr.*, the "young student to whom [as Hanford suggested] Milton entrusted the document in 1673 or 1674. . . ." The first fourteen chapters (pages 1–196) had been recopied by Skinner in preparing the treatise for publication by Elzevir's press* in Amsterdam. This portion of the theological* tractate contains the controversial chapters on the Son of God* and the Holy Spirit*, predestination* and other divine decrees*, the creation* of the world, and the death* of the body. Skinner's transcription, designed for the benefit of the printer rather than the twentieth-century scholar, replaced Picard's draft of these chapters and the marginalia of subsequent amanuenses— thus obliterating manuscript evidence that might have enabled Miltonists to date these chapters with greater accuracy and to ascertain with greater precision the state of Milton's beliefs at the time he was composing PL. (See also ECCLESIOLOGY.)

Plans for printing CD were abruptly dropped when it became evident that publication of the treatise would jeopardize young Skinner's political career. In 1677 Elzevir returned the manuscript at the request of Skinner's father; and after passing into the custody of Sir Joseph Williamson, Secretary of State, it remained buried in state archives until rediscovered in 1823 by Robert Lemon, deputy keeper of His Majesty's State Papers. Two years later, an edition of the Latin text and an English translation by Charles Richard Sumner were published in two quarto volumes by the Cambridge University Press; an American edition of Sumner's translation was printed the same year in Boston. Sumner subsequently revised his translation for the Bohn edition of Milton's prose (1848–1853). CM published a new edition of the Latin text prepared by James Holly Hanford and Waldo Hilary Dunn (1933–34) and reprinted Sumner's English translation. A new translation by John Carey appears in Yale Prose, 6, Maurice Kelley, editor.

On the date of Milton's treatise, its stages of composition, the nature and degree of its heterodoxy, and its value for the interpretation of PL, Milton scholars have disagreed strongly. Since its publication in 1825, a variety of dates have been proposed: 1) before 1641; 2) 1643–1645; 3) 1655–1658; 4) 1658–1660; and 5) 1660 or later. The testimony of Milton's early biographers* has been variously interpreted, and in his own account of the genesis of his tractate, scholars have found evidence for one, two, or even three stages of composition.

In his preface to CD, Milton himself declares that in his youth he had undertaken "an assiduous course of study, beginning with the books of the Old and New Testament in their original languages and going diligently through a few of the shorter systems of divines. . . ." In "imitation" of the latter, he was "in the habit of classing under certain heads whatever passages of Scripture occurred for extraction, to be made use of hereafter as occasion might require." Turning later to "some of the more copious theological treatises" and examining "the arguments advanced by the conflicting parties respecting certain disputed points of faith," he had been dismayed by their deficiencies in logical and exegetical method and their "deference to custom and the spirit of party" rather than to scriptural authority. Recognizing the need for "some methodical tractate of Christian doctrine" or "such a disquisition as might be useful in establishing my faith or assisting my memory," he had attempted to "compile for myself, by my own labour and study, some original treatise which should always be at hand, derived solely from the word of God itself, and executed with all possible fidelity . . ." (14 : 5–9).

Though Aubrey* and Wood* mentioned the manuscript of an Idea Theologiae in the possession of a member of the Skinner family, they gave no indication of its date of composition. The anonymous biographer (identified as Cyriack Skinner) listed "the framing a Body of Divinity out of the Bible" among works that the poet had begun after losing his eyesight and finished after the

Restoration. According to Edward Phillips, however, Milton was already at work on "a perfect System of Divinity" while still a schoolmaster in St. Bride's Churchyard. His students'* Sunday exercises had included "the writing from his own dictation, some part, from time to time, of a Tractate which he thought fit to collect from the ablest of Divines, who had written of that subject; *Amesius, Wollebius,* &c. . . ."

The problem of correlating these statements with one another and with the treatise in its present form has been further complicated by references (from about 1640 to 1652) in Milton's *CB* to an "Index Theologicus*." No such work exists among his surviving papers, and scholars have debated whether or not the theological index was an earlier version of *CD*. In Kelley's opinion it was apparently "concerned with temporal aspects of the church" and based on nonbiblical sources; it would appear, therefore, to have been an entirely different work from the system of divinity Milton was preparing at roughly the same time.

In 1920 James Holly Hanford argued, on the basis of handwriting and testimony of the anonymous biographer (*Studies in Philology* 17:309ff.), that in the last years before the Restoration Milton "carried forward . . . the actual composition of the document as we now have it" and that he had "practically finished the dictation of the treatise to his amanuensis by 1660, when the Restoration cut off all immediate hope of publication. . . ." The manuscript thus stood essentially "complete in the early sixties or before" and was therefore "very closely associated with *Paradise Lost*" chronologically (which, according to Aubrey, Milton had begun about two years before the Restoration). Hence the "theological detail" of the treatise "can and should be freely used in the interpretation of the poem."

Within the following decades Hanford's opinion of the value of the treatise as a gloss on the epic was questioned by Arthur Sewell (*A Study in Milton's*

"Christian Doctrine" [1939]) and defended by Maurice Kelley (*This Great Argument* [1941]). In Sewell's opinion, *CD* had been composed in three stages. After close study of the Scriptures and brief theological compendia (first stage), Milton attempted a "methodical tractate" based on Scripture (second stage) and finally a "reexamination" of traditional doctrines in the light of biblical testimony (third stage). This third version was never finished, and the surviving manuscript contains unresolved contradictions and several "layers of opinion." The Picard draft belonged to the second stage of composition (around 1658–1660) and represented an earlier and more orthodox version of the treatise than the surviving version; and it was the Picard draft (Sewell argued) that Milton utilized as a doctrinal guide for *PL*. After the first fourteen chapters the only passage in the manuscript that "plainly shows [Milton's] unorthodox view of the Trinity" is an addition made to the Picard draft by a later scribe. In Sewell's opinion, Milton apparently held Trinitarian* views as late as 1659; and, even though the later books of the epic show "the pressure of other opinion," the earlier books reflect a Trinitarian position. The "anti-Trinitarian" passages in the treatise were written *after* the early books of *PL*, and scholars should not "too uncritically assume" that the treatise could "be used as a comment on, and an interpretation of, the doctrinal basis" of the epic.

In defending the utility of *CD* as a gloss on *PL*, Kelley challenged Sewell's hypothesis of a third and unfinished stage in the composition of the treatise and Sewell's evidence for doctrinal discrepancies between the two works. In Kelley's opinion, Milton's own account of the genesis of his treatise clearly distinguished two rather than three phases in its composition. The first stage began while Milton was "still a boy" and ended with his "institution of a commonplace book" composed of scriptural passages arranged under general headings. The second stage began with Milton's "study of more voluminous treatises," and this attempt to compile a guide of his own making ultimately evolved into *CD*. Except for relatively unimportant additions by later amanuenses, the treatise as we know it was essentially complete when Picard made his draft around 1658–1660, "just before or during the period when Milton was dictating *Paradise Lost.*" There is no evidence that the treatise was subjected to extensive revision after Picard made his draft, and the latter probably contained the Arian* passages in the fifth and sixth chapters of the first book. Not only are *PL* and *CD* "apparently synchronous works," but "numerous parallel passages" indicate that they "agree in their theological doctrine." Nevertheless, the precise date at which Milton abandoned the orthodox positions that he had held earlier cannot, in Kelley's opinion, be ascertained. Though Milton expressed Trinitarian sympathies in the antiprelatical tracts of 1641, his subsequent remarks on this subject were ambiguous and noncommittal until the execution of the Picard draft. As late as 1644, Milton was still expressing hostility toward Arminianism* in *Areop.*

In W. R. Parker's judgment (*Milton,* pp. 1052, 1056) the entire treatise was composed over a period of three years ("between May 1655 and May 1658") rather than in two or three stages. The system of divinity mentioned by Phillips was merely "a preliminary work," and Milton's "attempt at an original compilation" utilizing the treatises of Ames* and other theologians was "begun about 1656." Like Hanford and Kelley, Parker believed that "the treatise stood essentially complete at least in first draft, *c.* 1658–60 . . . and that revisions made after the Restoration altered no important points of doctrine." Nevertheless, "internal evidence is of scant help in determining the date" of Milton's treatise, and "doctrinal points developed" therein cannot be "accurately dated with reference to either external events or Milton's published statements."

The organization and methodology of Milton's treatise have usually received less attention than its date, its stages of composition, and its doctrinal heterodoxy. These topics, however, are scarcely less important for understanding the nature and scope of the treatise and its relationship to *PL*. Sewell's objection that *CD* is "a patchwork thing, never conceived as a whole, an orthodox body of doctrine, altered, deleted, and amended as Milton's views changed" does scant justice to the systematic organization of the treatise or to its rigorous exegetical methods. Nevertheless this criticism points to inherent tensions in *CD* that are explicable primarily in terms of its genre and methods.

Essentially, *CD* belongs to the same literary genre as Amandus Polanus's *Syntagma Theologiae Christianae,* John Wolleb's* *Compendium Theologiae Christianae,* and William Ames's *Medulla SS. Theologiae.* It is a synopsis or "system" of theology"—a "methodical tractate"— and it belongs generically among the "many treatises of theology . . . wherein the chief heads of Christian doctrine are set forth sometimes briefly, sometimes in a more enlarged and methodical order" (14 : 3). The usual function of such compendia was essentially one of summarizing received opinion rather than of disputing controversial points of doctrine. Ecclesiastical debate and doctrinal dispute were normally prosecuted through other media.

Like the *Loci Communes* of Melanchthon and Peter Martyr Vermigli*, moreover, these treatises could serve as commonplace books, aiding memory and facilitating composition by defining essential doctrines, confirming them by various proof-texts, and arranging them under convenient topical headings. Milton himself declares that he intends to teach "no novelties of doctrine," but rather to assist the memory by "conveniently [reducing] into one compact body . . . and [digesting] under certain heads" materials "dispersed throughout the different parts of the Holy Scriptures. . . ." Justifying his procedure by biblical injunction (2 Tim. 1 : 13) and precedent, he maintains that the author of Hebrews had taught "the heads of Christian doctrine in methodical arrangement," and that St. Paul himself had delivered "some entire body of doctrine, formed according to a certain plan. . . ." Milton's methodology was firmly grounded, he believed, both on "Christian prudence" and on "divine command" (14 : 21–23).

It was also based, however, on humanistic rhetorical and pedagogical techniques. The "notebook-and-heading" method favored by Renaissance schoolmasters as an aid to the study and imitation of classical literature and to literary exercises had not only encouraged the use of private commonplace books as aids to reflection and composition, but had led to the publication of numerous topically organized manuals like Erasmus's *Copia Rerum,* which might assist the reader in inventing or "finding" appropriate arguments on a wide variety of themes. Similarly, the theological commonplace books of Reformation divines and the doctrinal compendia that Milton endeavored to "imitate" could serve as aids to meditation and composition, not only confirming the reader's memory and faith, but actually assisting him in selecting and deploying theological evidence in his own oral and written discourse. The chief heads in these manuals, then, were the commonplaces (*loci communes*) of Reformed doctrine; and the scriptural quotations arranged under these general headings functioned literally as "proof-texts," arguments based on divine testimony.

Structurally, *CD* is divided into two books ("Of the Knowledge of God" and "Of the Worship of God"), subdivided respectively into 33 and 17 chapters. Though Milton inherited this twofold division from earlier compendia, and perhaps also from the Ramist* method of classification through dichotomies, he specifically justifies this arrangement on scriptural and methodological grounds. Quoting 2 Timothy 1:13 ("the form of sound words . . . , in faith and in love"), 1 John 3 : 23 ("believe and love") and similar texts, he asserts that "Christian doctrine is comprehended under two divisions: FAITH*, or THE KNOWLEDGE OF GOD; and LOVE*, or THE WORSHIP OF

GOD." Though "distinct in their own nature, and put asunder for the convenience of teaching," these "two divisions . . . cannot be separated in practice" (14 : 23).

For his organization and choice of headings, in his definitions, and in his citations of proof-texts, Milton was frequently indebted to the compendia of Ames and Wolleb. The Latin proof-texts are usually taken directly from the Junius-Tremellius Bible* (which contained translations of the Old Testament by Tremellius*, of the Apocrypha by Junius*, and of the New Testament by Beza*, along with Tremellius's translation from the Syriac New Testament). On occasion, however, Milton translated directly from the sacred tongues.

In his discussion of major and minor topics Milton normally begins with a formal definition. Alternatively (or additionally) he may introduce a formal *divisio,* subdividing the topic into its parts and then taking these up in systematic order. Then he proceeds to the citation of proof-texts for his definition and/or its key terms. Having thus validated his doctrinal statements by scriptural testimony, he may on occasion draw further inferences from his texts or from his previous conclusions before progressing to the next topic. In discussing dubious points of doctrine he may at times introduce extended passages of philological analysis or theological speculation. Though these are an essential feature of his method of scriptural interpretation, they may seem at first reading digressive; and they are probably responsible for some of the adverse criticism directed against the treatise—charges of loose organization, uncertainty, and contradiction.

The philological techniques that Milton employs in his exegesis of Scripture reflect the influence of the Erasmian tradition, while his logical methods derive from Ramus and Downham* through his own *Logic.* Though the influence of Buxtorf's *Lexicon Hebraicum* is apparent in several passages, none of the 30 Hebrew entries in *CD* is in Milton's hand, and Harry Snyder Gehman has recently pointed out errors in vocalization and accentuation.

Despite occasional allusions to specific theologians (Calvin*, Luther*, Zwingli, Bucer*, Musculus, Beza, Polanus, Zanchius*, Placaeus of Saumur, and others), the immediate sources of *CD* remain for the most part unidentified. In several controversial chapters Milton fails to cite a single theologian or theological work by name. In certain instances, references to specific authors seem to have been derived from later works. In other cases, verbal resemblances to a contemporary theological treatise seem to have resulted from common indebtedness to an unidentified source. In Kelley's opinion, the specific sources of the Arminian and anti-Trinitarian views expressed in *CD* are, on the whole, uncertain; and the treatise exhibits dissimilarities as well as similarities to contemporary Arminian and anti-Trinitarian movements.

In addition to investigations of immediate sources, recent scholarship has compared Milton's religious thinking with that of particular theologians (Eusebius*, Lactantius*, Origen*, Ambrose*, Augustine*, Calvin, Curcellaeus, Arminius, Servetus*, Ochino*, and others) or reexamined it against the general background of patristic and Reformation controversy (*see* C. A. Patrides, *Milton and the Christian Traditions*). William B. Hunter, Jr. (*Bright Essence* [1971]) has compared Milton's views on the persons of the Trinity with the doctrines of the subordinationist fathers; and both Hunter and Patrides have reexamined Milton's theological vocabulary. Father Amadeus Fiore has reviewed Milton's treatise and epics in relation to seventeenth-century soteriology; and dissertations by Charles L. Childers and Roger Dale Chittick have reexamined his theology in terms of "historical Christianity" and the "Augustinian tradition" respectively. E. E. Cairns has discussed the utility of the treatise as a gloss on the epic; and J. T. Eisenring's recent book on *CD* analyzes its doctrines

from a Roman Catholic viewpoint. Arnold Williams has explored Milton's relationship to Renaissance commentaries on Genesis, and Harris Francis Fletcher has investigated Milton's possible indebtedness to rabbinical tradition and other facets of the Renaissance intellectual background.

Of Milton's alleged heresies*, his anti-Trinitarianism has received the greatest attention (*see* the studies by Hunter, Kelley, Patrides, L. A. Wood, J. H. Adamson, John A. Clair, Ruth Kivette, Roland M. Frye, and others). Adamson and A. J. Sambrood have reexamined Milton's views on the question of creation *ex nihilo* or *ex Deo;* Hunter and John Reesing, his materialism; George Williamson, his mortalism; and Geoffrey Bullough, his opinions on polygamy. For discussion, *see* HERESIES, MILTON'S; THEOLOGY; ARIANISM; SOCINIANISM; MORTALISM; MATTER; POLYGAMY; FATHER; SON; HOLY SPIRIT; INCARNATION.

Scholarship on the intellectual background of *CD* has, on the whole, been more successful in exploring its consistencies or inconsistencies with broader theological traditions or particular doctrinal movements than in ascertaining its actual sources. Milton had read widely in both patristic and Reformation literature and in the writings of liberal and conservative theologians. Though their arguments may have helped to formulate certain doctrinal issues for him, the principal factor in making up his own mind on these points would seem to have been his own reexamination of the controversial proof-texts in the light of his philological and logical principles. "I had not even read any of the works of heretics, so called," he declares (14 : 15), "when the mistakes of those who are reckoned for orthodox, and their incautious handling of Scripture, first taught me to agree with their opponents, whenever these opponents agreed with Scripture."

If the formal organization of *CM* represents the static aspect of Milton's method, the dynamic element in his methodology is his reliance on Scripture and the guidance of the Holy Spirit as the ultimate authorities in matters of doctrine. Though both aspects of his methodology are an inheritance from Reformation tradition, the latter sometimes led to original (and, from the viewpoint of Calvinist orthodoxy, heterodox) results.

In his citation of proof-texts and in the originality of his interpretations, he frequently goes far beyond his original models. In his dissatisfaction with "indolent credulity," as he writes in the Preface he is not content to produce simply another epitome of Reformed divinity like the "shorter systems" he had endeavored to "imitate." After a "diligent perseverance" in his plan for several years, he had recognized that "more than I was aware of still remained, which required to be more rigidly examined by the rule of Scripture, and reformed after a more accurate model." In his "unwearied search after truth" and his distaste for "implicit faith," he relies on the authority and "evidence of Scripture" alone, filling his "pages even to redundance with quotations from Scripture, that so as little space as possible might be left for my own words, even when they arise from the context of revelation itself." At the same time he insists on the importance of an individual and personal interpretation of the biblical revelation. It is "only to the individual faith of each that the Deity has opened the way of eternal salvation," and the man "who would be saved" (a conscious and possibly ironic echo of the phraseology of the Athanasian creed?) must "have a personal belief of his own. . . ." Milton has (he declares) "taken the grounds of my faith from divine revelation alone" rather than from "the faith or judgment of others . . . ," and in defending himself and his treatise against future charges of heresy he emphasizes the value of free "discussion and inquiry" and the importance of Christian liberty—"the liberty not only of winnowing and sifting every doctrine, but also of thinking and even writing respecting it, according to our individual faith and persuasion . . ." (14 : 3–15).

Sewell has not been alone in deploring the absence of an "orthodox body of doctrine" in Milton's treatise, yet his objection seems, in fact, to beg the question. For Milton, in his later years, an orthodox body of doctrine would have seemed a virtually unattainable goal, a remote objective to be approached and approximated rather than attained. The true doctrine stood revealed in the Scriptures, but it had not been definitively abstracted and arranged in systematic form. Its principles were scattered and dispersed throughout the sacred volume like the limbs of the mutilated virgin in *Areop,* to be gradually and progressively reassembled by conscientious researchers under the guidance of the Holy Spirit. The "perfect shape" of truth, who "came once into the world with her divine Master," has been "scatter'd . . . to the four winds"—and will not be completely reassembled "till her Masters second comming; he shall bring together every joynt and member, and shall mould them into an immortall feature of loveliness and perfection." As Milton recognized as early as 1644, the orthodox faith is rather a progressive process of rediscovery and revelation than an achieved body of dogma : "but he who thinks we are to pitch our tent here, and have attain'd the utmost prospect of reformation . . . is yet farre short of Truth. . . . The light which we have gain'd, was giv'n us, not to be ever staring on, but by it to discover onward things more remote from our knowledge. . . . To be still searching what we know not, by what we know, still closing up truth to truth as we find it . . . this is the golden rule in *Theology* as well as in Arithmetick . . ." (4 : 337–39). Milton's "methodical tractate," collecting, interpreting, and organizing the evidence of truth dispersed throughout Scripture, belongs, as he conceives it, to the Reformation program for the recovery and dissemination of the original biblical revelation. It is part of the search undertaken by the "sad friends" of Truth for the torn body of their martyred saint.

The "studie of scripture . . . is the only

true theologie," Milton declared in *Hire* (1659), and in the same work (6 : 78, 80) he expressed the need for "som wholsom bodie of divinitie . . . without schoole terms and metaphysical notions, which have obscur'd rather then explan'd our religion, and made it seem difficult without cause." This (it has been suggested) was a reference to his own *CD*; and it is significant that precisely at this time (in Hanford's opinion) Milton was apparently preparing his treatise for publication, with the aid of Picard.

"The Christian Doctrine," by Milton's own definition, "is that DIVINE REVELATION disclosed in various ages by CHRIST . . . concerning the nature and worship of the Deity, for the promotion of the glory of God, and the salvation of mankind." It is to be obtained not from man-made laws or philosophical schools but "from the Holy Scriptures alone, under the guidance of the Holy Spirit" (14 : 17–21). The Scriptures themselves, moreover, are "plain and perspicuous in all things necessary to salvation" and should be interpreted in no "more than one sense" (although in the Old Testament "this sense is sometimes a compound of the historical and the typical"). Not only is Scripture the sole "rule and canon of faith," but every believer possesses the right to interpret it for himself under "the guidance of the Spirit of God." Under the Gospel, we possess a "twofold Scripture," external and internal —"the written word" and "the Holy Spirit, written in the hearts of believers"— and though the former is usually "prior in point of reception," the latter is "far superior to all. . . ." Even "on the authority of Scripture itself, every thing is to be finally referred to the Spirit and the unwritten word." Finally, believers not only are forbidden "to pay any regard to human traditions, whether written or unwritten," but may not "trust implicitly . . . to the opinions of our forefathers, or of antiquity," nor "attach any due authority" even to "the venerable name of our mother church . . ." (16 : 249–85).

These are the basic theoretical and methodological assumptions underlying Milton's exposition of Christian doctrine. Proceeding according to these principles, he could and did achieve a systematic "body of doctrine" (even in the sense in which Sewell uses this phrase), but his system could be "orthodox" only in a highly specialized sense. By his own principles, Milton could not have subjected his creed to the authority of tradition or antiquity, church or state, without violating the superior authority of the biblical text and the supreme authority of the Spirit.

The exegetical methods that he follows in his treatise conform, on the whole, to the "requisites for the public interpretation of Scripture" as Milton understood them : "knowledge of languages; inspection of the originals; examination of the context; care in distinguishing between literal and figurative expressions; consideration of cause and circumstance of antecedents and consequents; mutual comparison of texts; and regard to the analogy of faith"; and attention to "the frequent anomalies of syntax. . . ." Finally, "no inferences from the text are to be admitted, but such as follow necessarily and plainly from the words themselves. . . ." Otherwise, we should be taking "the fallacies of human reasoning for the doctrines of God : for it is by the declarations of Scripture, and not by the conclusions of the schools, that our consciences are bound" (16 : 263–65). These principles, set forth in *CD* itself, were the guidelines that Milton followed in the composition of his treatise, and it is partly in terms of these principles that he defends himself and his work against charges (not unforeseeable) of heterodoxy.

One of the many paradoxes in the fate of *CD* is that it was, on Milton's testimony, a private "aid" to faith and memory, which he was nonetheless offering to the united church. Whereas the majority of Reformation compendia were essentially public rather than private documents—systematic statements of doctrines already accepted by a majority or a substantial minority of Protestant divines —Milton's treatise is avowedly the creed of an individual, the record of a personal quest for the divine doctrine dispersed throughout Scripture. Like *PL, CD* is a personal interpretation of the biblical revelation; Milton has conceived and executed his treatise as an aid to "establishing" his personal faith, and he defends it against future critics by insisting that it is essentially a personal creed, not a derivative heresy. It is as an individual that John Milton, in a dedication reminiscent of apostolic formulas, addresses his ecumenical and catholic epistle "To all the churches of Christ, and to all who profess the Christian Faith throughout the world. . . ."

Through all its various (and, for many scholars, undefinable) metamorphoses, Milton's treatise of divinity was, in spite of Sewell's criticism, conceived as an organic whole. It was a coherent system, but also a "living" system, constantly outgrowing itself and, in several notable instances, evolving significantly different attitudes toward the very categories with which it had begun. There is an inherent tension in the methodology underlying *CD*—between the topical categories that Milton had derived from his models, and the methods of scriptural exegesis that he had likewise inherited from Reformation divines. As his own examination of Scripture led him to question the "received" opinions of the Protestant churches, he found it increasingly difficult to remain within the very systems that he had chosen as formal models. The latter were, in fact, epitomes of an "orthodox body of divinity" (in Sewell's sense of this term), but Milton's "imitation" of the exegetical and structural methods of his predecessors sometimes resulted in highly personal or even idiosyncratic interpretations. Occasionally his unconventional doctrinal interpretations affected the formal organization of his work, as in the position of the chapters on predestination* and the divine decrees*. [JMS]

DE IDEA PLATONICA QUEMADMODUM ARISTOTELES INTELLEXIT (On the Platonic Idea as Understood by Aristotle). This thirty-nine-line Latin poem appeared in both the 1645 and 1673 editions of Milton's poems, but with no indication as to the date of composition. It may be the poem that Milton described in a letter to his former teacher Alexander Gill*. In this letter, *Epist* 3, dated July 2, 1628, Milton stated that he was enclosing verses which he had written for a Fellow in his college who was to participate in the commencement exercises of the year. Specifically, the Fellow was to engage in one of those disputations on philosophical questions which were a feature of the exercises at that time. As a disputant, he was required by custom to furnish verses on the question; but "being himself already long past the age for trifles of that sort, and more intent on serious things," he entrusted their composition to Milton, who obliged. (A date of 1631 has also been argued for the letter, and thus the poem.)

Further identification of these verses is lacking. It has often been assumed that they are rather the poem *Naturam,* but a number of scholars have pointed out that *Idea* fits Milton's description equally well. Indeed, in that it is a more "trifling" poem, it fits his description better. Absolute certainty in the matter, however, is impossible, although it is probably safe enough to assert that *Idea* belongs to Milton's Cambridge period and is an academic exercise of some kind.

Idea tackles a weighty philosophical issue—Plato's* theory of Ideas—in a lighthearted manner. According to Plato, the ultimate ground of reality lay not in the world disclosed to the senses, but in the realm of Ideas upon which the intelligibility and existence of that world depended. Thus there existed the Idea *Man,* which was responsible for the intelligibility and existence of men, as such. To this, Aristotle* objected that Ideas, rather than being outside the world of sense, were in some way present in it. There could not, then, be any Idea *Man* in separation from real men.

In *Idea* Milton assumes the role of a literal-minded follower of Aristotle who wants to know where the Idea *Man* can be found, a question anticipated, interestingly enough, by Plato himself in the *Parmenides*. The Idea *Man* does not lurk, Milton says, unborn in the brain of Jove. Perhaps, our poet speculates, he is a comrade of the stars or inhabits the moon, perhaps he dwells by the waters of Lethe or in some far-off expanse of earth. But no, Milton concludes, none of the seers or prophets before Plato ever mentioned this fabulous creature. Plato, then, must either recall the poets, whom he banished from his state for their fables, or go into exile himself.

Milton's tone is lightly ironical; his poem is a performance that deserves perhaps to have received more attention than it has. Scholars have generally ignored it despite the high praise of a few. Parker, for example, has described it as "a gay and good-natured burlesque . . ." (*Milton*, p. 104). C. S. Lewis was even more enthusiastic: in translating it, he noted the "goblin quality of the original" and hoped that his version would send "readers to explore for themselves such a neglected and exquisite grotesque" (*English* 5 : 195). His hope, however, has not been realized. [ERG]

DEATH. In Milton's view death is the result of and punishment for sin* : "After sin came death, as the calamity or punishment consequent upon it" (*CD* 15 : 203). Thus, Adam would never have died had he not fallen. Sin separates man from God, the source of life.

In *CD* Milton enumerates four degrees of death. "The first . . . comprehends ALL THOSE EVILS WHICH LEAD TO DEATH, and which it is agreed came into the world immediately upon the fall of man . . ." (15 : 203). "The second is called *spiritual death*; by which is meant the loss of divine grace, and that of innate righteousness, wherein man in the beginning lived unto God. . . . And this death

took place not only on the very day, but at the very moment of the fall. They who are delivered from it are said to be 'regenerated,' to be 'born again' . . ." (15 : 205). "The third . . . is what is called the DEATH OF THE BODY" (15:215). "The fourth and last degree of death, is DEATH ETERNAL, THE PUNISHMENT OF THE DAMNED . . ." (15 : 251).

Adam's dogmatic statement after the Fall* that "All of me then shall die" (*PL* 10. 792) emphasizes Milton's mature belief that the body and soul die together, since the soul never had any life of itself and the "separation of soul and body cannot be called the death of man" (15 : 217-19; *see* MORTALISM). Moreover, at the Last Judgment all men are to be resurrected, to either eternal bliss or eternal damnation.

Adam's discourse on death in *PL* is, however, highly speculative, since he is only beginning to understand the depth of his "doom" (10. 769f.). And it is not until Michael sets before him the "shape" of death through a vision of Abel's murder that Adam grasps the meaning of death as a foul and ugly terror, "horrid to think" and "horrible to feel" (11. 465). Adam's vision of death contrasts with Satan's encounter with the shapeless and indeterminate Death of Book 2, a personified description that incorporates the biblical Angel of Death and the skeleton in the Dance of Death and the Renaissance Triumphs of Death.

The death of Christ is central to the doctrine of the Atonement*. God requires "the rigid satisfaction, death for death" (*PL* 3. 212) as the means of preserving divine justice. Christ's death is both a "satisfaction" and "ransom" (*PL* 3. 212, 221), whereby "THE SATISFACTION OF CHRIST IS THE COMPLETE REPARATION MADE BY HIM . . . BY THE FULFILMENT OF THE LAW, AND PAYMENT OF THE REQUIRED PRICE FOR MANKIND" (*CD* 15 : 315-17). In this respect, death becomes a major paradox of Christian thought, by which death is the means to life, and provides Milton with a logical equivocation that allows him to pursue the fundamental mystery of God's justice. [EEE]

DEBATE. Milton was preoccupied with the art of debate throughout his life. Among his earliest extant writings are his school exercises in debate and his last publication is the polemical pamphlet *TR*. All together he composed more than twenty separate controversial tracts, and if one adds his school exercises (*Prol*) and the extensively revised second editions of several tracts, the number swells well beyond thirty. The range of topics is also great—religious doctrines, ceremonies, and government; political governments, their origins and laws; marriage customs and laws; educational theory and practice; and church-state relations—all of which Milton liked to think of as his program to make the Reformation flower in English soil by establishing full religious, domestic, and civil liberties*.

The debate form is frequently used to explain the structure of several of Milton's most celebrated poems. *L'Al* and *IlP* are often tied to Milton's school exercises in which he learned to argue both sides of a single topic. *Mask* has been described as an elaboration of its central event, the debate between Comus and the Lady. *PR*, with its rather minimal narration and description, largely consists of the arguments and counterarguments of Satan and Jesus. Finally, *SA* has been viewed as a series of defenses by a Job-like hero who resists the accusers confronting him. The last three works have often been labeled "dramatized debates."

In *PL* Milton brought the conventional epic debate to its full perfection. He displayed his mastery of different debate techniques especially in the Pandaemonium Council of Book 2, in Satan's disputes with Gabriel and Abdiel, and in the domestic quarrels of Adam and Eve after they have fallen. Although the Council in Hell is structurally parallel to the Council in Heaven, the latter is not so much a debate as a conversation between God and the Son, just as Adam and Eve never debate but simply converse before Book 9. Their opposite is Satan: he is never able to manage a conversation with anyone; he is always debating, even when he meets his son Death, and even when he talks to himself, as in his long soliloquy opening Book 4. Moreover, Satan in *PL* and in *PR* as well seems to be a kind of embodiment of strife that manifests itself in the form of verbal contests; he is the first cause not only of man's Fall* but of the art born of sin* —debate.

These associations in *PL* suggest that where there is no sin there is no debate, and once evil enters into the world, the need to confront it in debate is inescapable. Thus, since the Fall of Man from Paradise, where pure conversation and communion between men and between men and angels* and God was possible, debate has become one of the typical weapons of Christian warfare, but still a sign of corruption.

Milton felt obliged as a Christian to defend the truth publicly and zealously —he hated lukewarmness—and to denounce error vigorously wherever he saw it. As a Christian reformer, he had no time for "cloistered virtue" but felt that Protestants had a special duty to argue openly, and especially about matters not clearly decided by the Bible: "nothing more protestantly can be permitted then a free and lawful debate at all times by writing, conference or disputation" (6 : 13).

Besides this strong sense of religious duty, there are at least three other important reasons why Milton spent so much of his life as a debater: his environment, his temperament, and his education. First, the environment in England during the early seventeenth century was marked by revolutions in politics and religion. As Parliament began resisting the powers of the King and the bishops, a pamphlet war broke out in which opposing parties debated the rights of bishops to rule in both church and civil governments. Milton knew some of the men who opposed the bishops, and when they were attacked he joined the battle with a series of five hastily written tracts of his own. And once he started writing polemics, he could not seem to stop. The antiprelatical tracts were followed by his four divorce* tracts, his appeal for educational reform, his attack on censorship of the press, his two denunciations of tyrannical kingship, and so on. The number and variety of these pamphlets suggest the second reason: Milton seems to have had a naturally disputatious temperament.

Even though some scholars view Milton as a reluctant controversialist, others correctly picture him as taking no small delight in his role of revolutionary pamphleteer and official defender of the republic. It is noteworthy that he volunteered his services in the Puritan fight against the bishops; that he tried several times to instigate a public debate over divorce, and was quite disappointed when no worthy challenger picked up his gauntlet; that he seems to have enjoyed even the more unsavory side of polemics, such as trouncing his enemies' characters as much as their arguments, at times appearing gleeful as he heaped scornful epithets upon them; that in later life he was proud of the controversial prose he had produced with his left hand, particularly his *1Def* and *CD*; and that the end of his prolific period of pamphleteering came not when he chose but when he was officially silenced by the Restoration.

Milton learned how to debate at St. Paul's* and at Cambridge University, two schools that kept alive two very old traditions of learning, the classical and the medieval. These old traditions are important to know if one is to get even a brief glimpse of Milton's training in debate. Classical debate as an academic discipline began with Socrates' method of teaching by raising questions and objecting to the answers of his followers. Plato* beautifully embodied this method in his dialogue-debates, and Aristotle* analyzed it brilliantly in his logical and rhetorical textbooks. Of great importance for Western education were Aristotle's invention of the syllogism (formal proof) in logic* and the

enthymeme (short syllogism) in rhetoric*, and his distinction of the "means of persuasion" into the speaker's ethical character (*ethos*), the argument of a speech (*logos*), and the audience's feelings or passions (*pathos*). All later discussions of the arts of debate rely heavily on these key ideas.

Classical debate was developed further as rhetoric by the Romans. Cicero* created rich models for study in his political orations, and both Cicero and Quintilian* elaborated Aristotle's rules for rhetorical debate. Their practical Roman advice resulted in the widely popular method of dividing a speech into six parts: (1) introduction (*exordium*), (2) statement of the case (*narratio*), (3) outline of parts (*divisio*), (4) proof of the case (*confirmatio*), (5) refutation of opponent's case (*confutatio*), and (6) conclusion (*peroratio*). The Roman tendency to make rhetoric the center of all academic study was revived in the Renaissance.

Medieval debate may be said to begin with Peter Abelard's method of questioning the validity of both sides of every issue by his technique of *sic et non*. During the founding years of university education at Paris, Abelard laid the groundwork for the methods of arguing that grew to perfection in the writings of Thomas Aquinas and became the hallmark of Scholasticism. Whereas the Romans emphasized the Greek tradition of *rhetoric,* the scholastics stressed Aristotelian *logic* and became famous for their formal disputations: an assigned "Disputant" presented a thesis, an "Objector" countered with his antithesis, and then the Disputant tried to reach some sort of synthesis, often by making subtle distinctions. The most nearly perfect model of this education-by-debate technique is the *Summa Theologiae* of Aquinas*.

At St. Paul's Milton was educated in this form of argument. He began by writing *theses* according to the rules and models in his Latin textbooks. One of Milton's own theses survives and in it he argues in favor of early rising (it delights the senses, promotes health, improves study) and against sleeping late (it dulls the mind, especially the memory, and is a kind of death). The ability to argue on both sides of the same topic was stressed, so that his next assignment may well have been to refute his thesis on early rising and to argue in favor of sleeping late.

At Cambridge University in the early seventeenth century the curriculum was still heavily scholastic. Students were expected to attend almost daily the debates held within their own colleges and less often those held before the whole school. These debates were of two different types : disputations and declamations. Disputations were exercises in logic (symbolized for Cicero and Milton by a clenched fist), which continued the scholastic practice of having a disputant confront an objector in the hope of reaching a firmer grasp of some philosophical truth; too often, however, these exercises deteriorated in the later Middle Ages and the Renaissance to the level of empty formal procedures. Milton's *Prol* 5 (on the unity of form in animals) is a typical disputation; but his Fourth (on the destruction of physical bodies) only begins as a disputation and quickly turns into a satire on its own formalities. Declamations, on the other hand, were exercises in rhetoric (symbolized by an open hand) in which students were assigned to defend and attack philosophical problems or, more often, lighter topics in something like the manner used in the thesis at St. Paul's.

At Commencement and other important celebrations, formal disputations were regularly performed as the highlight of the festivities known as "Acts." The topic assigned for disputing in strict logical style was also elaborately presented in other art forms. First, declamations were delivered for and against the disputant's thesis, thus giving the topic a rhetorical introduction (e.g., Milton's *Prol* 2). Then printed verses were distributed to the audience in which the thesis was "argued" in poetic form (e.g., Milton's short Latin poems *Naturam* and *Idea*). Next, a student called a praevaricator or varier was asked to con-

duct a comic interlude in which he was expected to entertain by poking fun at the thesis, particularly by punning and with vulgar jokes (e.g., the "Prolusio" of *Prol* 6). Finally, the main event of disputant vs. objector was held. The thesis of the day, therefore, was debated not only with the tight-fisted rigor of the logician, but also with the open-handed persuasion of the rhetorician, the winning sweetness of the poet, and the meaningful humor and nonsense of the parodist.

The impact of these early experiences on Milton's later writing is not at all easy to trace in detail. Still, there are some clear links between his apprentice and journeyman debates. Three of his pamphlets, *DDD, Tetra,* and *Tenure,* reflect the logical formalities and even the language of disputations. For example, Milton sounds quite like a medieval philosopher when he uses Aristotle's four causes to define marriage in *Tetra* :

> it will be needful to take in all the fowr causes into the definition. First therefore the material cause of matrimony is man and woman; the Author and efficient, God and their consent, the internal *Form* and the soul of this relation, is conjugal love arising from a mutual fitness to the final causes of wedlock, help and society in Religious, Civil and Domestic conversation. (4 : 101)

Although the last phrase is purely Miltonic, all the rest is purely scholastic.

When Milton assumed the role of objector to another's thesis, as he frequently did with gusto, his method occasionally reveals how deeply ingrained was the habit of reducing arguments to formal syllogisms with major and minor premises, of attacking one or both premises, and of distinguishing levels of true and false meanings. An extreme example of this occurs in *Colas,* where Milton flaunts his scholastic jargon in the face of an opponent he considered poorly educated; over and over he throws out such phrases as "I deny your *major*," "I deny your *minor*," and "I grant [this meaning] but not [that one]" (4 : 242–43).

Other obvious marks of scholastic

debate appear in *CD*. Despite the heavily Protestant emphasis on scriptural proof-texts, many sections of *CD* borrow their technical language and philosophical procedure directly from the Catholic tradition of Aquinas and Suarez in which Milton was trained at Cambridge. Chapter 7 of the first book, for instance, contains many echoes of Milton's own disputations on prime matter* (*Prol* 4) and the unity of substantial form (*Prol* 5):

> But matter and form, considered as internal causes, constitute the thing itself. . . . For spirit being the more excellent substance, virtually and essentially contains within itself the inferior one; as the spiritual and rational faculty contains the corporeal, that is, the sentient and vegetative faculty. . . . It is acknowledged by the common consent of almost all philosophers, that every *form*, to which class the human soul must be considered as belonging, is produced by the power of matter. (15: 21–49)

Although there are these clear signs of Milton's early disputation exercises, the majority of his controversial works are not, strictly speaking, disputations but declamations. Milton preferred open-handed rhetoric to tight-fisted logic, especially in his antiprelatical and his political pamphlets. And since he was often trying to persuade the English Parliament to take action on specific issues, he used the traditionally polemical art of rhetoric. Although many editors of Milton's prose remind readers of his heavy debts to ancient rhetoric, especially to Aristotle and Cicero, the significance of this material may be easily overlooked.

The overall organization of Milton's polemics can be seen more readily if a reader is aware of the classical division of a speech into six parts; one of the things he will discover is a masterful manipulation of these parts to fit the sequence of arguments in *Areop*. More valuable for understanding Milton's debate itself, however, are the classical means of persuasion. Aristotle's emphasis on a speaker's need to win the emotions of his audience is helpful in appraising Milton's frequent eulogies of Parliament and his exalted

pictures of Englishmen as God's chosen people. Even more significant is Aristotle's judgment that the ethical proof is the most important means of persuasion. Because Milton agreed, as Cicero did, that the public image of a speaker is the most persuasive part of his argument, he revealed a great deal of his personal life in his debates, especially after his character had been questioned or attacked by his opponents, as in *RCG*, *2Def* and *3Def*. If readers recall that Aristotle and Cicero insist that a rhetorician take especially good care of how he himself appears to his audience, they can avoid misjudging Milton's advertisements of himself as signs of an egomaniac.

Recalling Cicero can also give perspective to the most troublesome aspect of Milton's controversial prose: his apparently unrestrained and even savage attacks on the personalities of his enemies. If the most potent means of persuading is indeed the image of a speaker's ethical character, as all the classical writers say, then the most vulnerable object to attack would naturally be an opponent's moral character. And Cicero's example might well be cited here, for even in his most virulent abuse of Bishop Hall* and Salmasius*, Milton never quite matched the ruthlessness of Cicero's public thrashing of Mark Antony in the *Philippics*. Only in his attack on Alexander More* in *3Def* did he go so far.

Although many critics simply deplore Milton's personal abuse of his opponents, others offer different explanations for it. Most popular is the one that says that since Milton's methods were commonplace among English pamphleteers for the past century, he should not be blamed for being a child of the age; after all, if the holy Thomas More can call Luther "an open incestuous lecher, a plain limb of the Devil, and a manifest messenger of hell," why should not Milton label the great scholar Salmasius "a monster, madman, liar, buffoon, pimp, parasite, and filthy swine"? Others emphasize the satiric quality of these passages and distinguish Milton's artistic ridicule from true personal abuse; they admire his talent for punning and his incredible capacity for inventing epithets.

Often Milton's prose debates are compared to Richard Hooker's* *Laws of Ecclesiastical Polity.* This inevitably leads to eulogies of Hooker's calm style and imperturbable good sense and to disparagements of Milton's passionate epithets and one-sided commitment. But, if one realizes that Hooker was writing a formal theological treatise at his leisure over many years and that Milton was rushing one tract after another to the printer (five in the course of a single year) in response to attacks on Puritans in a raging public debate that was as much political as religious, then one might feel the unfairness of weighing the works of these men on the same scale.

Very few masterpieces emerge from controversial writing. Most of it is so topical that no later reader is interested in it for its own sake. From the pile of Milton's debate literature only two tracts are widely read today—*Areop* and *Educ* —and a few others are picked over for their autobiographical revelations. Still, knowing about this material can help us see how Milton came to view all things in terms of polarities and why his poems are so often built up in blocks of contrasting patterns. [TRH]

DECLARATION OF HIS HIGHNESS: *see* ATTRIBUTIONS.

DECLARATION, OR LETTERS PATENTS, A. Milton translated this Latin prose work into English for Bràbazon Aylmer*, who published it anonymously around July 1674. It concerns the election of John Sobieski as King of Poland on May 22. It was Milton's last publication during his lifetime. He may have undertaken it for the money, which he needed; or possibly he saw a parallel between this warrior king elected through merit* and Oliver Cromwell*. Through Phillips we know that Milton translated *A Declaration,* and it was included in the 1698 edition of the prose. [WM]

DECORUM: *see* DICTION; STYLE AND LEVELS OF STYLE.

DECREES, DIVINE. Milton's doctrine of the divine decrees and his exploitation of this doctrine in epic* and tragedy* can best be understood against a dual background, theological and poetic. Accordingly, this survey will consist of three distinct parts : 1) an account of Milton's treatment of the decrees in *CD, PL, PR,* and *SA;* 2) a summary of sixteenth- and seventeenth-century controversies among Supralapsarians, Infralapsarians, and Arminians* concerning the nature and order of the divine decrees; and 3) a brief discussion of classical conventions for portraying the execution of the divine decrees in epic and tragedy. For fuller discussion the reader should consult Maurice Kelley's *This Great Argument: A Study of Milton's De Doctrina as a Gloss upon Paradise Lost* (1941) and the edition of the *Christian Doctrine* by Kelley and John Carey, in volume 6 of Yale *Prose.* (Kelley stresses the Arminian element in Milton's theology but observes that Milton disagreed with the Arminians on the subject of reprobation and that despite suggestive similarities between *CD* and Curcellaeus the sources of Milton's conception of the divine decrees and predestination have not yet been ascertained.)

According to *CD,* God's decrees belong to his internal efficiency, which is "independent of all extraneous agency" (14 : 63). Their execution pertains to his external efficiency, "whereby he carries into effect by external agency whatever decrees he has purposed within himself" (14:179). His decrees include whatever he "works or wills singly"—such as the creation* of the world and the removal of the curse from the ground—and are therefore distinct from actions that are performed by others or through cooperation between God himself and free agents (14 : 63). These decrees can be classified as either general or special.

Having defined God's general decree as that "WHEREBY HE HAS DECREED FROM ALL ETERNITY OF HIS OWN

MOST FREE AND WISE AND HOLY PURPOSE, WHATEVER HE HIMSELF WILLED OR WAS ABOUT TO DO" (14 : 63), Milton explicitly asserts the reality of both divine and human freedom. Though God's decree was in full accordance with his "perfect knowledge of all things that were to be created," it was "impelled by no necessity," and it would be absurd to separate his "decrees or will" from his "eternal counsel and foreknowledge," or to give them "priority of order." God "decreed nothing absolutely, which he left in the power of free agents" (14 : 65). Moreover, he himself laid down a "rule . . . according to which he would always have his decrees understood; namely, that regard should be paid to the conditionate terms attached to them" (14 : 67).

In defense of this "theory of contingent decrees" Milton argues that the alternate theory would not only make the Deity seem to "contradict himself, and appear inconsistent," but would also "entirely take away from human affairs all liberty of action, all endeavour and desire to do right" (14 : 69, 71). Since "the Deity purposely framed his own decrees with reference to particular circumstances, in order that he might permit free causes to act conformably to that liberty with which he had endued them," those "conditional events" which he voluntarily placed at man's free disposal "depend on the human will" (14 : 75). It is "wholly impossible, that God should have fixed by a necessary decree what we know at the same time to be in the power of man; or that that should be immutable which it remains for subsequent contingent circumstances either to fulfill or frustrate" (14 : 79).

Milton's argument for contingent decrees leads him, not surprisingly, to the problem of the Fall of Man* and the revolt of the angels*. In CD, as in PL, he stresses the free will* of men and angels alike :

> Whatever . . . was left to the free will of our first parents, could not have been decreed immutably or absolutely from all eternity; and questionless, the Deity must

either have never left any thing in the power of man, or he cannot be said to have determined finally respecting whatever was so left without reference to possible contingencies. . . . Seeing, therefore that, in assigning the gift of free will, God suffered both men and angels to stand or fall at their own uncontrolled choice, there can be no doubt that the decree itself bore a strict analogy to the object which the divine counsel regarded, not necessitating the evil consequences which ensued, but leaving them contingent; hence the covenant was of this kind: If thou stand, thou shalt abide in Paradise; if thou fall, thou shalt be cast out; if thou eat not the forbidden fruit, thou shalt live; if thou eat, thou shalt die (14: 79, 81).

Of God's special decrees the first and most important regards the begetting of the Son*, while the second concerns the angels (14:89). The principal special decree regarding man is predestination*, "whereby GOD IN PITY TO MANKIND, THOUGH FORESEEING THAT THEY WOULD FALL OF THEIR OWN ACCORD, PREDESTINATED TO ETERNAL SALVATION BEFORE THE FOUNDATION OF THE WORLD THOSE WHO SHOULD BELIEVE AND CONTINUE IN THAT FAITH" (14 : 91). The execution of the divine decrees thus includes generation, creation, and government of the universe (14 : 179).

In contrast to the systematic and comprehensive discussion of the divine decrees in the first book of CD, the second book (on the worship of God) alludes to them only in passing. Nevertheless, inasmuch as "the whole of our duty towards God and man" is comprised in "good habits," which in turn are the proximate causes of good works (17 : 27), every human virtue* appears to be related, either directly or indirectly, to the divine decrees and their execution. Several virtues, moreover, are specifically defined in terms of man's attitude toward the divine will. Wisdom*, for instance, is the virtue "WHEREBY WE EARNESTLY SEARCH AFTER THE WILL OF GOD, LEARN IT WITH ALL DILIGENCE, AND GOVERN ALL OUR ACTIONS ACCORDING TO ITS RULE" (17 : 27). Faith* is "TRUST IN

GOD . . . , whereby we wholly repose on him" (17 : 53), and hope* is "that by which we expect with certainty the fulfilment of God's promises" (17 : 57). Patience is the virtue "whereby we acquiesce in the promises of God, through a confident reliance on his divine providence, power, and goodness, and bear inevitable evils with equanimity, as the dispensation of the supreme Father, and sent for our good" (17 : 67). Its opposite or contrary vice—"impatience under the divine decrees"—is a temptation to which "the saints themselves are at times liable" (17 : 69). Obedience*, in turn, is "that virtue whereby we propose to ourselves the will of God as the paramount rule of our conduct, and serve him alone" (17:69).

In *PL* Milton depicts the promulgation and execution of several of the principal divine decrees—the creation of the world and man, and the government of the angels and man in their unfallen and fallen conditions. Several passages in the epic emphasize the interrelationship between God's internal and external efficiency and the execution of the divine decrees through the agency of the Son. During the War in Heaven*, the Father addresses his Messiah as (*PL* 6. 681–84)

Son in whose face invisible is beheld
Visibly, what by Deitie I am,
And in whose hand what by Decree I doe,
Second Omnipotence. . . .

Subsequently, in undertaking the mission of passing judgment on Adam and Eve after their fall, the Son summarizes his relationship with the Father in terms of decree and execution (*PL* 10. 68–70) :

. . . thine is to decree,
Mine both in Heav'n and Earth to do thy will
Supream. . . .

Again, when the Son in his prayer of intercession pleads for reconciliation with man, the Father replies that this has already been decreed (*PL* 11. 45–47) :

To whom the Father, without Cloud, serene.
All thy request for Man, accepted Son,
Obtain, all thy request was my Decree. . . .

References to the decrees governing the fallen or unfallen angels are frequent in *PL,* and even the devils utilize them as rhetorical *topoi* for persuading others or justifying their own actions to themselves. Belial argues that he and his fellows have been subdued by "fate inevitable . . . , and Omnipotent Decree, / The Victors will" (*PL* 2. 197–99). Satan, disguised as a cherub, flatters Uriel as the first of the seven spirits before God's throne to interpret the divine will through highest heaven and suggests that the angel is "likeliest by supreme decree" to obtain "Like honour" here below, "and as his Eye / To visit oft this new Creation round" (*PL* 3. 659–61). Immediately before the crucial temptation in Book 9, Satan couples the divine decree creating man with the assignment of angels to man's service as "flaming Ministers" and guardians (*PL* 9. 150–57) :

What he decreed
He effected; Man he made, and for him built
Magnificent this World, and Earth his seat,
Him Lord pronounc'd, and, O indignitie!
Subjected to his service Angel wings. . . .

The divine decree concerning Messiah's "metaphorical" begetting, or unction to his mediatorial office, provides the occasion for the revolt of the angels. In a passage strongly reminiscent of the language and imagery of the second psalm, the Father bids the assembled hierarchies (*PL* 5. 602) to "Hear my Decree which unrevok't shall stand"—a decree appointing the Son as "Head of the angels and as Vicegerent of the Father (*PL* 5. 603–14). Satan subsequently makes this edict the pretext for his rebellion. Exhorting Beëlzebub to remember "what Decree/ Of yesterday, so late hath past the lips/ Of Heav'ns Almightie" (*PL* 5. 674–76), he argues that

. . . new Laws thou seest impos'd;
New Laws from him who reigns, new minds
    may raise
In us who serve. . . .

(*PL* 5. 679–81)

Haranguing his troops at his own royal

seat, Satan subsequently complains that "by Decree / Another now hath to himself ingross't / All Power, and us eclipst under the name / Of King anointed" (*PL* 5. 774–77), and asserts that the angels are God's equals in freedom (*PL* 5. 786–99) : "Who . . . can introduce / Law and Edict on us, who without Law / Erre not . . . ?" On the other side, the Father himself, beholding "Rebellion rising," perceives "what multitudes / Were banded to oppose his high Decree" (*PL* 5. 715–17). Abdiel, condemning Satan's argument as blasphemy, bases his defense of the "just Decree of God" partly on the gulf between Creator and creature (*PL* 5. 813–25). On the authority of the second psalm and analogous passages in Scripture, Milton concludes that "however the generation of the Son may have taken place, it arose from no natural necessity . . . , but was no less owing to the decree and will of the Father than his priesthood or kingly power, or his resuscitation from the dead" (14 : 183, 185).

In developing the theme of the Fall, Milton emphasizes the contingent character of the divine decrees concerning free agents. Foreseeing Adam's transgression and clearing *"his own Justice from all imputation"* on the grounds that he had *"created Man free and able enough to have withstood his Tempter"* (2, pt. 1, p. 76), the Father asserts that he had created man "Sufficient to have stood, though free to fall" (*PL* 3. 99). Since they have been created free, Adam and Eve cannot "justly accuse" their maker of their fate,

As if predestination over-rul'd
Thir will, dispos'd by absolute Decree
Or high foreknowledge; they themselves decreed
Thir own revolt, not I: if I foreknew,
Foreknowledge had no influence on their fault,
Which had no less prov'd certain unforeknown.

They fall of their own volition :

. . . for so
I formed them free, and free they must remain,
Till they enthrall themselves: I else must change

Thir nature, and revoke the high Decree
Unchangeable, Eternal, which ordain'd
Thir freedom, they themselves ordain'd thir fall.
(*PL* 3. 114–28)

After Adam's fall, the Father again emphasizes man's moral freedom and his responsibility for his transgression :

. . . no Decree of mine
Concurring to necessitate his Fall,
Or touch with lightest moment of impulse
His free Will, to her own inclining left
In even scale.
(*PL* 10. 43–47)

Milton likewise emphasizes the freedom of the divine will and its independence from necessity. In sending the Son into chaos to create the world and man, the Father asserts (*PL* 7. 171–73) that his "goodness" is "free / To act or not, Necessitie and Chance / Approach not mee, and what I will is Fate."

The invasion of Sin and Death (later in the same book) in fulfillment of the curse pronounced by the Creator himself on mankind and on the earth leads to a renewed emphasis on the justice of the divine decrees. As the Father explains to his assembled angels, Sin and Death are merely his "Hell-hounds." He has drawn them thither to "lick up the draff and filth" resulting from "mans polluting Sin," and they are ultimately destined to be destroyed by the Son in preparation for the final renewal and purification of heaven and earth. "Till then the Curse pronunc't on both proceeds." The chorus of angels accepts this theodicy and, like the chorus in a formal tragedy, draws the appropriate moral inference :

. . . Just are thy ways,
Righteous are thy Decrees on all thy Works. . . .
(*PL* 10. 630–44)

At this point the emphasis shifts from the justice of the divine decrees in the eyes of heaven to man's emotional response to the decree of death and (subsequently) to the decree of exile. Knowing that he must die, Adam hails his future death-day as a "welcom hour" and questions the delay of divine justice :

> . . . why delayes
> His hand to execute what his Decree
> Fixd on this day?
> (*PL* 10. 771–73)

After his reconciliation with Eve, he declares that "If Prayers / Could alter high Decrees" (*PL* 10. 952–53), he would petition the Deity to forgive Eve's frailty and visit her sins on Adam's own head —an offer that unconsciously foreshadows the vicarious atonement of the Second Adam. In the following book the Father pronounces the sentence of exile (*PL* 11. 96–98):

> . . . to remove him I decree
> And send him from the Garden forth to Till
> The Ground whence he was taken, fitter soile

and Adam recognizes the necessity of submission to the decree for his expulsion (*PL* 11. 311–14):

> But prayer against his absolute Decree
> No more availes then breath against the winde,
> Blown stifling back on him that breaths it
> forth:
> Therefore to his great bidding I submit.

In *PR,* Milton emphasizes the imminent fulfillment of a divine decree—the future restoration of man through the woman's seed—by allowing Satan himself to broach the subject near the very beginning of the poem and to raise the important issue of the predestined time or occasion for fulfillment of the prophecy (*PR* 1. 52–59):

> . . . though since
> With dread attending when that fatal wound
> Shall be inflicted by the Seed of *Eve*
> Upon my head, long the decrees of Heav'n
> Delay, for longest time to him is short;
> And now too soon for us the circling hours
> This dreaded time have compast, wherein we
> Must bide the stroak of that long threatn'd
> wound.

In *SA,* as in *CD,* Milton considers the paradox of apparent contradictions in the divine decrees. Samson first raises the issue, obliquely and figuratively, by demanding why the *fiat lux*—the first stage in fulfillment of the decree of creation—does not apply to himself (*SA* 83–85):

> O first created Beam, and thou great Word,
> Let there be light, and light was over all;
> Why am I thus bereav'd thy prime decree?

The issue becomes more sharply defined in the course of Samson's first conversations with the Chorus; in the choral ode immediately preceding Manoa's arrival, Milton not only states the problem clearly in terms of apparent contradiction in the divine decrees, but also develops the related issue of the Deity's right to grant dispensation from his own laws and edicts (SA 300–314).

The dispensation from "National obstriction"—discussed here in relation to Samson's marriages with the woman of Timna and with Dalila—will subsequently recur in connection with the crucial episode in the drama, Samson's summons to participate in the Dagonalia. Though he flatly refuses to attend the feast on the grounds that "Our Law forbids at thir Religious Rites / My presence," (*SA* 1320–21), he later recognizes that God "may dispense with me or thee / Present in Temples at Idolatrous Rites / For some important cause" (*SA* 1377–79); and when he does decide to accompany the Philistine messenger, the issue has become not a conflict between divine laws but a subordination of the external written law to the internal and unwritten commands of the Spirit.

Milton's doctrine of the divine decrees represents a modification of Calvinist* views and a rapprochement with Arminianism. In emphasizing Adam's free will and moral responsibility, in declaring that God's own will was free and not bound by necessity, and in insisting that divine foreknowledge rendered Adam's fall certain but not necessary, Milton was affirming doctrines that would have been acceptable to perhaps the majority of Calvinist as well as Arminian divines. On the other hand, in asserting the conditional character of the decree of election, in denying that reprobation formed an integral part of predestination, in allowing fallen man a limited degree of freedom after the Fall, and in arguing that a necessitarian or deterministic view of the divine decrees tended to make the Deity the "author of sin," he advanced views that many Calvinists would have regarded as an Arminian heresy.

In the *Institutes* (ed. John T. McNeill, trans. Ford Lewis Battles), Calvin maintained that "Adam could have stood if he wished, seeing that he fell solely by his own will" (1. 15. 8). Divine foreknowledge was not the cause of predestination, and "subjecting one to the other is absurd" (3. 21. 5) : "When we attribute foreknowledge to God, we mean that all things always were, and perpetually remain, under his eyes, so that to his knowledge there is nothing future or past, but all things are present. . . . We call predestination God's eternal decree, by which he determined with himself what he willed to become of each man" (3. 21. 5). Arguing that God had predestined Adam's sin and foreordained the damnation of many of his posterity, Calvin ridiculed his opponents for objecting that God's plan for Christ's incarnation and mediation "depended on the ruin of man, which he foresaw" and for denying "that God decreed that Adam should perish for his rebellion." Whence "does it happen that Adam's fall irremediably involved so many peoples with their infant offspring, in eternal death unless because it so pleased God?" Though the "decree is dreadful" (*Decretum quidem horrible*), it "ought not to seem absurd . . . to say that God not only foresaw the fall of the first man, and in him the ruin of his descendants, but also meted it out in accordance with his own decision." God not only permitted Adam's fall and the damnation of the reprobate; he deliberately willed it (3. 23. 7–11; cf. 2. 12. 469).

Calvin's followers were divided among themselves as to the "order" of the divine decrees. Did the decree of election or reprobation precede or follow the consideration of man as fallen? This was a question of logical rather than temporal priority. According to the supralapsarian view, the predestination of a part of humanity to eternal life and the rest to eternal death was logically antecedent to the decree of man's fall. Adam's sin and the fallen condition of mankind are part of the God's eternal plan for manifesting the glory of his justice and mercy. In "the order of decrees," according to a modern commentator (Hastings *Encyclopedia, s.v.* Supralapsarianism), "it is first determined who are to be embraced in the one class, and who in the other; then the means are appointed—including creation, the Fall, sin, redemption—by which the end in each case is to be attained." According to the infralapsarian view, on the other hand, the decree of election considers mankind as a *massa damnata*, already fallen and under sentence of eternal death. In the opinion of several modern scholars, the supralapsarian doctrines of Beza* (Calvin's successor at Geneva) represent a departure from Calvin's more moderate views : James Orr maintains (Hastings, *s.v.* Calvinism; Sublapsarianism) that Calvin himself consistently interpreted the decree of election as a selection from the mass of mankind considered as already fallen and condemned. Nevertheless, as McNeill observes, a crucial passage in the *Institutes* (2. 12. 5) "briefly shows Calvin as favoring the supralapsarian as opposed to the infralapsarian view of the decrees of God." Arguing that Christ's incarnation* stemmed from God's eternal decree for men's salvation, Calvin appealed to St. Paul's account of "the lofty mystery of predestination" in Ephesians as evidence that "the fall of Adam is not presupposed as preceding God's decree in time; but it is what God determined before all ages that is shown when he willed to heal the misery of mankind."

After undertaking a reply to Dirk Coornhert (a liberal theologian who had challenged Beza's supralapsarian position), Jacob Arminius found himself unable to accept the high Calvinist doctrines he had set out to defend; in his opinion, their interpretation of the divine decrees tended to make the Deity himself the author of sin. After his death in 1609, his liberal position was supported and developed by such scholars as Episcopius, Uytenbogaert, and Grotius*; and in 1610 the Arminian party attacked both supralapsarian and infralapsarian positions in a *Remonstrance* to the States-General, whose chief author was Uytenbogaert. In opposition to the doctrine of absolute and unconditional decrees, the Remonstrants maintained (in the first of five articles) that the decree of election is conditional: "That God, by an eternal and unchangeable decree in Christ before the world was, determined to elect from the fallen and sinning race to everlasting life those who through His grace believe in Jesus Christ and persevere in faith and obedience; and, on the contrary, had resolved to reject the unconverted and unbelievers to everlasting damnation (John 3 : 36)." (See A. W. Harrison, *The Beginnings of Arminianism to the Synod of Dort* [London, 1926], pp. 148–51; and John T. McNeill, *The History of Calvinism* [New York, 1957], pp. 263–65. For the four following articles of the *Remonstrance,* see Harrison and McNeill.)

At the Synod of Dort, held in 1618–19 to pass official judgment on the Arminian doctrines, the infralapsarian position prevailed. Although Gomarus supported the extreme supralapsarian doctrine that "God had chosen certain individuals for eternal life, and decreed eternal death for others even before the Fall of Man," the "rest of the Synod seem to have modified the strict logic of Calvin and Beza so far as to call Election God's choice of individuals from the mass of fallen men, while Reprobation was merely leaving the rest to the natural results of their own fallen condition" (Harrison, p. 342). As finally drafted, the canons of the Synod on "The First Point of Doctrine, concerning Predestination, Election and Reprobation" defined election as "the immutable purpose of God by which, according to the free good pleasure of His will, of pure grace, He has chosen in Jesus Christ for salvation before the foundation of the world, out of the whole human race fallen by its own fault from its first innocence into sin and destruction, a certain number of men neither better nor more worthy than the rest with whom they were lying

in the same misery." The "decree of Reprobation," whereby some men are "non-elect, or left behind in the Eternal Election of God," for the manifestation of his justice, by no means makes "God the author of sin . . . , but reveals Him as a dreadful, irreprehensible, and just judge and avenger of sin." The Synod specifically condemns the doctrine that God's will to save "those who shall believe and persevere in the faith and obedience of faith, is the whole and entire decree of election to salvation" and the doctrine that "God has not decreed by His just will alone to leave any in the fall of Adam and in the common state of sin and condemnation, or to pass them by in the communication of the grace necessary to faith and conversion" (Harrison, pp. 347–56).

The divine decrees occupy a prominent position in the theological manuals and compendia on which Milton modeled his own treatise. Polanus's *The Substance of Christian Religion* (London,. 1600), pp. 47–48, defines "the decree of God" as "an essentiall inward worke of God, namely, the eternall purpose of Gods will, by which from all eternitie, he determined with himselfe, that all things should bee done, whatsoever . . ."; and in discussing the principal commonplaces of theology, Polanus includes a subsection "Of the decree of God, where also of the decree of predestination" (p. 52). In *The Marrow of Sacred Divinity* (London, 1638?), William Ames*, like Milton, treats the divine decrees as an aspect of the divine efficiency; according to his chapter "Of the Decree, and Counsell of God" (pp. 23–31), "The *Decree* of God is his determinate purpose of effecting all things by his almighty Power, and according to his counsell . . .": nevertheless God's will "doth not infer a necessity upon al future things, but a certainty only as touching the event." For Ames, "The Efficiency of God, is either Creation or Providence" (p. 31). (For Milton, as we have seen, creation and providence—along with generation—belong to the execution of the divine decrees.) By Ames's definition,

"Predestination is the decree of God of manifesting his speciall glory in the eternall condition of men." It includes both election and reprobation. Just as it is "called destination: because it is a certaine determination of the order of meanes unto the end," it is called a decree "because it containes a definite sentence to be executed by a certaine counsell" (pp. 103–6). Wolleb's *Abridgment of Christian Divinitie* (trans. Alexander Ross [London, 1656], 2d ed.) devotes a chapter to "the Works of GOD, and the Decrees of GOD in general" (pp. 30–38), defining "Gods decree" as "the internal action of the Divine will, by which he hath determined from eternity most freely and certainly of those things which in time are to be effected." His decree "in respect of the Creatures, is either general or special." His "general Decree is that by which he appointed to declare the glory of his power, wisdom and goodness, in the creation and conservation of all things," while his special decree, called predestination, is "that by which he appointed to manifest the glory of his grace, mercy, and justice, in the Election and Reprobation of the reasonable Creatures" (p. 38).

Finally, in the *Westminster Confession of Faith**, finished on November 26, 1646 (ed. S. W. Carruthers [Manchester, 1937]), the chapter *"Of God's Eternal Decree"* asserts that "GOD from all eternity did, by the most wise and holy counsel of His own will, freely, and unchangeably ordain whatsoever comes to pass: yet so, as thereby neither is God the author of sin, nor is violence offered to the will of the creatures, nor is the liberty or contingency of second causes taken away, but rather established." He has "not decreed anything because He foresaw it as future, or as that which would come to pass upon such condition." By "the decree of God, for the manifestation of His glory, some men and angels are predestined unto everlasting life, and others fore-ordained to everlasting death." As he has "appointed the elect unto glory," he has "fore-ordained all the means thereunto," but he has voluntarily passed by the "rest of mankind" and thus ordained them "to dishonour and wrath, for their sin, to the praise of His glorious justice" (pp. 94–96).

Insofar as God's efficiency comprehends (in Milton's belief) not only the generation of the Son, but the creation and government of the entire visible and invisible universe, the greater part of *CD* and *PL* could be regarded as either a doctrinal exposition or a poetic demonstration of the divine decrees. Though this discussion has been limited to passages that explicitly mention the divine decrees and edicts, these provide a restricted view of the subject; a complete survey of the problem would comprehend Milton's "vast Design" in its entirety :

> *Messiah* Crown'd, Gods Reconcil'd Decree,
> Rebelling Angels, the Forbidden Tree,
> Heav'n, Hell, Earth, Chaos, All. . . .

In conclusion, let us consider some of the literary techniques whereby Milton adapts his conception of the divine decrees to the formal requirements of the epic genre. In a poem that centers (as does *PL*) on an act of disobedience to a divine command and that explicitly affirms its intent to "assert Eternal Providence / And justifie the wayes of God to men," the poetic imitation of the divine efficiency becomes a technical problem of the first importance. Throughout the poem, Milton effectively exploits the conventions of epic machinery to emphasize the dynamic function of divine agency in the action of the poem. The first divine council, in Book 3, centers largely on God's "principal SPECIAL DECREE . . . RELATING TO MAN"—man's predestination or election to salvation on the conditions of repentance and faith. These are effects of spiritual regeneration, and after the Fall Milton portrays their gradual development in Adam and Eve through the inward ministrations of the Son. In the proleptic and retrospective episodes inserted into the fable, Michael's prophecy outlines the future struggle between divine and infernal efficiencies in world history, while Raphael's survey of celestial prehistory extends from the "metaphorical generation" of the Son (the occasion or pretext for Satan's revolt) to the creation of the world and man. The plot of *PR*, in turn, hinges on the obedience of the Son to the Father, the nature of his Messianic kingdom and the appointed means whereby he is to establish it, and on the due season that has been divinely set for initiating and fulfilling his mission. The action of *SA* centers on the paradox of a divine promise that at first seems incapable of fulfillment, on a divinely engineered occasion that apparently threatens the hero with deepest humiliation but actually leads to his greatest victory, on a spiritual tension between doubt and faith or impatience and patience under the "divine decrees," and (finally) on vindication of "th' unsearchable dispose / Of highest wisdom" and the triumph of God's "uncontroulable intent. . . ."

Milton's major poetry belongs to genres that had been traditionally associated with "divine efficiency" and the mysterious but inevitable execution of divine decrees. "'Tis Dionyse hath done it," exclaims Agave in Euripides' *Bacchae* (Oates and O'Neill, *The Complete Greek Drama*, 2 : 278). "Apollo, friends, Apollo was he that brought these my woes to pass; but the hand that struck the eyes was none save mine," declares Oedipus after his downfall (ibid., 1 : 411). ". . . and in all this there is nought but Zeus," Hyllus chants in the concluding line of Sophocles' *Trachiniae* (ibid., 1 : 499). In the *Iliad* "the will of Zeus" is accomplished, though its fulfillment entails the death of numerous heroes (Richmond Lattimore, *The Iliad of Homer*, p. 159). In the *Odyssey*, when "the circling of the years" arrives "in which the gods had spun" for the hero "his time of homecoming," they despatch a messenger to announce their "absolute purpose" to the nymph who detains him (Lattimore, *Odyssey*, pp. 27–29). Aeneas is divinely fated to "bring his gods to Latium" and thereby prepare the way for Rome's imperial destiny; at a crucial point in the fable Jove himself sends "my orders" to

set sail from Carthage for the sake of "Rome to be" (Rolfe Humphries, *The Aeneid of Virgil*, pp. 3, 95). In *Jerusalem Delivered*, "God Almighty from his lofty throne" chooses Godfrey as "chieftain" over the other crusaders and sends an angel to arouse him to action :

"Why frees he not Jerusalem distress'd?"
(Torquato Tasso*,
Jerusalem Delivered, trans. Edward Fairfax, ed. J. C. Nelson, pp. 2, 4).

In his epic and tragic imitation of the divine decrees Milton remains, on the whole, faithful not only to the doctrines of his theological treatise but also to the principles of poetic imitation and the literary conventions of his classical models. In his epics he is relatively free to portray the divine efficiency more directly than in his tragedy, employing the conventional epic machinery of councils and messengers to delineate the promulgation and execution of divine decrees. In his tragedy, on the other hand, where divine machinery cannot be directly portrayed, he utilizes other devices to emphasize God's dynamic intervention in the dramatic action. The sudden change in Samson's resolve once he has experienced the "rouzing motions . . . which dispose / To something extraordinary my thoughts," Manoa's recognition of God's "favouring and assisting to the end," and the final choral reflections on God's unexpected return to bear glorious "witness" to his champion—all of these are means of stressing the operative role of the divine efficiency in the central action of Milton's play. The "spirit of phrenzie" whereby Jehovah fills the Philistines with "mad desire / To call in hast for thir destroyer" fulfills the same function; it is a form of *ate* similar to the infatuation that Athena inflicts on the doomed suitors near the end of the *Odyssey* and the madness that the gods inflict on Ajax and Heracles and Pentheus in classical tragedy.

The motif of the divine promise in *SA* parallels the theme of the divine oracle in Greek tragedy. Despite the notable difference in the content of the oracles in the dramas of Milton and Sophocles, "divine prediction" is closely interwoven with the issue of faith in the reliability of divine testimony, for Samson no less than for Oedipus and Jocasta. "Aye, for thou thy self wilt now surely put faith in the god," Creon remarks to the fallen Oedipus (Oates and O'Neill, 1 : 414).

Other analogues further enhance the resemblances (and differences) between the poetic imitation of the divine decrees in *PL* and *PR* and in classical epic. Satan's announcement to his "gloomy Consistory" in *PR* concerning the advent of the woman's seed :

And now too soon for us the circling hours
This dreaded time have compast, wherein we
Must bide the stroak of that long threatn'd
    wound,

recalls Homer's allusion to the "circling of the years" to the appointed season of Odysseus's return, and indirectly underlines an implicit analogy between the themes of Ithaca recovered and Paradise regained; but it is also reminiscent of Virgil's reference to the time decreed, "as holy years wheel on," when Rome will conquer Greece and avenge the sack of Troy (Humphries, p. 13). Raphael's fruitless warning to Adam against disobedience —a mission intended to *"render Man inexcusable"*—parallels Hermes' visit admonishing Aegisthus against murdering Agamemnon and espousing Clytemnestra ("for vengeance would come on him from Orestes") and the prophet Halitherses' similar "warning to the suitors" against the "great disaster . . . wheeling down on them" because of their insolence against the household of the absent Odysseus (Lattimore, *Odyssey*, pp. 28, 43).

The direct infusion of divine power —into the Messiah at a critical moment in the angelic war and into Samson at the Dagonalia—and the inner regeneration of fallen Adam and Eve through the Son's mediation parallel the strength or wisdom that Olympian deities instill into their favorite heroes on crucial occasions in classical epic. The celestial scales whereby the "Eternal" prevents an open battle

between Satan and Gabriel in Paradise are a legacy from Homer's Zeus and Virgil's Jove, as well as from medieval traditions concerning St. Michael; and the literary formula whereby Milton introduces this episode ("now dreadful deeds / Might have ensu'd . . . had not soon / Th' Eternal to prevent such horrid fray / Hung forth in Heav'n his golden scales") is likewise an inheritance from Homeric epos. Milton represents the divine efficiency through the conventional techniques of the particular genres in which he is working, adapting them to the requirements of his biblical subject matter and his own theological doctrines. The fact that, unlike his classical predecessors, he is writing within a monotheistic system inevitably compels him to alter the conventions he has borrowed, but it also enables him to draw a more powerful image of divine monarchy and to give clearer and stronger definition to the divine decrees themselves. Unique, self-existent, eternal—the divinity of Judeo-Christian belief possesses a supreme monarchial authority far beyond the aegis of the classical Zeus. The latter might be immortal, but he was neither self-existent nor eternal; he was the grandson of heaven and earth, not their creator. His wife and daughter might quarrel with him or temporarily outwit him; in Milton's heaven, on the other hand, there could be only perfect unanimity between Father and Son. The Christian heaven—unlike Olympus—could accommodate no divided councils, no dissident gods. Dissident angels might momentarily disturb its peace, yet they would soon be expelled, condemned to execute the divine strategy in exile and to work out their own damnation with diligence. As the Absolute, Milton's deity possesses an absolute authority beyond the power of the Homeric and Virgilian thundergod; but this absolute ruler is also, in a sense, a constitutional monarch. He does not govern entirely by absolute decree, and some of his principal edicts are conditional.

Centering as it does on a divinely contrived temptation-ordeal, the action of all three of Milton's major poems portrays a continuous interplay between divine and human wills, a running dialogue between God and man as free moral agents. Divine decree and human decision complement each other, and their interrelationship is fundamental to an understanding of all three works. The critic who stresses divine action at the expense of human action—or vice versa—will misread Milton's epic and tragedy, as surely as he will misinterpret the *Aeneid* or the *Iliad* or *Oedipus Rex*. [JMS]

DEFENSE FOR HIMSELF: *see* PRO SE DEFENSIO.

DEFENSE OF THE PEOPLE OF ENGLAND, THE: *see* TRANSLATIONS OF MILTON'S WORKS.

DEFENSIO PRIMA: *see* PRO POPULO ANGLICANO DEFENSIO.

DEFENSIO SECUNDA: *see* PRO POPULO ANGLICANO DEFENSIO SECUNDA.

DEFOE, DANIEL (1660?–1731), journalist and novelist. Defoe maintains a religiously orthodox perspective in his critical comments on Milton's works, basing his judgment largely on the issue of scriptural integrity and preferring conventional interpretations of biblical history. In his zealous attacks upon Jacobitism in current periodicals, he often employs the rhetoric* of Milton's satanic council, which had become part of the language stock early in the eighteenth century. His remarks are to be found in his poetry, in *The Review* (Feb. 19, 1704–1711, June 1713), in prose works, particularly *The Political History of the Devil* (1726) where he accuses Milton of subscribing to the Arian heresy* in *PL*, and in his letters.

In the poetry and in *The Review* Defoe praises as sublime the art of his fellow poet and one-time neighbor. He is also aware of different public attitudes toward Milton's works. In *The Pacificator* (Feb. 15, 1700) Defoe attributes Blackmore's arsenal of poetic techniques for

Prince Arthur to "Giants . . . of Wit and Sense together" and includes in his list of exemplars Cowley*, Milton, Ratcliff, Rochester, Waller, Roscommon, Howard, and Behn (lines 127–34). In *The Reformation of Manners* (August [?] 1702) he observes the popular appeal of Rochester, commenting partially on changing taste and casting a realistic eye on public sentiment:

'Tis Wine or Lewdness all our Theams
    supplies,
Gives Poets Power to write, and Power to
    please:
Let this describe the Nation's Character,
One Man reads *Milton,* forty *Rochester.*
This lost his Taste, *they say,* when h' lost his
    Sight,
Milton had Thought, but *Rochester* had Wit.
The Case is plain, the Temper of the Time,
One wrote *the Lewd,* and t'other the *Sublime.*
                                        (1156–63)

In *Jure Divino* (summer 1706) he seeks poetic inspiration from Milton for his satire of man's corruption, expecting to expose the nature of sin and discover the means of man's adventitious escape from his dilemma: "Search the strict laws of his captivity, / And there almost as far as Milton see, / For no man e'er was here before but he" (Bk. 7, p. 14). Milton's description of Pandemonium* Defoe praises in a prose footnote to his satire as "the deepest laid Thought, most capacious and extensive that ever appear'd in print."

Defoe wrote more lines of poetry than Milton and, at one time, had hoped to be remembered for his verse. In 1705 and 1706 he had imitated Miltonic blank verse* at least three times in *The Review,* in "A Supplement to the Advice from the Scandal Club" (Jan. 1705), "Hymn to Truth" (Feb. 27, 1705), and "On the Fight at Ramellies," with the final sixteen verses in rhyme (Tuesday, May 21, 1706). Introductory verses of the "Britannia" portion of *The True-Born Englishman* (Dec. 1700–Jan. 1701), though rhymed, are also imitative of *PL*.

The pages of *The Review* list various reasons for approving Milton's poetry and certain justification for favoring one work over another. The beauty of the lyrics may prove less significant for him, however, than the moral of the tale. Although *PL* is acclaimed "the greatest, best, and most sublime Work now in the English Tongue," *PR* is judged "a Dull Thing, infinitely short of the former." Milton's imagined response reflects the diction of eighteenth-century theater reformers: "Well, I see the Reason plainly, why this Book [*PR*] is not liked so well as the other [*PL*], for I am sure it is the better Poem of the two, but People have not the same Gust of Pleasure at the regaining Paradise, as they have Concern at the loss of it, and therefore they do not relish this so well as they did the other, tho' it be without Comparison the best Performance" (Saturday August 18, 1711), a sentiment echoed in *The Family Instructor* (vol. 2, 1718). In an issue of *The Review* published while the *Spectator* essays on *PL* were appearing on successive Saturdays (*Spec.* 267—January 5, 1712, through *Spec.* 369—May 3, 1712) Defoe praises both Milton's epic* and Addison's* critical commentary (Saturday, March 29, 1712). He repeats his views on Milton's sublimity in *A Vindication of the Press: or, an Essay on the Usefulness of Writing, on Criticism, and the Qualification of Authors* (1718) where he attributes to Milton "the Foundation of Divine Poetry" (p. 12).

The Review provides commentary repeated in Defoe's later works. Milton's descriptive and narrative passages supply images that Defoe uses to advantage in arguing the moral turpitude of contemporary society. He admires Milton's poetic account of Adam and Eve enjoying "the Perfection of Conjugal Love towards one another," but their disobedience* is the more reproachful because their sin* negates order and restores chaos. Defoe not without some doubts accepts Milton's assertion that Adam and Eve had engaged in conjugal love before the Fall* (Saturday, Nov. 15, 1707). Milton's description of their love in the garden explains Satan's jealousy and malice when he observes "the happy Couple sporting together in the 4*th* Book" (Saturday, March 29, 1712).

Defoe accepts Milton's information that *"Adam knew his Wife Eve before the Fall,"* but he inquires about the implications of the conception of their twin son and daughter; do children conceived in a State of Innocence nevertheless bear "the Taint of Original Corruption"? If not, then credence is given the Mohammedan myth that the twins proved the ancestors of the prophet Mohammed. The possibility of the credibility of Moslem fideism causes Defoe momentary anxiety but in no way detracts from his confirmation of the bliss of the first couple in Eden; from the beauty of Milton's descriptions he would argue against the concept of concupiscence in Paradise before the temptation. (See E. G. Fletcher, *Modern Language Notes* 50:31, and B. Eugene McCarthy, *Milton Newsletter* 3:70).

The happiness of Adam and Eve in Paradise provides Defoe a basis for the examination of divorce* laws in *Conjugal Lewdness; or Matrimonial Whoredom. A Treatise Concerning the Use and Abuse of the Marriage Bed* (1727) in which he differs from Milton on an essential point. For Defoe, a marriage* conceived originally in love* and based upon "real merit, personal virtue, similitude of tempers, mutual delights" cannot be dissolved because a couple are disenchanted with each other. In this, he feels he cannot compromise himself with Milton's liberal position:

I say, I cannot think the Marriage can be lawful where there was not a resolved settled Affection, sincerely embraced before the Matrimony was contracted. I will not follow Mr. *Milton,* and carry it up to this, that it may be dissolved again upon that single Account. (p. 118)

In Defoe's mind, society is characterized by discord; *The Review* complains of political factionalism and corruption nurtured indiscriminately by intrigue or natural disaster whereby the least excuse affords opportunities to sustain the attack (Saturday, Nov. 15, 1707). Defoe exposes the nature of hypocrisy in his representation of the frontispiece to *PL* 2 (by Henry

Alrich, from the 1688 fourth edition) in which Sin is drawn with a fair face but shaped as a monster in her lower extremities, thus proving "the very Emblem of a *Jacobite High-Flyer"* (Tuesday, June 14, 1708; in his text, Defoe erroneously identifies the frontispiece as preceding *PL* 4, but with justifiable caution notes the possibility of error because he describes the engraving from memory). The imagery is sustained in a later essay, which deprecates Non-Jurors, Tory candidates seeking restitution of the Stuart monarchy while they profess loyalty to the Queen (Thursday, June 16, 1708).

Defoe's most exhaustive treatment of *PL* is in *The Political History of the Devil,* where his conventional praise of Milton's poetic power and aesthetic judgment is mitigated by the opinion he shares with the reformers in warning against the danger of charismatic evil characters : "so much poetic liberty is taken with the Devil" (p. 36). On this point, Defoe's sarcasm is unrelenting: Milton "has made a good PLAY of *Heaven* and *Hell*; and no doubt if he had liv'd in our times, he might have had it acted with our *Pluto* and *Proserpine.* He has made fine Speeches both for *God* and the *Devil,* and a little addition might have turned it *ala modern,* into a *Harlequin Dieu & Diable"* (pp. 68–69). For this reason, Defoe states his preference now for *PR*. *PL* depicts the power of Satan in too vivid fashion; the sequel narrates the victory of Christ without the anachronisms and inaccuracies located in the epic.

To Defoe's mind, the errors in *PL,* though charitably attributed to poetic license, unfortunately admitted into the scriptural account new information unique to the poetic version. A number of faults may be counted : (1) the fall of the angels resembles Ovid's* description of the "war of the *Titans* against *Jupiter," Metam.* 1. ix (p. 35); (2) Satan is restricted to circumscribed boundaries in a localized Hell* and thus likened in ludicrous fashion to a prisoner of Newgate rather than the roving agent he is depicted in biblical testimony (p. 30); (3) leaders of the armies

of Hell are given names ascribed in the Bible to the Devil himself (pp. 38ff.); (4) *PL* states that the Devil sought mankind's ruin as an affront to God and to disappoint the creation of "a new species . . . after his own image," whereas Satan's "more probable design," concludes Defoe, was to "see his rival damn'd with him" (pp. 57–58); (5) the nine-day period allotted Satan's descent after his expulsion from Heaven has basis neither in Scripture nor in philosophy (p. 78). (Summaries of Milton's "absurdities" are in a review of the 1729 French edition in the *Bibliothèque Raisonnée des Ouvrages des Savans de L'Europe* 3 [Juillet, Aout, Septembre 1729]:149–71). Defoe describes Satan's defection and assault upon mankind also in *Jure Divino* (Bk. 7, p. 20).

In chapter 5 of *The Political History,* Defoe discusses Milton's treatment of two major philosophical issues, the origin of sin in the angelic host and the role of Christ as Son of God*. On the first point, which he acknowledges Milton could not have answered to satisfaction because no tenable explanation is known, he represents the dilemma in his own Pindaric composition of 67 verses in iambic couplets of varied line length (pp. 65–68). On the second point, he complains that Milton has violated the orthodox conception of the Trinity: "He has indeed complimented GOD *Almighty* with a flux of lofty words, and great sounds, and has made a very fine Story of the *Devil,* but he has made a meer *je ne sçay Quoi of Jesus Christ"* (p. 69). These remarks predicate Defoe's enumeration of several anachronisms that suggest that Christ was begotten upon a date later than Creation and in a point of time* designated in Eternity. Defoe quotes from *PL* : "Hear my decree, which unrevok'd shall stand. / This day I have begot whom I declare / My only Son . . ." (5. 602–4). Thus Milton "lays an avow'd foundation for the corrupt Doctrine of *Arius,* which says, there was a time when Christ *was not* the Son of GOD" (p. 75). To his condemnation of Arianism*, Defoe adds his disapprobation of the anti-

Trinitarians and the modern followers of Socinus* who lead men toward atheism (p. 336).

In *Jure Divino,* Defoe writes that "Satan had no native enmity against man," but, instead, finding man "inclined to sin" took advantage of his weakness as a vindictive move against God (Bk. 7, p. 20). Satan's arrival on earth, as described at various points in *PL,* Defoe treats in "A Vision of the Angelick World" (1720); *A History of the Reality of Apparitions* (1727); and *A System of Magick; or, a History of the Black Art* (1727), pp. 81, 139. Letter 194 speaks of the Devil's intent to ruin mankind. Satan's methodology is described in *Apparitions,* where Defoe finds *PL* 4. 396ff. a source of information regarding Satan's power to alter his shape. In *A System of Magick,* Defoe describes the Devil in the shape of a toad "injecting lustful or loose and wandering Thoughts into [Eve's] chaste Mind" (p. 113); in "A Vision," he describes Eve's narration of her dream to Adam.

One curious error in Defoe's *Political History* is his substitution of Gabriel (p. 39) and Uriel (p. 298) for Ithuriel, placing them in possession of the magic spear in *PL* 4. 810–13. Defoe's erroneous attribution is doubtless owing to his faulty recollection of these two in their association against the devil. Gabriel, "Chief of th' Angelic Guards" (*PL* 4. 550), had forced Satan "out of Eden," and Uriel, whom Gabriel had assigned the watch, observed Satan's return to Earth and "forewarn'd the Cherubim" (*PL* 9. 54–61). The combination of Gabriel and Uriel appears again the following year in *A System of Magick,* where Defoe treats of Satan's reluctance to confront man in a physical guise. In the present, Satan prefers to maintain invisibility because of his fear of the two angels and his certain knowledge of the sharp watch they keep against him (p. 139). The supposition is that Uriel, having once lost sight of Satan entering Eden under covert shade (*PL* 4. 567–75), will not be thwarted a second time from preventing Satan's ingress to Earth.

The *Political History* reverses the Devil's early success and demonstrates the ineffectual character of Satan in the contemporary world where men have subsumed his powers. Defoe employs the image of a degraded Devil in ironic fashion to minimize Milton's own achievement. First, he explains the loss to the world of accurate history because the Devil has failed to write his own account of the past. Were the Devil to write history, he would, on first assessment, prove the inaccuracy of Milton's own presumptuous narrative of events. He would be in a position to provide accurate descriptions of nonhuman worlds rather than the English poet's falsified Heaven of "Hills and Dales, flowry Meadows and Plains" and Hell's "places of Retreat and Contemplation" (p. 71; cf. *PL* 8. 262,275), In retrospect, Defoe concludes that Satan would prove an inept "chronologer" because he is disobliged to tell the truth. By implication, Milton's work inevitably fails the test of historical truth because Man is not admitted to the secrets of the universe.

A small number of items in Defoe's commentary on Milton address themselves to the issue of rhetoric or diction*. In his note to *Jure Divino* (Bk. 7, p. 14) Milton's "Genius" allows "the best Ideas of the Matter of Original Crime, of any Thing put into Words in our Language." He frequently provides examples of sublime poetry from *PL,* but, in particular, he praises Milton's "Majestick manner" by which mortal actions are heightened and also placed within a moral perspective, as in *The Review* wherein Raphael reproves "*Adam* for his Rapture, and placing so much of his Happyness in the Embraces of his Wife, as a Woman," citing verses in *PL* 8. 579–85 (Saturday, March 29, 1712). He cites Milton's neologisms in defense of the Scandal Club in which "the Practice of taking any word, and making it a Phrase or Proper Name, stands upon Record, justify'd by the Example of *Milton* and *Dryden*" (Tuesday, July 4,

1704). He recommends the bold diction of authors who "make words signify something, which signified nothing before" in reference to the acronym *Smectymnuus**. Such linguistic techniques strengthen diction, he thought. Of Dryden and Milton in *The Review* he argues, "The like Freedom these Authors take with Quantities and Parts of Speech, making Verbs of Substantives, Participles, &c. and why may we not be allow'd to make an Adjective a Part of a Proper Name, or make a Word become a Phrase" (Tuesday, July 11, 1704). In his important letter to Harley (July–August 1704) Defoe lectures the newly appointed minister on the value of maintaining "Constant Epistolary Conversation" with "Severall forreign Ministers of State, and Men of Learning," in which the discussion of state matters is observed to be of incidental purpose. Such practices served Milton, whose general correspondence was "so woven with Politicall Observations that he found it as Usefull as any Part of his forreign Correspondence." In this letter, Defoe expresses the need for a "Supreme Ministry," that is, a prime minister, and educated leadership. He also appears to recommend his services to Harley for the purpose of acquiring intelligence in Scotland (Letter No. 14).

Milton and Defoe may have known one another. In 1664 Milton moved to Artillery Walk, Bunhill, a few hundred yards from Defoe's father's house. In his early years, Defoe could have seen Milton there. Milton was buried on November 12, 1674, at nearby St. Giles, Cripplegate, when Defoe was about thirteen years old. Of Milton's works, Defoe probably owned the sixth edition of *PL* (1695) with sculptures, and copies of *1Def.*

Passages in the prose and poetry of *The Political History* (May 7, 1726) appear to have provided source material for Jonathan Swift, Alexander Pope*, William Blake*, and Charles Dickens, material originating in Defoe's treatment of Milton's epic work. Defoe's prophetic description of Satan as historian curiously adumbrates Gulliver's own rhapsodic description of his future as historian when he envisions himself gifted with the eternal life of the Struldbruggs, prior to his meeting those unfortunates (*Gulliver's Travels*, October 28, 1726). Neither Defoe's Satan nor Swift's Gulliver can successfully assume Raphael's role as "Divine Historian" (*PL* 8. 6–7), for Satan is disinclined to speak the truth, and Gulliver's perception is always distorted by the limitations of his personal experience. Defoe and Swift are both skeptical of the validity of historical experience. Ultimate truth is to be found in Scripture.

Pope may be indebted to *The Political History* for his frivolous treatment of heroic imagery in chapter 12 of *Peri Bathous: Of the Art of Sinking in Poetry* (writ. 1727; pub. 1728), for the suggestion that the epic poem in absurdity becomes a Harlequinade, and for imposing the rhetoric of the stage upon his criticism of contemporary poetry. Defoe himself fares poorly in Pope's essay when he is compared to his disadvantage with Milton and Shakespeare.

Blake remembered Defoe's verses in *The Political History* (p. 66) on the admission of sin to Heaven, for "The Tyger" echoes the following passage (see R. Baine, *Daniel Defoe and the Supernatural* [1968], p. 54) :

How didst thou pass the Adamantine Gate,
　And into Spirit thy self insinuate?
　　From what dark state? from what deep place?
　　From what strange uncreated race?
Where was thy antient habitation found
Before void Chaos heard the forming sound?

Dickens dealt not with the nature of sin in Heaven but with the manner in which the Devil performs his temptations on earth. In his letter of November 3, 1837, he wrote that he had completed a reading of the *History of the Devil*. In *Oliver Twist* (1737–38) Fagin and Sikes are both depicted as agents of the Devil and the Devil incarnate. They entice their fellows to commit crimes imitative of the Devil when he insinuated himself upon Eve in Paradise and in his actions subsequent to the Fall (M. H. Law, *Publications of the Modern Language Association*, 40: 892–97). Milton's descriptions of the Devil's activity on earth Defoe found praiseworthy. Thus, four major English writers—Swift, Pope, Blake, and Dickens—show familiarity with Defoe's *Political History* and, in particular, with those sections treating *PL*. [IR]

DELILLE, ABBE (Jacques Montainer): *see* TRANSLATIONS OF MILTON'S WORKS.

DEMONS, DAEMONS. By *demon* is generally meant an evil spirit, a devil, an apostate angel. In the earliest Greek texts the term *daimon* is used to designate a spirit intermediate between the gods and men; such beings were believed to inhabit the four elements (especially the air) as well as minerals, dens, and caves. This belief lies behind St. Paul's reference to the chief of the evil spirits as "the prince of the power of the air" (Eph. 2:2). A later tendency was to identify daemons with gods. St. Paul is again a witness in that he used the term to describe the divinities to whom the Gentiles made sacrifices (1 Cor. 10:20). *Daimon* was rendered as *diabolus* in the Vulgate, from which, through the Anglo-Saxon, comes the word *devil*. Present-day connotations of *demon* should not obscure the fact that the term in the Renaissance, usually with the spelling "daemon" or "daimon," was applied to all sorts of spirits—real or fancied, good or evil. A compendium of Renaissance lore on the subject appears in Robert Burton's* *Anatomy of Melancholy* ("A Digression of Spirits," 1, 2, 1, 2).

Milton's discussion of the government of angels* in *CD* includes some remarks on demons. Angels are either good or evil, for it appears that many of them revolted from God by their own accord before the Fall of Man*. Their proper place is the bottomless pit, from which they cannot escape without permission, nor can they do anything without the command of God. But at times they are allowed to wander throughout the whole earth, the air, and heaven* itself in order to execute unwittingly the judgments of God. They retain much of what they possessed before their rebellion, such as their hierarchical order and their great knowledge; the latter, however, tends to aggravate rather than diminish their misery, so that they utterly despair of salvation. Their leader is the author of all wickedness and the enemy of all good; he has various names, among which are Beelzebub (Matt. 12:24) and Satan (Job 1:6) (15:107–11). In his discussion of the Fall of Man, Milton begins by pointing out that "this sin originated, first, in the instigation of the devil, as is clear from the narrative in Gen. iii. and from 1 John iii. 8" (15:181).

PL gives an imaginative portrayal of demons which, for the most part, is consistent with the exposition in *CD*. What Raphael refers to as "lik'ning spiritual to corporal forms" (5.573) results in a depiction of demons as possessing human bodies and emotions, along with taking part in war*, debate*, and games, but the basic doctrine is the same. Perhaps the only significant difference is that the names *Satan* and *Beelzebub* are used to designate separate individuals rather than as variant names for the same demon. Milton follows biblical accounts of Satan's leading a host of angels in rebellion and later seducing man. Present also are such traditional commonplaces as the fallen angels metamorphosed into pagan gods (1.364–505) and, to a lesser extent, as inhabiting the fire and air (1.430; 2.274–75, 397–402). This latter aspect is more pronounced in *PR*, where we find Satan addressing his followers as "Demonian Spirits now, from the Element / Each of his reign allotted, rightlier call'd / Powers of Fire, Air, Water, and Earth beneath . . . (2.121ff.).

In his earlier works Milton refers to daemons without connotations of evil. In *IlP* he speaks of "those *Daemons* that are found / In fire, air, flood, or underground" (93–96), spirits associated with the four elements like those named in *PR* but without any suggestion of evil. A somewhat different category is the Attendant Spirit of *Mask*—a demon in the MSS—

which is related somehow to the daemon that directed Socrates' life as described by Apuleius* and later developed by Augustine*. The "Genius" of the shore of *Lyc* may represent an allied tradition of local demideities. For full consideration see Robert H. West, *Milton and the Angels* (1955). [RF]

DENNIS, JOHN (1657–1734), poet, critic, and champion of Milton. Though his critical positions advance Dennis as a major critic of his age, he is inadequately known today and seems to have had little influence in his own age, as far as Milton is concerned. The present article therefore attempts to summarize Dennis's attitudes and critical analyses in some detail. In his discussions of Milton and his works, he was interested in the concept of sublimity in style and subject, the wide range that religion affords for poetry, the strategies of characterization, blank verse*, and decorum and epic* standards. He found Milton a literary reformer and innovator, and a genius because he surmounted mere rules and imitations unlike Dennis's contemporaries.

In the Preface to *The Passions of Byblis* (1692) Dennis indicates approval of Milton's blank verse amidst the controversy* that existed because of such antagonistic remarks as Thomas Rymer's in *The Tragedies of the Last Age* (1678). Sir Richard Blackmore's imitation of *PL* in *Prince Arthur* (1695)—imitation primarily in the use of blank verse, language, and certain subject elements—evoked objections to the too-frequent and inferior works that the epic had spawned (*Remarks on a Book Entituled, Prince Arthur, An Heroick Poem* [1696]). His comments on the fallen angels* stress Milton's wise decision to imbue them with something that is allied to goodness to make sure the effects of their fall would be more strongly recognized, for at their fall they had not yet conceived unrelenting hate against mankind. That is, Milton's fallen angels in the epic were not yet the devils that they appear to modern man, and Milton reasoned that their change from

angels to devils was not wrought all at once. The point, particularly as applied to Satan, has escaped some modern critics. *The Advancement and Reformation of Modern Poetry. A Critical Discourse* (1701) is a particularly strong statement of Milton's sublimity, a concept that is of pervasive influence in establishing Milton's reputation during the eighteenth century. A critic's view of what constitutes the sublime in terms of subject and language is the touchstone for the praise and dispraise of Milton and specifically of *PL* during this period. Dennis asserts the importance of "the Greatness of Ideas" to the achievement of the sublime "by infusing into the Poet, Admiration, and a noble Pride, which express'd, make the Spirit; which is stately and majestick till the last, and then it grows vehement, because the Idea which causes it, is not only great, but very terrible." The source of such sublime ideas in Milton, Dennis contends, is religion. While the ancients surpass the moderns (another important critical controversy of the age) because they incorporated poetry with religion, the moderns will have the advantage when they join Christian religion with poetry, as Milton has done.

Dennis develops his ideas of the sublime further in *The Grounds of Criticism in Poetry* (1704), and Milton is central to his position. The "Specimen. *Being the Substance of what will be said in the Beginning of the* Criticism *upon* Milton" recognizes first that Milton was "one of the greatest and most daring Genius's that has appear'd in the World," that his poem is "the most lofty, but most irregular . . . produc'd by the Mind of Man." Dennis stresses the sublimity that developed out of Milton's observations while at the same time he broke the rules of Aristotle*, "Not that he was ignorant of them, or contemn'd them. On the contrary, no man knew them better, or esteemed them more." The position of the eighteenth century was often that perhaps best illustrated in Dr. Johnson's* remarks; rules are rules and any breaking of them was to be condemned as indecorous. Dennis took the more seemingly modern opinion (not yet fully examined in Milton criticism) that Milton's functioning within tradition, though he altered that tradition, created "an Original Poem," "a Poem that should have his own Thoughts, his own Images, and his own Spirit," not properly to "be said to be against the Rules, as it may be affirmed to be above them all." His critical argument with Addison* in "Letters on Milton and Wycherley," which began in 1711 in replies to *The Spectator*, nos. 39 and 40 (see his *Reflections, Critical and Satirical upon a Late Rhapsody Called An Essay Upon Criticism*), is clear from the critical position here, a position that gives Milton the advantage over Homer* and Virgil*. Dennis was influenced by Longinus* and Hermogenes*, and though this leads him to praise the religious ideas of *PL* and the language in which they are cast, it also leads him to see Satan as properly Milton's hero because he bests the better (i.e., Man), and to find *PR* less than successful. For Dennis, the brief epic did not promote or hinder the violence, change, and variety of "Enthusiastick Passions."

In his letter "To Judas Iscariot, Esq., On the Degeneracy of the Publick Taste," dated May 25, 1719 (from *Letters to Steele and Booth* [1719], and reprinted in *Original Letters* [1721], 1 : 69–80), Dennis lashes out at his contemporaries by saying that they would find fault with Milton and damn him (as some in the eighteenth century did) because they prefer "that soft and effeminate Rhyme." To contrast the lack of attention from his countrymen before the publication of *PL* in 1688, the tributes to Milton by Selvaggi*, Salsilli*, and Manso* are reprinted. Dryden's* epigram given beneath the 1674 *PL* engraved portrait "is nothing but a Paraphrase" of Selvaggi's couplet. *Original Letters, Familiar, Moral and Satirical* (2 vols.) includes besides the aforementioned item a letter to Blackmore, dated December 5, 1716, 1 : 11, discussing epic poetry in answer to Blackmore's contention in "An Essay on the Nature and Constitution of Epick Poetry" (*Essays Upon Several Subjects* [1716], pp. 51–52) that the hero of *PL* is Adam. Allusions and quotations are also found in a letter to Thomas Sergeant, dated August 27, 1717, 1 : 33; Letter 3, "On the Writings and Genius of Shakespeare," dated February 8, 1711, 2: 398, 405; and "To the Spectator Upon His Paper on the 24th of April," 2 : 418, 429. Two other letters in the collection make noteworthy points. That "To H——C——," undated, 1 : 172–93, discusses the superiority of Milton's Morning Hymn, *PL* 5. 153–208 (which is quoted), to Sternhold and Hopkins's renditions of the psalms in standard ballad meter. Milton as a literary reformer is again Dennis's subject in "The Person of Quality's Answer to Mr. Collier's Letter : Containing a Defence of a Regulated Stage," dated January 1, [1705?], 2 : 236. "Letters on Milton and Wycherley" from *The Proposals for Printing by Subscription . . . Miscellaneous Tracts* (1721–22) offers observations on *Paradise Lost* in Letters 1–3, dated December 9, 1721; January 20, 1722; and January 24, 1722; the recipient was a friend, George Sewell, a medical doctor. Here, largely against the enthusiasms and strictures of Joseph Addison, Dennis, apparently annoyed that criticism he had published prior to 1712, when the *Spectator* papers appeared, had been ignored (or else plagiarized), charges others with not allowing "that *Milton* in the Sublimity of his thoughts surpass'd both Ancients and Moderns," with dwelling on elements in which Milton has equals rather than on those in which he surpasses others, with failing always to give a clear picture of Milton's sublimity, with not recognizing Milton's originality, and with Milton's leaving "ten times more to be understood than what he has exprest, which is the surest and noblest Mark, and the most transporting Effect of Sublimity." Again Dennis's position is noticeably "modern" and suggests the major failing of most eighteenth-, nineteenth-, and twentieth-century critics of Milton. But it should be pointed out that Dennis, who had little to say about any work other than *PL*, must be charged with the same criticism for such poems as *PR, SA,* and *Lyc.*

In *Remarks Upon Several Passages in the Preliminaries to the Dunciad* (1729), Dennis talks of Milton's poetical fire in *PL,* though again putting down *PR* for the lack of fire inherent in its subject. Dennis had the year before been attacked as one of the Dunces by Pope* in retaliation for Dennis's *Remarks Upon Mr. Pope's Translation of Homer with Two Letters Concerning "Windsor Forest" and the "Temple of Fame"* (1717). His strategy in the 1729 pamphlet is to use Milton as a foil against Pope's position that "the Force of Art" maintains poetical fire in order to place Pope in a category of poet lacking sublimity.

Milton was clearly a favorite author of Dennis's and his influence is seen in the background of Dennis's own poems and plays. Three specific items may be mentioned: "The Court of Death, a Pindarique Poem" (1695; rptd. in *Miscellany Poems,* 2d ed. [1697]) shows strong influence; *Iphigenia. A Tragedy. Acted at the Theatre in Little Lincoln-Inn-Fields* (1700) alludes to and quotes from *Educ,* p. [vi]; and *The Invader of His Country: or The Fatal Resentment. A Tragedy* (1720) gives two lines from *L'Al* as a marginal note to the Prologue, p. [xiii]. [JTS]

DENTON, WILLIAM: *see* ADAPTATIONS.

DERBY, ALICE, COUNTESS DOWAGER OF: *see* EGERTON FAMILY.

DESPAIR. Despair "takes place only in the reprobate," according to Milton's *CD* (bk. 2, chap. 3), and he illustrates this vice by citing the examples of Judas (Matt. 27 : 5; Acts 1 : 18) and Cain (Gen. 4 : 13). Like doubt, it is an opposite of hope*—but with a significant difference. Pious men, such as David and Peter, are "sometimes liable" to doubt, "at least for a time"; but they do not utterly despair. The distinction is significant, for it underlines the difference between Milton's Moloch and his Samson, the strongest of

the angels* and the strongest of men. Moloch despairs; Samson doubts. The parallel and the contrast between the two fallen champions is significant, for both were, in fact, tainted with the stigma of suicide. "And Samson said, Let me die with the Philistines" (Judges 16 : 30). In the eyes of many commentators on this passage, Samson was, in fact, a suicide, dying by his own volition and by his own hand. Nevertheless the point was disputed. As Don Cameron Allen observed in *The Harmonious Vision,* chapter 4, Donne* regarded Samson as "the first of Biblical suicides and a justifier of self-destruction," while Francius Collius maintained on the contrary "that Samson died a martyred avenger of Israel's Jehovah." Milton himself takes pains to exonerate Samson from this charge; as the Chorus observes, he is an involuntary suicide: "self-kill'd / Not willingly, but tangl'd in the fold / Of dire necessity. . . ." Moloch, on the other hand, does not (to be sure) die by his own hand, but he nevertheless wills his own destruction. Milton describes him as "fiercer by despair," preferring "not to be at all" rather than be less in strength than the Almighty. His look denounces "Desperate revenge," and (as Belial correctly observes) he "grounds his courage on despair / And utter dissolution. . . ." Our "final hope / Is flat despair . . ," exasperating the Almighty to spend his rage. That must "end us, that must be our cure. . . ."

The etymology of *despair* suggests its diametric opposition to hope; and in medieval iconography the words are often contrasted through images of conflict, sometimes through antithetical positions. Since suicide was commonly regarded as an unpardonable sin* (inasmuch as the felo-de-se could never repent and receive absolution), despair was often represented emblematically by images of suicide. In Spenser's* *The Faerie Queene* (bk. 1, canto 9) Despayre tempts Redcrosse to stab himself and, thwarted in this design, "chose an halter . . . And with it hung himself, unbid unblest." Milton is able to exploit such associations between suicide and despair both in his portrait of Moloch and in his drama of Samson, creating deliberate ambiguities by references to Samson's "swoonings of despair, / And sense of Heav'n's desertion" and his "one prayer" for "speedy death, / The close of all my miseries, and the balm"—dropping hints of suicide but ultimately refuting them by a verdict of death by accident. Phrases like "death's benumbing Opium as my only cure" may resemble the "sad cure" that Belial ridicules in Moloch's desperate revenge and the "happie ease" that Spenser's tempter promises St. George; but they occur (significantly) *before* Samson's encounter with Dalila and Harapha and *before* he feels the "rousing spirits" that will lead him to his final victory over his enemies and to his own accidental death. Samson does not fall into despair in the sense in which Milton defines this term in *CD*—in the sense in which Moloch (*PL* 2) and Satan (*PL* 4) experience despair. In countering Harapha's accusation of presumption, he refuses to despair of God's final pardon. In theological terms, his weakness is not the true despair of the reprobate but the doubt (and the "impatience under the divine decrees") to which even the pious are liable. In the course of the drama this is converted into its logical contrary —hope, the devout affections toward God "by which we expect with certainty the fulfillment of God's promise" (*CD* bk. 2, chap. 3). Samson dies not as a suicide but as a hero of faith. [JMS]

DEXTER, GREGORY: *see* PRINTERS.

DICTION. Milton's diction may be examined from two necessarily overlapping perspectives: the general character of his vocabulary and the functions and effects of words in context.

Scholarly examinations of the general character of Milton's vocabulary have often been concerned with two issues: the extent to which Milton's vocabulary is native or borrowed from other languages (especially Latin) and the extent to which his vocabulary is innovative, current, or

archaic. One of the earliest commentators on *PL* (Patrick Hume*, *Annotations on Milton's Paradise Lost,* 1695), calling attention to the "Old and Obsolete words" and the "Obscure parts" of the work, set out to explain and render into "Phrases more Familiar" such terms as "with hideous Ruine," "Adamantine chaines," "Obdurate Pride," and many others. Hume's implied judgment of obscurity in Milton's vocabulary was made explicit by some eighteenth-century critics. The general eighteenth-century view that Milton's vocabulary is alien and archaic was voiced by Addison* when he said that Milton "infused a great many Latinisms" into English (*Spectator,* no. 285) and by Francis Peck*, who cited among the many "old" words in Milton, "minstrelsy," "murky," "carol," and "chaunt." Although some eighteenth-century critics, most notably Dr. Johnson*, condemned some features of Milton's diction (Johnson said Milton "wrote no language" but a "Babylonish dialect"(*Lives of the Poets* [1905], 1 : 190–91)), many admirers of Milton appreciated what they thought to be his "quaint uncouthness of speech" (for accounts of the eighteenth-century views of Milton's diction, see R. D. Havens, *Influence of Milton on English Poetry* [1922], pp. 63–68, and Lalia Phipps Boone, *SAMLA Studies in Milton,* ed. J. Max Patrick [1953], pp. 114–15).

The critical opinion that Milton's diction is highly foreign and highly archaic survives into the twentieth century, notably in the evaluation of T. S. Eliot* and Ezra Pound (*Polite, Essays* [1937], p. 192). This attitude was summarized in a statement, later revised, by James Holly Hanford in the first edition of *A Milton Handbook* (1927), who said that Milton's diction, unlike that of Shakespeare* and other Elizabethan dramatists, ". . . has little relish of the speech of men. Where their [the dramatists'] anomalies are colloquial and idiomatic, his [Milton's] are the product of a preference for the unusual and recondite in vocabulary and construction, which leads him to archaism on the one hand, and to the substitution of foreign idiom, particularly Latin, for native on the other" (p. 233).

Yet generalizations about the nature of Milton's vocabulary need to be made with reference to clear linguistic standards. For example, does the label "Latinate" or "alien" mean that the proportion of foreign borrowings (in one poem, or all poems, or all works) is higher than the norm proportion for other poets and writers of the seventeenth century? If an individual word is labeled "foreign," does that mean that the word is of ultimate or immediate foreign origin (e.g., "angel" vs. "alleostropha")? Does "archaic" mean that a word went out of currency in 1550, 1600, 1650, or when exactly?

Asking these and other more exacting questions, modern criticism has begun to question the generalizations about the nature of Milton's vocabulary. Some modification of the view that the vocabulary is alien is made in the scientific and statistical studies of George P. Marsh (*Lectures on the English Language*, 4th ed. [Charles Scribners, 1864]). Making a careful distinction between Milton's total vocabulary in a given poem (i.e., each word counted once) and the proportional vocabulary of that poem (i.e., the number of times Milton uses a word, excluding proper names and articles), Marsh finds that although Milton's total vocabulary contains many foreign words, yet his proportional vocabulary contains fewer foreign words. That is, the poet has many foreign words at hand but he uses them with restraint. Furthermore, among the Greek and Latin borrowings that appear often are "air," "angel," "force," "glory," "grace," just," "mortal," "nature," and "part." Marsh finds that the proportion of native words in *L'Al, IlP,* and *PL* 6 is 90%, 83%, and 80% respectively (pp. 125, 128; later studies have modified these figures somewhat).

Several investigations of Milton's vocabulary in the twentieth century confirm a more moderate view of its Latinate or foreign element. Examining *Lyc,* a

poem "as far removed as possible from daily life both in content and artistic method of presentation," G. C. Taylor finds that even in this "rarefied" poem, more than 80% of the total vocabulary is from Old English (*Notes and Queries* 178 : 56–57). R. M. Lumiansky, extending and correcting the approach of Marsh, finds that the proportional vocabulary of *L'Al* is 81% native if proper names, prepositions, conjunctions, and articles are included and 75% if they are excluded. Further, although the total vocabulary appears to be only 68% native, actually about 98% of the words in the poem were in use before 1500 (*Modern Language Notes* 55 : 591–94). Lalia Phipps Boone has also reexamined Marsh's figures in her analysis of *PL* 6 and finds that not only is the proportional vocabulary more native than foreign (although Marsh's 80% is too high), even the total vocabulary is more native than Marsh had estimated. Consequently Boone, like Marsh, Taylor, and Lumiansky, concludes that the latinity of Milton's poetic vocabulary has been overemphasized.

Joshua H. Neumann, in a detailed and thorough study of Milton's prose vocabulary, reaches a similar conclusion. In treatises like *Colas* (1645), *Apol* (1642), *RCG* (1642), and *Way* (1659), Neumann finds that the native words are much more characteristic of Milton's vocabulary than the foreign words and that, moreover, the native words often give the prose style "its color, and vigor, its homely flavor, and, on occasion, its downright earthiness" (*Publications of the Modern Language Association* 60 : 114).

The generalization that Milton's vocabulary is archaic may also be qualified by consideration of the proportion of archaic words. There are certainly archaic words to be found in the poetry ("foughten," "frore," "wonns," "welkin," "darkling," "drear," "ychained," "yclept," "swinkt"), yet the archaic words, according to Helen Darbishire, form a relatively small proportion of the poet's vocabulary. Rather than being archaic, "the groundwork of his diction is the racy natural

English that people speak" (*Essays and Studies* 10 : 41–42; on Milton's archaic diction see H. C. Wyld, *Some Aspects of the Diction of English Poetry* [1933], pp. 22–24).

Although the greater proportion of words in Milton's vocabulary may be current (for his time), Milton's linguistic innovations are significant and numerous enough to require special mention. William B. Hunter, examining the poetry (*Essays in Honor of Walter Clyde Curry* [1954], pp. 241–59) and Joshua H. Neumann, examining the prose, find that Milton's many lexical innovations entitle him to be considered an enricher of the English language. These neologisms are created by various linguistic processes including borrowing, invention of present and past participles, functional shift (i.e., changing words from one part of speech to another; *see* Hunter, p. 253, List 3), affixation, and compounding (with either native or borrowed words).

All of these processes can create words that are striking in their appropriateness and freshness, but the processes of affixation and compounding are particularly interesting. By joining classical or romantic prefixes or suffixes to words already in the language (prefixes— *arch, dis, mis,* or *em, in* or *en, anti, sub*— and suffixes— *ean, ian, ous, eous, ize, ist, ism, ant*), Milton can create careful distinctions between words. Neumann points out that Milton probably invented the word "sensuous" to avoid the negative connotations of "sensual." The flexibility that these inventions allow is clear when Milton uses the distinction between two words with different suffixes to advance an argument. In *Ref* he says "Antiquaries" are those "whose labours are useful and laudable, while "antiquarians" are those "whose work is a hinderance to Reformation" (3 : 14). Milton frequently uses the suffixes "ean" and "ian" to make sonorous adjectives from personal and place names: "Adamantean," "Atlantean," "Pharisaean," "Cathaian" (Neumann, p. 111). Nor does the poet neglect native affixes; with the native prefix "un"

he creates many words that are commonplace today : "unprincipled," "unaccountable." These words can be arranged in forceful groups, as when the savior speaks harshly of the idolatrous tribes of Israel, who are "unhumbled, unrepentant, unreform'd" (*PR*, 3. 429).

The number and variety of compound words in Milton's prose and poetry is great and is evidence, as Neumann says, of "the diligence with which Milton searched the coffers of the language round" (p. 115). Many of the compounds are epithets and are composed of an adjective or an adverb plus a participle (ill-taught). In the prose Milton formed many words with "church," "idol," and "law" (law-giving, law-prudent). Among the compounds that are familiar today are "arch fiend," "awe-stroock," "full-grown," "half-starved," "love-lorn," "never-ending," "well-balanced," "far-sighted,' "hotheaded." Other compounds, though less familiar today, are nevertheless striking and forceful in their contexts : "baby-rhetoric," "dinner-doctrine," "slip-skin" ("evasive"), and "tongue-fence" ("a debate"). Some of the compounds are nonce words, used for their effectiveness on one occasion : "the many-benefice-gaping mouth of a Prelate" (*Ref* 3 : 19), "the now-only law-giving mouth of charity" (*Tetra* 4: 175). (For a detailed description of compounds see Neumann, pp. 114–16, and Hunter, p. 244.)

The value of the various descriptive criticisms of Milton's vocabulary cited here is the correction they give to an earlier overemphasis on Milton's Latinity and archaism. The criticisms do not deny, however, that there are unusual words (whether foreign borrowed, neologisms, archaisms, and so forth) in Milton's vocabulary and that these words have effects in the contexts in which they appear. Indeed, the exhaustive study of E. M. Clark shows clearly that the number of words of foreign origin varies according to the poetic context (*Studies in Phililogy* 53: 220–38).

Milton's diction may also be understood from the point of view of the functions and effects of words in context. In viewing diction with respect to context, one more nearly approximates the sixteenth- and seventeenth-century rhetorical stance (*see* RHETORIC). Many, though not all, Renaissance rhetoricians, following the lead of the classical rhetoricians, suggest that the speaker or writer consider five steps or stages in preparing his work: *invention, disposition, elocution, memory,* and *utterance* (for a representative 16th century definition of these terms, see Thomas Wilson, *The Arte of Rhetorique,* 1553). Elocution (closest to the modern concept of style) is the stage wherein the writer chooses those words, figures of speech, and figures of grammar* that will make the thoughts that he has already formulated (*invention*) and ordered (*disposition*) forceful and clear to the audience. The concept that a writer and particularly a poet first formulates his thoughts and then chooses the right words (and other devices of style) to convey those thoughts forcefully is often expressed in a clothing metaphor. In an early poem, Milton, for example, asks his "native language" to "from thy wardrope bring thy chiefest treasure; / . . . those richest Robes, and gay'st attire / Which deepest Spirits, and choisest Wits desire : / I have some naked thoughts that rove about / And loudly knock to have their passage out; / And wearie of their place do only stay / Till thou hast deck't them in thy best array" (*Vac,* lines 17–26). For various interpretations of the clothing metaphor in Renaissance criticism, *see* Rosemond Tuve, *Elizabethan and Metaphysical Imagery,* pp. 61–78.

But just as clothing must be suitable to the occasion at which it is worn, so style (including diction) must be suitable to the kind of poem (or in the broader sense, the kind of writing) that the poet is attempting (*see* STYLE AND LEVELS OF STYLE). This suitability or appropriateness of style to genre is called *decorum.* Milton praises *decorum* as "that sublime Art" and further specifies that *decorum* teaches "what the laws are of a true Epic Poem, what of a *Dramatic,* what of a *Lyric*"

(*Educ* 4 : 286). According to the commonplace concept of poetic decorum the "fittest style" for an epic* or heroic poem is the lofty or high style, the "fittest style" for the lyric is the middle style, the "fittest style" for the pastoral* poem is the lowly style, and so forth for other genres of poetry.

Diction, as part of style, must also vary from "high" to "low" according to the context in which it appears. A working definition of what makes diction lofty, and by implication what makes it mean or lowly, is formulated by Aristotle* in the *Poetics*: "That diction . . . is lofty and raised above the commonplace which employs unusual words. By unusual, I mean strange (or rare) words, metaphysical, lengthened—anything in short that differs from the normal idiom. . . . For by deviating in exceptional cases from the normal idiom the language will gain distinction . . ." (chap. 22).

Milton's Latinate or classical diction, so often the subject of adverse criticism and misunderstanding, often functions to elevate a poem or a passage in a poem to the lofty dimension that is appropriate to the genre and subject. Helen Darbishire throws light on exactly this decorum in *PL* when she says that Milton needs a large infusion of words like "loss irreparable," "inextinguishable fire," "immutable, immortal, infinite," and "ineffable joy," in the poem (formation by Latin affixation) because the subject of the poem transcends the bounds of the finite and everyday—it contradicts earthly limitation. Semantically, of course, the words defy limitations of time and space since the prefixes suggest "beyond"; but aesthetically the words also defy the everyday and hence elevate because they are unusual.

Many of Milton's classical words in the poems give elevation and loftiness to the style not only because they are unusual, but because they also allow for precision, surprise, and subtle extensions of meaning and theme. Milton often uses Latinate words primarily in their etymological rather than their derivative or acquired English sense to bring ideas into sharp focus as when Adam speaks of submitting his "obvious brest" to the chastising hand of heaven (*PL* 11. 374). By drawing on the Latin meaning of "obvious" as "exposed, lying open," Milton makes emphatic Adam's repentance as well as his vulnerability (Wyld, p. 13). Examples of words used primarily in the etymological or Latin sense abound and their specific effects in the contexts of the poems should be noted by the careful reader ("while night *invests* / the sea," *PL* 1. 207–8; "there went a *fame* in Heaven," 1. 651; "Let none *admire* that riches grow in Hell," 1. 690–91; "his look *denounc'd* [i.e., proclaimed] / Desperate revenge," 2. 106–7; "for speed *succinct*," 3. 643; *see also* Bernard Groom, *The Diction of Poetry from Spenser to Bridges* [1955], pp. 74–94).

Even more often, however, Milton achieves elevation, interest, precision, and surprise by drawing on both the etymological and derivative sense of a word, that is, by making the word do "double duty" (Walter A. Raleigh, *Milton* [1900], p. 208). Two values of the word *individual* come significantly into play in the passage in which Eve recalls Adam's first words to her. As she fled from him, Adam told her that he had given of his own flesh and bone "to have thee by my side / Henceforth an individual solace dear; / Part of my Soul I seek thee, and thee claim / My other half . . ." (*PL* 4. 485–88). The word *individual* carries the derivative sense of "other" and Eve is the "other being" that Adam felt compelled to seek. But *individual* also has the Latin meaning of "undivided" or "unseparable," suggesting in this passage as elsewhere in the poem (5. 609–12), that Adam and Eve are joined together in a unique, exemplary, and fruitful union, a union that significantly contrasts with Satan's infertile self-embrace (Mario A. DiCesare, *Language and Style in Milton: A Symposium in Honor of the Tercentenary of Paradise Lost*, ed. R. D. Emma and J. T. Shawcross [1967], pp. 3–6). By using two values of the word *voluble*, Milton gives both an immediate physical description of the snake and a dramatic anticipation of an important moral action. As the snake approaches Eve, he is ". . . voluble and bold, now hid, now seen" (*PL* 9. 436). The etymological meaning of *voluble* refers to the "coiled" movement of the snake, but the derivative English sense, "talkative," anticipates the all too effective talkativeness of the snake when he seduces Eve (Christopher Ricks, *Milton's Grand Sytle* [1963], p. 108). Similarly, the word *illustrious* carries two values in the description of the hair of Uriel, which hangs "Illustrious on his Shoulders" (*PL* 3. 627). The etymological meaning refers to the light that shines from the hair while the derivative meaning suggests the great dignity of Uriel, "One of the seav'n/ Who in Gods presence, neerest to his Throne / Stand ready . . ." (*see insinuating* in *PL* 4. 348–50; *fallacy* in *PR* 1. 154–55).

Examining *PL*, Christopher Ricks describes the precise way that Milton dramatizes the effects of the Fall by using the etymological meaning of a word in one context and the derivative meaning in another context. Before the Fall, language, like man, is in a state of innocence and purity; words do not refer to man's sin because man is not sinful. Consequently, when Milton describes a scene in Paradise before the Fall, he suppresses the derivative meaning of the word *error* and insists, rather, on its etymological meaning, "wandering" : ". . . the crisped Brooks, / Rowling on Orient Pearl and sands of Gold, / With mazie error under pendant shades / Ran Nectar . . ." (4. 237–40). Because the word *error* appears in context along with words that refer to good and innocent sights and sensations, Milton in effect reminds the reader that "error," which now (its derivative meaning) has only an evil denotation, was once innocent when man was innocent. The effect of the Fall, then, is to "infect" language (Satan says that he will reside in man until he infects man's "thoughts, his looks, words, actions"—10. 607–8) and the word *error* comes to refer only to man's evil: "I also err'd in overmuch admiring," "I rue / That errour now" (9. 1178 and 1180). The fall has "degraded language too, and turned these innocent notes to tragic" (Ricks, p. 111; for a similar argument concerning "lapse" *see* p. 111).

Milton's use of Latin words in both their etymological and derivative senses may be considered a kind of pun* (*syllepsis*). Puns are, indeed, an important part of Milton's diction and are found in many forms including *syllepsis* (a word used once with two meanings), *paronomasia* (repetition of words close, but not identical in sound—"At one slight *bound* high overleap'd all *bound*," *PL* 4. 181) and *antanaclasis* (repetition of a word with a shift in meaning—"Much ostentation vain of fleshly *arm*, / And fragil *arms*," *PR* 3. 387–88).

Furthermore, puns, like foreign and other kinds of unusual diction, may give distinction or delight to a passage. Puns allow the reader to see multiple meanings simultaneously. The fact that a pun can be an instrument of delight or distinction as well as of derision has been obscured by some eighteenth-century evaluations of the pun as "false wit" (Addison) and the punster as a "low wit" (Johnson). Although a modern audience along with the eighteenth century might smirk at a pun, yet for Milton and his seventeenth-century audience the pun was a flexible device of diction that could be used for many effects. In that most somber part of *PL* when the poet must change his "Notes to Tragic," he puns on the word *world* to make emphatic the new sorrow of man's condition:

. . . foul distrust, and breach
Disloyal on the part of Man, revolt,
And disobedience: On the part of Heav'n
Now alienated, distance and distaste,
Anger and just rebuke, and judgement giv'n,
That brought into this World a worlde of woe
(9. 6–11)

Yet, in a description of the beauties of Paradise, a pun on *aires* serves to elicit delight in the beauty of the scene:

The Birds thir quire apply; aires, vernal aires,
Breathing the smell of field and grove, attune
The trembling leaves . . .
(4. 264–66)

Aires in its primary sense refers to the "breezes" that move through the "trembling leaves." But the musical denotations of *quire* and *attune* suggest a musical denotation for *aires* as well: "melody." William Empson explains, "The airs attune the leaves because the air itself is as enlivening as an air; the trees and wild flowers that are smelt on the air match, as if they caused, as if they were caused by, the birds and leaves that are heard on the air; nature, because of a pun, becomes a single organism." Referring to a critic who would condemn such a passage because it uses a pun, Empson concludes, "A critical theory is powerful indeed when it can blind its holders to so much beauty" (*Some Versions of Pastoral* [1950], p. 157).

Milton does, of course, use puns for derision, most interestingly so when he allows a character to pun in order to dramatize the character's faults. But the reader must be attentive to the degree of derision that the poet intends, for there are careful modifications. Eve's punning reply to the serpent when they have come to the tree—"we might have spar'd our coming hither, / *Fruitless* to mee, though *Fruit* be here to excess" (9. 647–48)—dramatizes her all too typical jauntiness and levity at the moment of crisis. But Satan's string of artillery puns in his exhortation to the new-made devils implies a more severe condemnation of the speaker simply because they are bad puns:

But that I doubt, however witness Heaven,
Heav'n witness thou anon, while we discharge
Freely our part; yee who appointed stand
Do as you have in charge, and briefly touch
What we propound, and loud that all may
    hear.
(6. 563–67)

As one nineteenth-century critic observed, "the wit . . . is worthy of newly-made devils" (W. S. Landor, quoted in Ricks, p. 67).

Other special kinds of diction that

may give distinction to the language are compound words, words lengthened by affixation (Aristotle recommends both compounding and lengthening to achieve distinction, *Poetics* 22), epithets, the grandiose nominative of address (e.g., "Thrones, Dominations, Princedoms, Vertues, Powers,"—*PL* 10. 460, and 5. 601, 772; *PR* 1. 44), proper names (especially in sonorous lists—*PL* 1. 396–99; *PR* 2. 19–24, 186–90, 351–61, and 3. 270ff.), Italianate words and phrases (*the air adust* [*l'aria adusta*], *the blanc moon* [*bianca luna*], and probably *harald, sovran, sdein, imparadise*), and occasionally archaic words (although archaic diction often effects lowering; see Hilda Hulme, *Language and Style in Milton* . . . , pp. 75–78, on *wonns, gride, frore, wight*). The reader should also examine the effects of these various kinds of diction in poems that are not of epic dimensions.

Although much may be said of Milton's lofty diction, attention to it should not obscure, for the reader, the flexibility of Milton's language. The diction is not lofty in all poems (or throughout all poems) because lofty diction is not everywhere appropriate. In an early English hymn, a metrical version of Psalm 136, the diction is simple, sensuous, and sings well: "Let us with a gladsom mind / Praise the Lord, for he is kind / For his mercies ay endure, / Ever faithful, ever sure." The diction of a poem that E. M. W. Tillyard calls a "humorous but kindly epitaph on a homely person" is simple and homely: "Here lies old *Hobson*, Death hath broke his girt, / And here alas, hath laid him in the dirt, / Or else the ways being foul, twenty to one, / He's here stuck in a slough, and overthrown" (*The Miltonic Setting, Past and Present* [1938], p. 121). The problem of style and meaning in *Lyc* is, of course, complex but one certainly finds some rustic, homely diction (*rathe, scrannel, Canker, Taintworm, weanling, uncouth, swart star*) appropriate to the pastoral setting. (For discussions of levels of diction in the prose, *see* F. E. Ekfelt, *Philological Quarterly* 25 : 46–69, and E. N. S. Thompson,

Philological Quarterly 14 : 1–15. Ekfelt finds a "homely graphic language" in the prose, and Thompson sees the most distinctive feature to be "simple, vigorous, home-spun phrases.")

The flexibility and range of Milton's diction is apparent even within poems. In *Lyc*, for example, Milton uses not only homely words but delightful, melodious words ("Bid *Amarantus* all his beauty shed") and even harsh words (*shove away, Blind mouthes, for their bellies sake*). These variations in diction accord, however, with a careful and flexible decorum. The harsh diction is found in St. Peter's invective condemning the clergy (112–31) where a more melodious, sonorous diction would be inappropriate. Such careful variations in diction are apparent in the other major poems including *SA*, *PR* (*see* B. K. Lewalski, *Milton's Brief Epic: The Genre, Meaning and Art of Paradise Regained* [1966], pp. 332–42), and *PL*.

That *PL* shows variations in the level of diction and that the variations are decorous was noted by Pope* : "Milton is not lavish of his exotic words and phrases everywhere alike, but employs them much more when the subject is marvellous and strange as in the scenes in Heaven and Hell, than where it is turned to the natural and agreeable as in the pictures of Paradise. In the lower sort of narration the character of the style is simplicity and purity" (quoted by Darbishire, p. 44). More recently, John Steadman, pointing out that "Like *Lycidas, Paradise Lost* is music scored for more than one instrument," explains the rhetorical and poetic theories underlying the stylistic variation in *PL* (*English Studies* 47 : 329–41). According to the theorists, the style of a poem should be appropriate to the subject matter, the speaker, and the "end" of the poem. The "end" of the high style is to cause admiration, of the middle style to cause delight, and of the low style, to teach. In *PL*, when the subject is the cosmic and marvelous, Latinate, polysyllabic, sonorous words are prominent, as in the description of the discharge of Satan from heaven :

Him the Almighty power
Hurl'd headlong flaming from th' Ethereal Skie
With hideous ruine and combustion down
To bottomless perdition, there to dwell
In Adamantine Chaines and penal Fire,
Who durst defie th' Omnipotent to Arms.
(1. 44–49)

But when the subject is the sorrow of a simple woman, plain words predominate: "So cheard he his fair Spouse, and she was cheard, / But silently a gentle tear let fall / From either eye, and wip'd them with her haire" (5. 129–31). The arrival of Raphael is dignified and grand—"Like Maia's son he stood, / And shook his Plumes, that Heav'nly fragrance fill'd / The circuit wide" (5. 285–87)—but the angel finds Adam "as in the dore he sat." Thus there is much lofty diction in the descriptions of public or universal events and much plain diction in the descriptions of domestic and private life.

Significantly, the kind of plain, familiar diction that characterizes many of the early domestic scenes in *PL* comes to be a more notable feature of the style in the last four books of the poem. The shift in diction corresponds to a shift in subject for in these books "the domestic character of Adam and Eve in their trial becomes the focus of interest" (Harold Fische, *Language and Style in Milton* . . . ,p. 57). The prayer that Adam and Eve offer "in lowliest plight repentant" after their trespass (10. 1086ff.) and the labors imposed on them by the curse (10. 1053ff.), require a "lower pitch." Humbler words are appropriate to man's humbler condition (J. M. Steadman, p. 339).

Milton's diction also shows fine variations according to speaker. When the poet speaks in his own voice (*in propria persona*) he may use quite elevated diction. But when he creates the dialogue of different characters, he accommodates the diction to the stature, capacities, or purposes of the character. One may contrast, for example, the diction in the poet's invocation to his heavenly Muse* when he says that he will soar "with no middle flight" (1. 1ff.) with Eve's plea to Adam ("Forsake me not thus," 10. 914–36) made in her "lowlie plight." The diction

of God the Father* is an interesting case of decorum according to speaker and the speaker's purpose. God, of course, is omnipotent and omniscient and hence could be given the most exalted, lofty kind of diction. But God's purpose, or Milton's purpose through him in many of the speeches, is to make clear certain concepts to man's understanding. According to the rhetoricians, a lower, barer diction is the best medium for instruction (J. M. Steadman, *Language and Style in Milton* . . . , pp. 193–232). Hence, in many of God's speeches, the diction is quite bare. Simple, monosyllabic words are notable when God explains with startling conciseness and austerity why and whereof man will fall:

So will fall,
Hee and his faithless Progenie: whose fault?
Whose but his own? Ingrate, he had of mee
All he could have; I made him just and right,
Sufficient to have stood, though free to fall.
(3. 95–99)

(This argument can also account for the prominence of plain diction in *PR*, since much of that poem is given over to argumentation and the "revelation of moral purpose.") For other discussions of lowered diction *see* Arnold Stein, *Answerable Style* [1953], pp. 127–28; C. A. Patrides, *Language and Style in Milton* . . . , pp. 102–19; and Harold Fische, *Language and Style in Milton* . . . , pp. 30–64. [KDC]

DICTIONARIES AND ENCYCLOPEDIAS. Responding to the need for better instruments to aid in the study of ancient languages and literatures, the dictionaries of the Renaissance were not only sources of linguistic information about the ancient languages, but often were also compendia of biographical, historical, geographical, and mythological information as well. Among the dictionaries that filled the need for encyclopedic as well as linguistic learning were the *Elucidarius Carminum et Historiarum vel Vocabularius Poeticus* (1498) of Herman Torrentinus, the *Dictionarium* (1502) of Friar Calepine, the *Thesaurus linguae latinae* (1531) or the

Dictionarium seu latinae linguae thesaurus (1532) of Robert Stephanus (Estienne), the *Dictionarium historicum, geographicum, poeticum,* (1553) of Charles Stephanus (Éstienne), the *Thesaurus Linguae Romanae et Britannicae* (1565) of Thomas Cooper (with encyclopedic items in a separate dictionary at the end of the volume—*Dictionarium Historicum & Poeticum*); and the *Thesaurus Graecae linguae* (1573) of Henri Stephanus. Other standard reference manuals of mythology*, history, and legend include Lilius Giraldus, *De Deis Gentium* (1548); Natalis Comes, *Mythologiae* (1551); Verderius (V. Cartari), *Imagines Deorum Lexicon Geographicum Poeticum & Historicum* (1551); and Vencenzo Cartari, *Le Imagini con la Spositione de i Dei degli Antichi* (1556).

At St. Paul's School*, Milton may have used some of these reference works. The school had copies of Calepine's *Dictionarium,* Robert Stephanus's *Thesaurus* (probably the 1543 ed.), Thomas Cooper's *Thesaurus,* and a *Dictionarius* that was probably the lexicon of Charles Stephanus. Further, the works of Giraldus, Comes, and Cartari were recommended by some educators as reference texts for student composition.

Talbert and Starnes argue that Milton frequently consulted the compendious and well-indexed dictionaries (especially those of Calepine and Charles and Robert Stephanus) while composing his poems (*Classical Myth and Legend in Renaissance Dictionaries* [1955], pp. 226–339). Because the dictionaries concentrated much widely dispersed information in their pages, they would have been valuable tools for the blind poet, dependent on readers. Comparing passages from the dictionaries with passages from Milton's works, Talbert and Starnes find similarities in phrasing (e.g., in entries under Cassiopea, Joshua, Muses, Pandora), similarities in details of a story, especially those details not found in other accounts (e.g., under Cotytto, Elysium-Hesperian Gardens), and even similarities in apparent errors or odd associations (e.g., under Hermione, Briareos) that suggest to them

that Milton turned to the dictionaries to refresh his memory of historical, legendary, and mythical persons and places.

One of the more persuasive arguments for Milton's use of a dictionary concerns an allusion to Echo in *Mask*. In both phrasing and meaning, Milton's account of Echo is like an entry on Echo in Charles Stephanus's *Dictionarium*.

Mask:

Sweet Echo, sweetest Nymph that liv'st unseen
  Within thy airy shell . . .
Canst thou not tell me of a gentle Pair
  That likest thy Narcissus are?
    Or if thou have
Hid them in som flowry Cave,
  Tell me but where
Sweet Queen of Parly, Daughter of the Sphear,
  So maist thou be translated to the skies,
And give resounding grace to all Heav'ns Harmonies

            (229–30, 235–42)

Dictionarium:

  Echo, Nympha, nullo oculo visa, et a Pane, pastorum deo, mirum in modum adamata: quae quidem physice coeli harmoniam significare dicitur, Solis amicam, tamquam domini, et moderatoris omnium corporum coelestium, ex quibus ipsa componitur atque temperatur. . . .

The nymph in both Stephanus and Milton is living unseen, is the daughter of the sphere, and gives "resounding grace" to all "Heaven's Harmonies." The usual account of the myth, however, does not refer to Echo as the daughter of the sphere nor does it associate her with heavenly harmony. Thus Talbert and Starnes conclude that this "unusual conception" of Echo strongly suggests that the *Dictionarium* was Milton's "immediate inspiration" for the passage (p. 249).

Yet the general argument that Milton consulted the dictionaries as he wrote must be carefully qualified. Milton's classical erudition, his wide reading in the ancients, certainly brought him to the original classical sources of the myths, legends, and histories to which he alludes in the poetry, and his capacious memory might well have allowed him to recall these allusions in their original contexts. Thus the dictionaries may not be primary sources for the poet. Indeed, in his *1Def*, Milton castigated those who "seem rather to have turned over phrase-books and lexicons and glossaries than to have perused good authors with judgment or profit" (7 : 67). The dictionaries and encyclopedias were probably most useful to Renaissance writers, John Steadman points out, "as handbooks designed to assist composition and description; as guides for making the most effective practical use of classical materials rather than as rival or alternative sources. . . ." (*New Aspects of Lexicography* [1972], p. 29). Furthermore, since the dictionaries and encyclopedias themselves were often eclectic and synthetic digests of academic and literary commonplaces (as Talbert and Starnes acknowledge, p. 340), it is often difficult to say that Milton even refreshed his memory with any *one* source. Milton's conception of the Genius in *Arc* (44–49), for example, may be drawn from Polydore Virgil, Erasmus*, Cesare Ripa, Perottus, and Virgil*, as well as the dictionaries of Calepine and the Stephanus brothers.

Although it is often difficult to prove that Milton consulted any one reference work, the poet did most certainly know the Greek *Thesaurus* of Henri Stephanus (he alludes to this work in his *Marginalia*, 18 : 287, 318, 323, 326, 327) and the *Thesaurus* of Robert Stephanus. According to the early anonymous biographer of Milton and to Edward Phillips, the poet's nephew, Milton was compiling a Latin dictionary or thesaurus of his own in the "manner of Stephanus." Milton began his dictionary about 1655 and continued it "even very near to his dying day." Although the dictionary was not published (Phillips explains that the papers "were so discomposed and deficient, that it could not be made fit for the Press," several later lexicographers claim to have used Milton's dictionary in their own

work (*Linguae Romanae Dictionarium . . . A New Dictionary in Five Alphabets,* 1693; Adam Littleton, *Latin Dictionary,* 1719; and Robert Ainsworth, *Thesaurus Linguae Latinae,* 1736). The editors of the *Linguae Romanae* describe Milton's dictionary as "a Manuscript Collection in three Large Folio's digested into an Alphabetical order, which the learned John Milton had made, out of Tully, Livy, Caesar, Sallust, Quintus Curtius, Justin, Plautus, Terence, Lucretius . . . in short out of all the best and purest Roman Authors." [KDC]

DIGRESSION, THE: *see* CHARACTER OF THE LONG PARLIAMENT.

DIODATI, CHARLES. Charles Diodati was born in London, probably in 1609. His father, Dr. Theodore Diodati, was a well-known and widely respected London physician born in Geneva and educated at the University of Leyden. Dr. Diodati traveled to England about 1598, married an English woman, and became a British subject in 1628. Charles Diodati developed a deep friendship with Milton when they were schoolmates at St. Paul's*. They shared an intense desire for learning, and no doubt began visiting at each other's home. Their dispositions seemed complementary, for the young Milton's gravity and studiousness contrasted with Charles's more outgoing and lighthearted temperament.

Charles matriculated at Trinity College, Oxford, on February 7, 1623; he received the B.A. degree on December 10, 1625, and the M.A. degree on July 8, 1628. Milton remained a student at St. Paul's approximately two years after Charles was graduated; and on February 12, 1625, Milton, then sixteen years old, was admitted to Christ's College*, Cambridge. While the two boys attended different universities, they maintained their close relationship by letter writing and by visits during vacation periods.

Shortly after admission to Oxford, Charles wrote his one published poem, a tribute to William Camden*, which is included in *Camdeni Insignia,* the volume of tributes issued in 1624 at Oxford. Camden, a distinguished Headmaster of Westminster School and a prolific scholar, had attended both St. Paul's and Oxford; and perhaps the similarity of his educational background to Charles's as well as his reputation as a scholar helps explain why Charles wrote a poem for the commendatory volume. The two extant letters from Charles to Milton, written in Greek and undated, may also have been composed during his Oxford years, 1625–26. Other correspondence from Charles to Milton, similar to these letters, presumably was written, but does not survive. The first letter, which may have been composed during the summer of 1625, anticipates an excursion with Milton that has been delayed by bad weather (12: 292–93). Charles looks forward to their learned discourse when they travel together. In the second letter, written while Charles was visiting in Chester, probably during the spring of 1626, Charles complains that he has no close companion with whom he can converse, but he is enjoying the scenic beauty of nature (12 : 294–95). He then humorously chides Milton for his continuous study and tireless booklearning that are depriving him of the joys of youth. But in the Lent term of 1626, Milton had been suspended from Cambridge because of a quarrel with his tutor, William Chappell*; and from London, while at home, he replied to Charles's second letter with the Latin poem *El* 1. In this verse letter Milton alludes to his harsh tutor and to the indignities that he could not suffer. He enjoys his exile in London since he is pursuing his studies and enjoying himself with reading drama. The poem concludes with the news that he will be returning shortly to Cambridge. Milton probably went back for the beginning of the Easter term on April 19, and he was assigned to another tutor, Nathaniel Tovey*.

El 6, another verse letter, also replies to correspondence from Charles that does not survive. It alludes to Charles's letter, which was in verse (presumably

Latin) and which was written during the Christmas season, on December 13, 1629. Apparently Charles apologized for his verses in the letter, and suggested that the holiday festivities, described with great exuberance, do not favor poetic composition. *El* 6 employs a debating technique that supports but also refutes Charles's suggestion, for Milton argues that wine and feasting have encouraged the composition of the gay elegiac poets (e.g., Ovid*, Anacreon, Pindar, Horace*, and Charles also) but not of the epic* poets. The epic poet is an ascetic, ever chaste and temperate, but only Homer* is cited as an example; and Milton does not mention himself or his aspirations in connection with epic poetry. He concludes by telling Charles about his current writing, *Nat.* Around this time Milton may also have composed his Italian sonnets, and Charles, to whom *Sonn* 4 is addressed, may have criticized them. *Sonn* 4 describes a dark-complexioned beauty by 'vhom the speaker is smitten, maybe the same lady, named Aemilia, celebrated in *Sonn* 2. It has been suggested that the lady may have been related to or acquainted with the Diodati family. *L'Al* and *IlP* were also probably written during Milton's later university years, around 1631. Critics have fancied that Milton is contrasting his own temperament with Charles's, or is employing again the debating technique of *El* 6.

On April 16, 1630, Charles matriculated as a theology student at the Academy of Geneva, where his uncle, Giovanni Diodati*, was a renowned theologian. His translation of the Bible into Italian had been published in 1607. How long Charles remained at the Academy is uncertain, but he stayed there at least through September 1631. He left the Academy, abandoned the ministry as a prospective career, and turned to medicine, which he seems earlier to have contemplated. No records indicate that Charles enrolled as a medical student at a university in England or elsewhere, but he was learning the profession. He was studying medicine under his father's supervision;

he was observing his father at work; and evidently he began practicing as a physician, probably in the outlying counties west of London.

Milton's last two surviving letters to Charles, both written in November 1637, are in Latin and illustrate the classical epistolary art practised by Cicero* and emulated by the Italian humanists. In the first letter Milton humorously rebukes Charles for not having recently corresponded with him and for not having visited with him (*Epistol* 6). He alludes also to Charles's medical training. Charles evidently replied quickly, but his letter does not survive; and Milton, in turn, wrote the second letter (*Epistol* 7). Apparently Charles mentioned that he was now a practising physician; and Milton, after congratulating him, writes a remarkable tribute to their friendship. Milton also mentions that he has been reading Greek and Italian history, and he inquires about domestic difficulty in the Diodati family, which derived from Dr. Theodore Diodati's hasty remarriage after his first wife's death.

In 1638 while preparing to travel abroad, Milton could have consulted with Charles, who might have given him letters of introduction and who would have provided information about Switzerland and about his uncle, Giovanni. While in Geneva, Milton, as he mentions in *2Def,* met daily with the uncle (8 : 126–27). Perhaps, too, Charles or another of the Diodatis in England, Switzerland, or France introduced him to Elie Diodati, a distant cousin to Theodore. From Elie Diodati, who had befriended Galileo*, who had translated some of the astronomer's writings from Italian into Latin, and who had performed other valuable service for him, Milton may have received a letter of introduction that allowed him to visit with Galileo in Florence.

While traveling abroad, Milton heard news of Charles's death. Though the cause is unknown, his death may be attributable to the plague. On August 27, 1638, Charles was buried at St. Anne's, Blackfriars, London. Over one year later Milton composed *EpDam,* a pastoral* elegy observing the conventions established by classical prototypes and reflected earlier in *Lyc.* But *EpDam,* unlike *Lyc,* is more suffused with the tone of personal loss. Charles's personality and character are described. Damon, who is Charles, is identified as having been the intimate friend of the speaker, who is Thyrsis (Milton). Charles's virtue, his temperance, his gaiety, his delightful conversation, and his interest in medicine are all mentioned. *EpDam,* in short, is Milton's poignant tribute to the dearest friendship of his youth. The poem was published apparently in 1640 for private distribution among Diodati's family and friends and Milton's acquaintances on the Continent. [ACL]

DIODATI, GIOVANNI [OR JEAN] (1576–1649), uncle of Milton's friend Charles Diodati* and distinguished Genevan divine, for many years Professor of Hebrew and Theology at the Academy of Geneva. He is now chiefly remembered for his translation of the Bible into Italian (Geneva, 1603, 1607, 1646), to which Milton refers approvingly. The work is still regarded as among the best of all Protestant versions. Less notable are his French version (1644) and his *Pious Annotations upon the Bible,* which was translated into English in 1643. Diodati made several visits to his relatives in England, and Milton visited him in Geneva in late spring of 1639 when returning from his Italian tour. All six of Milton's references to him appear in his controversial works (i.e., *Tetra* [4 : 109], *2Def* [8 : 126], *3Def* [9 : 118, 206, 232, 276]). [DJD]

DIODORUS SICULUS, historiographer of Agyrium, who lived in the late first century B.C., was the author of the *Bibliotheca Historica,* a forty-book history of the world from the origin of man to the year 59 B.C. Books 1 to 5 and 11 to 20 of the work are preserved, and fragments of the rest survive in the works of other authors. Written in Diodorus's native Greek, it is essentially a compendium of earlier writers, and in this its value consists, since it preserves the work of such authors as Ephorus, the most important historian of the fourth century. It covers, too, areas of which we would otherwise know little, such as the gap left between the end of Herodotus's* narrative and the beginning of that of Thucydides*. Such a compilation is as valuable as its authorities, for Diodorus has little to contribute on his own account. His chronology is confused in its attempt to relate Greek and Roman annals, nor does he always disentangle the inconsistencies and even contradictions that result from the multiplicity of his sources.

The *Bibliotheca* is a work of popular appeal, suited to its period, that of the early empire when worldwide Graeco-Roman civilization created a demand for such handbooks of its past. The book deals with Egypt, as the cradle of civilization, with Assyria, India, Scythia, Arabia, Ethiopia, as well as Greece and Rome and the conquests by which Julius Caesar extended the empire as far as Britain. In a prefatory discussion of his aims Diodorus makes clear that he values history chiefly as a source of moral exemplars. A knowledge of the past is instructive in that it commemorates good deeds and witnesses to evil ones, a conception of the use of history that descends, of course, to the Renaissance. We are given a very moral interpretation of events, with good men praised and bad ones execrated, and with rewards and punishments stressed wherever possible. Unlike some ancient historians, Diodorus chose, too, to incorporate myth and legend into his narrative of the earliest times, and in the syncretic manner of his age he liked to relate foreign, for example Egyptian, mythology to that of Greece. The *Bibliotheca* was thus a source of mythological as well as of historical lore for the scholars of the Renaissance, and it was one of the seminal books of the period. The Latin translation of the first five books by Poggio Bracciolini (1449) was widely read, and it was one of the first classical texts to be translated

into English (by John Skelton, whose version is based on Poggio's Latin).

In the sixteenth and seventeenth centuries the *Bibliotheca* was naturally an important work of reference for writers like Spenser* and Milton with their interest in epic* and historical themes and in mythology*. The first five books of the *Bibliotheca,* which survive complete, provided much of this mythological material, for which Diodorus favors natural explanations. For example, the gods of Egypt, originally the four elements, eventually gave their names to singularly heroic mortals. Osiris, Belos, and the rest, to whom Milton refers in *Idea*, thus became part of human history. *PL*, which incorporates through metaphor some of that history, makes effective use of Diodorus. For example, in Book 2 Hell's "frozen continent" of ice and snow is compared to

> that *Serbonian Bog*
> Betwixt *Damiata* and *Mount Casius* old,
> Where armies whole have sunk . . .
> (2. 592–94)

The information comes from Diodorus, who in the course of outlining the geography of Egypt (1 : 30, 5–7) describes the sand-covered lake of Serbonis in which whole armies have disappeared. The *Bibliotheca* contributes also to one of the loveliest of the similes, where Satan in Book 4 reaches the end of his dangerous journey at the borders of Eden and is met by the "odorous sweets" of the garden, like more recent travelers who, having rounded the dangerous Cape, sail into the

> *Sabean* Odours from the spicie shoare
> Of *Arabie* the blest, with such delay
> Well pleas'd they slack thir course . . .
> (4. 162–64)

The account in the *Bibliotheca* (3 : 46–47) of Arabia Felix, fortunate home of the Sabaeans, enlarges upon the divine ambrosial fragrance of myrrh and balsam and cassia that pervades the land and stirs the senses even of those who sail along the coast as the summer off-shore winds carry it to passing ships. Even in Diodorus's prose the account of the paradisal shore is deeply evocative. (It has been pointed out also that the other important feature of Diodorus's blest Arabia is that the fragrant forests are infested by snakes whose bite is incurable.) There are other references to Arabian odors in the poems, and the symbolic figure of Orpheus*, to whom Milton refers in *IlP*, *Lyc*, and *Educ* (4 : 280) appears in the *Bibliotheca* as not only the greatest of singers but the most learned of men in divine matters (4 : 25).

Brit draws on Diodorus among others for its account of the state of civilization that prevailed in the island at the coming of Caesar*, and particularly for the Britons' honesty as traders, "thir dealing, *saith Diodorus,* plaine and simple without fraud" (10 : 50). Diodorus (in 5 : 21) does indeed present the Britons as men of simple virtue, living in the ancient manner without luxury and its consequent vices. The *Bibliotheca* has, however, a more pervasive effect upon *Brit* than the providing of particular facts. Diodorus's deliberate use of materials he knows to be legendary, as the only evidence for the earliest times, affords authority for Milton to do likewise. In the apologia with which he begins, Milton concedes that we know nothing certain of Britain before Caesar's time, and that the stories "of oldest seeming" are now dismissed as fables, but he adds that such fables have often been found to contain relics of truth, and alludes to the example of Diodorus and Livy* (10 : 3). Diodorus is also useful in controversy. In *1Def* he is cited as an incontrovertible authority for the argument that throughout history men have, as by a law of nature, risen up against tyrannical rulers. Salmasius* had asserted that the Egyptians never attempted to depose their kings; Milton refutes him from Diodorus (7 : 292–95). Similarly, Diodorus's opinion that anciently kingdoms descended not by inheritance but by eminent service to the people denies Salmasius's claim that kingship derives unlimited power from the ancient "jus patrisfamilias" to which it owes its origin.

Milton seems, indeed, to have thought highly of Diodorus and his conception of a historian's task. In 1657, in a letter to Henry de Brass*, he names Diodorus with Polybius*, Cicero*, and others as one who has handed down certain precepts that will instruct de Brass correctly in "what is suitable for the historian ("Quid autem conveniat Historico") (12 : 102–3). *See* HISTORIOGRAPHY. [KW]

DIONYSIUS THE AREOPAGITE, an early convert of St. Paul (Acts 17 : 34) and reputed author of several theological works that became widely known during the later Middle Ages and Renaissance. The true author of the Dionysian writings, sometimes called the Pseudo-Dionysius, has not been identified; he is thought to be a follower of the fifth-century Neoplatonist*, Proclus. The most celebrated of these writings, "Peri tes ouranias hierarchias" (*Celestial Hierarchy*), divides the nine angelic orders into three groups: seraphim, cherubim, and thrones; dominations, virtues, and powers; principalities, archangels, and angels*. (All are names to be found in Scripture.) Although certain theologians from the beginning and Renaissance scholars, notably Erasmus*, were openly sceptical of the authenticity of Dionysius, the *Celestial Hierarchy* forms the basis of a well-established tradition of belief about the formal organization of the heavenly hosts. Milton was certainly aware of this tradition, and though like most scholars of his day he placed no dependence on Dionysius as a canonical authority, he refers to a hierarchical establishment among the angels in *RCG*, *PL*, and *CD;* and he employs the Dionysian names for the orders, though never in a way consistent with the Dionysian scheme. [PS]

DISOBEDIENCE. Of the many thematic oppositions that Milton uses, *disobedience* and its opposite, *obedience*, are given perhaps the greatest prominence by their appearance as the key thematic words in the opening lines of both *PL* and *PR*. He will sing, Milton says in the first four words of *PL*, "Of Man's First Disobedience"; and in the first four lines of *PR* he announces that having sung of disobedience he will "now sing" of obedience.

> I who e're while the happy Garden sung,
> By one mans disobedience lost, now sing
> Recover'd Paradise to all mankind,
> By one mans firm obedience fully tri'd.

He has, however, already sung of both in *PL*, and although he concentrates on Christ's perfect obedience in *PR*, he does not compartmentalize the themes of disobedience and obedience. Theme and antitheme clarify and define each other both within and between the two poems.

The ultimate source of Milton's antithetical use of Adam and Christ is the epistles of St. Paul. The disobedience-obedience antithesis, in particular, finds its clearest statement in the following passage from Paul : "For as by one man's disobedience many were made sinners, so by the obedience of one shall many be made righteous" (Romans 5 : 19). The echoes of this passage in the opening lines of *PR* are obvious, and the same basic antithesis lies behind the opening lines of *PL*. In addition, the Pauline epistles are an essential basis for Milton's conceptualization of the relationship between man and Christ in *CD*, such as the frequent references to Paul in, say, Book 1, chapters 14–22, attest.

Even more important than Paul for understanding Milton's conception of obedience and disobedience, however, is Milton's own definition of those terms in *CD* (17 : 69). "Obedience," he says, "is that virtue whereby we propose to ourselves the will of God as the paramount rule of our conduct, and serve him alone." Disobedience is simply the opposite.

All the major poems are concerned with the themes of obedience and disobedience to the will of God, and all are exemplary to the reader. Within the context of cosmic warfare and the vast perspectives of generations of struggling humanity in *PL* and within the stringent but archetypal compactness of *PR* and *SA*, six exemplary figures stand out: Satan, Christ, Adam, Eve, Abdiel, and Samson.

Satan and Christ, as the great exemplars of disobedience and obedience, respectively, represent the extremes by which all of the other characters are measured. Each is necessary to establish the range of obedience and disobedience, but Satan as the constant adversary throws into relief both the disobedience and obedience of Adam and Eve and the obedience of Christ. Not only does he represent the extreme furthest removed from the perfect example of Christ; he also serves as the foil who reveals the homologous relationship between Adam and Christ.

Adam is the human figure who learns from his own experience and, vicariously, from the revelations of Raphael and Michael (of Satan and past disobedience from Raphael and of Christ and future obedience from Michael). Both qualities meet in him. In fact, Adam's gradual recognition of the full significance of both disobedience and obedience is perhaps the central thread of the narrative progression of *PL*. Toward the end of the final book Adam can say to Michael,

> Henceforth I learne, that to obey is best,
> And love with fear the onely God.
> (12 : 561–62)

But he has arrived at this point through hearing Raphael's "terrible example" of the War in Heaven*, which is framed, incidentally, at its beginning and end by Raphael's quite explicit explanation and warning concerning disobedience; through his own experiential knowledge of the harrowing consequences of disobedience; and, finally, through Michael's panorama of lonely just men amid the sinful and suffering multitudes. Adam and Eve fluctuate between the polarities of disobedience and obedience represented by Satan and Christ, with emphasis upon movement toward obedience as they become less like Satan and more like Christ.

Abdiel, who is Milton's invention rather than a traditional character, is a mediating figure between the perfect example of Christ and the aspiring but limited human capacities of Adam and Eve. Although an angel, he is much more accessible to human emulation than is the perfection of Christ. He faces the same adversary as Adam and Christ, and, like

Christ, he perseveres in obedience to God.

SA is not so explicitly concerned with the themes of obedience and disobedience as are the other two major poems. Yet when one recalls Milton's definition of obedience in *CD* as "that virtue whereby we propose to ourselves the will of God as the paramount rule of our conduct, and serve him alone," it becomes clear that Samson's agon, too, is a struggle to understand and obey the will of God. There is no Satan to serve as foil and adversary here, however; instead, Samson faces embodiments (and instigators) of his own weaknesses in the persons of Manoa, Dalila, and Harapha. Down to the encounter with Harapha, Samson even serves to some extent as his own foil—the evocations of the former Samson serving as a contrast to his "new" heroism. In defeating Harapha, he not only defeats a heathen adversary but also disposes of a comic and distorted image of his former self. From that point on he is in accord with the will of God. Like Adam and Eve, he is an example of both disobedience and obedience, representing the human potentialities for both, and finally he provides an eminently human example of heroism that triumphs through obedience. [WAM]

DIVINE PERMISSION. The problem of divine permission is best approached through two questions: Why does God permit moral evil* (and specifically, Why does he not restrain Satan?)? and Why does he permit suffering? The answers are bound up with the issues of free will* and predestination*, which exercised so many seventeenth-century minds. Milton affirms that although God could not and did not create evil, he is concerned with the production of it in one of two ways: "either, first, he permits its existence by throwing no impediment in the way of natural causes and free agents . . . ; or, secondly, he causes evil by the infliction of judgments, which is called the evil of punishment" (*CD* 15:67).

Since the problem is crucial for an epic written to justify the ways of God to men, Milton faces it early in *PL*, pointing out (1.210ff.) that Satan could not have risen from the burning lake without God's concurrence, which is given in view of the ultimate triumph of good. For the average reader, the difficulty looms largest in the account of the War in Heaven*, a three-day conflict that might seem pointless, since God could have ended it at any time, had he not chosen to sit "Consulting on the sum of things, foreseen / This tumult, and permitted all, advis'd" (6.673–74). Many readers from Dr. Johnson* on have argued cogently that this part of the poem is a failure; others accept an explanation along the line of Madsen's (*Publications of the Modern Languages Association* 75: 519–26): God gives both men and angels* an opportunity to prove their loyalty; men must fight as though everything depended on us, knowing and trusting that ultimately everything depends on God.

The limits on Satan's activities are emphasized again in *PR*. Christ's serenity rests in part on the knowledge of those limitations: "do as thou find'st / Permission from above; thou canst not more," he says to the Tempter (1.495–96); and again: "But I endure the time, till which expir'd, / Thou hast permission on me" (4.174–75; see also 3.251, and 4.394–95). When Satan's power does expire, he falls.

Ultimately the mystery of the divine permission of evil lies in the fact that God always brings good out of evil. Though the end that a sinner (or Satan, for that matter) has in view is something evil, from it God always produces a good and just result, "thus as it were creating light out of darkness" (*CD* 15:77). The structure of *PL*, as Summers and others have shown, rests on this contrast, creation succeeding destruction. Adam's famous "felix culpa" speech (*PL* 12.469–78), echoing the long tradition that Lovejoy traces, makes the same point.

Besides permitting the evil of sin, God permits the physical evil of suffering. This may fall on good and wicked alike. Its effect on the former is to induce greater self-knowledge (or the suffering may be a punishment for some former sin), while it may persuade the latter to forsake his sins (*CD* 15 : 77). The utility of such suffering is brought out in the last two books of *PL* : through it man learns true patience; moreover, the force of one man's example can show others how to suffer (see especially 12.360–61). The Christ of *PR* is a special case of this, since the poem revolves around his exemplary function; in the wilderness he lays down the rudiments of his great warfare (1. 156–58). Samson, too, is one whom patience finally must crown (*SA* 1296).

Milton sees both the apparent triumph of evil and the consequent suffering of the just as part of a larger plan, to the exposition of which he devoted his talents. His purpose as an inspired poet was to celebrate "what [God] works, and what he suffers to be wrought with high providence in his Church, to sing the victorious agonies of Martyrs and Saints" (*RCG* 3: 238). Sin and Death, triumphantly let loose on earth by Satan, are God's hellhounds, his means of purifying the earth (cf. *PL* 10. 629–39). Man, "delivered from sin and death by God the Father through Jesus Christ, is raised to a far more excellent state of grace and glory than that from which he had fallen" (*CD* 15 : 251). The interplay between man's free will and God's grace gains for man entrance to the paradise within. [MCP]

DIVORCE, MILTON'S VIEWS ON.
Milton's views on divorce were a logical outgrowth of his concept of marriage* as a spiritual companionship, a "Godly society" (*DDD* 3, pt. 2, 415), an institution created for "the apt and cheerfull conversation of man with woman" (*DDD* 3, pt. 2, 382). Alone among his contemporaries, he regarded "mutual solace" as the primary end of marriage (John Halkett, *Milton and the Idea of Matrimony* [1970], p. 30). Such an elevated view of marriage was in sharp contrast to that of adherents of either English law, which had developed from Catholic canon law, or that of continental reformers, both of which advocated divorce regulations that recognized only the physical and sexual aspects of marriage. Viewing marriage as a sacrament, canon law permitted two kinds of separation. *Divortium a vinculo matrimonii* (divorce from the bond of matrimony) declared the marriage void *ab initio*, on such grounds as precontract (which might nullify in various ways the validity of a marriage), entrance into holy orders, or impotency; either party could remarry, but children born of such a broken union were regarded as illegitimate. *Divortium a mensa et thoro* (divorce from bed and board) was a mere separation, granted for such grounds as adultery or cruelty; neither party could remarry, and the children were regarded as legitimate. Continental reformers, in contrast, permitted only *divortium a vinculo matrimonii*, on the grounds of adultery and desertion; the innocent party could remarry, and the children were regarded as legitimate. For Milton neither view was acceptable, because both paid heed only to the physical side of marriage. In their place he recommended absolute divorce for incompatibility, which he saw as the most serious impediment to a successful marriage, as well as for other common grounds; remarriage for either party; and the return of marriage and divorce from both ecclesiastical and civil jurisdiction to the individual couple or to the husband alone, whom he saw as having the God-given right to make decisions on so essential an aspect of his life.

Of the common grounds for divorce, Milton has the most to say about adultery, which he can scarcely condone but which he asserts may be a mere "accident" and hence excusable. Furthermore, he argues that an adulterous woman takes nothing from her husband, especially if he is ignorant of her trespass. To allow divorce for this momentary and forgivable transgression but not for the permanent and unpardonable one of incompatibility is manifestly illogical and unjust. In the same way, frigidity, although it seriously hampers the sexual pleasures to be expected in marriage, does not in itself make the marriage intolerable, as does incompatibility. Milton sees heresy* or idolatry, for which canon law allowed only *divortium a mensa et thoro*, as roughly analogous to incompatibility; but there is at least the possibility of saving the unbeliever. Desertion as a ground for divorce is virtually untouched in any of Milton's writings. He regards it, like the other common grounds, as far less demanding of absolute divorce than incompatibility, which more than the other grounds frustrates the true purpose of marriage.

The genesis of this view may lie in Milton's own first marriage, which took place in May or June 1642 and which was temporarily interrupted shortly thereafter when his young bride left to visit her parents. His difficulties in persuading her to return to him and his chagrin and injured pride at being spurned may well have turned his mind to thoughts of divorce, as Edward Phillips asserted (Darbishire, *Early Lives* [1932], p. 65). However, Milton never stressed desertion as a ground of divorce, even failing to mention it in his first edition of *DDD* (1643). Furthermore, there is no reason to believe that he regarded Mary as incompatible; on the contrary, his vigorous attempts to induce her to return suggest that he regarded her as eminently suitable to him.

It is far more likely that his interest turned to divorce in 1643 through a coincidence of personal, occasional, and long-range causes. The unfortunate start of the marriage must have brought to Milton's attention the hazards of matrimonial life. On June 12, 1643, Parliament called for the convening of the Westminster Assembly* to recommend church reforms. And Milton's interest turned to marriage and divorce at this time as part of a general plan to write on various aspects of English liberty. As he noted in *2Def* (1654), after considering ecclesiastical problems in the antiprelatical tracts, he turned to a consideration of domestic problems: "Reflecting, therefore, that there are in all three species of liberty,

without which it is scarcely possible to pass any life with comfort, namely, ecclesiastical, domestic or private, and civil; that I had already written on the first species, and saw the magistrate diligently employed about the third, I undertook the domestic, which was the one that remained" (8 : 131). This threefold division of interests is supported by the tripartite structure of *CB*, of which the "Index Oeconomicus" contains many passages on marriage and divorce.

Unfortunately, Milton's references to divorce in the "Index" cannot for the most part be dated with assurance. Some of the items are merely reports on ecclesiastical versus civil jurisdiction or on divorce among royalty, which have little connection with the ideas he was to develop in the divorce tracts. Thus Parker asserts that "Milton's interest in the problem of divorce even before his marriage, which one might like to believe, is . . . without substantiation in the Commonplace Book entries" (*Milton*, 2 : 879). However, in a passage possibly dated "1642–1644(?)" (Yale *Prose* 1 : 409), Milton cites "Pro divortio vide Bodin. repub. 1. I. c. 3 [In defense of divorce see Bodin*]" (18 : 156). In the passage noted, "Bodin argues, with many authorities, that when husband and wife are not truly married minds, as well as bodies, they may be divorced" (Yale *Prose* 1 : 409). Herein could lie the beginnings of Milton's interest in divorce. "There is some reason to believe that, in a not very urgent way, Milton had had a favorable opinion of divorce before he was deserted" (Sirluck, Yale *Prose* 2 : 138).

Milton's first tract on the subject, *DDD*, was published about August 1, 1643, probably timed to appeal to the Westminster Assembly, which had convened on July 1. The revised and expanded edition, addressed to the Parliament as well as to the Assembly, appeared about February 2, 1944. The pamphlets advocate the greater significance of incompatibility as a deterrent to a happy household than any of the commonly accepted grounds for divorce.

In order to lend scriptural support to

his view, Milton asserts that the Mosaic law, Deuteronomy 24 : 1 ("When a man hath taken a wife, and married her, and it come to pass that she find no favor in his eyes, because he hath found some uncleanness in her : then let him write her a bill of divorcement, and give it in her hand, and send her out of his house"), as stated in Matthew 5 : 17 ("Think not that I am come to destroy the law, or the prophets : I am not come to destroy, but to fulfill"), was not abrogated by the Gospel and is therefore available for the use of Christians. "Christ cannot have repudiated the Mosaic permission because of the eternal morality which lay behind its inclusion in the law" (Arthur Barker, *Modern Language Review* 35 : 156). His argument that Christ's injunction against divorce save for fornication, Matthew 5 : 32 ("But I say unto you, That whosoever shall put away his wife, saving for the cause of fornication, causeth her to commit adultery"), was merely a reference to the first marriage, made in Paradise* and therefore perfect, was to undergo various modifications. By the time he wrote *Tetra* (published March 4, 1645), Milton saw the "uncleanness" of Deuteronomy 24 : 1 and the "fornication" of Matthew 5 : 32 as virtually synonymous. Arguing from the point of view that marriage was instituted for man's happiness, Milton asserts that Christ would not establish a restriction on divorce to act as an obstacle to attaining that happiness.

However, as early as his translation of *Bucer* (published about August 6, 1644), Milton seems to be reconsidering the authority of the Mosaic law. He renders without modification Bucer's qualified enthusiasm for the Old Testament edict: "Wee beeing free in Christ are not bound to the evil Laws of *Moses* in every circumstance" (4 : 23). Bucer's point is that although the laws of the Old Testament are good to follow, the Christian is free to accept or reject them.

By 1659, Milton's view has further developed. He never loses confidence in the validity of incompatibility as a ground

for divorce, but he now looks to the Gospel rather than to the Mosaic law for guidance. In *CivP,* he asserts that "the state of rigor, childhood, bondage, and works, to all which force was not unbefitting" (6 : 25) has yielded to a "free, elective and rational worship" (6 : 26) of the Gospel. In that same year, in *Hire,* he even more strongly asserts that the law and the Gospel are God's "two great dispensations" (6 : 50) to man, but the Gospel is "now the only dispensation of God to all men" (6 : 46). He tacitly admits the irrelevance of the law to Christians; but his focus here may be on the ceremonial rather than on the moral law.

In chapter 27 of *CD,* Milton clearly states his view of the supremacy of the Gospel to the Mosaic law, and he leaves no doubt here that he is speaking of the moral law. "On the introduction of the gospel, or new covenant through faith in Christ, the whole of the preceding covenant, in other words the entire Mosaic law, was abolished" (16 : 125). "The whole law itself [is] annulled . . . [and] no part can be now binding upon us" (16 : 131–33). However, the moral force of the Mosaic law, that which is eternal and beneficial to all men, remains in effect. Although "the whole of the Mosaic law is abolished by the gospel . . . the sum and essence of the law is not hereby abrogated . . . Matthew 5 : 17, 'think not that I am come to destroy the law, or the prophets; I am not come to destroy, but to fulfill' " (16 : 141–43). His distinction here between "abolishing" and "abrogating" is an important one. "In the revelation of God's law, certain modes of expression, like the Mosaic system, may be abolished, but the essential demands are unchanging and unabrogable. The forms may pass away, but the substance is eternal. . . . The Mosaic law of divorce and the Decalogue remain binding insofar as they received the sanction of the Holy Spirit, were just and equitable, and consulted the love of God and of neighbors" (Maurice Kelley, *This Great Argument* [1941], pp. 60–61). In declaring the entire Mosaic law abolished (but not abrogated),

Milton replaced "the outward with an inward Law conceived as ethical and rational in character, and identified with the law of nature (of which indeed the Moral Law was itself a formulation); so that the essence of the Law is not abolished but accepted and obeyed in a new spirit of free and voluntary activity" (A. S. P. Woodhouse, *Puritanism and Liberty* [1951], p. 65).

Thus, through his consideration of the seeming contradiction between Deuteronomy 24 : 1 and Matthew 5 : 32, and the need of all men to some recourse from an unsupportable marriage, Milton came to see the possibility of Christian liberty*, which frees Christians from the rigors of the Old Testament law to the grace of the Gospel. "As he showed most fully in the *Christian Doctrine,* Christian liberty meant, in brief, the advance of the regenerate man from restrictive, external subjection under the Mosaic law to the positive, inward, and voluntary freedom of service and self-direction attained through faith in the gospel of Christ" (Douglas Bush, *English Literature in the Earlier Seventeenth Century* [1952] p. 248). [AA]

DOBSON, WILLIAM: *see* TRANSLATIONS OF MILTON'S WORKS.

DOCTRINE AND DISCIPLINE OF DIVORCE, THE. Milton's first divorce* tract, *The Doctrine and Discipline of Divorce: Restor'd to the Good of Both Sexes, From the bondage of Canon Law, and other mistakes, to Christian freedom, guided by the Rule of Charity,* was published anonymously and without being registered or licensed about August 1, 1643 (the date on Thomason's* copy), in London; the printers* were Thomas Paine and Matthew Simmons*. That it was addressed to the Westminster Assembly*, which had convened in July to assist in church reorganization, is suggested by part of the subtitle : *Seasonable to be now thought on in the Reformation intended.* There are apparently no variants among extant copies of the first edition; what

appears to be a variant in the errata sheet of the William Andrews Clark Memorial Library copy proves under close examination to be merely a hand-correction. This text can be read in *CM* by referring to the textual notes to the 1644 edition. Through a system of arrows and brackets, Lowell Coolidge combines the first and second editions in Yale *Prose* 2. The only separate edition of the 1643 text is in *The Prose of John Milton,* ed. J. M. Patrick and A. M. Axelrad, 1968.

The second edition of the tract, which appeared by February 2, 1644 (the date on Thomason's copy), was also probably printed by Matthew Simmons. Only the initials "J.M." appear on the title page, but Milton's full name follows the prefatory address "To The Parlament of England, with the Assembly." Like the previous edition, this one was unregistered and unlicensed. Lowell Coolidge, collating twelve copies for the Yale *Prose,* found that "no two . . . are identical" (p. 219); additional copies also differ in certain details. All copies lack the original leaf G2 (pp. 43–44), which Parker hypothesizes read, "I shall never disswade my soul from such a creed" (*Milton,* p. 879); some copies contain a substitute G2. The textual emendations by hand are probably not by Milton, as suggested by so obvious an error as "sel[ves]" for "indicental" on p. 73 of the University of London copy (Parker, *Milton,* p. 880). An even more remarkable "correction" on this misprint pointing away from Milton's having made the emendations is found in the Newberry Library copy, where the word, as in several extant copies, is correctly printed as "incidental." However, the "corrector" (surely not the author), knowing that he was expected to make a change in this word, altered the "c" into a "d" by adding an upstroke and altered the "d" into a "c" by crossing out the upstroke; after rendering the correct word into "indicental," he proceeded to write "incidental" in the margin! (See also the discussion of Claud A. Thompson in *Papers of The Bibliographical Society of America,* 68: 297–305.)

The third edition of *DDD*, a close reproduction of the second and probably by the same printer but from newly set-up type, appeared in 1645. It was unregistered and unlicensed. The fourth edition, likewise unregistered and unlicensed, also appeared in 1645. The text is the same as that of the third, but with numerous changes in typography, spelling*, and punctuation. "There is no reason to believe that Milton was responsible" for these variants (Yale *Prose* 2 : 218).

The central argument of the first edition is that incompatibility is as valid a ground for divorce as any other, including those most commonly accepted, such as adultery, desertion, and frigidity. Early in the tract he states this view in a "thesis" which, although never methodically developed, underlines not only this work but all his later treatments of the subject : *"That indisposition, unfitnes, or contrariety of mind, arising from a cause in nature unchangable, hindring and ever likely to hinder the main benefits of conjugall society, which are solace and peace, is a greater reason of divorce than naturall frigidity, especially if there be no children, and that there be mutuall consent"* (*The Prose of John Milton*, p. 147).

In adopting this view, Milton forsakes his condemnation of the Mosaic law in *RCG* (1642), now equating the "uncleanness" of Deuteronomy 24 : 1 with incompatibility. His argument is clear cut : the Mosaic law, given to the ancient Jews and specifically not abrogated by Christ (Matt. 5 : 17), is available for the use of Christians. To the objection that Christ commanded that "What therefore God hath joined together, let not man put asunder" (Matt. 19 : 6), Milton replies that Christ here refers only to the first marriage, made in Paradise and, as perfect, indissoluble. Later marriages are separable or inseparable according to their closeness to the perfection of the original institution. To the stronger objection that Christ prohibited divorce except for "fornication" (Matt. 19 : 9), Milton presents two different replies. First he asserts that Christ made this severe prohibition to amaze the Pharisees and any other men who had been abusing the Old Testament law, by setting up a standard applicable only to the first marriage. Then he avers that Christ "declares that no accidental, temporary, or reconcilable offence, except fornication, can justifie a divorce" (*The Prose of John Milton*, pp. 179–80), thereby reinforcing the Mosaic permission to divorce for offenses that are not accidental, temporary, or reconcilable (i.e., uncleanness). The extreme narrowness of this view of Christ's statement did not leave Milton with a very convincing argument, and in the second edition he carried the point further.

Milton is especially careful to strike a balance between the evil nature of man since the Fall* (hence his need for the laxity of the Mosaic law) and his inherently good nature (hence the possibility of his attaining the liberty* that raises him beyond the law to the Gospel). But Milton is not yet ready to go far in the matter of Christian liberty and natural law. In a passage considerably revised for the second edition, he does assert that "Wee find also by experience that the Spirit of God in the Gospel hath been alwaies more effectual in the illumination of our minds to the gift of faith, than in the moving of our wills to any excellence of vertue, either above the *Jews* or the Heathen" (*The Prose of John Milton*, p. 167). As Arthur Barker observes, "The statement introduces a ticklish theological problem, and is itself ambiguous. It is clearly connected with the idea that the gospel does not *require* a perfection higher than the unattainable standard set by the law to show the necessity of a redeemer; but it also implies that it does not *enable* the Christian to a greater degree of perfection than could be attained by the Jews and, what is even more significant, by the heathen" (*Modern Language Review* 35 : 158).

Other ideas are perhaps more adequately developed in this early, somewhat tentative work. Milton asserts that marriage* and divorce are properly civil rather than ecclesiastical matters, as evidenced by long tradition. He sees the authority to declare a marriage void as wrested from the husband by the medieval church and still withheld by Canon law. Marriage, which is not a true sacrament, is a thing "indifferent," a matter not subject to ecclesiastical scrutiny; and its dissolution must be left up to the conscience of the individual couple or the husband alone. The institution of marriage was created for man, he maintains, not man for the institution. In taking this stand, Milton is not far from the views of continental reformers, who regarded a marriage as dissolved by adultery or desertion, a position to be accepted in the Westminster Confession* (24 : 5, 6). For Milton this Protestant attitude fell short of permitting what was to him the most urgent ground, incompatibility. The spiritual nature of marriage, he asserts, not the physical and sexual, is its true value. In addition, he supported remarriage for both parties in cases of adultery or desertion. His arguments are especially sharply focused in his assertion that Canon law, by an over-literal interpretation of Scriptures (which must be read in the light of human reason and human needs), has created the seeming paradox of Christ's forbidding divorce despite the Mosaic permission.

Probably the most interesting point of the first edition of DDD is what it does *not* consider: desertion. Beyond a brief note that Paul refers to remarriage after desertion, Milton is strangely silent on this subject in light of his domestic situation. The personal element of the book is a vexing question, one that ranges from the extreme of seeing Mary Powell as the inspiration for the tract ("The divorce pamphlets . . . were a direct result of his unfortunate union with Mary Powell," Arthur Barker, *Milton and the Puritan Dilemma* [1942], p. 63) to viewing the work as objective and impersonal ("The *Doctrine and Discipline* . . . had no connection whatever with his own domestic life," Chilton Latham Powell, *English Domestic Relations: 1487–1653* [1917], p. 230). According to Edward Phillips, his

uncle, unable to persuade Mary to return from Forest Hill* in September 1642, was "so incensed . . . that he thought it would be dishonourable ever to receive her again, after such a repulse; so that he forthwith prepared to Fortify himself with Arguments for such a Resolution, and accordingly wrote . . . *Doctrine and Discipline of Divorce*" (Darbishire, *Early Lives* [1932], p. 65). However, Phillips is not always a reliable witness, and since there is no advocacy of desertion as a ground for divorce in the first edition, it can hardly be seen as an attempt to justify dissolution on that ground. Supporters of the now almost universally rejected 1643 marriage date could point to the absence of reference to desertion as evidence of the later date. However, this assumption would require Milton to write the tract during his honeymoon. The safest view is probably that the unfortunate start of the marriage brought to Milton's attention the difficulties in obtaining a divorce, and he perhaps decided to universalize from his own limited experience. That Milton himself wanted a divorce, or even that he found Mary objectionable as a mate, cannot be deduced from the text of either of the first two editions of DDD, nor did Milton himself say anything elsewhere bearing on this matter.

There are no extant comments on DDD between its first appearance in July or August 1643 and the revised version of January or February 1644, despite Milton's claim *"that some of the Clergie began to inveigh and exclaim on"* the tract (*Bucer* 4 : 12). During these months Milton studied the background of divorce literature and legislation, so that he might better *"reinforce the question with a more accurat diligence"* (ibid.). The result of his study was for all practical purposes an entirely new tract. It employs the same basic arguments, but its formal structure of a preface and two books, each divided into chapters preceded by short introductory synopses, suggests an awareness of the rambling and diffused effect of his earlier argument.

The preface, "To The Parlament of

England, with the Assembly," is a clear turning away from the Westminster Assembly, so eagerly appealed to in 1643, to what Milton hopes will be a more receptive body. His disappointment in the Assembly was based not only on its not responding to his tract but its drawing up a statement (not published until 1651) accepting only adultery and desertion as grounds for divorce, thereby discountenancing his efforts. In its style the dedication paves the way for the eloquence of *Areop.* Milton attacks custom and error, and glorifies truth, with a vigor and verve that will extend to the whole of the later work. As in many passages throughout his writings, Milton makes clear that he seeks not a large and undiscriminating audience, but one that is judicious and small in number, a "fit audience . . . though few." The obvious compliment to the Parliament is laid on somewhat thick, but their support, in view of the Assembly's coolness and possible hostility, must be won. With special pride, he notes that he has written in his native tongue, to glorify both his land and his language. By signing his full name to the prefatory address, Milton leaves no doubt that he has authored this tract as well as its earlier version. His full name had already appeared on the title page of *RCG* (1642), but this is its first appearance within the body of a text and therefore clearly with his knowledge and consent.

The much greater length of the body of the second than that of the first edition of *DDD*—almost twice the length—evidences a need to support the points of the earlier tract with more compelling arguments. Most of the added material is in the nature of expanded commentary; many small and insignificant verbal changes show close attention to detail.

Milton does not abandon his earlier stand that the Mosaic law, the "expresse law of *God*," delivered by "an author great beyond exception," is eternal and immutable, hence not abrogated by the Gospel. In the first edition he had argued that as such it is not a dispensation, not a relaxation of standards of virtue for the

hard-heartedness of the Jews; therefore, it is meant for Christians as well as for Jews. Now, expanding a single sentence of the earlier argument into three entirely new chapters (2, chaps. 4, 5, and 6), he shows how it is applicable to Christians even if it was, after all, merely a dispensation to the Jews.

In a similar manner, he expands and elaborates earlier points, indicating more possible facets of each aspect of his argument. For example, he strengthens his view that "mutual consent" really is the husband's decision, since "the absolute and final hindring of divorce cannot belong to any civil or earthly power, against the will of both parties, or of the husband alone" (3, pt. 2, 498). Divorce was designed primarily for men, but women reap unexpected blessings from it. His argument that a repelled wife is fortunate to be cast off by an unloving husband may strike some readers as sophistic.

Although Milton is still some distance from the views he was to adopt later, he is more than formerly interested in the concept of Christian liberty. "The whole drift of his argument . . . is against obedience to the letter of any law which the spirit dislikes, and toward the radical assertion of Christian liberty which he finally made in *Of Christian Doctrine*" (Merritt Y. Hughes, *John Milton: Prose Selections* [1947], p. lx).

Desertion as a ground for divorce is introduced into this revised tract, but only as an addition to a phrase that had already appeared in the first edition. Thus "Afterwards [marriage] was thought so Sacramentall, that no adultery could dissolve it" (*The Prose of John Milton*, p. 145) becomes "Afterwards [marriage] was thought so Sacramentall, that no adultery or desertion could dissolve it" (3, pt. 2, 383). There is little justification for reading autobiographical meaning into this addition. [AA]

DOLLE, WILLIAM: *see* PORTRAITS.

DONI, GIOVANNI BATTISTA (1593–

1647). Public lecturer in Greek in Florence during the latter part of Milton's trip to the continent, Doni may have met Milton through Florentine friends, who suggested that he could help discharge a request that Lukas Holste* had made of Milton (see *Epistol* 9). Holste, librarian at the Vatican, had desired information concerning a manuscript in the library at Florence, but such materials were not available for any kind of note-taking. Doni was in Rome when Milton wrote to Holste, and Milton suggests that Holste contact him. Whether Doni was asked or was able to comply is unknown. [JTS]

DONNE, JOHN: *see* METAPHYSICAL POETS, MILTON AND THE.

DORÉ, GUSTAVE: *see* ILLUSTRATIONS.

DORIAN, DONALD C(LAYTON) (1900–1963), scholar, born in Paris, earned a doctorate from Columbia University and then was associated for his entire professional life with Rutgers University as professor and administrator. Dorian's main contribution to Milton studies is his published dissertation, *The English Diodatis* (1950), a scholarly investigation of the family and of Milton's relationship with them. He also edited *Educ* for the Yale *Prose* and discussed various problems in the minor poems such as the much-debated two-handed engine of *Lyc* and the autobiographical significance of *L'Al* and *IlP*. [WBH]

DORT, SYNOD OF: *see* ARMINIANISM.

DOUGLAS, JOHN: *see* LAUDER, WILLIAM.

DOWNHAM (OR DOWNAME), GEORGE (ca. 1563–1634), Anglican bishop and logician. He was the son of William Downham, bishop of Chester, and the elder brother of John Downham*, a Puritan divine of Milton's acquaintance. George matriculated in Cambridge University as a pensioner from Christ's College* in November 1581, took his B.A. degree in 1585, and became university lecturer on logic* there in 1590. Attaining a reputation as perhaps the best Aristotelian-Ramist in the field, he climaxed his career as a logician with the publication of his *Commentarii in P. Rami Regii Professoris Dialecticam* (Frankfurt, 1601). A strong Calvinist, he published a sermon against Arminianism* in 1604. From 1608, he became an adamant defender of episcopacy as a divine institution. In 1616, James I* nominated him bishop of Derry, Ireland, to which post he was consecrated on October 6 of that year. A successful career in this office ended with his death on April 17, 1634.

It was not Downham's ecclesiology but his Ramist* logic that Milton approved and utilized. Twice in *Animad* he cites Bishop Downham's *Dialecticks* in support of a logical point he is making against the Remonstrants, implying that these prelatical respondents can hardly ignore the authority of their own "Patron" (3 : 115, 135).

Downham was most influential in Milton's *Logic*. After the text proper, Milton appends "An Analytic Praxis of Logic from Downham. On the Third Chapter of the Dialectic of Ramus" (11 : 487). But the text itself also draws heavily from Downham, as Thomas S. K. Scott-Craig has shown (*Huntington Library Quarterly* 17 : 1–16). Downham's chapter on form illuminates Milton's logical hard line against Trinitarianism : no beings can differ in number without differing in essence (see *CD* 14 : 309–11; and *Logic* 11 : 59). And in the Preface to *Logic* Milton follows closely Downham's definition and distribution of the arts. Regarding causality, both Milton and Downham follow the traditional fourfold division of causes into formal, efficient, material, and final, with efficient divided into primary and one or more secondary causes.

Another George Downham, son of John and nephew of the logician, studied at Christ's College, Cambridge, from 1626 to 1634. Milton, who attended there from 1625 to 1632, probably knew him, but there seems to be no evidence of later contact or influence. [GLM]

DOWNHAM (OR DOWNAME), JOHN
(1577?–1652), Puritan divine, the son of
William Downham, bishop of Chester. His
elder brother, George*, was a logician
whose work Milton knew. John received
his B.D. degree from Christ's College*,
Cambridge. In November 1630, he be-
came rector of Allhallows the Great in
London and held this office until his
death. He wrote several popular treat-
ments of Puritan doctrine, among which
were *The Christian Warfare against the
Devil, World and Flesh* (1604; 4th ed.,
1634); *The Sum of Sacred Divinity*
(1630?); and, in collaboration with others,
*Annotations upon All the Books of the
Old and New Testament* (1645).

Downham was active in the religio-
political world of London. In 1640 he
joined with other Puritan ministers in
petitioning the Privy Council against the
church policies of William Laud*, Arch-
bishop of Canterbury, who was forcing
uniformity of worship. In June 1643,
when the Puritan Long Parliament passed
a strict ordinance for licensing* (i.e., cen-
soring) books, Downham became one of
twelve divines appointed for the licensing
of books of theology. Any one of them
could approve a book for publication.

It was against this printing ordinance
that Milton directed the unlicensed *Areop*
the following year. Also in 1644 Down-
ham licensed Milton's *Bucer* (entered
in the Stationers' Register on July 15),
despite the fact that Milton had pre-
viously been condemned for his (un-
licensed) *DDD.* Downham was perhaps
generally more tolerant than his col-
leagues; in early 1649 Parliament ordered
the seizure of the Englished Koran that
he had licensed, and the Council of State
examined Richard Royston for printing a
kind of sequel to *Eikon Basilike** called
The Papers which passed at Newcastle,
which Downham had likewise approved.

In 1647 Downham was one of fifty-
eight London ministers to sign the *Tes-
timony* published by the "Sion College"
Presbyterians as a blast against current
heresies*. Regarding Milton, most inter-
esting is the section describing "Errors

touching Marriage and Divorce," for it
includes an excerpt from Milton's *DDD,*
condemning "J.M." for his shocking
proposition.

Milton seems never to have mentioned
John Downham in his writings. But even
if there was no direct influence, Down-
ham's books are a valuable repository of
the commonplaces of seventeenth-century
Reformed theology that illuminate Mil-
ton's works for the modern reader. [GLM]

DRAMATIC PLANS. Milton's dramatic
jottings—roughly one hundred subjects on
biblical, British, and Scottish history—fill
seven pages in *TM.* Because of their use
of the Italian *e,* they are usually assigned
to the early 1640s, shortly after Milton's
return from his continental journey.
(However, Milton had adopted the Italian
e inconsistently before his trip to Italy.)
Though it is impossible to establish a
terminal date with precision, several com-
mentators have suggested 1642 in part
because in September the theaters were
officially closed by act of Parliament.
Moreover, the notes apparently reflect the
same awareness of the value of "Dra-
matick constitutions . . . to a Nation" that
Milton expressed in *RCG* (1641), the same
sense of "what religious . . . use might be
made of poetry . . . in divine and human
things" that he revealed in *Educ* (1644).
It has also been suggested that some of
these dramatic subjects may have ap-
pealed to Milton because of their topical
relevance; several of the British and
biblical subjects could be developed for
dramatic commentary on the English
political and ecclesiastical situation be-
tween 1639 and 1642.

Though most of these entries are
merely notes—possible themes for dra-
matic treatment rather than settled plans—
the sketches for tragedies on Dinah,
Abijah, and Phineas are more detailed;
and the drafts for tragedies on the Fall
of Man*, the sacrifice of Isaac, and the
execution of John the Baptist are devel-
oped even more fully. Some of these
sketches contain act divisions, suggestions
for the content of particular speeches or

songs, the basic outline for the structure and development of the plot, and notes for the roles of the prologue, the chorus, and various major or minor characters. Most of the remaining biblical entries are merely titles, and in many instances they are followed by brief references to scriptural sources. In several cases additional titles have been inserted in the same entry, and it is not always possible to determine whether these are merely alternative titles for the same drama or the titles of separate dramas on distinct though interrelated themes. The British and Scottish entries, on the other hand, indicate subjects rather than titles. Moreover, they lack the resounding Greek and Latin epithets that occur so frequently in the biblical list—titles such as "Thamar Peplophorus," "Salomon Gynaecocratumenus or Idolomargus aut Thysiazusae," and "Amaziah Doryalotus."

Though most of Milton's jottings were notes for tragedies, they also include suggestions for two pastoral* dramas and for a heroic poem on Alfred. The biblical subjects, drawn primarily from the Old Testament, constitute slightly less than two-thirds of the entire number of entries; and it is significant that the dramatic sketches developed in greatest detail concern scriptural themes. Many of the more detailed plans exhibit a concern for plot structure, noting possibilities for the complication and resolution of the action. Neoclassical principles are evident in Milton's general fidelity to the unities of time, place, and action, his use of the critical terminology inherited from the commentaries of Donatus or from Renaissance neo-Aristotelian and neo-Horatian theory, and his inclusion of many of the stock figures and devices of Senecan tragedy: nurse, messenger, ghosts, chorus, and the like.

For his scriptural entries his chief source was the Bible itself, though he occasionally alluded to secondary sources. In Parker's opinion (*Milton*, pp. 190–92), Milton "picked up a Bible, leafed through it, and jotted down ideas as they were suggested to him"—and perhaps never gave a second thought to most of these notes. In contrast to the detailed outlines for dramas on the fall of Adam, the sacrifice of Isaac, and a few other scriptural subjects, the theme of Samson remains undeveloped. Though the title "Dagonalia" foreshadows his future tragedy *SA*, the entry provides no information beyond the title and a brief reference to Judges 16. Another entry indicates that Milton considered another drama on the exploits of Samson, but scholars have not reached agreement on the number of subjects mentioned in this entry: "Samson pursophorus or Hybristes, or Samson marriing or in Ramath Lechi."

An early interest in the subject of *PL* is apparent in four different drafts for a tragedy on this subject, as well as a note for a sequel, "Adam in Banishment." On the first page of dramatic outlines, after two canceled lists of *dramatis personae* for an untitled play on Adam's fall, Milton outlines a five-act tragedy entitled *Paradise Lost*. Later in the manuscript he introduces still another sketch for a drama on this subject, concluding with a note to himself: "compare this with the former draught." In this sketch the title *Adams Banishment* has been canceled, and the caption *Adam unparadiz'd* substituted. Though no act division is specified, James H. Hanford has suggested a tentative division into five acts. For a comparison of these versions, see W. R. Parker, *Journal of English and German Philology* 34 : 225–32; John S. Diekhoff, *Philological Quarterly* 28 : 44–52; Grant McColley, *Philological Quarterly* 18 : 73–83; W. Schork, *Die Dramenpläne Miltons* (1934); Maria Wickert, *Anglia* 73 : 171–206. After *Adam unparadiz'd* Milton appears to have evolved still another plan, beginning with a prologue by Lucifer (instead of Moses, as in the third version, or Gabriel, as in the fourth version). Edward Phillips claimed to have seen the first ten lines of Satan's apostrophe to the sun (*PL* 4) several years before Milton actually began the epic. These verses "and some others" were designed for "the very beginning" of the tragedy.

For the thirty-odd British subjects for tragedy, Milton drew on various historians. Except for a single entry on the earlier stage of the Roman occupation of Britain, these stories range from the period of the Anglo-Saxon* invasion to that of the Norman conquest. Though Milton does not specify sources for all of these entries, he cites Speed* and Holinshed* on several occasions and refers less frequently to Bede*, Stow*, Geoffrey of Monmouth*, and William of Malmsbury*. He apparently consulted the 1587 edition of Holinshed's *Chronicles,* the 1615 or 1631 edition of Stow's *Annales,* and the 1623 or 1627 edition of Speed's *History of Great Britain.* Milton's annotated copy of Jerome Commelin's* edition of *Rerum Britannicarum Scriptores* (Heidelberg, 1587), now in the Harvard College Library, contains the histories of Bede, Gildas*, Geoffrey of Monmouth, and other historical writers (Parker, *Milton,* pp. 841–42; Yale *Prose* 5 : 4). For the five Scottish subjects, Milton relied on Holinshed. Two of these entries are significant inasmuch as they show an interest in stories that Shakespeare* had woven into *Macbeth.* Milton proposes a tragedy on Macbeth, introducing the "matter of Duncan" through Duncan's ghost—in conventional Senecan manner—and a separate tragedy on Kenneth's murder of Malcolm Duffe and his death at the hands of Fenela. [JMS]

DRAMATISTS, GREEK. Aeschylus, Sophocles, and Euripides, fifth-century Greek writers, are praised in the epistle to *SA* as "the three Tragic Poets unequall'd yet by any, and the best rule to all who endeavour to write Tragedy." Acquaintance with their work Milton considered essential for the best critical judgment of style, plot, and the other artistic aspects of tragic drama, or at the least of the "Dramatic Poem" at hand (1 : 333). But when "Gorgeous Tragedy" is personified in *IlP* as "Presenting *Thebes,* or *Pelops* line, / Or the tale of *Troy* divine" (97–100), the myths evoked are those favored by the Greek dramatists

collectively. On the basis of these lines, however, they cannot be individually identified, nor are they differentiated in the debate on Athens in *PR* (4. 261–66, 331–52).

Aeschylus (525–456 B.C.) is mentioned only once before the publication of *SA.* During a discussion of Aeschylus's play *The Suppliants* in *1Def,* Milton enunciates some principles of dramatic exegesis, and then applies them to character, scene, and the speeches quoted in Greek with Latin translation, in order to prove that, by using lines 370–71 out of context, Salmasius* had misrepresented the playwright's treatment of kingship (7: 307–11). Despite the small notice taken of Aeschylus previously, *Prometheus Bound* may have served as one of Milton's principal Greek models in composing *SA.* Resemblances between the tragedies are structural and situational, and among the more salient are a hero in captivity and chains; a soliloquy at or near the beginning in which he laments his plight; a string of visitors that includes a sympathetic chorus and others who are friendly or hostile and who come to him one by one in a *post hoc* rather than a *propter hoc* sequence; scenes restricted in the older, pre-Sophoclean manner to no more than two speaking parts aside from the chorus; and an outcome in which destructive violence, though without death in the case of the Titan, overtakes the protagonist.

Sophocles (496–406 B.C.), the man and his plays, is referred to much more often than his older contemporary. In *RCG,* first of all, the "wise Poet *Sophocles*" is linked with "the sad Prophet Jeremiah" (15 : 10 quoted) and John "the great Evangelist" (Rev. 10 : 9–10 paraphrased) in recognizing how irksome is the dispensing of displeasing truth, so that Tiresias is brought into *Oedipus the King* (316–17) "bemoaning his lot, that he knew more then other men" (3 : 231). In the pamphlets Milton finds support for his polemical points in three other instances in Sophoclean plays. To illustrate his contention that the prelates "are the men who have wounded religion, and their stripes must heale her," Milton quotes from *Electra* (624), where the "wise Virgin answer'd her wicked Mother who thought her selfe too violently reprov'd . . . *'Tis you that say it, not I, you do the deed, / And your ungodly deeds finde me the words*" *Apol* 3 : 319). In *1Def*, right after examining Aeschylus's *The Suppliants*, and continuing the refutation of Salmasius's assertion that kings in Greece were not subject to the laws, Milton adduces evidence from three plays by Euripides—*Orestes, The Suppliants,* and *The Heracleidae*—as well as from Sophocles' *Oedipus the King* and *Antigone* (7 : 311). The pedagogical scheme in *Educ* calls for tragedy at two separate points in the curriculum. Earlier, along with "the study of Economics" and of "some choice Comedies, Greek, Latin, or *Italian,*" the tragedies to be taken up are those "that treat of Household matters, as *Trachiniae, Alcestis,* and the like"; somewhat later the *"Attic* Tragedies of stateliest and most regal argument" will be studied, together with "Histories, *Heroic Poems,* . . . all the famous Political Orations." The distinction drawn is between the former group of works on domestic or private and the latter group on political or public subjects. Further, students are to memorize some of the dramatic and rhetorical texts, which should be "solemnly pronounc't with right accent, and grace, as might be taught," the purpose of such exercises being not to perfect them in languages but rather to "endue them even with the spirit and vigor of *Demosthenes* or *Cicero, Euripides,* or *Sophocles*" (4: 284–86). Milton habitually associates these two tragedians, alike exemplary when writing about household or regal matters, and accords them the highest honor. They are among the "choycest wits of Athens," or more properly of ancient Greece, whom he regarded as masters to be emulated in poetry of the various kinds : in the "diffuse" epic*, Homer*; in "Odes and Hymns," Pindar and Callimachus; and as for "Dramatic constitutions," therein *"Sophocles* and *Euripides* raigne." They

reign over dramatic literature, aside from the Bible, with its "divine pastoral Drama in the Song of *Salomon*" and "majestick image of a high and stately Tragedy" in "the Apocalyps of Saint John," without rivals (*RCG* 3 : 236–38). Only with the epistle to *SA* would Milton admit the third member, Aeschylus, to their illustrious company.

Oedipus at Colonus is commonly regarded as the Greek drama that equals or surpasses *Prometheus Bound* in the closeness of its affinities with *SA*. The most obvious similarity between the Sophoclean and Miltonic tragedies consists of a hero who is blind and whom divine intervention leads to a triumphant death. In addition, each protagonist is in exile on foreign soil, and attempts are made, and resisted, to bring him "home"; his powerlessness through most of the play contrasts with his past prowess and final triumph; each has been the subject of prophecies at birth; each experiences familial loyalty, from father or daughters, and familial betrayal, by wife or sons and uncle, and each gets his revenge on the betrayers. The tragedies can be jointly contrasted with *Oedipus the King* in two respects: in their being "episodic" alongside a play whose plot was for Aristotle* the pattern of organic unity, and in the opposite movements of their central figures from wretchedness to glory. In another respect *SA* is more similar to the *Tyrannus* : in the dramatic irony that pervades both. Milton's management of the chorus is sometimes considered Sophoclean (W. R. Parker, *Milton's Debt to Greek Tragedy in SA* [1937], p. 249).

Euripides (480?–406 B.C.), though he was often paired with Sophocles, received, by comparison, greater and more diverse kinds of attention. Numerous citations to his plays, some of them noted above, can be found in the controversial prose. In *Tenure* a speech of "the Heathen King Demophoon" in *The Heracleidae* (423–24), the same speech that would be subsequently repeated in *1Def* (7 : 311), contributes to a refutation of the proposition that "Kings are accountable to none but God" (5 : 11–13). Again in *1Def* (7 : 351) words of Euripides' Theseus are taken from *The Suppliants* (352–53, 403–6) to show that sovereignty resides in the people. In *2Def* (8 : 75), when viewing his blindness as a sign of divine favor and the increased devotion of friends as confirming this view, Milton says that he shares with some of them the feelings expressed by Orestes and Pylades in an exchange in *Orestes* (795) and that he knows the sentiments uttered by Theseus to the protagonist in *Heracles* (1398, 1402). At the end of the section on the "muselesse and unbookish" Spartans in *Areop,* Euripides is mentioned as affirming in *Andromache* (590–93) "that their women were all unchaste" (4 : 300). In several instances he is presented as having a special relationship with revealed truth. Paul was thought to have quoted him at 1 Corinthians 15 : 33 (epistle to *SA* 1 : 331; *Areop* 4 : 307), but the verse in question had become proverbial and its source was a fragment probably of Menander. A passage from *The Suppliants* (532–34), meant to show the playwright an unconscious but better interpreter of Scriptures about death, especially Job 34 : 14–15, than many Christian theologians are, appears in Greek, without translation, in *CD* (15 : 237–39). Lines extracted from the plays twice serve as epigraphs of prose works, lines 438–41 of *The Suppliants,* in Greek and in Milton's translation into English blank verse, being printed on the title page of *Areop,* and lines 298–301 of *Medea,* in Greek and untranslated, on that of *Tetra* (4 : 293, 63). The poetry provides two of the references to this author or his works. In the last tercet of Sonnet 8 ("Captain or Colonel") he is "sad *Electra*'s Poet" whose "repeated air" saved Athens—about to be sacked in 404 B.C. until a Spartan officer sang the first chorus of the tragedy, according to Plutarch* in his Life of *Lysander*; and a reminiscence of the closing scene of *Alcestis* dominates the first quatrain of *Sonn* 23 ("Methought I saw"). That Milton's attitude toward Euripides was compounded of familiarity and

fondness would be apparent even without the further evidence. His daughter Deborah is reported in Johnson's* *Life* to have designated Ovid's* *Metamorphoses* and Euripides as the reading, after Homer, that most delighted her blind father. As a young man, Milton purchased, in 1634, *Euripidis Tragœdiæ,* a bilingual edition, Greek with Latin, published in two volumes at Geneva in 1602, and his copy with marginalia for each play is the most heavily annotated book owned by him now extant (18 : 304–20). In it he carefully underlined the dramatist's many antifeminist statements. A glimpse of his earlier acquaintance with the dramatist, at Cambridge, is supplied by *Prol* 1, wherein some students are mocked for their declamations of parts of *Orestes* (12 : 121).

His preference for Euripides with an admiration for Sophocles almost as great would seem to conform—the extent and profundity of his interest aside—to the taste of his own as of the previous age; but his apparently late discovery of an exemplar for tragedy in Aeschylus and the consequent elevation of him to their lofty level represent a significant revaluation (see Madeleine Doran, *Endeavors of Art* [1954], p. 14). Very few Greek tragedies were Englished before the eighteenth century : none by Aeschylus; one by Sophocles, *Electra,* only in 1649; and as many as four by Euripides in the sixteenth century, but these include one from an Italian adaptation, one that remained in manuscript, and two lost, one of which may have been in Latin (Alfred Harbage, *Annals of English Drama, 975–1700* [1964]). It is most unlikely that Milton knew any of these versions or any tragedy out of the Greeks in English before he produced his own in their manner.

His verse does not often exhibit verbal echoes of theirs—much less often than once was supposed. J. C. Maxwell denies all such echoes from Aeschylus (*Review of English Studies,* n.s. 3 : 366–71), while P. W. Timberlake illustrates the older tendency in greatly overstating the case for Euripidean influence (*Essays in Dra-*

matic Literature, ed. Hardin Craig [1935], 315–40). Recent editors such as Merritt Y. Hughes and Douglas Bush have been more judicious than their predecessors in annotating borrowings. Among the textual parallels that are striking enough to be generally remarked are the denunciations of women in Euripides and Milton. The outraged antifeminine attitudes vented in and by *Hippolytus* (616–48) are reflected in an irate speech with which Adam when fallen greets Eve (*PL* 10. 888–908; and cf. lines 894–97 with *Medea,* lines 573–75), and also in the choral comments following upon Dalila's departure (*SA* 1034–45, 1053–60). The entire third episode of the tragedy is Euripidean, Dalila recalling famous iniquitous female characters such as Medea that the playwright could so powerfully portray. He could also portray the opposite type in an Alcestis, and Milton followed him there too, associating the "espoused Saint" of *Sonn* 23 with that idealized wife. Additional characteristics common to the two poets are their penchants for presenting closely reasoned debates and for having a soliloquy open their dramas. The latter device occurs not only in *SA* but also in *Mask,* and Satan's soliloquy in Book 4 of *PL* (32ff.) was originally designed to begin, in just that way, a tragedy on the Fall. Yet no specific play by Euripides, despite his importance in other respects to Milton and his art, has been imitated in *SA* to the extent that specific plays by Sophocles and Aeschylus have. [JP]

DREAMS. The fullest account of dreams in Milton's writing occurs in chapter 6 of Manfred Weidhorn's *Dreams in Seventeenth-Century Literature.* Chapter 8 of Walter Clyde Curry's *Chaucer and the Medieval Sciences* (Barnes and Noble, 1960), which Weidhorn uses extensively, is also helpful in providing a background for understanding the traditional concepts that underlie Milton's treatment.

Milton draws upon a sustained tradition of dream literature extending from fourth century (B.C.) Greece down to his own time (see Weidhorn, Curry, and Lynn Thorndike, *A History of Magic and Ex-*

perimental Science); but his use of dreams is literary rather than "scientific," and only in a few places does he make use of the technical vocabulary of the codifiers and interpreters of dreams. He is far more interested in the aesthetic and literary possibilities of dreams than in their classification or causes, although he does establish the universal learning expected of the epic poet by alluding to the technical vocabulary of dream lore in a few passages—most notably in *PL* 4. 799–809, and 5. 100–121.

The most important dreams occur in *QNov,* in *El* 3, in *Sonn* 23, in Books 5 and 8 of *PL,* and in Books 2 and 4 of *PR.* Those in *QNov* and *El* 3 are relatively simple and conventional. The former contains Milton's first diabolic dream—if a dream rather than an apparition. In the guise of a Franciscan, the Devil appears in the Pope's chamber and convinces him that he should undertake a plot to blow up the English king and parliament. The dream serves an important function in initiating the plot and magnifying its importance by attributing it ultimately to the devil. In *El* 3 the dream is simply a means of achieving the transition from the state of mourning to the vision of Lancelot Andrewes* in Heaven. Except for Milton's characteristic use of light, it is a conventional pastiche of *loci amoeni,* with a few Christian details, also conventional, added. The dream in *Sonn* 23 differs from the other dreams in that it is isolated from any narrative context. The rather indistinct vision and the dreamer's emotional response are presented, then suddenly dissolved to waking reality, leaving the reader with a strong awareness of the contrast between the dream and the poet's waking consciousness.

Eve's dream (*PL* 5. 1–121) has been the subject of more critical commentary than any of the others, mainly because it is so closely related to the problem of the transition from innocence to guilt. The dream itself, with its abrupt discontinuities and sudden shifts in perspective, is an accurate approximation of the dream experience. Roused by a voice that she thinks is Adam's, Eve walks alone through a moonlit landscape until she comes to the forbidden tree. An angelic figure appears and addresses the tree. As Eve watches, he plucks the fruit and eats. Then, in the midst of praising the fruit, he turns and offers it to Eve. Suddenly there is no distance between them.

> So saying, he drew nigh, and to me held,
> Even to my mouth of that same fruit held part
> Which he had pluckt; the pleasant savorie smell
> So quick'nd my appetite, that I, methought,
> Could not but taste. Forthwith up to the Clouds
> With him I flew.
>
> (5. 82–87)

Then, just as suddenly,

> My Guide was gon, and I, me thought, sunk down,
> And fell asleep.
>
> (5. 91–92)

But what seems to be sleep is actually the fading of the dream, as she awakes to find Adam bending over her.

In accord with seventeeth-century dream theory, Adam plausibly—but mistakenly—identifies the dream as a *somnium animale* (see Curry, pp. 203–8) consisting of distorted parts of their conversation on the previous evening— although he admits that it contains "addition strange." The reader, however, has been shown Satan,

> Squat like a Toad, close at the eare of *Eve*;
> Assaying by his Devilish art to reach
> The Organs of her Fancie, and with them forge
> Illusions as he list, Phantasms and Dreams,
> Or if, inspiring venom, he might taint
> Th'animal Spirits that from pure blood arise.
>
> (4. 800–805)

Knowing more than Adam, the reader infers that the dream is shaped by Satan, a diabolic dream. (See William B. Hunter, *ELH, A Journal of English Literary History* 4 : 255–65.)

The dream may, as Grant McColley believes (*Harvard Theological Review* 32: 210), have been suggested to Milton by an exegetical tradition that held that Eve was twice tempted by Satan, at first unsuccessfully. If so, Milton brilliantly resolved the dangers of repetition and prolixity by placing the first temptation, which closely resembles yet diverges from the later successful temptations, in a dream.

Satan is obviously seeking to pervert Eve's will—at the very center of all sensual impressions, at a time when reason is in abeyance. Stanley Fish believes that he fails to gain Eve's assent. Noting the hiatus between "I, methought, could not but taste" and "Forthwith up to the Clouds / With him I flew," Fish says, "We have missed the deed itself and passed to its effects. . . . Satan is unable to make Eve go through the motions of disobedience, even in her fancy" (*Surprised by Sin* [1967], p. 222). Rather than succumbing in her dream, Eve, in Fish's view, resists Satan's efforts, and the dream, rather than foreshadowing the Fall*, "stands in the sharpest . . . contrast [to] it" (ibid., p. 225). Satan has, however, planted the idea of disobedience* within Eve at a deeply subconscious level through images that she need not approve of, but that she has nevertheless experienced. She could of course use this vicarious experience as a warning and strengthen her will against the actual temptation. Remembering the experience, Eve says "mee damp horror chill'd," and she is "glad" to have wakened. Adam, suspecting that the dream is "of evil sprung," is "sad" but reassures Eve,

> Evil into the mind of God or Man
> May come and go, so unapprov'd, and leave
> No spot or blame behind.
>
> (5. 117–19)

As Fish says, the response of Adam and Eve to the dream "militates against the *inevitability* (not the fact) of their later failure" (p. 225). At any rate, Milton stresses their innocence until their wills succumb. After the morning hymn, which immediately follows the dream, we are told that they are "innocent" (5. 209), and even at the moment just before Satan's final speech of temptation Eve is described as "yet sinless" (9. 659). Nevertheless, the dream is "there," and Eve's response reverberates beyond the immediate context of her account of the dream in Book 5.

Adam's two dreams in Book 8 are used as transitional and distancing devices. His colloquy with God is opened and closed with sleep, and in both instances he "dreams" of what is actually happening. The dreams present a distanced account of actual events, and they end by merging with reality. In both instances, Adam wakes, as Keats says, to find that his dream is true. (See William B. Hunter, *Modern Language Quarterly* 9 : 277–85.)

Christ's dream in *PR* 2. 263–84, is presented as a natural dream caused by his hunger.

> He slept
> And dream'd as appetite is wont to dream,
> Of meats and drinks.
>
> (2. 263–65)

But, significantly, he dreams of Daniel, who would not defile himself with Nebuchadnezzar's meat and wine but grew fat on pulse and water, and of Elijah who was fed at Cherith by ravens and in the wilderness by an angel who prepared a meal that sustained him for forty days and nights. Although a natural dream based on Christ's bodily hunger and perhaps on Milton's memory of passages in 1 Kings, it also suggests, prophetically, the Providence* of God toward those who trust in Him.

The dream in *PR* 4. 397–431, is, like Eve's, a diabolic dream. As Christ sleeps,

> at his head
> The Tempter watch'd, and soon with ugly dreams
> Disturb'd his sleep.
>
> (4. 407–9)

Against a backdrop of rain, lightning, and rushing wind,

> Infernal Ghosts, and Hellish Furies, round
> Environ'd thee, some howl'd, some yell'd,
> some shriek'd,
> Some bent at thee thir fiery darts, while thou
> Sat'st unappall'd in calm and sinless peace.
> Thus pass'd the night so foul till morning fair
> Came forth with Pilgrim steps in amice gray;
> Who with her radiant finger still'd the roar

> Of thunder, chas'd the clouds, and laid the
> winds,
> And grisly spectres, which the Fiend had rais'd
> To tempt the Son of God with terrors dire.
>
> (4 : 422–31)

Burton* comments on this kind of dream in *The Anatomy of Melancholy* :

> Sometimes by dreams . . . , the devil in several shapes talks with them: in the Indies it is common, and in China nothing so familiar as apparitions, inspirations, oracles; by terrifying them with false prodigies, counterfeit miracles, sending storms tempests, diseases, plagues . . . he raiseth such an opinion of his deity and greatness, that they dare not . . . offend him. (Holbrook Jackson, ed., 3 : 325.)

This dream, however, is an indication of Satan's spite and desperation rather than of any hope to succeed. It is a crude and ineffective gesture, but, as in many of the dreams, it does serve as a transition. Although Christ calls the storm and the apparitions of the dream "false portents, not sent from God, but thee," they suggest the violence that Christ must yet experience, and, more immediately, they are a prelude to Satan's use of force shortly afterward as he attempts to impose a physical dilemma upon Christ by placing him on the pinnacle. The dream to some extent foreshadows this use of force, and it also heightens, by contrast, the sudden reversal in which Satan falls as Christ stands triumphant. [WAM]

DRING, THOMAS: *see* PRINTERS.

DRYDEN, JOHN (1631–1700), an admirer, imitator, and frequent critic of Milton's poetry. His epigram *Lines on Milton,* written for the 1688 folio edition of *PL,* is one of the earliest English poetic tributes to Milton's epic, and one of the most generous :

> Three *Poets,* in three distant *Ages* born,
> *Greece, Italy,* and *England* did adorn.
> The *First* in loftiness of thought Surpass'd;
> The *Next* in Majesty; in both the *Last.*
> The force of *Nature* cou'd no farther goe:
> To make a *Third* she joynd the former two.

Dryden's contemporaries would probably have understood the last three lines as conventional hyperbole rather than literal preference (some perhaps recognizing the epigram to be an amplification of a complimentary Latin distich presented to Milton during his stay in Rome in 1638 by someone named Selvaggi* and published with the 1645 *Poems*). They would at the same time have seen that Dryden awarded Milton the highest honors by ranking him with ancient masters of epic, the genre generally estimated as the most elevated, and by claiming for *PL* the unique power to "adorn" English literature as Homer* and Virgil* had endowed antiquity.

Dryden's remarks about Milton in his critical writings, though not bound like the epigram by the conventions of poetic hyperbole, often make the same handsome evaluation. Twice in the *Apology for Heroic Poetry* (1677) Milton is linked in easy company with Homer, Virgil, and Tasso*, and *PL* is there declared "undoubtedly one of the greatest, most noble, and most sublime poems which either this age or nation has produced." In the *Discourse concerning the Original and Progress of Satire* (1693) Dryden wrote of Milton's work, that it must be acknowledged that, although "his event is not prosperous like that of all other epic works . . . his thoughts are elevated, his words sounding, and that no man has so happily copied the manner of Homer, or so copiously translated his Grecisms, and the Latin elegances of Virgil." Still later, in the *Dedication of the Aeneis* (1697), he again associated Milton with Homer, Virgil, and Tasso, although allowing the English writer to plead for *PL* as a heroic poem on the model of the other three only "if the giant had not foiled the knight, and driven him out of his stronghold, to wander through the world with his lady errant; and if there had not been more machining persons than human in his poem."

Perhaps the strongest evidence for Dryden's high estimate of *PL* was his request to Milton in 1674 for permission to transpose the epic into a dramatized version in his own rhymed verse (which became the "opera" called *The State of Innocence*, entered at Stationers' Hall in 1674, but published first in 1677 and again in 1684, 1690, and 1695). By choosing it for such adaptation, he ranked *PL* in interest not only with Homer and Virgil, from whose works he made English translations, but with his greatest predecessors in his own language, Chaucer* and Shakespeare*, whose writings he also considered appropriate for his translation or adaptation. Such efforts were intended to adorn English literature of his own time with the poetic riches of the past rendered in the literary language of the later seventeenth century.

Strongly implied in Dryden's tributes to the greatness of Milton—in the epigram, the critical essays, *The State of Innocence*—is his sense of admiring from a distance not created entirely by Milton's elevation. The epigram, in its marmoreal conventionality and by the phrasing of its opening line, sets Milton in an age that seems as "distant" from his praiser's as Homer's or Virgil's. One would not guess it to have been written to a fellow poet whom Dryden had known and visited. Even in his less formal prose criticism, one is surprised to find this recollection of Dryden's in the *Preface to the Fables* (1700), "Milton has acknowledged to me, that Spenser* was his original," with its unusual reminder that these men were contemporaries who met and conversed with each other. The very fact that Dryden requested permission to recast *PL* only seven years after its first publication, and within Milton's lifetime, suggested that he must have thought it as appropriate for transposition into contemporary verse as plays by Shakespeare written half a century earlier.

Dryden's view of *PL* as a literary monument expressed his awe of Milton's achievement but also his sense that it was not altogether suited to the tastes of contemporary readers. Those attitudes are often mingled in his critical essays. For example, in the *Original and Progress of*

Satire (1693) he considered that, as Milton tried "everywhere to express Homer, whose age had not arrived to that fineness, I found in him a true sublimity, lofty thoughts, which were clothed with admirable Grecisms, and ancient words, which he had been digging from the mines of Chaucer and Spenser, and which, with all their rusticity, had somewhat of venerable in them." Similarly in the earlier *Preface on Translation* (1685) he had objected that Milton's "antiquated words, and the perpetual harshness of their sound" identified his poem with an age "not arrived to that fineness" Dryden saw in his own time. Milton's diction gave his verse a "rusticity" to be contrasted with the recent "refinement" of English poetry so often admired in Dryden's critical essays.

If Milton's diction contributed to the "rusticity" of his epic, in Dryden's view, its lack of the "ease" and "graces" to be found in the "refined" poetry of the age was due also to absence of rhyme. The use of blank verse* rather than heroic couplets seemed to him Milton's greatest offense against contemporary taste, for which Dryden judged him most severely, perhaps because he had early committed himself in printed controversy to defending the theoretical superiority of rhyme, perhaps because here (the following quotation from the *Original and Progress of Satire* implies) lay Milton's practical inferiority to himself: "for whatever causes he alleges for the abolishing of rhyme . . . his own particular reason is plainly this, that rhyme was not his talent; he had neither the ease of doing it, nor the graces of it; which is manifest in his *Juvenilia*, or verses written in his youth, where his rhyme is always constrained and forced, and comes hardly from him, at an age when the soul is most pliant, and the passion of love makes almost every man a rhymer, though not a poet." Milton's matchingly condescending estimate of the youthful Dryden's rhyming gifts was remembered by his widow, who reported his opinion of Dryden as "no poet, but a good rimist."

Dryden's terms of contrast between *PL* and the contemporary style of which he was the most successful practitioner were used by other poets, for example in commendatory verses prefixed to his revision of the epic and to his *Absalom and Achitophel*. A satirical awareness of these terms is shown in the answer Milton supposedly gave to Dryden's proposal for *The State of Innocence*. The reply plays on the fashion in dress for tags, metal knobs worn at the ends of laces: "Well, Mr. *Dryden*, says *Milton*, it seems you have a mind to *Tagg* my Points, and you have my Leave to *Tagg* 'em, but some of 'em are so Awkward and Old Fashion'd that I think you had as good leave 'em as you found 'em." This answer is a further example of the current contrast, whether Milton actually said it, or whether the phrasing was attributed to him after his friend Marvell* used the same wordplay to contrast the blank verse of *PL* with Dryden's fashionable rhymes in Marvell's commendatory lines prefixed to the second edition of 1674. Awareness of the unfavorable terms used to distinguish his poem from others of the time is certainly shown in Milton's contentious paragraph on "The Verse" added in 1668 to the fifth binding of the first edition of *PL*. There, perhaps with Dryden's heroic verse and critical arguments in mind, he dismissed rhyme as the "Invention of a barbarous Age, to set off wretched matter and lame Meeter; grac't indeed since by the use of some famous modern Poets, carried away by Custom, but much to their own vexation, hindrance, and constraint. . . ." His own blank verse he claimed no "defect, though it may seem so perhaps to vulgar Readers," but rather an "example" to be esteemed, "the first in *English*, of ancient liberty recover'd to Heroic Poem from the troublesom and modern bondage of Rimeing."

The distance, then, from which Dryden praised Milton was more theoretical than chronological. While the older poet was still alive Dryden felt no inappropriateness in asking to revise *PL*, and the results in *The State of Innocence* suggest that the distance was insurmountable.

Dryden's "opera" is so gross a vulgarization of its original that it sounds almost like burlesque when we listen to the coquetry of Eve, the peevishness of Adam, or such cheery bombast from the devil as we hear in the following speech soon after his fall from heaven :

So, now we are ourselves again an host,
Fit to tempt fate, once more, for what we lost;
T' o'erleap the etherial fence, or if so high
We cannot climb, to undermine his sky,
And blow him up, who justly rules us now,
Because more strong: Should he be forced to
    bow,
The right were ours again: 'Tis just to win
The highest place; t'attempt, and fail, is sin.
                                    (5. 128)

If it were not for the unevenness of the verse, Dryden's introduction of some serious philosophical debating, and his praises of PL in the prefatory remarks quoted earlier from the *Apology for Heroic Poetry*, one would judge him to have been making fun of the epic as, for example, the style of his own heroic plays had been mocked in Buckingham's *The Rehearsal*. The cruditiy of his adaptation shows no genuinely felt appreciation, no understanding in his early admiration for *PL*. Dryden himself is said to have confessed more than twenty years later to the critic John Dennis* (who recorded the remark in a letter dated May 25, 1719) that at the time of revising Milton's poem he "knew not half the Extent of his Excellence" (in which view Dennis dryly concurred).

Despite the insensitivity to Milton's language shown in *The State of Innocence,* despite his critical objections to Milton's diction* and verse forms, Dryden continued throughout his life to read the other's works and to make use of his reading. There are echoes of *Nat* in *Heroique Stanza's*; of *Lyc* and *Areop* in *Annus Mirabilis;* of *SA* in *Aureng-Zebe, Oedipus* and *All for Love*; of *PR* in *Absalom* and *Achitophel* and *The Medall*. Especially Dryden drew upon *PL* for poetic materials, which he learned to use with far more subtlety than he showed in *The State of Innocence*. Milton's description of Satan

from the opening of Book 2, for example, contributed to the mock-heroic portrait of the playwright Thomas Shadwell in *Mac Flecknoe* [1678] :

The hoary Prince in Majesty appear'd,
High on a Throne of his own Labours rear'd.
                                    (106–7)

It is largely by Miltonic allusion that Dryden makes us see evil in Shadwell's sovereign dullness or danger in bad verse. Returning to the same lines sixteen years later in his poem to the playwright Congreve, he contrasted the genuine sovereignty of his friend's plays with the vicious successes (in Dryden's former posts of Poet Laureate and Historiographer Royal) of Shadwell and Thomas Rhymer:

But now, not I, but Poetry is curs'd;
For *Tom* the Second reigns like *Tom* the first.
. . . .
Yet this I Prophesy; Thou shalt be seen,
(Tho' with some short Parenthesis between:)
High on the Throne of Wit; and seated there,
Not mine (that's little) but thy Lawrel wear.
                              (47–48, 51–54)

This double allusion to Milton's description and his own mock-heroic adaptation of it enabled Dryden to blend knowingly playful compliment with an elevated prophetic tone : the sophisticated poet who can rightly value his friend's art measures him by high heroic, by Miltonic, standards.

PL contributed expressions for many of Dryden's works. But for his finest long poem, *Absalom and Achitophel,* Part 1 [1681], it provided the large design and much of the heroic manner, as well as many details intricately woven into the language of the poem by allusion, imitation, and parody. The professed scene is an earlier, Old Testament world, recalled in language associated with a natural "Paradise" in which King David once ruled "undisturb'd," as it were, by the upheavals of fallen history. Its action is the temptation and fall of Absalom, the "Natural" hero whose "manly beauty" and "motions all accompanied with grace" recall descriptions of unfallen Adam. His tempter is "Hells dire Agent," Achitophel, portrayed in an extended analogy with Satan as "A Name to all succeeding Ages Curst," a "fiery Soul," a "daring Pilot," with a son as "shapeless" a deformation of nature as Satan's progeny, and supported by villains listed in an ironic parody of Milton's catalogue of fallen angels*. Absalom is seduced by speeches introduced in a comparison with serpentine "Venome" and alluding richly throughout to Satan's. The damage wrought by his fall, compared to floods and plagues such as disrupt Milton's natural world, is averted through heavenly intervention, marked by Miltonic thunder —"Th'Almighty, nodding, gave Consent;/ And Peals of Thunder shook the Firmament"—and the poem ends, like *PL,* with the poet's heroic vision of a "new time" in which "The mighty Years in long Procession ran" in a history "Restor'd" according to divine consent. Such connections between *Absalom and Achitophel* and Milton's epic are so elaborate and so insistent that they direct us to read Dryden's story—an episode from contemporary English politics satirically disguised in the biblical analogy—as a reenactment of Milton's archetypal drama. The parallels with *PL* help to give universal significance to the local modern situation: they demand that the reader understand the petty and passing circumstances of this world as instances of the recurring patterns of history and that they be interpreted in the light of the noblest values, preserved in such great works of literature as Milton's epic. Dryden's ways of using *PL,* begun in *Mac Flecknoe* and later revived in the tribute of Congreve, are so richly varied, elaborated and extended in *Absalom and Achitophel* that they are central to the poem's subject and its meaning.

By making *PL* a context—literary and therefore moral—in which *Absalom and Achitophel* may be interpreted, Dryden paid a tribute as generous as his epigram on Milton. By drawing attention to the ways in which his own poem was in the heroic manner and also specifically Miltonic, by relating *Absalom and Achitophel*

explicitly in design and detail to Milton's poem, Dryden acknowledged his older contemporary as a vital contributor to an ancient and ongoing tradition. After Dryden, to write heroic verse in English was to write like Homer and Virgil, and like Milton, who "joynd the former two." [AF]

Du BARTAS, GUILLAUME de SALLUSTE, SIEUR (1544–1590). The voluminous works of this Huguenot statesman and poet were highly popular in England in the late sixteenth and early seventeenth centuries. To a great degree, he popularized the idea that poetry should be dedicated exclusively to Christian uses. *L'Uranie,* his poetic manifesto, is noteworthy for transforming Urania*, the muse of astronomy, into the muse* of Christian poetry. Other writers may have effected the transformation earlier, but it was this poem that made her into the guardian of the movement. His subsequent works, especially the two *Sepmaines,* became models for those who wished to concentrate on Christian subjects rather than the more customary epic and amatory ones. The first of these poems is a hexameron*, an elaborate retelling of the creation* story; the second and longer poem, which Du Bartas never finished, is a compendium of Old Testament stories. In both poems, he incorporated encyclopedic amounts of learning into his narrative, although fortunately he handled his materials in sprightly fashion.

Milton was familiar with Du Bartas in the translations of Josuah Sylvester (1563–1618), particularly his rendering of *Les Sepmaines* as the *Devine Weekes and Works.* Sylvester's Du Bartas was at the height of its considerable popularity during Milton's childhood, and he probably read it while still quite young. Certainly the psalm paraphrases that he completed at age fifteen contain verbal echoes of Sylvester's translation. Influence on his poetry was studied by Charles Dunster in *Considerations on Milton's Early Reading* (1800) and by George C. Taylor in *Milton's Use of Du Bartas* (1934). According to Taylor, "no other work of the Renaissance had a more important and definite influence on *Paradise Lost* than Sylvester's translation of Du Bartas"; but although he adduced an impressive number of parallels to support his thesis, it requires modification. By no means ignorant of Renaissance commonplaces, Taylor did not take them sufficiently into consideration in making his case. Subsequent research has underscored how many of his parallels involve just such commonplaces available to Milton in a variety of authors. Consequently, Du Bartas no longer seems particularly impressive as a source for specific ideas and details. More recently, William B. Hunter, Jr., has argued that Sylvester's *Du Bartas* and metrical versions of the Psalter were the prime factors in shaping Milton's prosody (*Philological Quarterly* 28 : 125–44). His view, however, has not been widely accepted.

That some influence existed seems reasonable. Milton's muse in *PL* owes something to Du Bartas's Urania, and in general the two authors' attitudes toward Christian poetry accord with each other, suggesting at least a general influence. Also to be considered is the impact of Du Bartas's style, particularly in Sylvester's translation. Encouraged as a child to read him for his piety and erudition, Milton doubtless valued his unusual images and humor as well; and it is probably in the passages where he himself is not deadly serious—in, for example, the scenes of pastoral* comedy in *PL*—that the older writer most notably survives. The elephant that makes the other animals laugh by wreathing "his Lithe Proboscis," Adam's lack of concern "lest Dinner cool"—such figures and details reflect the spirit of Du Bartas. [ERG]

DU BOCCAGE, MARIE ANN: *see* IMITATIONS.

DU CHESNE, ANDRE (1584–1640), "the father of French history." Du Chesne was a prodigious writer and editor whose works Milton consulted during the period 1642–1647. Milton's notes from his *Histoire D'Angleterre, D'Escosse et D'Irlande* (Paris, 1614; 3 ed. 1641) were recorded only in *CB*. Two entries appeared under the topic "Marriage"*; both asserted that marriage with a person of a different religion was dangerous, especially if one were head of state. Milton here judged the danger inherent in an English marriage alliance with a Catholic country. Under "Property and Taxes," he recollected the subsidy voted in 1624 for the recovery of the Palatinate by his quotation on parliamentary control of subsidies. Milton also knew Du Chesne's edition of the anonymous *Encomium Emmae* from his *Historiae Normannorum Scriptores Antiqui* (Paris, 1619). This work provides valuable evidence of the struggle between the Danes and English, which Milton incorporated in *Brit*. [RMa]

DU GARD (TYPIS DU GARDIANIS): *see* DUGARD, WILLIAM.

DU MOULIN, PETER (Pierre, the Younger; 1601–1684), Anglican divine. Born in Paris, du Moulin studied at Sedan and Leyden before attending Cambridge. He was the son of Pierre du Moulin (1568–1659), a cleric and a prolific author, and brother of Lewis (1603–1680), reputedly translator of part of *Eikon* into Latin. In 1640 du Moulin received the degree of Doctor of Divinity from Leyden, reporting that he held the living at St. John's, Chester, though no confirmation is known. He was ejected from the rectory at Wheldrake, Yorkshire, in 1641. He then engaged in tutoring in Ireland and England during the Civil War period, and became rector of a parish in Kent in 1646. He held the latter post, except for a brief period in 1660, until his death. His writing against the government not being known, he was made Doctor of Divinity at Oxford in 1656. With the Restoration he became a chaplain to Charles II* by virtue of a prebend at Canterbury, where he lived in his later years.

In answer to *1Def* (1651), which had

attacked Salmasius* and *Defensio Regia, pro Carolo I,* du Moulin wrote *Regii Sanguinis Clamor ad Coelum Adversus Parricidas Anglicanos* ("The Cry to Heaven of the King's Blood against the English Parricides") during the summer of 1652; it was completed before September 17/27, 1652. *Clamor* was published by Adrian Vlacq*, the Amsterdam printer who was later to make clear that he was unconcerned with political positions and sought simply to capitalize financially on the controversy as any businessman would. The author was not given, but a dedication to the king was signed by Vlacq. Du Moulin had sent the manuscript to Salmasius, who gave it to Alexander More* (or Morus in Latin) to have published. More wrote the dedication, and thus the first reports of authorship in letters from the Continent calling More the author and Salmasius author of the dedication were understandably in error. Even the semi-official *Mercurius Politicus* reported in its issue of September 20-30, 1652, that More was the author. In the wake of his identification slanderous rumors circulated widely about personal misconduct by More. In 1654 when Milton finally came to answer *Clamor* with *2Def,* as he had previously been officially ordered to do, he wrote as if More were the author and employed the slander that he had heard to confute the invective of his antagonist. Basically Milton's stance in *2Def* is that those who accuse people of misconduct should be blameless themselves. This, therefore, demanded two main attacks : the author of *Clamor* (that is, More) was guilty of heinous crimes, which are recited, and he, Milton, had been falsely calumniated, which is evident from the record of his personal life as set forth in the tract. Primarily *Clamor* had denounced the crimes of the parricides against royalty, against the people, and the like, and attacked Milton as their spokesman in *1Def* on personal grounds. It included two Latin poems : one praising Salmasius, one of 245 lines condemning Milton. In *2Def* Milton tries to make Salmasius partially culpable by arguing

that he had solicited the support of others. (Salmasius had died on August 24/ September 3, 1653.) *Clamor* was published three times in 1652 by Vlacq and again in 1661 ("Editio Secunda") by Vlacq. There is supposed to have been a Flemish translation in 1652 by James (?) Stermont, but no copy is known.

Before he wrote *2Def* Milton was aware that More was probably not the author of *Clamor.* Isaac Vossius* had learned that it was "written by some anonymous Englishman, but transmitted to Salmasius and published by" More, as he reported in a letter dated October 8, 1652. Vlacq wrote to Samuel Hartlib*, Milton's friend, that More was not the author, sometime before October 29, 1652. Nicolaas Heinsius* likewise corrected Abraham Gronovius* on this point on information from Vossius. Du Moulin later said that he thought Milton actually knew that he was the author. But Milton, unarmed with the name of the real author or any information about him that he would need for his strategy of refutation, chose to treat More as author. More answered *2Def* in *Fides Publica,* 1654, to which he added a *Supplementum* in 1655. He denies authorship and says that he knows the real author's name though he is not personally acquainted with him. Milton's rejoinder in *3Def* argues that More may not have been the author but that he is at least culpable by having had the tract published and by having contributed the dedication.

In a collection of poems and various prose pieces entitled *Parerga* (Canterbury, 1670; reissued, 1671), du Moulin confessed his authorship of *Clamor,* and thus Milton's early biographers* Aubrey*, Wood*, and Toland* got the ascription correct. However, the Anonymous Biographer (Cyriack Skinner*) and Edward Phillips continued to cite More. Du Moulin reprinted his poem on Milton in *Parerga,* and commented that since Milton was unwilling to accept being in error, he was kept safe from reprisals. Similarly, Abraham Hill, treasurer of the Royal Society, told Aubrey that Milton knew the name of the author from the Dutch ambassador before publishing *2Def,* but this did not deter him. *Parerga* is in three books with separate title pages and pagination; books two and three in which the poem and comments occur (2:36–42, and 3:141–42) have publication dates of 1669. The poems are also found in British Museum MS, Burney 406, ff. 64–71. A manuscript note by du Moulin in his *Historie des Nouveaus Presbyteriens Anglois et Eccossois* (1660) in the Canterbury Cathedral copy (cat. Z.9.18) also indicates his authorship of *Clamor.* There are allusions to Milton in his *A Replie to a Person of Honour* (1675) on pages 10, 40, 45. [JTS]

DUBRAU, THEODORE: *see* CONSIDERATIONS . . HIRELINGS.

DUGARD, WILLIAM (1606–1662), printer for the Cromwellian government and friend to Milton. From 1644 onward Dugard was Headmaster of the Merchant Taylors' School, although he was suspended from this post for a few months in 1650. He also was author of *Rhetorices Elementa* (1648) and *Graeca Grammatica* (1654). Around March 15, 1649, he printed *Eikon Basilike** with four prayers allegedly written by Charles I* given as an integral part of the volume. The manuscript had been delivered to him by Edward Simmons, the late king's servant, who had also brought the manuscript of the work without the prayers to its first printer, Richard Royston, around December 24, 1648. Between these two publications the prayers had separately been licensed on February 23, 1649, by James Cranford to John Playford. Although Dugard was ordered arrested on March 16, he was released when the license was produced; Cranford was imprisoned instead. On February 1, 1650, Dugard was ordered imprisoned for attempting to publish Salmasius's* *Defensio Regia.* He was confined to Newgate Prison on February 20, and his press and post as headmaster of the Merchant Taylors' School were taken from him. He seems to have been released

by April 2, when the press was restored to him; he reassumed his headmastership on September 25. Apparently as a result of these brushes with the government, he was brought to the attention of the Council of State* and became an official printer for it.

On February 24, 1651, Dugard printed *1Def,* his work being noted as "Typis Du-Gardianis." Dugard was also responsible for the second edition (Madan, no. 2), also published in 1651. The various continental pirated editions continued to cite Dugard's press, and they give no indication of the actual place of publication or of the printer. A Dutch translation in 1651 (Madan, no. 11), by G. de Hoere from his press at Gouda, indicates that it has been translated from the Latin of the copy printed in London "by Du Gardianis." The exact date of the first publication of *1Def* is given in *Nouvelles Ordinaires de Londres,* no. 34, February 24–March 9, 1651, p. 136, a governmental news sheet produced for a continental audience and printed by Dugard. This and various volumes make clear that Dugard used a New Style calendar; that is, he dated the new year from January 1 rather than from March 15. Around December 24, 1651, although the title page gives 1652, Dugard printed John Phillips's *Responsio Ad Apologiam Anonymi**; again the press is "Typis Dugardianis." Three Dutch pirated editions in 1652 continue this ascription.

Dugard was in trouble in 1652 over the Racovian Catechism*. This tract was registered to him on November 13, 1651, and was ordered seized by the Council of State on January 27, 1652. Two days later he had the registry canceled. He was examined by the Council and implicated Milton as the licenser. But the matter seems not to have caused him any cessation of his work. He published John Dury's* French translation of *Eikon* in 1652, with the title page reading *"A Londres* Par *Guill. Du-Gard,* Imprimeur du Conseil d'Etat." He was also the printer of *Scriptum Parlamenti Reipublicae Angliae,* the Latin version of *A*

Declaration of the Parliament of the Common-Wealth of England (against the Dutch), in 1652. A memorandum from the Council of State on July 20, 1652, requests Dugard to speak with Milton concerning the printing of *A Declaration*. The Latin version appeared on July 29, and it has thus often been assigned as Milton's work. (*See* ATTRIBUTIONS.)

One last item should be mentioned concerning Dugard. During 1660 when those who had written against the monarchy or had served the Interregnum government were being apprehended, Dugard harbored James Harrington*, author of *The Common-Wealth of Oceana, The Prerogative of Popular Government*, and *The Rota*. Dugard was apparently not out of the good graces of the new regime. [JTS]

DUNS SCOTUS, JOHANNES (ca. 1265–1308), Franciscan scholastic. Despite the fact that Duns figures in one of Milton's most famous comparisons (*Areop* 4 : 311 : "our sage and serious Poet *Spencer* . . . I dare to be known to think a better teacher then *Scotus* or *Aquinas*"), there has been almost no analysis to show the influence upon him of this compeer of Aquinas*, who has figured largely in Milton scholarship. W. C. Curry has argued (*Milton's Ontology, Cosmogony, and Physics* [1957], pp. 167ff.) that Milton's distinction of several kinds of matter is indebted to Duns's expansion of some ideas of Avencebrol and that the comparison of the Scale of Nature* to a tree in *PL* 5. 479–83, may reflect the same image in Duns. Duns viewed prime matter* as being not pure potentiality but as embodying positive reality to some degree, and this may also be Milton's view (*PL* 2 and *CD* 1 : 7). Finally, Milton's strong affirmation of freedom, in turn involving the primacy of the will, seems to some extent analogous to Duns's view that the will causes its own decisions and is not properly subordinate to the intellect, as Thomas had argued. God wills anything because he wills it and thus it is good; he does not will it because it is good (an intellectual judgment).

Adam and Eve, endowed with freedom, are also endowed with the possibility of using their free will* to sin. But such parallels, if they exist, between Milton and Duns have never been explored. [WBH]

DUNSTER, CHARLES (1750–1816), editor and miscellaneous author. A graduate of Oriel College, Oxford, Dunster held various posts before becoming rural dean of West Sussex and rector of Petworth. His later writing dealt mainly with the New Testament, for example, *Consideration of the Hypothesis that St. Luke's Gospel was the First Written* (1808). In 1791 he published an edition of John Philips's* *Cider* "With Notes Provincial, Historical and Classical." The poem, a parody* of Miltonic style, is amply related to its Miltonic sources in the notes. In 1795 his important variorum edition of *PR* appeared; it included new notes and an introduction written for the edition by him and new remarks by Robert Thyer (1709–1781), whose comments had been lost in transit and reproduced from memory. Dunster states his reasons for producing this edition in the preface : "The *PARADISE REGAINED* of our great English poet has never had justice done it either by critics or commentators. As it has been generally and unjustly under-rated, so it has been negligently and scantily illustrated" (p. i). Dunster's concluding epitome of the poem (p. 267) notes that it "has something of the *didactic* character; it teaches not merely by the general moral, and by the character and conduct of its hero, but has also many positive precepts every where interspersed. It is written for the most part in a style admirably condensed, and with a studied reserve of ornament. . . ." *Considerations on Milton's Early Reading and the Prima Stamina of His Paradise Lost* (1800), one of the first scholarly studies of Milton's relationship with contemporary authors, investigates Milton's debt to Joshua Sylvester in his translation of Guillaume Du Bartas's* *Divine Weeks and Works*. Dunster finds that debt in Milton's early paraphrases of Psalms 114 and 136 and various other poems (through *Lyc*). He offers many parallels, which citations *"go near* to evince, that the author of *PARADISE LOST* had made an early acquaintance with his predecessor in Sacred Poetry. This might be strongly corroborated, and a much larger extent of obligation might be pointed out from various parts of his two great Poems . . ." (p. 119). [JTS]

DUPRE, NICOLAS FRANÇOIS (RAMOND DE ST. MAUR): *see* TRANSLATIONS OF MILTON'S WORKS.

DURY or DURIE, JOHN (1596–1680), a descendant of forebears who were leaders of Scottish Presbyterianism. When his father, Robert Dury, was banished from Scotland for treason against James VI, he was taken to the Continent, and in 1609 he settled in Leyden, where his father had become pastor of a British Presbyterian congregation. Very early Dury attained the mastery of Latin, French, and German that was later apparent in his vast correspondence. He was educated in the University of Leyden and in the Huguenot Academy at Sedan. In both places he became aware of the deep rifts in Protestant thought, to the healing of which he was to dedicate most of his life. He received Presbyterian ordination, and in 1624 he was called as minister of a congregation of English-speaking Presbyterians at Elbing, Germany, where he met Samuel Hartlib* and began his long and fruitful association with this friend of Milton. It appears that at Elbing also he received strong incentive for his life's purpose to unite Protestants, for Caspar Godemann, chief minister of Gustavus Adolphus there, proposed the role to him, and elicited his "Vow of Perseverance in the Worke," which he faithfully kept. At Elbing too he met English diplomatist Sir Thomas Roe, who successfully urged him to transfer his activity to Britain and to seek the mediation of the Anglican Church between the Lutheran and the Reformed Churches.

When Dury reached London in 1630, he did not find attitudes responsive to his ideal of Protestant union. There already was tension between King and Commons; Charles* himself was interested in European Protestantism only because of the plight of his sister in the Palatinate; Laud* and the King were essentially Anglo-Catholics hostile to dissent from the Establishment; and the doctrine and polity of the Anglican Church rendered it unsuitable for membership in an organically unified Protestant church. Soon, however, he revived his acquaintance with Hartlib, and in him found a zealous co-worker for his prime project. Several low churchmen, particularly Archbishops Abbot and Ussher* and Bishop Hall*, encouraged him by giving him letters of recommendation to Lutheran and Reformed divines abroad. From 1631 through 1633 he negotiated with Swedish and German clerics without clear indication of progress. After his return to London in 1634 he was ordained an Anglican priest, in an effort, it appears, to give him greater status, appointed one of the royal chaplains, and preferred to a benefice in Lincolnshire. In mid-1635 he returned to his missionary efforts on the Continent, where he met a mixed response. His most severe setback came in Sweden, when Queen Christina*, reversing the policy of her father, expelled him from her realm. His continued loyalty to the royalist cause in Britain was evidenced by his appointment as chaplain and tutor to Mary Stuart, Princess of Orange, whom he served for two years. After a short period as pastor of the Merchant Adventurers in Rotterdam, he returned to London to assume duties as a member of the Westminster Assembly*. During the ensuing nine years he found in Hartlib an energetic ally in the cause of Protestant union, and with him and with Milton he became engrossed in schemes for the reform of schools and libraries. In 1645 he married an aunt of Lady Ranelagh*, and thus enlarged his place in Milton's circle. He and Milton had met perhaps as early as 1641 and certainly by 1644. Dury was one of Hartlib's friends who must have read *Educ* closely. The relationship must have ripened, for Dury translated *Eikon* into French in 1652. But in *3Def* Milton boldly cites his letters from Holland, which assert that Alexander More* was not the author of the *Clamor*, an error of ascription that Dury evidently wished to correct. Instead, Milton attacked the authority of Godofred Hotton, the source of Dury's information.

Dury's evangelistic nature caused him to develop an active interest in the conversion of the Jews, and, after a long correspondence with Rabbi Menasseh ben Israel, he took a leading part in the successful effort to have the expulsion of Jews from Britain revoked. Despite his earlier royalist sympathies, he found favor with Cromwell* and with Parliament, which granted him an annuity. Throughout his later years he oscillated between England and the Continent, still tireless in his quest for church union. He was rebuffed in Britain at the Restoration, and in 1662 he removed to Cassel in Westphalia, where he continued his activities with diminishing success and where he died on September 26, 1680. Dury was a prolific writer of open letters and tracts on the many significant matters that interested him. He was often assisted in their publication by Hartlib. J. M. Batten (*John Dury* [1944], pp. 213–22) lists ninety-eight works by title and date. [DAR]

DWIGHT, TIMOTHY: *see* INFLUENCE IN AMERICA, MILTON'S.

EAST, MILTON AND THE. Milton's knowledge of the Indian background—its rivers, its mountains, its splendor and pomp—is surprisingly close. More than this geographical knowledge that he reveals in his poems is his acquaintance with, and understanding of, Indian thought.

The business members of Milton's family may have been in contact with the members of the East India Company. Milton, working as Secretary for Foreign Tongues* in the time of Cromwell, would have been acquainted with some aspects

of Indian life (Cromwell granted a charter to the East India Company in 1657). Milton's knowledge of the East and especially of India has been profitably used by him in his epics. He uses the classical myths* mostly to give to his epic *PL* antiquity and remoteness. The varied references to the Scriptures give to the epic a certain credibility and authenticity. He brings in the East and the Indian background largely to satisfy a contemporary interest and lend to the poem freshness and originality. Ormuz and Ind, Agra and Lahore, Damasco, Morocco and Trebisond, Congo and Angola would have given to the seventeenth-century reader the fascinating picture of an El Dorado.

Milton traces the origin of the Pigmean race to the region "beyond the Indian Mount" (*PL* 1.781), the Himalayas. While describing "the bad eminence" of Satan, Milton refers to the fabulous "wealth of Ormus and of Ind" and comments,

High on a Throne of Royal State, which far
Outshon the wealth of *Ormus* and of *Ind*,
Or where the gorgeous East with richest hand
Showrs on her Kings *Barbaric* Pearl and Gold,
Satan exalted sat.

(2.1–5)

One can see the ceremonial pomp, ostentation, and grandeur of the Mogul emperors reflected in these lines. Whether Milton with his puritanical bias is favorably disposed toward this magnificence and splendor of the oriental monarchs is doubtful. But his rich poetic imagination is able to get a lurid picture of oriental pomp either through the records of the East India Company or through intimate conversation with the members of that body. (*See also* GEOGRAPHY, MILTON AND.)

Milton describes Satan's journey as he approaches Paradise:
As when a Vultur on *Imaus* bred,
Whose snowie ridge the roving *Tartar* bounds,
Dislodging from a Region scarce of prey
To gorge the flesh of Lambs or yeanling Kids
On Hills where Flocks are fed, flies toward
   the Springs
Of *Ganges* or *Hydaspes, Indian* streams.

(3.431–36)

Both the rivers, the Ganges and the Jhelum (Hydaspes), have their springs in the Himalayas. Satan moves from the Himalayas, from the Tibetan region to the barren plains of Sericana, "where *Chineses* drive / With Sails and Wind thir canie Waggons light." Similarly, Satan's journey through Hell is likened to the fleet of ships sailing from Bengala :

As when farr off at Sea a Fleet descri'd
Hangs in the Clouds, by *Aequinoctial* Winds
Close sailing from *Bengala,* or the Iles
Of *Ternate* and *Tidore,* whence Merchants bring
Thir spicie Drugs: they on the trading Flood
Through the wide *Ethiopian* to the Cape
Ply stemming nightly toward the Pole. So seem'd
Farr off the flying Fiend.

(2. 636–43)

Ternate and Tidore figured very much in the records of the East India Company at that time. Drake touched at Ternate in 1579 and claimed prior rights of discovery for the East India Company. Equally important was Bengala for the seventeenth-century coastal trade. It is no erudite allusion to a region held marvelous because unknown, dragged in to add opulence to the rhythm and suggestion to the meaning, but a fact as relevant as Ternate and Tidore themselves.

Satan, being sent out of Paradise with a warning from Gabriel (at the end of Bk. 4), waits for a suitable opportunity to enter Paradise. Of the seven days during which Satan goes round and round the earth, three are spent in moving from east to west on the equatorial line, four in moving round from pole to pole, that is, from north to south and back.

Sea he [Satan] had searcht and Land
From *Eden* over *Pontus,* and the Poole
Maeotis, up beyond the River *Ob*;
Downward as farr Antartic; and in length
West from *Orontes* to the Ocean barr'd
At *Darien,* thence to the Land where flowes
Ganges and *Indus*; thus the Orb he roam'd
With narrow search.

(9. 76–83)

The precision and accuracy with which Milton describes Satan's wanderings, astronomically as well as geographically, is superb. Satan goes northward over Pontus (the Black Sea) and over the pool Maeotis (Sea of Azov); from there he continues on beyond the Liberian river Ob (that flows into the Artic sea); on over the North Pole he goes down the other side of the globe, and comes to the Antarctic regions. This is his journey, north and south. Along the equatorial line he travels westward from the Syrian river Orontes to the Isthmus of Darien, continues further on round to India, passes first the Ganges and then the Indus. This brings him to the east of Eden. The order of passing from Ganges to Indus is noticeable. Accurate knowledge of these rivers, their origin and the regions through which they flow, is easily discernible in this passage.

Adam and Eve wish to entertain their guest, the angel Raphael, with delicacies culled from the best fruits of East and West. Eve promises Adam the most delicious fare for Raphael.

from each tender stalk
Whatever Earth all-bearing Mother yields
In *India* East or West, or middle shoare
In *Pontus* or the *Punic* Coast, or where
Alcinous reign'd, fruit of all kindes, in coate
. . . .
She gathers.

(5. 337–43)

Milton refers to the fruitful and plenteous aspect of Mother Earth in India and elsewhere. India figures in his mind's eye.

But the most poetic and realistic picture that Milton presents is that of Adam and Eve after their fall desperately trying to cover their bodies with leaves. To their great shame and consternation Adam and Eve realize that they are naked. Their innocence and purity are now replaced by guilt and shame. The eating of the fruit of the Tree of Knowledge has brought them only a painful realization of their nakedness and guilt. As Milton describes,

Into the thickest Wood, there soon they chose
The Figtree, not that kind for Fruit renown'd
But such as at this day to *Indians* known

In *Malabar* or *Decan* spreds her Armes
Braunching so broad and long, that in the
    ground
The bended Twigs take root, and Daughters
    grow
About the Mother Tree, a Pillard shade
High overarch't, and echoing Walks between;
There oft the *Indian* Herdsman shunning
    heate
Shelters in coole, and tends the pasturing
    Herds
At Loopholes cut through thickest shade:
    Those Leaves
They gatherd.
                            (9. 1100–11)

The leaves of the banyan tree in India
are large enough. These trees have such
strong limbs that they support the main
tree and stand as sturdy pillars. The
Indian summer brings many a rustic or a
shepherd to the cool shade of such a tree,
which spreads itself over a large area. It
stands for ages and ages as a benevolent
sentinel of humanity. In fact it is not one
tree, it is a synod of many trees, the
mother tree supported by the limbs of its
daughters. This is indeed a faithful picture
of the Indian tree with its usefulness to
the herdsmen, and it well captures the
sylvan atmosphere. The summer heat and
the cool, refreshing shade of the tree are
easily imaginable. One gets the impression
that Milton may have seen a drawing of
a tree of this type, so common in South
India, or have heard it described by a
returned traveler.

Milton mentions with pleasure and
pride populous cities of the East. In order
to give an idea of futurity to Adam,
Michael takes him to the top of a hill
where

His Eye might there command wherever stood
City of old or modern Fame, the Seat
Of mightiest Empire, from the destind Walls
Of *Cambalu*, seat of *Cathaian Can*
And *Samarchand* by *Oxus, Temirs* Throne,
To *Paquin* of *Sinaean* Kings, and thence
To *Agra* and *Lahor* of great *Mogul*
Down to the golden *Chersonese,* or where
The *Persian* in *Ecbatan* sate, or since
In *Hispahan,* or where the *Russian Ksar,*
In *Mosco,* or the Sultan in *Bizance,*
Turchestan-born; nor could his eye not ken
Th' Empire of *Negus* to his utmost Port
Ercoco and the less Maritim Kings
Mombaza, and *Quiloa,* and *Melind,*

And *Sofala* thought *Ophir,* to the Realme
Of *Congo,* and *Angola* fardest South.
                            (11. 385–401)

These names would have meant pomp
and luxury, fabulous wealth and fantastic
delights to the readers of Milton's age.
Equally fascinating and exotic is the pic-
ture of the East presented in *PR.* The
picture moves rapidly, unfolding the mag-
nificence of the East. Satan directs the
attention of the Son of God* to the
colorful East,

Assyria and her Empires antient bounds,
Araxes and the Caspian lake; thence on
As far as *Indus* East, *Euphrates* West,
And oft beyond; to South the *Persian* Bay,
And inaccessible the *Arabian* drouth:
Here *Ninevee,* of length within her wall
Several days journey, built by *Ninus* old,
Of that first golden Monarchy the seat,
And seat of *Salmanassar,* whose success
Israel in long captivity still mourns.
                            (3. 270–79)

Civilizations of the East figure vividly in
this account.

In all these references one can see the
familiarity with which Milton speaks of
India and the East, mostly based on his
intimate acquaintance with men who have
come

From *India* and the golden *Chersoness,*
And utmost Indian Isle *Taprobane,*
Dusk faces with white silken Turbants
    wreath'd.
                            (4. 74–76)

Apart from these references to India
based on intimate knowledge, the similar-
ity between Indian and Miltonic thought
is strikingly significant. In *Mask* and in
the last poetical compositions—*PL, PR,*
and *SA*—Milton repeatedly presents the
conflict between good and evil.* He
strongly affirms that virtue may be assailed
but can never be overcome. He holds the
view that God purposely puts man in the
midst of plenty so that he may be tempted
and tested. Not that God distrusts his
chosen beings, but he would like to give
them an opportunity to express their un-
flinching faith in him. Also Milton believes
in a militant type of virtue, virtue that is

positive and dynamic, not the type of "cloistered virtue" that "slinks out of the race." So these great poems of Milton reveal to us his philosophic speculation and his preoccupation with the eternal problem of man's relationship with God. Triumphantly he pleads that God's ways are just, essentially just and justifiable to men. Milton's God is more an embodiment of justice, moral law, and righteous indignation than of simple love. Milton's thought is especially akin to the philosophic thought expounded in the *Gita*.

The *Gita*, the most refreshing and enlightening philosophic exposition of Indian thought, is a part of the Sanskrit epic *The Mahabharata*, and embodies the message of Lord Krishna to Arjuna on the battlefield. It recognizes that different types of men should have different ways of attaining perfection. It typifies mainly three distinct methods of transcending human limitations—"Jnana Marga," "Bhakti Marga," and "Karma Marga." The *Gita* emphasizes the need for unquestioning faith in God. It discusses the relationship between God and man.

An intellectual can approach God through "Jnana" or wisdom, through spiritual enlightenment. Or one can do one's duty, "Karma," unmindful of the reward. It may be done as an act of faith in God. Even the ordinary man can attain salvation through implicit faith in "Bhakti" and unswerving loyalty to God. The *Gita* repeatedly harps on this point, that those who believe in God with no mental reservations will be nearer and dearer to Him. The tone of the *Gita* is authoritative because it is the Lord who is addressing the erring, struggling humanity symbolized by Arjuna. The message is for the man whose vision becomes clouded, though temporarily; who has lost his reasoning power and fallen into despair; who fails to differentiate the right from the wrong, the wrong from the right.

Milton expresses a somewhat similar view in *PL* and *PR*. He also believes that perfection lies in right conduct and belief in reason.* As Adam expresses his sense

of relief on beholding a pleasant vision, Michael immediately warns him:

> Judg not what is best
> By pleasure, though to Nature seeming meet,
> Created, as thou art, to nobler end
> Holie and pure, conformitie divine.
> *(PL* 11. 599–602)

Milton here states that human standards of judgment or appreciation are not perfect. Our judgments are clouded by our ignorance, and we become perfect only when we can penetrate through this mist.

Later, Adam shows his unflinching faith in God and says,

> Henceforth I learne that to obey is best,
> And love with feare the onely God, to walk
> As in his presence, ever to observe
> His providence, and in his sole depend.
> (12. 561–64)

Adam is now aware of his relationship with God. There is perfect acquiescence in God's ways. This realization, as Michael suggests, is the sum total of wisdom.

In *PR* Milton emphasizes the need for man to govern all his passions and desires before he can aim at perfection. The Son of God tells Satan,

> Yet he who reigns within himself, and rules
> Passions, Desires, and Fears, is more a King;
> Which every wise and virtuous man attains.
> (2. 466–68)

The concept of a perfect man as given in the *Gita* is also the same. Lord Krishna says,

> Pain follows pleasure,
> He is not troubled;
> Gain follows loss,
> His is indifferent.
> (*Gita,* trans. Swami Prabhavananda, p. 63)

The insistence here is on detachment from worldly pleasures and self-control. He who is not a slave to his passions or desires is a perfect man. "A serene spirit accepts pleasure and pain with an even mind and is unmoved by either. He alone is worthy of immortality" (*Gita,* p. 40). This serenity is in no way to be equated with stoicism. Milton in large measure comes near to the Indian thought that one who does his duty with faith in God is releasing himself from bondage and is attaining the bliss of Heaven; to him; therefore, pain and pleasure have no meaning. He can accept them with equanimity, surrendering himself to God's will.

PR also suggests renunciation. The Son of God speaks lightly of glory, pomp, and other such worldly objects. He says,

> But why should man seek glory? Who of his own
> Hath nothing, and to whom nothing belongs
> But condemnation, ignominy, and shame?
> (3. 134–36)

In *PL* Milton advocates implicit faith in God, which in Indian terms is "Bhakti." Raphael's advice to Adam is based on this essential doctrine of obedience to God. Adam can retain the love of God "If [he] be found obedient." But this is not subordination of oneself to a higher authority. The votaries of God serve Him voluntarily. As Raphael says,

> freely we serve
> Because wee freely love, as in our will
> To love or not; in this we stand or fall.
> (5. 538–40)

Freedom means the free service of God.

In *PR* also, Milton reveals the same attitude; the Son of God says,

> To know, and knowing worship God aright,
> Is yet more Kingly, this attracts the Soul,
> Governs the inner man, the nobler part,
> That other o're the body only reigns,
> And oft by force, which to a generous mind
> So reigning can be no sincere delight.
> (2. 475–80)

Reassuringly, the Deity in *PL* says,

> Man shall not quite be lost, but sav'd who will,
> Yet not of will in him, but grace in me
> Freely voutsaft. . . .
> (3. 173–75)

Man's prayers will definitely be answered. God's grace comes to those who believe in Him. In similar terms Lord Krishna emphatically utters,

> Quickly I come
> To those who offer me
> Every action
> Worship me only,
> Their dearest delight
> With devotion undaunted.
> (*Gita*, p. 120)

Both epics—*PL* and *The Mahabharata*—undoubtedly demand a superlative faith in God. It is the essential requisite to become ennobled and perfect. Worship of God, implicit faith in him, and unswerving loyalty to him are some of the tenets expressed in the two epics.

Indian philosophic thought also envisages the doctrine of doing duty for the sake of duty. This is "Nishkāma Karma," disinterestedness, or doing duty without expectation of reward. One who practices "Karma Marga" does everything cheerfully, deriving strength from a belief in God. He develops a spirit of detachment and indifference to the results of action. He feels that he has to work, but he should leave the outcome to God.

In *PL* Michael tells Adam,

> Nor love thy Life, nor hate; but what thou livst,
> Live well, how long or short permit to Heav'n.
> (11. 549–50)

Man's primary duty is to do his work with faith in God and in himself. He need not be too much involved or entangled in worldly ties. Progressively he should detach himself from mundane interests.

The two epics, *PL* and *The Mahabharata*, produce the same aesthetic response (*Rasa*) in their readers. The dominant note in these epics is one of serenity and bliss attained through spiritual enlightenment. The purpose of the poets in both epics is to produce an atmosphere of tranquility. The aesthetic pleasure or the emotion we feel on reading these epics is "Sānta." All human limitations are transcended. A calm of mind, all passions spent, prevails. This is true of *SA* and of *PR*.

PL and *The Mahabharata* show the path of deliverance from mundane fetters. They emphasize the need for absolute faith in God and reveal the transformation of man into a spiritual being. Man may lose the world of material prosperity, but he gains spiritually and is regenerated and ennobled. In its universality of theme, its sublime thought, and its transcendental vision, *PL* is close to the Sanskrit epic *The Mahabharata,* which, of course, Milton may not have known. [MVRS]

ECCLESIOLOGY. From the beginning to the end of his career as a controversialist*, Milton was deeply involved with the problems of church government and discipline, and no less with the related question of the true nature of Christian worship. On worship he wrote extensively but intermittently throughout his prose, and the bearing of his interest in that subject extends in an especially interesting way toward his poetry. But his concern with church government was more generally a reflection of the political development of Puritanism and relates specifically to the problem on which the unity of that movement foundered, namely, the relationship of church and state. (*See* POLITICS.) On this issue there were important durable elements in Milton's views as well as those that were relatively mutable.

Like most Puritans, he believed that the church was or should be a holy community. And again like most Puritans, he thought of its members as endowed with a special liberty* that was their new birthright through their redemption by Christ. Ideally there should have been no conflict between Christian liberty and the claims of the church as a holy community, and when Milton began to write he evidently believed in their complete concord. When, however, it became painfully apparent to him that there could indeed exist a conflict between them, his faith in Christian liberty remained constant, subject to hardly any redefinition. It was his view of the church, therefore, that changed, and in this respect Milton's ecclesiology appears as an evolution toward something like a vanishing point, a stage where the historically real, partic-

ular church seemed to interest him far less than an almost abstract vision of the universal church more fully concordant with his sense of Christian liberty.

Milton's belief in Christian liberty had one peculiar aspect that underlies all his writings, from *Ref* (1641), all the way through *TR* (1673). He began and ended with the conviction that the church existed for the sake of enlarging within its members their sense of godliness, by which he meant not merely an outward rectitude, but the inward knowledge of one's likeness to God in whose image Man was created. He called this knowledge and the sense of heroic dignity it inspired *magnanimity,* an ability "to correspond with Heav'n" (*PL* 7. 511), whether in terms of matching one's life against ideal, almost celestial standards, or of communicating through the Spirit within the equal communion of saints and angels in the worship of God. From thence followed his belief in voluntarism, the most significant of all Milton's principles with respect to the relationship of the individual to the church and of both to the state. And voluntarism is another name for his belief in Christian liberty.

What essentially changed in his ecclesiology happened within a relatively brief span of time—between the antiprelatical tracts and *Areop*—in direct response to an alteration of his understanding of voluntarism itself, and thereafter the consequences involved him progressively in a drastic redefinition of the claims church as well as state might legitimately make upon the conscience or the Christian liberty of the truly regenerate man. His first tracts seem to have been written in an exalted mood, his arguments tempered by the millenarian faith that by the special grace* of God England collectively was being inclined to a voluntary and essentially uniform Presbyterian* reformation of the church. (*See* MILLENNIALISM.) He saw her, therefore, as already transfigured by what she implicitly was, a true Kingdom of God, within which it was a contradiction in terms to think of compelling the spirit of any believer. Then within several years, during which he experienced the problems of his marriage* and the hostile reaction to his publications on divorce*, it became forcefully clear to him that "New Presbyter" was "but Old Priest writ large." Out of his disillusionment there emerged more clearly his unmovable concern with the inviolability of the individual conscience, the only sure foundation for either a personal or social reformation. There could be no other basis for the work of divine grace in human life than the unrestrained encouragement of God's Spirit animating men alone or in fellowship with one another to live on earth a measure of the heavenly godliness they would enjoy in the hereafter.

The corollary of Milton's concern with the freedom of conscience or Christian liberty was thus a special regard for the efficacy and authority of the Holy Spirit* in all matters of religion, for not only did the Spirit directly inspire each responsive Christian to a life of godliness, but it was also the means by which his understanding could be enlightened to comprehend and accept the authority of Scripture. What Puritan did not know that the Word of God could only be read with the help of the Spirit by which it had been composed by Moses, the Evangelists, the Prophets, and the Apostles? No church of itself had such an implicit authority over the conscience of any man as did his own understanding of the Word by the Spirit, nor did even a generally accepted interpretation of Scripture have such authority except by the voluntary assent of Christians taught by the Spirit to see the truth. Hence the Puritan dilemma was essentially over the question of subjective as against communal authority in knowing and acting on God's will and the imperative of his law. In their days of opposition under a state-established church that conceived God's law in terms unacceptable to them, the earlier Puritans regularly invoked the claims of their conscience and the authority of the Holy Spirit. But when they were in authority, what were they to say to those who invoked against them the

same claims of conscience and the freedom of the Spirit? What besides force, and not free assent, could judge between competing and contradictory claims as to what Scripture and the Holy Spirit authorized the magistrate to enforce in the name of religion? One hears the dilemma in the words of Oliver Cromwell* as he pleaded with his Presbyterian brethren after he had crushed them in the battle of Dunbar: "I beseech you in the bowels of Christ. . . . He will pour out his Spirit upon you; and you shall understand his words, and they will guide you to blessed reformation indeed."

Milton saw that the problem went beyond a clearly inadmissible forcing of conscience and was most critical with respect to the political right of Christians to install or support only those civil authorities who would protect religion as it was rightly and spiritually defined. But for Presbyterians this meant their right to install or support only magistrates who would impose their ecclesiastical system, to which all others must conform, a right even more vehemently denied in the name of the Spirit by the more sectarian Puritans. Setting Spirit against Spirit, Puritans were nerved to rely on their inner assurance of rightness and to make as much as possible of the sanctity and the near-infallibility of that assurance. It is in this respect that Milton's belief in magnanimity, his belief in himself as made in God's image, steeled him in the sense of his own rectitude to assume a public role and justify the truth of his convictions. Such assurance he called a "pious and just honouring of our selves . . . above which there is no higher ascent but to the love of God which from this self-pious regard cannot be asunder" (RCG 3 : 260–61), and in PL Adam's magnanimousness was part of the authority inherent in him and by which he was empowered to govern the rest of God's creatures.

But one can be sure only of one's own possession of such a justifiable conviction. Others might be mistaken, or one might be mistaken about them. Milton, for example, was prone to assume that those he actively supported enjoyed the same justifiable assurance of godliness as he did, and so he was happy to believe at first that Parliament was led by extraordinary men, that God had poured out a measure of spiritual bounty on his countrymen at large, and thus that England and the true church of Christ were becoming effectively one. Conversely, as his disenchantment extended (and eventually spread very wide), his sense of personal justification became a self-isolating conviction, until at last he stood spiritually alone, a church of one man, as was said of him.

Paradoxically, only then did he seem easiest in his mind, assured of at least himself as a living temple of faith, and most content to address himself to no particular church but the universal one within which he and his ideal readers (as he invariably imagined them to be) communed on that level of Christian understanding that came to serve him as the surrogate for the congregational communion of the church of the visible saints. This was implicitly his posture in the last major poems, as it was explicitly his posture in the high apostolic address opening *CD* : "JOHN MILTON, ENGLISHMAN, To all the churches of Christ, and to all who profess the Christian Faith throughout the world, Peace. . . ."

Milton's movement from his proud affirmation of England as a national church to his equally proud and opposite affirmation of membership in none but the universal church was not altogether unique, although with few others in his time was the range of the span so wide and the manner of the movement so distinctive. Nevertheless, it was along this kind of gradient that many radical Puritans moved, the verb *to move* itself being characteristically used by Puritans to express the workings of the Holy Spirit in their lives. What most of them sought at each station of the way was a visible church within which they might discern the shape of another one that was unearthly and whose fellowship was eternal. In Milton's case the movement began within the Church of England and ended

in something close to a Baptist* or even Quaker* way of thinking, an ecclesiastical evolution that illustrates one phase of the reciprocal movement described by Ernst Troeltsch between the churchly type of broad, comprehensive institution and the sectarian type of separating Christian community. The Puritan understanding of the church was not, therefore, arbitrarily mutable, but responsive rather to two ideals, the one embodied in the isolated communities of the primitive church, the other in the evangelical vision of a universal Christianity, both of which, as types, were defended in Puritan ecclesiology.

Between its reformation under Henry VIII and the onset of the Puritan Revolution, the English Church was a national episcopal institution ambiguously justified by parliamentary law and divine right, a *via media* between Roman Catholicism and the more radical Protestantism of the Calvinist and sectarian churches. Within it those who came to be called Puritans, those favoring the weakening or the abolition of the episcopal form and the movement of the church in the direction of ecclesiastical Calvinism*, were at first accommodated and then, under the first two Stuarts, subjected to a policy of harassment and exclusion. But between 1638 and 1640 Archbishop Laud's* attempt to force the episcopal system on Scotland led to a successful Scottish Presbyterian rebellion that forced Charles I* twice to convene in England Parliaments bent, among other things, on ecclesiastical reform. Indeed, with the convening of the second of these, the Long Parliament (as it was to be called) in late 1640 the ecclesiastical tensions latent in the established order reached a breaking point and in the excitement of the new possibilities that seemed to be opening before England, Milton, with many others, was drawn into the public debate on the reformation of the church.

His interest, he was to claim, was particular as well as general. At one time he had thought with his family that he had a clear calling to the ministry, but whether he was as he claimed "church-outed by the prelates," or yielded to the irresistible calling of his gifts as a poet to find some alternative way to serve the church by writing, he had by this time given up the idea of a vocation within the church but not of a vocation in its service. Thus, in the opening phases of the Puritan Revolution he was seized by an extraordinary sense of urgency on behalf of a reformation whose apparently accelerating course seemed providentially guided. Like many of those most enthusiastically possessed by the excitement of events, he was almost persuaded that in the renewal of the church the Kingdom of God was at hand. And for himself it was as if, he wrote, God had commanded him to take up a trumpet and blow a clarion call to his countrymen, rousing them to fulfill their prophetically destined reformation. There was no doubt to him, at any rate, that the real meaning of the events of 1640–41 was religious and not political.

Though not all his contemporaries and few historians would agree with him as to the meaning of those events, religion nonetheless was uppermost in the minds of many who took part in the opening debates of the Long Parliament. Certainly it was foremost in the hopes of those outside Parliament who almost immediately launched an energetic campaign in the press and pulpit, through petitions and addresses to both Houses, to get prelacy abolished. Up to a point the campaign could count on considerable Parliamentary support, especially on such specific matters as excluding the bishops from the House of Lords and eliminating or curbing the power of the ecclesiastical courts. But there emerged gradually a reluctance among a sizable element in Parliament to eliminate episcopacy root and branch, as most Puritans desired. It was this hesitancy to which polemic on both sides was addressed, and though the principal antagonists were at first chiefly spokesmen for the Church of England and the Presbyterians, even from the outset there were heard the voices of the more radical sects

beginning to question the assumption shared by the other two, that there had to be a national church. But sectarian opposition to the Presbyterian positions was not yet fully aware of itself, particularly among Congregationalists, and this accounts for the fact that Milton's advocacy of Presbyterianism could incorporate elements that were shortly to become anathema to those he thought he was supporting.

They were all agreed, however, on the need to do away with episcopacy, and on this there were two essential considerations never altogether isolated in debate but which can be stated in the form of two questions theoretically to be resolved. Was episcopacy justified by divine law or any other basis? And could the Church of England in its established form be rooted out of the structure of English political life without threatening the life of the state, especially the institution of monarchy? To both these questions Milton turned in *Ref*'s two parts. The first book examined the prelatical arguments *against* reformation derived from Scripture, custom, tradition, and patristic authority. The second book was more particularly devoted to the prelatical contention that episcopacy and monarchy were indissolubly united and that prelacy alone, by suppressing heresies and schismatic sects, prevented total confusion in the state. Rebutting the first set of arguments, Milton tended to denigrate the early church fathers and their age in such a way as to imply that his own age was more spiritually enlightened and therefore closer to the Gospels which, in any case, did not authorize episcopacy but rather a Presbyterian form of church polity. The second set of arguments, by which it was claimed reformation would upset the state, he treated as sophistries, arguing that prelacy had in fact been responsible for far more tumult, bringing the nation to its present troubled condition, whereas a Presbyterian reformation was in keeping with the true genius of English political life. In all this Milton's real vision seemed set not within the actual terms of English political realities but rather as if England was to be transformed in some imminent Second Coming of Christ. And such a vision went beyond his mere tactical need to enlarge his argument by associating a reformation according to Scripture with every conceivable good. The truth was that at this time church reformation signaled for him the dawning of a new millennial age.

Milton's subsequent two tracts were polemical responses, the first, *PrelE*, to a rather involved exchange of tracts and reprints that set out the positions of both sides from their origins in Elizabeth's reign, while *Animad* was a point-by-point commentary on Bishop Hall's* Remonstrance against an attack upon him by the Presbyterian ministers known as the Smectymnuans*. In these works Milton went even further in discrediting patristic traditions and the authority of the church itself in favor of the authority of Scripture and the Spirit. Similarly, the Remonstrant's appeal to the light of reason he countered with an evocation of the higher reason of Scripture or grace. But "reason," as in *RCG* did not mean a rational argument for Presbyterianism, or an effort to harmonize divine and natural law in the manner of Richard Hooker's* great defense of the Elizabethan establishment in *The Laws of Ecclesiastical Polity*. Rather, it meant the ground or basis of ecclesiastical authority as evident in Scripture. And behind Milton's continual invocation of the evidence of Scripture there loomed larger and larger the special authority of the Holy Spirit. It was the Spirit above all that Englishmen were to acknowledge as the guiding genius of their reformation. Then, to account for the long historical delay in the Spirit's work in England, Milton began evolving the idea of its gradually emergent progressive revelation since John Wyclif's day, reappearing again in greater force in Elizabeth's age and now providentially in their own time. How else, without this preparation, wrote Milton in *Animad,* could they and their fathers "have been able to have receiv'd the sudden assault

of [God's] reforming Spirit warring against humane Principles, and carnall sense . . . that still cry'd up Antiquity, Custome, Canons, Councels, and Laws" (3 : 145–46). Significantly, there followed upon this passage his most expressly apocalyptic outburst, a great millenarian hymn of thanks for the gifts of the Spirit. (*See* APOCALYPSE.) What Milton was vindicating so enthusiastically was above all the singular spiritual authority upon which he conceived the advance toward reformation to be securely grounded; for what must be clearly distinguished in his ecclesiological arguments is the main and ultimately spiritual authority by which he justified the church, as against the specific forms of government and discipline at issue. It was his own tendency to blur the questions of spiritual authority and ecclesiastical forms, so as to make the church the vehicle of the Spirit, which led him progressively toward sectarianism.

On the actual nature of the church itself he advocated throughout the antiprelatical tracts what seemed like an orthodox Presbyterianism but really was not, since he neither fully grasped, nor could have accepted had he really understood them, the essential postulates of the Presbyterian position. With respect to church government he indeed argued for Presbyterian forms : particular churches of ministers, elders, and laymen; the ministers elected by their congregations and installed in office by a simple ceremony replacing ordination; the churches organized regionally into councils or presbyteries of ministers, and comprehensively or nationally in a general assembly. But it must have shaken his former tutor, the Smectymnuan Thomas Young*, with the rest of his committee, to note Milton's astounding assumption that all this could be built up on a purely voluntary ground, by the free motion of the Spirit in men, and to see the whole parochial system completely undercut by Milton's attack upon hireling clergy, to which was added his praise of ministers who would serve freely or for only the modest competence of voluntary donations offered at the discretion of each congregation. Milton's view was that it was preferable that those called to the ministry be indifferent to creature comforts, or should otherwise be possessed of independent means, since men God had inclined to his free service should rightly expect no reward but one that was truly heavenly. The implications here are radical and drastic, although they were not yet spelled out, for so to sever from its economic base the roots of a national church was in effect to deny it the traditional means for its survival.

And Milton's Presbyterian friends should have been perturbed by his emphasis, already sectarian in outline, on the clergy-right of laymen, the royal priesthood of each spiritually gifted Christian to preach, lead in prayer, and otherwise minister to his fellows in the church. But even more crucial in separating him from those he was defending were his suggested constraints upon the church's prerogatives of ecclesiastical censure, particularly where it might apply to those sects and heresies that Milton took to be a sign of the Spirit's great and beneficent working in this "age of ages." With all these signs it is not surprising that even Milton himself, in *RCG*, should begin to seem aware that on this point especially their agreement might founder, as he considered momentarily the possibility that, in seeking to impose conformity, a Presbyterian church polity might look for support to the magistrate's sword. Hence he warned that Providence alone was to bring English Christians into conformity. There was to be no "despising the mighty operation of the Spirit . . . by using the way of civil force and jurisdiction." But he quickly added that he could not imagine any such "crookedness, any wrinckle or spot should be found in presbyterial government." He was soon to be disabused on this point.

Milton did not anticipate the defects of a Presbyterian reformation because he was imaginatively enraptured by its possible effects on the work and worship of the church. His warmest interest was not in church organization and discipline, but in worship and the office of preaching. Neither at that period nor later did he disagree with the Presbyterian conception of preaching and worship except in a degree of emphasis reflecting his special sense as a layman and poet of involvement in the church's devotional offices. And it is in that sense that the theme of worship always seemed to strike a responsive chord within him, touching his instincts as a poet with a devotional vocation, as in the apocalyptic prayers in *Ref* and *Animad,* where what emerges most clearly is his self-image as an inspired devotional spokesman for his countrymen. Worship, like poetry, he conceived to be a gift under the direct inspiration of the Holy Spirit. The sin of prelacy above all was evident in its misdirection of this power of devotion into a descending carnality. Its liturgy, unauthorized by Scripture, left no room for the power of the Spirit in prayer ("promised only to the elect"), without which free outlet a man's spiritual gifts might atrophy within him to his mortal danger. The repetitiousness and cold formality of set worship he contrasted with the fervor or zeal of extemporary prayers, just as the chants and the litanies of the established liturgy were colder than the enthusiastic hymn-singing of the Puritans.

Milton could recognize, in *Apol*, the "expedience of set forms" in worship, probably remembering that the Presbyterians were by no means averse to a directory of worship, only to the specific use of the prelatical Book of Common Prayer. However, Milton distinguished between *allowing* and *enforcing* set forms and seemed to expect that, with full reformation, liturgical helps would wither away and, with the help of the Holy Spirit, become entirely unnecessary. Similarly, he imagined the ideal minister as someone whose essential gift it was to be a peculiar vehicle for the flow of grace in the inspirational stream that began in the fountainhead of God. In *Animad* he pictured the preacher as the mediator of the quickening power of the Spirit in terms strikingly applicable to his own conception of the work of the poet, just as in *RCG* he equated with each other the minister and the poet. The minister's work was "to be the messenger and herald of heavenly truth from God to man, and by the faithfull worke of holy doctrine, to procreate a number of faithfull men, making a kind of creation like to Gods by infusing his spirit and likenesse into them, to their salvation, as God did into him, . . . raising out of darksome barrennesse a delicious, and fragrant Spring of saving knowledge and good workes" (*Animad* 3 : 164).

With such idealized conceptions of reformed worship and discipline, Milton's ecclesiology in the antiprelatical tracts, despite their polemical effectiveness, appears essentially enthusiastic, in the inspired sense of the word, a poet's vision of a church and of its worship, in keeping with such a poem as *SolMus,* and akin to his highly idealized sense of the poetic function itself. There was thus an unexpressed tension within his views, in which were opposed the spiritual to the worldly form of the church. And hence in *RCG,* when Milton wished to establish the axiomatic nature of discipline as the universal attribute to which all things conformed, it is highly significant that he began with its heavenly forms, the music of the spheres, the symbolic proportions of the heavenly New Jerusalem, and, in a rapturous burst of prose imagining the disciplined worship of the saints in eternity, he concluded by asking who could doubt that God would leave a pattern of discipline for his worldly church below, a pattern really seen in perfection in voluntary worship. Who indeed? But if the worldly church were too brilliantly illumined by the light of its heavenly forms and the choraling together of saints and angels, whatever visible church he espoused would be sure to appear embarrassingly inadequate whenever its earthly nature would show too grossly. In any event, after the antiprelatical tracts Milton no longer found in the Presbyterian New Jerusalem the shape of the true church that had once descended from heaven with its Master.

The Presbyterian ecclesiastical campaign of the early stages of the Puritan Revolution eventually began to bear fruit in the piecemeal abolition of episcopacy, to further which, in July of 1643, there was convened at Parliament's behest the Westminster Assembly* of Divines. The function of this body was to advise Parliament on the settlement of religion to be enacted by law, and given its overwhelming Presbyterian majority it was all but certain that the Assembly would recommend a Presbyterian national church. However, there were a small number of ministers included, known by the way they differed from the majority as the Dissenting Brethren, and in short order their position earned for them as well the name of Independents*. Although they were Presbyterians doctrinally, in worship, and in the matter of the organization of individual congregations, they believed in "Presbyterianism independent" rather than in "Presbyterianism dependent"; that is to say, they wanted for their congregations, and for such as believed as they did, an accommodation allowing their autonomy within a centralized Presbyterian national church. Actually they would have preferred an altogether decentralized national church organized more or less in the kind of loose federation found in the New England Congregational system and later to be established during Oliver Cromwell's Protectorate.

Balanced against both kinds of ministers in the Assembly were members of Parliament, most of whom were Erastian* in their views on the nature of the relationship of church and state, believing that ultimately the state, for political reasons, was justified in prescribing the kind of church to be nationally established. Milton's emerging identification with the Independents against the Presbyterians can be traced by way of the divorce tracts and *Areop,* although none of these works was primarily motivated by his concern for the church. The fact is, however, that his divorce tracts alienated him decisively from the Presbyterians, some of whom explicitly condemned him for such publications. Yet, notwithstanding his movement toward a more radical position, Milton remained—and he made this plain especially in the *Areop*—an Independent, not a separatist, believing still that Christian liberty was compatible with a broadly accommodating national church, one that might still provide the framework for a holy community of Englishmen. But he had also lost much of the enthusiasm that had enabled him to think of church reformation as the basis for a larger renewal of life. By the end of the first civil war he was more inclined to hope that no new ecclesiastical tyranny would arise to interfere with the only aid Christians needed in regulating church matters, the free working of the Holy Spirit, and this was to remain his essential position until the closing days of the Puritan Revolution.

When Milton next appeared as a controversialist, it was on behalf of an Army revolution that had purged Parliament, brought the defeated King Charles to trial and to the verge of the scaffold, and was about to make of England a republic. The Army's actions were in some part attributable to the religious insecurity of the minority Independents and sects whose power the Army most directly represented. Nevertheless, their revolution was political and, whatever the ultimately religious basis may have been for Milton's sympathies with it, his defense of their actions was also largely political. But now an important element in the whole situation was that the Royalist cause was upheld from within Puritanism by active Presbyterian propaganda. Milton's response to this led him further toward a complete rupture with their ecclesiastical program and to a sustained attack in *Tenure*, in *Eikon* and in *Peace* upon the moral authority of the Presbyterian ministerial leadership. Yet these leaders no longer represented the real threat to Milton's ideal church which, as he obliquely identified it in his sonnets to Cromwell and Sir Henry Vane*, came

now from the leading classical Independent ministers, chief among whom was Cromwell's chaplain, John Owen*, and many of whom enjoyed a quasi-official status in the new circles of power. What Milton feared of them, as of their Presbyterian and prelatical predecessors, was their disposition to limit toleration more narrowly than he would have liked, and to insist still upon a state-established and supported church.

To be sure, Cromwell himself, the effective leader of the state, was generously inclined toward a large toleration of all sects and churches agreeing in the fundamentals of Christian faith, but he was loath to surrender his duty of encouraging the emergence of a sanctified nation through the medium of a loosely federated national church, the maintenance of which would mean preserving the parochial system for organizing congregations and collecting tithes. The settlement of the church thus came to hinge particularly on the issue of tithes, a matter that became one of the main areas of religious disagreement between the government and its more radical supporters. The other issues were the actual limits of toleration that began to emerge under the new regime, and millenarianism, or the question of the conformability of Cromwell's successive governments to the sectarian sense that the nation was to be ruled principally in the interests of the saints who, as prophesied for the last days, were to rule with Christ. In common with the Baptists and more radical sects, Milton was one of those who watched critically the continued maintenance of tithes and the persistence of an officially sanctioned persecution of heretics. He was far less sympathetic to the millenarian or Fifth Monarchist criticism of the later phases of Cromwellian rule in the Protectorate government.

Somewhere in the interim between 1654 and 1658, possibly in beginning to work on *CD*, Milton had become even more radically sectarian in his sympathies than had been indicated in his previous publications. For although on doctrinal grounds and in relation to congregational discipline and worship he could have subscribed to much of the Independent Savoy Declaration of Faith (1658), he clearly found unacceptable Independency under its state establishment of 1654. Either the Savoy Conference or Cromwell's death induced him to write the two treatises representing his most extreme positions on the church, with which he hoped to influence the politically restored Parliamentary Rump in the radical campaign for the disestablishment of Independency.

CivP and *Hire* were received in complementary relationship to one another as two parts of one argument. The object of his attacks Milton bluntly stated to be the un-Christian dependence in the English church, when reformation had already gone so far, on force and hire in religion. The first tract rested on four interlocking arguments that taken together he treated as the golden rule of Christian liberty. The first was that there could be no authority in religion other than Scripture as illumined for each man by the light of the Holy Spirit. On that basis there could be no warrant for the jurisdiction of any kind of church discipline or censure except upon those who willingly submitted themselves to the authority of the congregation censuring them. Even then the jurisdiction could extend no further than to spiritual limits, with no recourse whatever to corporal punishment or the mulcting of fines. Nor could even spiritual discipline be efficacious unless it was inwardly acceptable to the conscience of the individual being censured. The second argument Milton developed from a consideration of the distinct and different natures of Christ's government in his church and the ends of the civil magistrates. The first kind of government was expressed in the faithful belief and the charitable practice of evangelical religion and concerned only the regenerate, who were "wrought on by divine grace" and who, if as individuals they could not be compelled in matters of conscience by the church, could cer-

tainly not be compelled spiritually by the civil magistrate, whose jurisdiction extended only to the outward man. The third argument was properly a definition of Christian liberty as the redemption of the regenerate from the bondage of legalism in religion, a redemption that must be outwardly nullified if civil fear was made a means to religious ends. Last, Milton argued, there was no just end that any state could profess that was compatible with the exercise or threat of force in religious matters. In sum, the only valid role of the state in religion was the protection of all professing Christians from intimidation or constraints aimed at coercing them in their consciences.

Seen as a whole, Milton's defense of Christian liberty in *CivP* was methodical yet quite impersonal, notwithstanding the depth to which his own conscience was committed to its principles. By contrast there was more revealed of his own nature as a rather idiosyncratic and radical Puritan, both in the contemptuous animus against hireling clergy in *Hire,* and in the ideal image of the ministerial servant of God that stood behind his contempt. In the earlier part of that work Milton demolished with characteristic thoroughness the justification of tithes as a way of maintaining the ministry of free Christian churches. Neither the Old Testament with is precedents and types, nor the New Testament with its itinerant evangelical ministry, nor even the examples of the imperial patronage of the church in early centuries provided any warrant for its practice. Yet how then were the ministers of the church to live?

Milton's answer is enormously revealing, for what emerges from the latter part of the work is an intensely conceived image of a church whose prototype may seem to be the practice of some contemporary Baptist churches, but which more remotely and authentically suggests the example of the primitive Christian communities among which Paul, Peter, Timothy, John, and other itinerant founders of Christianity lived and worked. It was not necessary, Milton suggested, to imagine that churches needed the constant attendance of their ministers. They were properly to be thought of as communities of the faithful, ideally very small, who might come together anywhere, no matter how humble the house or barn, and where the brethren were all pious and worthy enough to minister in some way to one another. From time to time they might be visited by itinerant preachers, none of whom should stay for more than a year or two at the most—that long if they were founding the church—but more likely only briefly, for one or several meetings. Such ministers in their calling would ideally be self-chosen, self-dedicated individuals needing no other ordination than their responsiveness to the power in them of the Holy Spirit. In general they would be content with the expenses of their journeys and a mere sufficiency for their barest necessities. The church Milton thus imagined would seem almost to exist in a primitive, spiritually Arcadian golden age, except for its partial resemblance in fact to some contemporary Baptist communities. More suggestively, it seems to anticipate the frontier churches that were to emerge in the United States and its territories in the late-eighteenth and nineteenth centuries.

The methodical clarity of the 1659 tracts probably derives from Milton's work on the *CD*, then most likely in hand and completed later when the Restoration had turned all Puritans into disestablished Nonconformists. In the doctrinal treatise ecclesiology is not isolated in any single section but emerges coherently from the sequence within which Milton developed the broader aspects of his discussion of faith and worship, or belief and practice. He began his actual consideration of the church where for most Puritans it properly began, under its primal aspect as the Mystical or Invisible Church. As he defined it, the timeless Mystical Church stood in somewhat the same relationship to the universal church (which was not tied to any place) as the latter stood to the particular gathered congregation of visible saints. In that sense it was only a

more universal Universal Church. "The mystical body called *The Invisible Church* is not," he wrote, "confined to place or time, inasmuch as it is composed of individuals of widely separated countries, and of all ages, from the foundation of the world" (16 : 61, 63, 67).

The link between the visible saints and the Invisible Church was in predestination*, however conditionally Milton, now an Arminian*, defined it, for predestination was the effective cause of the fellowship that "consists in a participation through the Spirit" in the various gifts and merits of Christ, and of the church, in both its invisible and visible forms. The relationship of the invisible church to the visible one is mediated entirely through the consciousness of every individual believer as an aspect of imperfect glorification, which is his own awareness of his advance in spiritual perfection, and is, therefore, a sense of blessedness beginning now but culminating in the final millennial consummation of the Kingdom of Glory, when the invisible and visible churches become one (1 : 25). Or, in the words of *Nat,* "And then at last our bliss / Full and perfect is, / But now begins."

The nature of this bond of communion in the invisible church, its discipline, so to speak, is the Covenant of Grace which, since the New Testament, is no longer the written law but the unwritten law of God; this, in the regenerate, under the influence of the Holy Spirit, is daily tending toward a renewal of its original brightness, that is, the more perfect illumination of the unfallen Adam. Since the covenant is written into the hearts of believers by the Holy Spirit, it is in turn the saints' assurance of their enfranchisement from sin through Christ, and the basis of their real and practical Christian liberty (1 : 27). Thus Christian liberty is, as it were, an aspect of fellowship in the Invisible Church, the internal realm of the Covenant of Grace and—this is important—it is theologically prior to that lesser or external sealing of the covenant which is merely outwardly represented in the sacraments and in the visible church within which the sacraments may be administered. The effect of this sequence of ideas, it will be seen, is to enshrine as the highest certainty, above the church, and as the truest embodiment of the visible church, the temple within, or the conscience of the true believer.

The authority of the visible church, therefore, resides in the Christian liberty or the unforced assent of the believer who seeks, by voluntarily gathering himself to others of the same faith, some outward sustenance of his need for spiritual fellowship, particularly in the common need and desire to worship God. Such a gathering is an "assembly of those who are called" because its first and efficient cause is predestination, which in Milton's sense means the calling of all men, whether or not every one so called to salvation perseveres in his call and is saved as one of the regenerate. Despite this admission that the visible church might number in its midst many who are, in the eternal sense, unregenerate, it must consider itself as a gathering of visible saints, since in charity every man professing salvation and living in apparent godliness must be accepted as regenerate, no one being humanly able to judge otherwise (1 : 25, 24).

In the government of the visible church the primary distinction Milton made was between the universal visible church and particular visible churches or congregations, thus excluding from any consideration, as perforce illegitimate, a national church. The universal church he defined essentially in the terms of *Hire,* but with the significant addition that among its component elements, and in full parity or equality with congregations or particular churches, was included the individual Christian, either by himself, or as he joined himself to others worshiping God through Christ. While men should worship together, "such as cannot do this conveniently, or *with full satisfaction of conscience,* are not to be considered as excluded from the blessing bestowed by God on the churches (16 : 235). And it is in keeping with both the heightened individualism of this

ecclesiology (where each man individually is a temple of faith) and Milton's special sense of the true ministry as an itinerant one, not tied to any particular church, that both the ministry and church membership are not defined by him in terms of particular churches but rather pointedly in relation to the universal church, as if both members and ministers might freely attach and detach themselves from congregations. Thus the visible church begins to assume in Milton's account of it not a static character but rather a fluid identity, as if it were really the secondary manifestation, the mere place and time, where the seeker, the wayfaring Christian, pauses to set up his altar to God.

Even the minimal distinctions between minister and laymen tended now to be reduced, Milton conceded in the argumentative context of the late tracts. Ministers are *all* people who respond to a divine calling that may be either extraordinary or ordinary in its nature (1 : 29). Such an extraordinary calling, for example, Milton described his own to be in the second book of *RCG* specifically in reference to his calling as a polemical advocate of reformation, but no less as a sacred poet. Those best known whose calling had been extraordinary were mainly the prophets, evangelists, and apostles in Scripture. Later the extraordinarily called appeared again as reformers and such as those who, preaching or writing, served the universal church in some unusual capacity. A minister with an extraordinary calling was approved exclusively in his own and in God's eyes.

The ordinary minister of the particular church was by contrast responsive both to his own sense of calling and to the approval of a congregation, and shared his responsibilities with his deacons and elders. The laying on of hands was imposed on all church officers, lay and cleric, on their assumption of office, and was merely a blessing and not a form of ordination, for in the fulfilling of their functions nothing spiritually distinguished the minister from the rest of the congregation. Conversely, any qualified member of the church might preach, lead in prayer, baptize, or administer the Lord's Supper, as long as the spiritual end of the mutual coming together was thereby served. There is a suggestion that Milton felt that there was less ambiguity when laymen rather than ministers performed such offices, since it was generally more desirable, for example's sake, and for the prevention of offense or suspicion, as well as being in itself more noble, honorable, and godly to render unpaid service in the church. But for their services ministers might be paid a small recompense, provided it was freely offered (1 : 31).

Again Milton thought the congregation should be small enough to need no more than a private home for its worship, the possibilities of mutual edification apparently decreasing with the increase in congregational size. The discipline of a small congregation would, moreover, be in keeping with the spiritual intimacy of its members, all of whom were joined one to another in a covenantal relationship, an agreement Milton imagined as frequently renewed by the individual, as often as he passed "from one particular church to another." Discipline was to be in the hands of the whole church and not of the pastor specifically. It was to begin with forbearance or forgiveness, but could proceed through persuasion and admonition to excommunication. Civil power, needless to say, had no role whatsoever in such a church, civil power being no less than a derogation of the church's higher spiritual power (1 : 31, 32).

Christian worship in its broadest sense Milton saw as comprising all good works, but logically beginning as the expression of one's faith, whether offered alone, in a gathered church, or within the universal church. Its primary sphere was inward, evincing itself first as an inclination of some emotion, an impulse of the spirit whenever the believer's faith in God was involved with external things in the forms of such feelings as love, hope, gratitude, fear, and so forth (2 : 3). In true religion these inclinations could never be divorced from external worship, which is why

prayer, for Milton, had to be spontaneous and individual, related to the spiritual and affective reality of distinct circumstances. But such circumstances being generally found in the common experiences of all the saints, there was no less individuality in communal worship than in praying alone.

Yet it is notable that Milton treats, as if indifferently, the virtues of public and private prayer, certainly with far less insistence on the necessity of communal worship than is to be found among contemporary ministerial treatises on worship. Praying, Milton carefully indicates, may be properly offered alone or in company; and if in company each Christian might (in the Quaker fashion) sometimes silently frame "within himself his petition relative to some subject on which they had agreed in common." No liturgical forms whatever were necessary in worship, nor was any order more seemly than another. It was necessary, of course, to distinguish differences between kinds (or genres) of worship, as if by a decorum suitable to their occasion, these being broadly the kinds appropriate for "the invocation or adoration of God and the sanctification of his name in all the circumstances of life. Under invocation are included" he wrote, "supplication and thanksgiving" (17 : 71). Thus Milton consistently treated the Lord's Prayer as a model of supplication, rather than as a set prayer. The hymns of his prose works were prayers of thanksgiving and supplication; the great hymn of Adam and Eve in *PL* 5 was an invocation to the universality of creaturely praise, which Milton conceived as the highest expression of the devotional understanding of the two unfallen parents of mankind. But their invocation of universal praise was really itself a kind of hyperbolical thanksgiving offering.

Milton's views of preaching, the central element in Puritan worship, are sparsely touched upon in *CD*, probably because preaching's evangelical and edifying functions, its procreative role in the mission of grace, were so well understood and axiomatic, that it needed little comment. Its exercise required above all the finest spiritual gifts, and comprised prophesying (what was known as "opening" the Scripture) and teaching (1 : 29). Its end was that same quickening of an aroused spirit in another which might be the consequence of communal prayer or psalm singing (cf. *SolMus*), and which should properly always be the consequence of the conscious reception of the sacraments (1 : 28). Under the liberty of the Gospel anyone qualified might preach, as anyone might lead in prayer, baptize, or administer the Lord's Supper. Nor was the sacrament* of communion a vehicle of grace as such; rather it was a confirmation of God's promises to the elect, quickened within them by the Spirit as a special consciousness. Its administration might be public or private, actual (as in the communication of bread and wine), or symbolic, that is to say, celebrated in the "many opportunities . . . open to [the Christian] through life of evincing his gratitude to God, and commemorating the death of Christ, though not in the precise mode and form which God has instituted" (16 : 205). Yet if the consciousness of the sacrament of communion did not necessarily reside in any distribution of the elements, it did exist presumably as the consciousness of participation in a sacramental act, and might extend to other comparable sacramental acts that Milton described, such as the solemnizing of private vows of self-dedication, and the public vows taken individually and by the whole of a covenanting church as the act by which it became a gathered church (2 : 4).

Milton's tendency clearly was to relegate to the area of spiritual indifference, to the so-called *adiaphora,* all formal structures, devices, distinctions, ordinances, and orders of the church, without depriving them of their sanctity. No particular ecclesiastical forms being commanded, the freedom of the Christian was almost unlimited in the way he chose to respond to the Spirit, and the response itself determined the validity of the act, not the prescription of any form. The

purpose was perpetual spiritual renewal, with no institution to be allowed to harden into an ecclesiastical formality. Thus even the institution of the Sabbath as the Lord's Day was a matter of indifference with no intrinsic spiritual authority in it, only the "voluntary duty" the members of the church might find convenient. In such things there was to be balanced against the inviolability of one's conscience a decent respect for the opinions of one's truly Christian fellows, keeping as one's guide the need to renew perpetually the spiritual meaning of each occasion for worship.

It cannot be pretended that this whole tendency of Milton's ecclesiology to move from closed to open forms, from real to symbolic communality, from the visible or universal church to the Kingdom within as an outward enfranchising spirit, is merely good Puritan doctrine and practice. Nor was his movement toward defining *himself* as a church simply a movement toward spiritual inwardness. Quietism was simply not in Milton's nature. And at least in not being quietistic he remained very typically Puritan, accepting as the consequence of his election and justification the duty of publicly and energetically testifying to his calling as a saint within the communion of visible saints. Thus we come to what seems like a paradox, for on the uncontradicted testimony of his early biographer, John Toland*, Milton in his later years withdrew from regular church membership and public worship. Perhaps it was for the sake of conscience. Another tradition records his contempt for the conventicle pastors. His own words, in *Educ,* tell us how trying he found preaching, which strained his high standards. There is as well the judgment on the church at the end of *PL* in the Archangel Michael's prophecy of its corrupt degeneration, contrasted as it is with the persevering few individuals who are God's "living Temples, built by Faith to stand, / Thir own Faith not others" (12. 527–28).

Yet whether Milton would have abandoned congregational worship, the public profession and testimony of his faith, if he had had no alternative calling as a poet to an extraordinary ministry within the universal church, may be fairly asked. *CD* theoretically justified such a calling, which was precisely the one he had publicly declared as his vocation in *RCG* years earlier, when he had solemnly and sacramentally covenanted with his ideal readers to write for them "a work doctrinal to a nation." But in the terms of his identity with his nation in the later years, that sacred work of religious edification and worship would not have been conceived as a patriotic religious undertaking, but as an act of communion shared with the Christian readers of England in the universal church, and for readers not even confined to that time or place.

In one of the more solemn moments of his youth, after his twenty-first birthday, and on the morning of Christ's Nativity, he had seen himself as a poet-priest anticipating the general worship of all Christians in homage to the holy birth. Then later, in the enthusiasm of his hopes for a national and universal reformation, he again saw himself anticipating and leading the worship of all Britain in its final apocalyptic transfiguration. But in *PL* his gaze was level as he addressed himself to the universal church, "Standing on Earth . . . / . . . I Sing with mortal voice, unchang'd." Though he knew he had imaginatively worshiped in heaven, he spoke not so much to exalt as to edify a certain remnant, others like himself, and "all who in the worship persevere / Of Spirit and Truth" (7. 23–25; 12. 532–33). In the last analysis Milton's poetry was his church. [MF]

CONTRIBUTORS TO VOLUME 2

AA   Arthur Axelrad. California State University, Long Beach, Calif. 90801.

ACL   Albert C. Labriola. Duquesne University, Pittsburgh, Pa. 15219.

ARC   Albert R. Cirillo. Northwestern University, Evanston, Ill. 60201.

AW   Austin Woolrych. University of Lancaster, Lancaster, England.

BEM   B. Eugene McCarthy. College of the Holy Cross, Worcester, Mass. 01610.

CK   Carole Kessner. State University of New York, Stony Brook, N.Y. 11790.

DAR   Donald A. Roberts. Vineyard Haven, Mass. 02568.

DJD   Daniel J. Donno. Queens College, Flushing, N.Y. 11367.

EEE   Edward E. Ericson. Northwestern College, Orange City, Iowa 51041.

EHD   Edgar Hill Duncan. Vanderbilt University, Nashville, Tenn. 37205.

EHH   Elizabeth H. Hageman. University of New Hampshire, Durham, N.H. 03824.

ERG   E. Richard Gregory. University of Toledo, Toledo, Ohio 43606.

FF   French Fogle. Claremont Graduate School, Claremont, Calif. 91911.

GDM   Gilbert D. McEwen. Whittier College, Whittier, Calif. 90608.

GFB   Gillian Fansler Brown, Tulane University of New Orleans, New Orleans, La. 80118.

GLM   George L. Musacchio. California Baptist College, Riverside, Calif. 92504.

HFR   Harry F. Robins. University of Arizona, Tucson, Ariz. 85711.

ILD   Ivar Lou Duncan. 3627 Valley Vista Road, Nashville, Tenn. 37205.

IR   Irving Rothman. University of Houston, Houston, Texas 77004.

JDe   James Devereux, S.J. University of North Carolina, Chapel Hill, N.C. 27514.

JEH   Joan E. Hartman. Staten Island Community College, Staten Island, N.Y. 10301.

JFH   John F. Huntley. University of Iowa, Iowa City, Iowa 52241.

JHS   James H. Sims. University of Oklahoma, Norman, Okla. 73069.

JMS   John M. Steadman. Huntington Library and Art Gallery, San Marino, Calif. 91108.

JP   Joseph Pequigney. State University of New York, Stony Brook, N.Y. 11790.

JTS   John T. Shawcross. City University of New York, New York, N.Y. 10031.

JWH   Jack W. Herring. Baylor University, Waco, Texas 76703.